THE COOKING DEMO BOOK

- This book emphasizes the use of fruits, vegetables, whole grains and beans.
- Recipes are low in fat, saturated fat, sodium and cholesterol, while staying high in fiber and flavor.
- Ingredients are common and inexpensive.
- The featured recipes come together fast and present themselves beautifully.
- Recipes are also a vehicle for teaching vital information about nutrition and cooking preparation techniques.
- Dishes are well-tested and taste great!

By Judy Doherty, PC II, Publisher and Professional Chef
Food and Health Communications

For more cooking information, visit us online:
www.foodandhealth.com

Download our new Salad Secrets App for the iPhone for over 50 of our best salad recipes with photos - you can email them to clients right from your phone.

The Cooking Demo Book

Everything you need to succeed in over 130 cooking demonstrations.

Judy Doherty, PCII
Food and Health Communications
Louisville, Colorado
www.foodandhealth.com

Food and Health Communications

P.O. Box 271108

Louisville, CO 80027

www.foodandhealth.com

Printed in the United States

This book is printed in ebook, epub, workbook and CD-ROM formats. For special licensing, contact Food and Health
Communications at 800-462-2352 or through
their website at foodandhealth.com

ISBN-13: 978-1456538446

ISBN-10: 1456538446

License to Copy

LICENSE TO COPY The Cooking Demo Book and Materials

PLEASE READ THE FOLLOWING BEFORE MAKING ANY COPIES OF COOKING DEMO II ("CDB").

As the original purchaser and current subscriber of Food & Health Communications, Inc.'s CDB, you are permitted to make copies of CDB, or any portion thereof, only (1) for your internal use or provision to your lay clients or patients, (2) for educational, non-profit purposes, and (3) for use at a single site. This permission neither transfers any ownership rights to you nor creates a relationship between you and CDB or Food & Health Communications, Inc. (Food & Health).

Without further prior written permission from Food & Health, you may not use CDB or any portion or copy thereof: for commercial purposes or gain; as part of another publication or work distributed for commercial purposes or gain; or for any other purpose other than as stated above. Without further prior written permission from Food & Health, CDB, or any portion or copy thereof, may not be distributed any further than as stated above, and no additional copies may be made. Inquiries for such permission may be made to Food & Health at P.O. Box 271108, Louisville, CO 80027 or by calling 800-462-2352 or via email through foodandhealth.com.

You may not alter, edit, or revise any copy of CDB without the prior written approval of Food & Health. The changes in reproduction refer only to physical changes in our articles made in the reproduction process. For example,

you can't "white-out" a name as author of an article, insert your own name, and photocopy the article. Changes in the way you actually use a recipe (for example, doubling the ingredients to allow for an increased serving size, or use of cashews instead of peanuts) do not implicate copyright law, and therefore are not prohibited by the federal Copyright Act or by the language of the photocopy language.

Each copy must include the relevant author's name and credits as originally provided in CDB, and must display the following notice in easily legible print on the first page of each copy:

© Food & Health Communications, Inc. www.foodandhealth.com.

The materials provided in CDB and any copies thereof are provided for informational purposes only. Neither CDB nor Food & Health makes any representations about the suitability of these materials for any other purpose. These materials are provided "AS IS," without any express or implied warranty of any type, and any individual or entity using these materials assumes all responsibility and risk for such use. Neither CDB nor Food & Health shall have any liability whatsoever for any use of these materials.

This book is dedicated to my son, Nicholas Doherty, who loves to cook in the kitchen with me.

If you'd like to cook with your family, here are some projects for kids.
• Two year olds can help set the table or stir lettuce in a bowl.
• Five year olds can assemble fruit plates.
• Ten year olds can be responsible for packing their own lunches every day.
• Thirteen to eighteen year olds can make dinner. After they learn to cook, let them plan and execute a meal entirely on their own.

If you start cooking at home more frequently while teaching your kids to help, you will find yourself with an able and enthusiastic sous-chef, a healthier child, more quality time with your family, a fatter wallet from reducing restaurant attendance, and better meals for all.

Table of Contents

Let's Get Started!

Cooking Demos for All!

People in the process of giving food demonstrations have a lot on their minds. They're trying to form coherent sentences while following a recipe, manipulating ingredients, avoiding drips and spills, monitoring audience engagement, following food safety best practices, working with cooking equipment, and trying not to set anything on fire. That's a lot to worry about at once! Plus there's the whole preparation process, not to mention cleanup and lessons learned "for next time." We've put this book together in order to facilitate mindful, creative, and healthy cooking demonstrations and just generally make this process easier. This first section outlines key strategies for outstanding presentations, so be sure to check them out before you move on to the actual lessons.

What's Included?

This section features the following handouts...
- Cooking Demo Success Tips
- Food Safety Tips for Cooking Demos
- Ideas for Cooking Demo Themes
- Seven Steps for a Successful Regional Class
- Show and Tell for a Healthy Kitchen
- The Wellness Kitchen
- SuperStar Cooking
- Food Demo Organizer

Bringing USDA's MyPlate and the Dietary Guidelines for Americans Along...

Our cooking demo information includes plenty of nutritional guidance and advice from the USDA's MyPlate and the Dietary Guidelines for Americans. Keep an eye out for tips that will make your cooking demonstration healthier and even more educational. Visit choosemyplate.gov for more information on MyPlate.

Cooking Demo Success Tips

1. Choose the right recipe(s).
When you plan your cooking demos, be sure to pick recipes that could appeal to your audience. Remember that your group will probably include a wide range of types -- this could be everyone from experienced chefs to people who have never even turned on their ovens.

2. Include example foods.
Purchase a variety of food products that feature health lessons you would like to discuss during your demo. These are especially handy tools to fill the void that comes up while you wait for something to cook. Try bringing salt-free canned tomatoes, oven-ready lasagna noodles, broth, flavored oil sprays, spice mixes, etc.

3. Practice.
Confidence is the key to cooking demonstration success. Practice your recipes in front of friends and family before going in front of strangers. Remember, practice really can make perfect!

4. Provide handouts.
Offer handouts with recipe details and/or health information. Encourage everyone to follow along and take notes while you're demonstrating various recipes.

5. Get organized.
Double check equipment and shopping lists to make sure that you will have everything you need. Drop by the demo kitchen a few days in advance. Organize your work area before participants arrive (protip: items you will use first should be closest to you), and keep it neat during the demonstration. Clean as you go.

6. Remember your appearance.
Wear comfortable shoes and professional clothing.
- Black pants and a white shirt or chef's coat create a simple, professional look, especially when combined with a colorful bib apron.
- Your hair should be tied back or otherwise secured.
- Go easy on the makeup, wear very little jewelry, and completely avoid nail polish.
- Have an extra apron on hand in case of spills.
- Keep towels nearby. Wipe your hands on them, not your apron.
- It helps to stand a few inches away from the counter. This will keep your clothes cleaner.

7. Prepare ahead.
Prepare all recipes as far ahead as possible. Chop vegetables, measure ingredients, cook pasta, etc. This is why we provided "make ahead options" in most recipe leader guides. They will help your demo move quickly

and keep your audience interested. This strategy also comes in handy when you have limited cooking equipment. For example, if you want to make a pie but don't have an oven, you can bake one pie ahead of time and show the group how to assemble another during class.

8. Check the mike.
If you are using a lavaliere microphone, insist on fresh batteries. There is nothing worse than losing power and having to wait on replacements during your demo.

9. Check the power.
Make sure your equipment is hooked up (correctly) to a functional power source. Before you start, test your set-up by running every single appliance at once.

10. Remember your sense of humor.
It is hard to guarantee that every single part of any endeavor will go perfectly. Laugh in the face of adversity and improvise.

11. Find a helper.
Audience participation promotes engagement. Ask for volunteers to help monitor the microwave/stove/oven, assemble dishes, and prepare ingredients. That way you can concentrate on your presentation.

12. Keep your audience involved.
Like we said, ask for volunteers. Be sure to have them wash their hands before they start. You can also ask questions and check the group's understanding as you go.

13. Finish the dish.
Give presentation tips that will help participants show off the final product. Try a sprinkling of chopped herbs or top a dish with a rainbow of colorful veggies and/or fruits. We have provided garnish and presentation tips in most recipe leader guides.

14. Encourage questions.
Encourage questions, but don't let them derail your train of thought. Before you begin, tell the group that you would love to hear any and all of their questions, but only at the end of the presentation. Take questions while dishing up samples and not one minute sooner. This helps keep your demo moving and prevents you from becoming distracted while you are trying to cook.

15. Keep food safe.
Follow the food safety tips that we outlined in the Food Safety Lesson of this kit. Remember, when in doubt, throw it out.

Food Safety Tips for Cooking Demos

Food safety is important, especially during cooking demonstrations. Sadly, typical demos often occur in less than ideal conditions with no sink, very little space, inadequate refrigeration, etc. While these tips are not meant to be all-inclusive, they are meant to help you prepare for your cooking demo as safely as possible.

- **Four critical areas of focus:**
  - Wash hands and food surfaces often.
  - Separate: don't cross contaminate.
  - Cook to proper temperatures as quickly as possible.
  - Refrigerate chilled items promptly.

- **Don't depend on the site** to have adequate facilities and supplies for handwashing, refrigeration, and cooking unless you've checked it out first. Make sure you have a back up plan, even if everything seems to be working and available.

- **Use a separate set of implements** for raw and ready-to-eat food. These sets should include everything from cutting boards to bowls to utensils and beyond. Keeping separate sets of implements ensures that you don't cross contaminate fresh or cooked food with raw food. In a cooking demo, you are moving rapidly and trying to keep your audience entertained. Even if you do have running water and adequate washing/sanitizing facilities, you might not have time to keep track of what utensil has been used when. Stay safe and use separate sets. Placing items on trays is another way to move things around without losing track of which works with what.

- **Emphasize to your helpers** that implements for raw and ready-to-eat foods (as well as the actual foods) should be separate. Do not serve any food that gets contaminated.

- **Bring plenty of paper towels** and a couple of big trash bags. One trash bag can be for trash, while the other can be for dirty implements. Paper towels are important for wiping your hands and cleaning up. Cloth towels are not sanitary and should be avoided.

- **Bring hand soap** and fingernail brushes so that you and your helpers can wash your hands at a nearby faucet. If there is no running water, bring a water carrier with a spout. Dry your hands with paper towels.

- **Bring perishable foods** to the site in a good ice box or cooler filled with ice. Use a thermometer to check that the interior temperature remains below 45 degrees F.

- **Judge the conditions** at your demo kitchen. If they're not up to snuff, serve food that you prepared off-site under more sanitary conditions. Then you'll just need to demo enough to outline what to do with each recipe.

- **Bowls of ice water** help keep small bowls of food cold during meal prep and sample tasting sessions.

- **If you're slicing and dicing** fruits, vegetables, etc, it is important to wash them well before the demo and transfer them to the site in plastic bags. Or you can bring pre-washed, pre-sliced food to the demo.

- **Hot plates** are good for keeping hot foods hot when electricity is available. Propane camping stoves or butane stoves are excellent if you do not have electricity. Did you know that you can rent these?

- **Bring a portable sanitizer** for counters and other food contact areas. A pump spray bottle (labeled "bleach water") filled with 1 quart of water and 1 tsp of bleach works very well.

- **Bring clean, disposable cups,** plates, and/or serving utensils for samples of the finished product.

- **Plan ahead for leftovers**, particularly during warm weather. Before giving anything away, ask yourself: can the recipient take it home quickly, can they cool it and keep it cool, and will they reheat it correctly?

Resources

- A food safety consumer education campaign called Fight Bac focuses on hand washing, avoiding cross contamination, cooking to proper temperatures and chilling quickly. Check it out at *www.fightbac.org*.
- Check out the USDA's tips on food safety at *http://www.fsis.usda.gov/*
- The National Restaurant Association Educational Foundation has an excellent book, called *Applied Foodservice Sanitation* (ISBN:0-915452-17-0). The text discusses applied measures for the prevention of foodborne diseases and the HACCP system.
- The USDA hotline (*800-535- 4555*) has excellent information about handling meat and poultry.
- *Don't Get Bugged* is a game for food safety education by the University of Nebraska Extension. For more information, visit *http://lancaster.unl.edu*.

We have assembled these tips from professionals on the foodsafe listserv. Special thanks go to Cindy Roberts, USDA/FDA Foodborne Illness Education Information Center, and Carl Custer, Staff Officer Food Microbiologist, USDA/FSIS/OPHS/SRO. This advice is based on the resources above, our own experience, and that of other health professionals.

Ideas for Cooking Demo Themes

Themes make cooking demos fun and interesting while attracting an audience that shares a common interest. Make sure to give your demo a title that outlines a specific benefit for attendees. In other words, instead of calling a class "Cooking 101," try "Heart Healthy Meals in Minutes." We've listed some of our favorite theme ideas below, many of which can be combined with some of the lessons in this book.

Holidays - Try a theme like Healthy and Delicious Holiday Gift Ideas, Hosting the Perfect Healthy Holiday Party, Diabetic Holiday Desserts, Trimming Favorite Holiday Recipes, Healthy Holiday Baking Valentine Dinner for Two, 4th of July, etc...

Regional - Many parts of the United States have regional dishes that can be made healthier. Consult restaurant menus and cookbooks for ideas. Local chefs can also be very friendly and willing to help. Sometimes they'll even guest star in a cooking demo to promote their restaurant. Try to catch chefs during off-peak periods so they're not too busy to talk with you.

Seasonal - Each month of the year provides a bounty of seasonal fruits and vegetables. Some ideas for seasonal themes include Summer Picnic Basket, Winter Citrus Desserts, Summertime No Cook Meals, Spring Berry Dishes, An Apple A Day, etc. Check out Cooking Light and Eating Well magazines for ideas. If you file your cooking magazines by month, you can retrieve multiple years of September issues, etc. This will give you more options that fit various seasonal themes.

Sport themes Take advantage of opportunities to highlight the importance of exercise. Why not try a Super Bowl, Olympics, World Series, or World Cup theme?

Family - Movie night is a common family bonding activity, so why not build a theme around healthy movie snacks? Or, for more family fun try a Family Reunion centered presentation or Ways to Eat Healthy on Vacation.

Health - Relate themes to your population or a timely message. Some examples include: Phytochemicals for Better Health, Soy, Flax, Ethnic Favorites Made Healthy, Getting to 5 A Day, etc..

Quick - This is one of our most popular recipe types by far. There are many ways to riff on this theme. Try Speed Scratch (the art of preparing a homemade meal with preassembled ingredients), Quick and Healthy, 7 Ingredient Meals, 15 Minute Meals, Weekday Meals, No Cook Meals, Speedy Vegetarian, Healthy Boxed Meals & Convenience Foods, etc.

Budget - These seem to be the second most popular type of recipe on the planet. Some budget theme options include Spend Less and Get More Nutrients, Stretching Your Food Budget, Making Every Food Dollar Count, Inexpensive Meals in Minutes, etc...

Ethnic - Help people break out of a kitchen rut by featuring new and interesting ethnic cuisine. Try Latin Style Meals in Minutes, Asian, Italian, Mediterranean, etc...

Ingredient - People are almost always fascinated by an exploration of a few of the current healthiest ingredients. You can also do an in-depth exploration of a particular ingredient, like garlic. This is a great opportunity to feature health stars such as greens, garlic, cruciferous vegetables, pasta, potatoes, etc.

Nutrient - Help your audience learn about specific nutrients like calcium or selenium. Try putting together a presentation on Getting More Fiber, Boning up on Calcium, Increasing Folic Acid for Better Heart Health (or pregnancy), etc.

Age - From toddlers to seniors, age appropriate demos work very well and allow you to focus on particular foods and interests.

Vegetarian - Many people are curious about vegetarian lifestyles, even when they personally would never give up meat. Build a demo around vegetarian options and explore common misconceptions.

Building a Better Brown Bag - Show attendees how to pack a better lunch, either for themselves and their children (or both).

Dessert - What better way to boost attendance than by featuring everyone's favorite course? Chocolate Without Guilt, Diabetic Desserts, Heart Healthy Fruit Desserts, are all options for a fun demo theme.

Herbs - Show participants how to grow an herb garden or demonstrate how to use fresh and dried herbs to flavor meals. Try something along the lines of Herbs for Flavor and Health.

Farmer's Market - Farmer's markets are taking off all across the country. You can come up with great meals based on produce that is local and in season. It is fun to use a market basket approach - come in with a bunch of ingredients and make something great!

7 Steps For a Successful Regional Class

Melissa Hight, Family & Consumer Science Educator at the North Carolina State University Cooperative Extension Service, has presented a number of Southern cooking classes. We think Melissa's format is fantastic and could be adapted for any region in the United States.

A) Start with the history or other interesting locale trivia. Melissa's presentation starts with a history of Southern foods and ways of life, both past and present, and also includes heart disease risk factors.

B) Outline how your regional or ethnic foods fit into MyPlate. Melissa explains where most Southern foods fit into MyPlate, emphasizing local agricultural products such as peanuts, sweet potatoes, okra, corn, tomatoes, wild greens, beans, and berries.

C) Serve lowfat, healthy samples of favorite regional or ethnic foods. Melissa serves lowfat chicken salad, healthy hearty collards, black-eyed peas and lemon cake squares. Some of the seasonings include: a ham-flavored broth made from ham hocks and smoked turkey meat. The cake is made with natural applesauce as a replacement for oil and the chicken salad is made with yogurt and nonfat mayonnaise. Modified recipes are given to attendees in their handout package, so that they can make them at home if they'd like.

D) Explain how to lighten up recipes while pointing to actual ingredients and items. Melissa usually brings the following items to her demos:
- Canned, evaporated skim milk
- Nonfat sweetened condensed milk
- Nonfat dry milk
- Nonstick cooking spray
- Applesauce
- Baby food prunes, apricots
- Butter sprinkles
- Fat skimming utensils & a meat rack

E) Bring along local restaurant menus to explore how to eat out without overindulging in fat and calorie heavy meals. Melissa hands out local restaurant menus, then students identify what traditional Southern foods they see. Melissa she writes down what is spotted as they go along, then the class uses this list to talk about the way those foods are prepared and how that affects the amount of fat and calories they contain.

F) If possible, offer hands on cooking in your class. Melissa divides her students and ingredients into four groups to prepare Southern Style Chicken Nuggets. She even shared her recipe with us:

Southern Style Chicken Nuggets:
    8 boneless skinless chicken breast halves (cut into 6-8 nuggets each)
    3 cups crushed corn flakes
    1 cup all-purpose flour
    1 tsp paprika
    1 tsp salt
    1 tsp pepper
    1 cup lowfat buttermilk

1. Trim any visible fat from chicken breasts and cut into nuggets. Place chicken and buttermilk in plastic zip top bag; seal and refrigerate 15 minutes, turning once.

2. Heat the oven to 400° and line jelly roll pan with aluminum foil; spray with nonstick cooking spray. Place cornflakes, flour and spices in blender. Cover and blend on medium speed until cornflakes are reduced to crumbs; pour into bowl.

3. Remove chicken nuggets and place in cornflake mixture to coat. Place coated chicken pieces on aluminum foil covered pan. Let chicken sit for 5 minutes and spray lightly with nonstick spray.

4. Bake approximately 20 minutes or until chicken nuggets are crisp and no longer pink in the center. Serves 8.

G) Offer a list of books or further resources for ethnic/regional healthy cooking. Check out some of the following...

http://www.eatingwell.com/recipes_menus/collections/healthy_asian_recipes. Cooking Well presents a fantastic online collection that features healthy Asian recipes. Take a look at the link above to find everything from appetizers to entrees.

http://www.foodnetwork.com/healthy-italian/package/index.html Craving Italian? Swing by the Food Network's collection of healthy Italian recipes and pantry tips.

Everyday Indian by Bal Arneson is a lovely cookbook that features healthy Indian recipes and explores Indian food.

http://www.southernliving.com/food/healthy-light/healthy-southern-recipes-00417000069405/ Southern Living presents a wide range of lightened up Southern dishes. Explore their recipe archives for gorgeous photos and helpful hints.

Show and Tell for a Healthy Kitchen

Here is a list of supermarket items that we like to discuss with attendees. People love to learn about new, delicious foods that will make their lives easier!

Pre-Chopped Vegetables:

There are many delicious veggie options in both the produce and freezer sections of the grocery store. Some great examples include...

Frozen diced onion

Frozen sliced bell peppers

Minced garlic in water or oil

Chopped basil in water

Canned tomatoes with basil, onions, peppers, spices, etc are delicious. These cans include a bunch of different, flavorful ingredients, all in one place. Choose no-salt-added and reduced sodium options in order to stay in alignment with MyPlate recommendations.

Prepared produce. Check out the produce section for pre-chopped stir fry mixes, cole slaw mixes, broccoli slaw, salad mixes, diced fruit, veggie sticks, and more.

Frozen vegetable medleys have come a long way since peas and carrots. There are now stir fry mixes, festive vegetable mixes, Italian vegetable mixes, etc. Watch out for high sodium and fat content by checking sauce packets and nutrition information.

Healthy Products That Save Time

The grocery store is chock-full of healthy, flavorful products to help save time in the kitchen. Here is a brief list of our favorites...

Spice mixes. Don't miss Italian Seasoning, Apple Pie Spice Mix, Pumpkin Pie Spice Mix, Poultry Seasoning, Chile Powder, etc.

Sauces. Look beyond worcestershire and soy sauce. Why not try teriyaki sauce, garlic Tabasco sauce, Hoisin Sauce, or Sriracha?

Salsa. A little bit of salsa goes a long way and adds tremendous flavor to pasta, rice, and more.

Instant brown rice is a healthy whole grain that cooks in 5 or 10 minutes.

Fat free tortillas. You can also find lowfat versions in most areas of the country. These can be toasted or used as wrappers for various sandwiches or burritos.

Pasta sauces are a whole class of sauces unto themselves. Be sure to stay aware of their sodium content.

Ground, skinless turkey breast and other turkey breast products are available, along with all sorts of flavored chicken tenders.

Unique shapes and flavors of pasta enable you to serve healthy whole grains several times a week without sacrificing variety. Some of our favorites are fusilli, bowtie, and wagon wheel.

Exotic or rare produce is always fun to slice and taste. Try kiwi, starfruit, exotic winter squashes, dinosaur kale, passion fruit, etc.

Cup-of-meal. There are now soups, cereals and mashed potatoes that make great take-along snacks and meals.

Nifty Fat Replacers

Quite a few common grocery store finds make great replacements for fats and oils in cooking and baking projects. We especially like...

Lighter Bake, baby food prunes, Smucker's Baking Healthy and apple sauce. These all easily replace the fat in baking. Switch all or half of the fat with the full amount of applesauce or half the amount of pureed prunes. Prunes work best in dark-colored baked goods like brownies, spice cakes, muffins and banana nut bread.

Silken tofu makes unbelievable cheesecakes, cream pies, puddings, and even Caesar Salad Dressing.

Broths add a lot of flavor (and almost no fat) to savory dishes. Keep an eye on the sodium content and choose low-sodium options where possible.

Vegetable oil cooking sprays are available in a wide range of flavors. Olive oil cooking spray is great to mist over a salad that has been tossed with vinegar. You'll get much less sodium than you would if you use fat free salad dressing. For fun sprays on a budget, make your own by adding oil to a new, food-grade spray bottle.

Calcium Fortified Products

These are varied and include everything from orange juice to milk, yogurt, sweetened cereal, waffles, spaghetti, apple juice, Knox gelatin, tofu, soy milk, instant oatmeal, frozen yogurt, rice, and more.

Calcium is the number one mineral added to food. Often these products are high in sugar, so keep an eye out for healthy options and stick to lowfat or fat free versions.

Buyer Beware

Reduced fat foods are often still high in calories. They make good examples when teaching the importance of label reading. Reduced fat cookies are usually not low in calories, for example. Neither is reduced fat peanut butter, reduced fat chips, or reduced fat ice cream. Bring along regular versions of reduced fat foods so that your audience can see the lack of a significant calorie difference.

The Wellness Kitchen

The secret to preparing quick, healthy meals is keeping your kitchen stocked with nutritious foods.

You certainly do not need all the foods mentioned here in order to cook in a healthy way. This list just provides ideas and suggestions for ingredients to have on hand to prepare great meals.

Pantry

Stock your pantry shelves with a variety of beans, pasta, tomatoes, and tomato sauces. Here is a list that will help you get started:

- Lowfat chicken broth
- Black beans (canned or dry)
- Kidney beans (canned or dry)
- Pinto beans (canned or dry)
- Assorted whole wheat pastas - Try spaghetti, angel hair pasta, rotini, penne, and/or macaroni.
- Pasta sauce
- Cooking oil sprays. (You can make your own by adding oil to a new, food-safe spray bottle).
- Tuna packed in water
- Tomatoes - Try some of the new varieties that have seasonings and other vegetables added. These will save a lot of time.
- Salsa
- Soups - These make great quick meals and can also be used as delicious sauces for many dishes.
- Flavored vinegars

Spice Shelf

The spice shelf is important. If you are cooking with less fat, you'll really need to depend on various herbs, spices, and seasoning mixes for flavor. Here is a list of some of our favorites...

- Italian Seasoning mix - This is good for pasta and other dishes. It contains oregano, basil, marjoram and thyme.
- Tabasco or hot pepper sauce - These are great for spicing up Latin and Asian style dishes.
- Garlic powder - This powder saves tons of time.
- Black pepper- Try ground or fresh cracked.
- Dried basil - This herb is great in many dishes.
- Dried oregano - Oregano is delicious in Italian, Mediterranean, and Latin style dishes
- Cumin - This is tasty in Latin style dishes and chiles.
- Rosemary - Rosemary is especially good on poultry.
- Cinnamon - This is great to use to top fruits or add to your coffee.
- Apple pie spice - This is delicious in fruit desserts

- Pumpkin pie spice - Try it on winter squash and pumpkin pie.
- Ground ginger - This one is a must for stir frys.
- Sesame oil - A little dash adds flavor to stir frys.

Refrigerator

- Fresh fruit is a healthy snack and seems naturally wrapped for people on the go.
- Broccoli is an easy vegetable to prepare and steam.
- Lettuce can be bought already prepared if you are in a hurry.
- Vegetable sticks can be bought already sliced for easy snacks.
- Shredded cabbage is great to add to slaws.
- Mustard
- Minced garlic
- No salt added ketchup
- Nonfat plain yogurt
- Vanilla flavored yogurt
- Your favorite fat free salad dressings
- Fat free mayonnaise
- Lowfat deli meats
- Fat free cheese or reduced fat cheese
- Skim milk
- Parmesan cheese

Your Kitchen Counter

- Bananas
- Fresh fruits (like peaches) and other produce (like avocados and potatoes) that are store better at room temperature.
- Tomatoes

Freezer

- Frozen vegetables - Use these in everything from soups to pasta to stir frys, or just by themselves.
- Frozen fruits - These come in handy in fruit desserts, fruit syrups for pancakes and waffles, and for smoothies.
- "Planned-Overs" - These are essential. Make large batches of your favorite foods and freeze them for a later date.
- Lean meat, poultry, and/or fish - These should be frozen in portion-sized packages so you don't have to thaw more than you need.
- Bread - Whole grain bread, pitas, tortillas, and more will stay fresh and ready for use in your freezer.

SuperStar Cooking

14 Tips for Smooth Cooking Demos

#1 If you are using a lavaliere microphone, insist on fresh batteries. There is nothing worse than losing power and having to wait on replacements during your demo. This happened to me on the second day of a workshop, when my voice was already tired after 6 hours of talking the day before. Never assume that the audiovisual department will check these things

#2 Check your power source. At one of my presentations, the engineers hooked up 2 burners and 2 microwaves to the same outlet. This overloaded the poor outlet and we lost power completely for part of the first day. Run all your appliances at once for a minute or two to make sure all is well with your power supply.

#3 Keep a sense of humor. If the problems I describe don't happen, odds are good that something else will. Laugh in the face of adversity and improvise.

#4 Appearance is everything. Wear comfortable shoes and comfortable, professional clothing. My favorite outfit is black pants and a white blouse/chef's coat with a blue bib apron. My hair is always tied back, makeup is kept light, jewelry is minimal and I never, ever, wear nail polish. Keep an extra apron handy in case you spill something, and be sure to wipe your hands on towels (keep them nearby) instead of your clothes. It helps to stand back from the counter -- that way you will not lean into your food.

#5 Make a selection of dishes that can appeal to a wide variety of people. Remember that everyone from the health conscious to the higher fat intake crowd could be there, and you will likely be giving presentations for a widely mixed group.

#6 Explore new, time-saving food products. This will keep your audience interested and add credibility to your presentation. Think about trying salsa, flavored canned tomatoes, oven-ready lasagna noodles, broth, flavored cooking oil sprays, prepared produce, spice mixes, and instant brown rice.

#7 Make sure you prepare all recipes as far ahead as possible. Have some pre-finished dishes where

applicable. People tend to get bored very quickly when they have to watch you measure ingredients.

#8 Emphasize the microwave for speedy meals.

#9 Have an assistant to help monitor the microwave and stove so you can concentrate on your presentation and questions. If you can't have a hired one, find a volunteer from the audience. The odds are pretty good that someone will be happy to take the stage.

#10 Provide visuals of the finished dish. Give presentation tips like sprinkling with chopped herbs or Parmesan and using colorful veggies and fruits. Here is an excellent opportunity to explore portion sizes and how to arrange your plate according to MyPlate and the Dietary Guidelines for Americans.

#11 Encourage questions, but don't let them derail your train of thought. Before you begin, tell the group that you would love to hear any and all of their questions, but only at the end of the presentation. Take questions while dishing up samples and not one minute sooner. This helps keep your demo moving and prevents you from becoming distracted while you are trying to cook.

#12 Provide handouts with recipes, cooking tips, and ingredient substitutions for your audience to follow. Handouts are an excellent tool to have available - you can refer to them and make other points while you are waiting for something to cook. My favorite one is the Fat Saver Guide; I use it to talk about recipe substitutions all the time.

#13 Organization is indispensable! Make a list of everything that you will need for the demo. This list should include equipment, ingredients, and utensils. Make a list of what you need to do before the demo and also what you will do from start to finish during the actual demo. Lists are easy to follow and allow you to relax and stay organized.

#14 Confidence is the KEY to success. Practice your recipes in front of friends and family before going in front of strangers. This will help you develop proper timing and memorize your directions. A well-practiced presentation lends an aura of expertise to the presenter. With practice, you will be able to move smoothly from start to finish. Just be sure to practice your speech while actually cooking.

Food Demo Organizer - Page 1

Copy this page and use it as a handy to-do list to keep you organized through all phases of your cooking demonstrations.

Step 1. Several weeks before the demo

Determine the theme and title of your cooking demo. Write all steps that you will have to do to advertise it (posters/announcements, sign up sheets, etc).

_____
_____
_____
_____
_____

Step 2. Several weeks before the demo

Make a list of all the topics that you would like to cover. Write down a list of handouts or props that you might use to further your point.

_____
_____
_____
_____
_____

Step 3. Several weeks before the demo

Make a list of recipes that you would like to demonstrate. Do a dress rehearsal of these recipes for interested family and friends.

_____
_____
_____
_____

Step 4. Several weeks before the demo

Make an equipment/supplies list for the recipes. Here are a few suggestions:

- Read up on food safety tips and determine if you need to bring handwashing supplies, paper towels, and separate implements for raw and cooked food.
- Do you need a microwave or stovetop?
- What pots, pans, and dishes do you need?
- What utensils do you need for cooking and serving?
- Do you need a cutting board or mixing bowls?
- Do you need any appliances such as a can opener, food processor or blender?
- Will you need oven mitts or pan holders? What about an apron or towels?
- Will you require a refrigerator, freezer or cooler? How about ice?

- What do you need to present the finished dish?
- What do you need for audiovisual equipment?

_____
_____
_____
_____
_____
_____
_____
_____
_____
_____
_____
_____
_____
_____

Step 5. One week before the demo

Make a shopping list for all the groceries you'll need during your cooking demo. Remember to include cooking oil spray and water.

- Paper Goods: Do you need supplies for serving samples? If you do, you might need plastic utensils, plates, cups, and/or napkins.
- Ziploc bags are great for storing prepared/premeasured ingredients, while paper towels are a must for any clean up.
- Do you need food items for a show and tell pantry?
- In some cases, you may want to bring a finished, prepared dish and serve tasting samples. Then you would need to bringing a second set of ingredients in order to show how to prepare the featured food. Make sure you allow for multiple options on your list.

_____
_____
_____
_____
_____
_____
_____
_____
_____
_____
_____
_____

Food Demo Organizer - Page 2

Step 6. One week before the demo
Make a list of what you need to prepare ahead of the demo. For example, you may want to premeasure all ingredients (including seasonings), chop all vegetables and fruits, cook pasta or rice ahead of time, cut meat into bite-size pieces, open new jars or bottles (so you don't struggle in front of your audience), etc.

_____

_____

_____

_____

_____

_____

_____

_____

_____

_____

_____

_____

_____

_____

Step 7. Several days before the demo
Print handouts and gather props/equipment.

Step 8. Two days before the demo
Go grocery shopping. Double check all your lists to make sure that you have everything you need.

Step 9. The day before the demo
Prepare all items from your list in step 6. If you are doing multiple recipes, it helps to label everything and write down which recipe it accompanies (Color coding? We say yes). Keep ingredients for each recipe together and organized.

Assemble everything you need from handouts, cooking equipment, supplies for tasting, recipe ingredients, to props and your demonstration outfit. Load your car with the nonperishable items you'll need.

Step 10. Demo Day
Arrive at the demo site early. Get everything set up in an organized fashion and in the order you will need it to cook. Test the equipment. Do a "dry run" rehearsal. Look at your demo area from the audience - can they see well, is there anything obstructing their view, etc? Placing handouts on chairs makes everything run more smoothly during the actual presentation.

Take a deep breath and have fun! A sense of humor will take you through even the greatest challenges.

Step 11. After Your Demo
Gather feedback from your audience. This can be done formally with a quiz or worksheet, or informally by hosting a quick discussion while participants are eating their samples.

Take the time to write down what you would do differently next time. Also, write down what your participants seemed to like the best. Did they have good questions that you think you should cover in more depth next time?

If you do cooking demos often, you may want to make a separate storage area for your supplies. That will make them easier to gather and organize the next time.

What my participants liked the best:

_____

_____

_____

_____

_____

_____

_____

_____

What would make my demo smoother next time:

_____

_____

_____

_____

_____

_____

_____

What questions was I asked? How can I address these questions next time? Would other props or handouts come in handy?

_____

_____

_____

_____

_____

_____

_____

_____

_____

_____

Leader Guide: Antioxidants

Target Audience:
This presentation kit is intended for audiences from age 14 to seniors. It is suited for general audiences and covers wellness, aging, cancer prevention, and nutrition.

Lesson Objectives:
• Participants will learn the role of antioxidants and the importance of consuming them.
• Participants will identify sources of antioxidants.
• Participants will explore how to prepare foods that are rich in antioxidants.

Lesson Rationale:
Health authorities have indicated that good nutrition is one of the most important factors in determining long-term health (along with limited alcohol consumption and avoidance of tobacco products). Poor diet plays a major role in the development of four of the top seven killers in the United States: heart disease, cancer, stroke, and diabetes. Students who have the skills to select and prepare nutritious foods can positively impact their present and future health.

Lesson at a Glance:
This lesson introduces participants to new recipes and teaches cooking skills. It also provides nutrition and dietary information that is consistent with the Dietary Guidelines for Americans and MyPlate.

Lesson Materials:
This lesson contains:
• Leader and activity guide
• 3 pages of copy-ready handouts and recipes
• 1 coloring page for children, titled "Color Me Fruity."
• Word document file with recipes

Preparation:
___ Review leader guide
___ Review handouts
___ Select activities
___ Copy, collect, and prepare materials for lesson

Introduction:
Ask your audience if anyone can define the word "antioxidant." Then ask for those who take vitamins with antioxidants to raise their hands.

Discussion:
Use the Antioxidant Fact Sheet to provide answers to the following questions...
• What are antioxidants?

• What can they do for me?
• Where can I find antioxidants?

Conclusion:
Have participants brainstorm ways to incorporate more antioxidant-rich foods into their diets. Use the Smart Substitutes handout to illustrate strategies for replacing nutrient-poor foods with nutrient-rich foods. If possible, choose one of the food activities listed in the next section.

Activity Ideas:

Activity 1 - Can You Find the Missing Link?
1. Using the Antioxidant Fact Sheet, make a display of foods that are high in antioxidants. Group the foods by the type of antioxidants they contain. Here is a heart healthy list of antioxidant sources...
• Vitamin C - Citrus fruits, strawberries, broccoli, bell peppers, tomatoes.
• Vitamin E - Nuts (especially almonds), seeds, vegetable oils, dark green leafy vegetables, whole grains, fatty fish.
• Selenium - Lean meat, fish, cereal, dairy products, Brazil nuts.
• Beta-carotene - Dark green, deep yellow and orange fruits and vegetables (like carrots, oranges, winter squash, sweet potatoes, cantaloupe, tomatoes, kale, and spinach).
2. Ask participants if they know what these foods have in common. Encourage guessing!
3. Confirm (or provide) antioxidants as the correct answer. Hand out copies of the Antioxidant Fact Sheet before discussing each group of foods. Explore how some foods contain more than one type of antioxidant.
4. Explain the importance of obtaining antioxidants from food and eating a variety of foods. Don't let that call for variety serve as a green light for overeating, however. Remember, according to the USDA's MyPlate, you should enjoy your food, but generally eat less of it, keeping portions small.

Activity 2 - Cooking Demo
Prepare a few simple dishes using the recipes featured at the end of this program.

Activity 3 - Antioxidant Memory Quiz
1. Arrange examples of high-antioxidant foods on a table.
2. Allow participants to view them for a set length of time.

Leader Guide: Antioxidants

3. Have participants return to their seats, where the display of foods is not in view, then have them all make a list of the foods they saw.
4. Using a blackboard, dry-erase board, or overhead projector, make a group list of the foods that they made in their own lists.
5. At the end, unveil the foods once more and check to see which ones they remembered.

Activity 4 - Kids "Color Me Fruity"

1. Have kids color the cartoon sheet "Color Me Fruity."
2. While they are coloring, serve them a variety of fresh fruit and vegetables as snacks.
3. Explain the importance of eating a variety of colors from fruits and vegetables. Have the kids color a rainbow and then see if they can name one fruit or vegetable that is the same color as each aspect of the rainbow. You can also provide cut pictures of fruits and vegetables for them to paste in their rainbow.

Activity 5 - Antioxidant Trivia Party

1. Ask the following antioxidant trivia questions. You can reward correct answers with fruit, vegetables, dried beans, etc.
   1) What is another name for free radical scavengers.
      Answer: Antioxidants
   2) True or false? There are hundreds, maybe thousands, of substances found in food that act as antioxidants. *Answer*: True
   3) Name four health benefits of antioxidants.
      Answers: Vary, but should include at least some of the following -- they may help lower your the risk of cardiovascular disease, they may help slow the aging process, they may help inhibit the growth of certain cancers, and/or they may enhance the health of your eyes.
   4) You should get your antioxidants from _____.
      Answer: Food
   5) Name the three MyPlate food groups that contain the most antioxidant rich foods.
      Answer: Vegetables, fruits, and grains. These should take up lots of space on your plate at every meal!
   6) What are the four most commonly studied antioxidant nutrients?
      Answer: Vitamin E, vitamin C, selenium, and carotenoids

   7) True or false? Thanks to soil depletion, you should be concerned about getting enough selenium in your diet.
      Answer: False. We eat a variety of foods from a wide range of geographic areas. Most contain ample selenium in the soil.

Leader Guide: Antioxidant Recipes

Open Faced Fruit Sandwich
Makes 16 sample servings

4 slices whole grain bread (frozen)
4 Tbsp peanut butter
2 cups assorted fruit: banana, strawberries and kiwi

Directions:
1. Arrange bread on cutting board.
2. Spread 1 tablespoon of peanut butter on each slice.
3. Place 1/2 cup of fruit slices in an attractive pattern on top of the peanut butter.
4. Slice bread into triangular quarters and serve immediately.

Equipment needed:
___ Cutting board
___ Table knife (to spread peanut butter)
___ Paring knife (to cut fruit and finished sandwiches)

Shopping list:
___ 1 loaf 100% whole grain bread
___ Natural, unsalted peanut butter
___ Assorted fresh fruit (such as bananas, strawberries, and kiwis)
___ Napkins for serving

Cooking skill/nutrition lesson:
This recipe teaches the audience how to make a healthy snack using nut butter, fruits and whole grain bread. It requires no cooking and highlights the use of fresh fruit instead of (or in addition to) jelly. Since people should fill one quarter of their plate with fruit at each meal (according to the USDA), this is a great way to sneak in fruit in a more creative setting. While you prepare the sandwiches, discuss how to purchase and store fruit. Peanut butter spreads more thinly and evenly on frozen bread.

Demo preparation:
1. Wash your hands before you handle the food.
2. If possible, wash the fruit in cold, running water.
3. Place bread, peanut butter, and fruit near the cutting board.
4. Place knife next to the cutting board.

Make ahead:
You can make most of the sandwiches just before class starts so that you will have enough for everyone to taste.
Garnish/presentation tip: Place the sandwich triangles on a small, attractive plate.

Number of sample servings: 16

Antioxidants Rock! Smoothie
Makes 12 sample servings

1 cup orange juice
1 cup vanilla-flavored light yogurt
1 banana
1/2 cup strawberries
1/4 cup wheat germ
Pinch cinnamon

Directions:
1. Place all ingredients in blender and blend until smooth.
2. Serve immediately. Pour into 2 ounce tasting cups.

Equipment needed:
___ Measuring cups
___ Cutting board
___ Paring knife
___ Blender
___ Attractive glass (to show final product)

Shopping list:
___ 1 quart orange juice
___ 1 container vanilla-flavored light yogurt
___ 1 banana
___ 1 pint strawberries
___ 1 jar wheat germ
___ 1 jar ground cinnamon
___ Small cups and napkins (for samples)

Cooking skill/nutrition lesson:
This recipe demonstrates how to make a smoothie.

Demo preparation:
1. Wash your hands before you handle the food.
2. Wash all fruit in cold, running water where possible. Remove cores or seeds and place fruit in plastic bag.
3. Measure ingredients.
4. Place the blender in the center of your table and arrange all ingredients around it.

Make ahead:
You can make this recipe ahead of time and keep it refrigerated for up to 4 hours.
Garnish/presentation tip: Pour the smoothie into a tall glass and garnish with a sliced strawberry and colorful straw.

Number of sample servings: 12

Leader Guide: Antioxidant Recipes

Vegetables with Tomato Hummus
Makes 25-30 sample servings
Vegetables:
1 cup baby carrots
1 cup broccoli florets
1 cup cherry tomatoes
1 cup celery sticks
1 cup cauliflower florets

Tomato Hummus:
15 oz can garbanzo beans, drained and rinsed
1/3 cup tomato paste
Juice of 1 lemon
1 tsp garlic powder
2 Tbsp olive oil
1/2 tsp ground cumin
1/4 cup tahini paste (Look in kosher food section)
1/2 cup water
Directions:
1. Arrange vegetables on a large platter in an attractive fashion. Place a bowl for dip in the center.
2. Make dip by placing all tomato hummus ingredients in a blender or food processor.
3. Process on high speed until a smooth paste forms. Spoon the dip into the center bowl and serve immediately. You can also refrigerate it for later use -- it keeps for up to one week in the refrigerator.
Shortcut: Add half of a 6-ounce can of tomato paste to 2 cups prepared hummus. Swirl a little tomato paste in for garnish.

Equipment:
___ Measuring cups
___ Measuring spoons
___ Cutting board
___ Vegetable peeler
___ Chef's knife
___ Paring knife
___ Blender or food processor
___ Spatula
___ Can opener
___ Attractive platter
___ Bowl for dip

Shopping list:
___ 1 bag baby carrots
___ 1 head fresh broccoli
___ 1 pint cherry tomatoes
___ 1 package celery sticks
___ 1 head cauliflower or 1 bag cauliflower florets
___ 1 15-ounce can garbanzo beans
___ 1 6-ounce can tomato paste
___ 1 lemon
___ Garlic powder
___ Olive oil
___ Ground cumin
___ Tahini paste
___ Napkins
___ Miniature cups (for samples)

Cooking skill/nutrition lesson:
The USDA asserts that half your plate should be fruits and vegetables at every meal. This recipe provides a creative way to make sure you're getting enough vegetables in your diet. Plus, legumes like garbanzo beans can count either as a protein food or as a vegetable. What versatile treats!This recipe requires no cooking and very little prep time, especially if you buy the pre-cut veggie from your grocery store.

Demo preparation:
1. Wash your hands before handling the food.
2. Wash, peel, and cut the vegetables. Arrange them on an attractive platter and cover the whole thing with plastic wrap.
3. Measure all ingredients for the hummus and place them, along with utensils, within reach of the blender.

Make ahead options:
You can make this entire recipe ahead of time. You can also buy prepared hummus at most grocery stores if you just want to pass out sample servings of this dish.

Garnish/presentation tips:
Arrange the vegetables in an attractive circular fashion around the dip bowl on a large round or square platter. Place the bowl of dip in the center. Arrange some sliced veggies on top of the hummus or decorate it with chopped tomatoes.
Tastings: serve 1 tablespoon of hummus dip in a small container with 2-3 pieces of vegetables.

Number of sample servings: 25-30

Leader Guide: Antioxidant Recipes

Maple Cinnamon Sweet Potato
Makes 16-20 sample servings

4 large, orange-fleshed sweet potatoes (about 1 pound)
4 Tbsp light maple-flavored pancake syrup
1/2 tsp ground cinnamon

Directions:

1. Wash sweet potatoes under cold running water; remove all exterior dirt.
2. Pierce potatoes with a fork and place them in a microwave oven for 6-8 minutes each. Try to keep the potatoes from touching.
3. Microwave on full power until fork tender, turning once halfway through cooking.
4. Slice potatoes in half lengthwise, fluff with a fork and top with 1 tablespoon of syrup and a pinch of ground cinnamon. Serve hot.

For tastings, place 2 tablespoons of mashed sweet potato in a small cup with a spoon.

Equipment:
___ Measuring spoons
___ Microwave oven
___ Paring knife
___ Fork
___ Plate for final presentation

Shopping list:
___ 4 large orange-fleshed sweet potatoes
___ 1 bottle light pancake syrup
___ 1 jar ground cinnamon
___ Mini-cups (for samples)
___ Forks and napkins (for samples)

Cooking skill/nutrition lesson:
This lesson teaches participants an easy, fast way to prepare a sweet potato. Here are quick nutrition facts from the North Carolina Sweet Potato Commission.

- One cup of cooked sweet potatoes provides 30 mg (50,000 IU) of beta carotene (Vitamin A). It would take 23 cups of broccoli to provide the same amount.
- Sweet potatoes have four times the US Recommended Daily Allowance (USRDA) for beta-carotene when eaten whole, skin and all.
- Sweet potatoes are a great source of vitamin E and are virtually fat-free, which makes them a real vitamin E standout. Most foods that are rich in vitamin E, such as vegetable oils, nuts and avocados, contain a hefty dose of fat. Just two thirds of a cup of sweet potatoes provides 100% of the USRDA for vitamin E, without the unwanted fat.
- Sweet potatoes provide many other essential nutrients including vitamin B6, potassium, and iron.
- Sweet potatoes are a good source of dietary fiber, which helps to promote a healthy digestive tract. Sweet potatoes have more fiber than oatmeal.
- Sweet potatoes are virtually fat-free, cholesterol-free and very low in sodium. A medium sweet potato has just 118 calories.

Demo preparation:
1. Wash and pierce the sweet potatoes.
2. Assemble all ingredients near the microwave.
3. Precook sweet potatoes about 3/4 of the way before class starts.
4. When class sits down, show them the sweet potatoes and explain what you have done so far.
5. Finish cooking the sweet potatoes then demonstrate how to finish the process and serve one on a plate by cooking them the rest of the way, then topping with cinnamon and syrup.
6. Serve small scoops of finished potato in small cups for tasting samples. It is fun if you can give the large potato used to show presentation of the final dish to one of the participants for helping or answering a trivia question about antioxidants or sweet potatoes.

Make ahead options:
You can cook sweet potatoes ahead of time and just finish them in front of the audience.

Garnish/presentation tips:
Fluff sweet potatoes with fork, drizzle with syrup in a fine stream, and sprinkle the cinnamon over the potato. Dash a little of both onto the plate itself. If you want to make this dish a little fancier, consider serving fresh salsa on the side.

Number of sample servings: 16-20

Antioxidant Recipes

Open Faced Fruit Sandwich

4 slices whole grain bread (frozen)

4 Tbsp peanut butter

2 cups assorted fruit: banana, strawberries and kiwi

Directions:

1. Arrange bread on cutting board.
2. Spread 1 tablespoon of peanut butter on each slice.
3. Place 1/2 cup of fruit slices in an attractive pattern on top of the peanut butter.
4. Slice bread into triangular quarters and serve immediately.

Serves 4. Each serving (one open-faced sandwich): 256 calories, 11 g fat, 1.5 g saturated fat, 0 mg cholesterol, 295 mg sodium, 35 g carbohydrate, 5.5 g fiber, 7 g protein.

Vegetables with Tomato Hummus

Vegetables:

1 cup baby carrots

1 cup broccoli florets

1 cup cherry tomatoes

1 cup celery sticks

1 cup cauliflower florets

Tomato Hummus:

15 oz can garbanzo beans, drained and rinsed

1/3 cup tomato paste

Juice of 1 lemon

1 tsp garlic powder

2 Tbsp olive oil

1/2 tsp ground cumin

1/4 cup tahini paste (look in Kosher food section)

1/2 cup water

Directions:

1. Arrange vegetables on a large platter in an attractive fashion. Place a bowl for dip in the center.
2. Make dip by placing all tomato hummus ingredients in a blender or food processor.
3. Process on high speed until a smooth paste forms. Spoon the dip into the center bowl and serve immediately. Shortcut: Add half of a 6-ounce can of tomato paste to 2 cups prepared hummus. Swirl a little tomato paste in for garnish.

Serves 10. Each serving (1/2 cup of veggies with 1/4 cup hummus: 129 calories, 7 g fat, 0.5 g saturated fat, 0 mg cholesterol, 134 mg sodium, 12 g carbohydrate, 3.5 g fiber, 5 g protein.

Maple Cinnamon Sweet Potato

4 large orange-fleshed sweet potatoes (about 1 pound)

4 Tbsp light maple-flavored pancake syrup

1/2 tsp ground cinnamon

Directions:

1. Wash sweet potatoes under cold running water; remove all exterior dirt.
2. Pierce with a fork and place them in a microwave oven for 6-8 minutes per potato. Try to keep the potatoes from touching.
3. Microwave on full power until fork tender, turning them over once about half way through cooking.
4. Split potatoes in half lengthwise, fluff with a fork and top each one with 1 tablespoon of syrup and a pinch of ground cinnamon. Serve hot.

Serves 4. Each serving (1 potato): 143 calories, 0 g fat, o mg cholesterol, 44 mg sodium, 34 g carbohydrate, 3.5 g fiber, 2 g protein.

Antioxidants Rock! Smoothie

1 cup orange juice

1 cup vanilla-flavored light yogurt

1 banana

1/2 cup strawberries

1/4 cup wheat germ

Pinch cinnamon

Directions:

1. Place all ingredients in blender and blend until smooth.
2. Serve immediately or refrigerate until ready to consume - up to 4 hours.
3. Pour into two tall glasses.

Serves 4. Each serving (1 cup): 117 calories, 1 g fat, 0 g saturated fat 1 mg cholesterol, 26 mg sodium, 23 g carbohydrate, 2 g fiber, 4.5 g protein.

Antioxidant FAQs

What are antioxidants?

Antioxidants are 'free radical scavengers.' Oxygen free radicals are produced as part of normal cellular activity, as well as from exposure to pollution and radiation. Antioxidants stop these free radicals, which would otherwise damage cells and contribute to the development of conditions like heart disease and cancer. Free radicals also appear to contribute to the aging process. There are hundreds, maybe thousands, of substances in food which act as antioxidants. The ones that have been studied the most are vitamin C, vitamin E, selenium and some of the carotenoids (like beta-carotene, lycopene, lutein and zeaxanthin).

Health benefits

There are no clear answers yet about exactly what antioxidants can do. Some likely health benefits include:

- Cardiovascular - may lower the risk of heart disease and stroke
- Cancer - may decrease the risk of cancer
- Eyes - may prevent cataracts and age-related macular degeneration
- Aging - may help slow age-related decline in memory and cognitive function

Antioxidant requirements

No recommendations exist for antioxidant intake in general. However, the Food and Nutrition Board made recommendations for specific antioxidant nutrients:

- Vitamin C - women should get 75 mg/day, while men should get 90 mg/day. Smokers should get about 35 mg/day more than that. Do not consume more than 2000 mg/day.
- Vitamin E - women and men should get 15 mg/day, but no more than 1000 mg/day.
- Selenium - women and men should get 55 mcg/day, but absolutely no more than 400 mcg/day.
- Carotenoids - No recommendations have been fixed because not enough is known about carotenoids.

Food labels still use Daily Values, which are based on older recommendations (75 mg for vitamin C, 13.5 mg for vitamin E, 70 mcg for selenium).

Get your antioxidants here!

Whenever possible, get your antioxidants from foods - primarily fruits, vegetables and whole grains. Some studies have found antioxidant supplements may be damaging to smokers. Plus, no one knows the long-term risks of these supplements. On the other hand, many studies have shown that people who eat the most antioxidant-rich foods have the lowest rates of chronic disease. By choosing a wide range of foods, you will also get the whole spectrum of antioxidants as well as all the other nutrients and fiber that whole foods offer. That's one of the reasons that the USDA's MyPlate recommends eating small portions of a wide variety of foods. You'll get more vitamins, nutrients, fiber, and antioxidants that way.

The antioxidant power of foods has been measured in units of Oxygen Radical Absorbance Capacity (ORAC). High-ORAC vegetables include kale, spinach, broccoli, beets, Brussels sprouts, and red bell peppers. High-ORAC fruits include prunes, raisins, blueberries, blackberries, strawberries, plums, oranges and grapes.

Sources of specific antioxidants include:

- Vitamin C - Citrus fruits, strawberries, broccoli, bell peppers, tomatoes.
- Vitamin E - Nuts (especially almonds), seeds, vegetable oils, dark green leafy vegetables, whole grains, fatty fish.
- Selenium - Meat, fish, cereal, dairy products, Brazil nuts.
- Beta-carotene - Dark green, deep yellow, and orange fruits and vegetables (like carrots, oranges, winter squash, sweet potatoes, cantaloupe, tomatoes, dark green leafy vegetables).

Antioxidant fun facts

- There are about 600 different carotenoids - we still have a lot to learn about them!
- The selenium content of food varies greatly depending on the soil where the plants were grown, but this is not a concern in the U.S. because we eat food grown in a variety of locations.
- Our bodies protect themselves by producing their own antioxidants, but normal aging and environmental factors can lessen our ability to do so. That's where whole, colorful foods enter the picture!

By Cheryl Sullivan, MA, RD

Antioxidant Smart Substitutes

Instead of:	Use:
Beverages:	
Punch, soda	100% fruit juice
Breakfast:	
Bagel, donut	Whole grain cereal, skim milk, fruit
Sweetened cereal	Oatmeal with fruit and skim milk
Lunch:	
White bread	100% whole wheat bread
Hamburger	Veggie burger with lettuce & tomato
Peanut butter and jelly sandwich	Peanut butter and fruit sandwich
Deli sandwich	Vegetable soup, salad, grain bread
Snacks:	
Chips with dip	Tortilla chips with salsa
Snack chips	Fruit, nuts, vegetables
Dinner:	
Spaghetti with meat sauce	Spaghetti with marinara sauce and veggies
Iceberg lettuce	Assorted dark, leafy greens
Butter or margarine bread spread	Nut butters
Meat	Fish
Dessert:	
Ice cream	Fruit and yogurt smoothie

Ways to get more nutrients:

- Eat **fresh fruit for breakfast**. Put it on cereal, eat it as a side dish, or throw it in a smoothie. Try 100% fruit juices for a great start to your day.

- Take **fruit and vegetables with you for snacks.**

- Eat a **salad for lunch**. Choose one with lots of dark green lettuce and fresh vegetables. Use lowfat dressing or order dressing on the side to keep your salad healthy and low-cal.

- Eat **vegetable soup for lunch or dinner**. Make a big batch of vegetable soup and freeze it in single serving portions.

- Choose **fish** (baked or broiled) for lunch or dinner.

- Sprinkle **nuts** over yogurt, cereal or fruit. They add crunch, flavor and lots of nutrients. Go easy on them if you are trying to lose weight since they are high in fat and calories.

- Serve at least **2 vegetables with dinner**. The USDA asserts that half your plate should be fruits and veggies, while only a quarter should be a protein source. A large salad can often add up to three servings, while a stir fry dish is a flavorful way to eat a variety of vegetables in one meal.

- Eat **fruit for dessert**.

- Choose **whole grain products** in place of refined grain products wherever possible. For example, choose 100% whole grain bread or crackers.

- Serve **brown rice instead of white rice**. Choose whole grains instead of refined grains. The USDA claims that at least half the grains you eat each day should be whole grains.

Follow ChooseMyPlate.gov's advice and make half your plate fruits and vegetables! The other half should be divided between lean protein and whole grains.

Color Me Fruity!

27

Leader Guide: Beans

Title:
Bean Magic

Target Audience:
This presentation kit is intended for general audiences age 14 and up. It covers topics of wellness, heart disease, diabetes, weight loss, and nutrition.

Lesson Objectives:
• Participants will learn about the health benefits of eating beans.
• Participants will be able to name at least three different types of beans.
• Participants will learn how to prepare dishes using and/or featuring beans.

Lesson Rationale:
Health authorities have indicated that good nutrition is one of the most important factors in determining long-term health. Poor diet plays a major role in the development of four of the top seven killers in the United States: heart disease, cancer, stroke and diabetes. Students who have the skills to select and prepare nutritious foods can positively impact their present and future health.

Lesson at a Glance:
This lesson introduces participants to new recipes and teaches cooking skills. It also provides nutrition and dietary information that is consistent with the Dietary Guidelines for Americans and MyPlate.

This lesson contains:
• Leader and Activity Guide
• 3 pages of copy-ready handouts and recipes
• Word file with recipes

Preparation:
___ Review leader guide
___ Review handouts
___ Select activities
___ Copy and collect materials for lesson

Activity Ideas:
Introduction: Welcome your audience, then ask them to offer examples of types of beans. (i.e.: black, pinto, kidney, etc). Explain the difference between mature and immature beans.

Ask your audience to name 3 different benefits of eating beans. Here is a list:
• Beans are an excellent source of soluble fiber, which lowers cholesterol and helps control blood sugar.
• Beans are a source of vegetable protein without satu-

rated fat or cholesterol. They provide about 6-7 grams of protein in each 1/2 cup serving.
• Beans can be counted as either a protein or a vegetable, according to the USDA's MyPlate food guide.
• They are also excellent source of folate, which helps prevent birth defects.
• Beans are low in fat but high in nutrients. They're full of iron, calcium, potassium, B vitamins, phosphorus, magnesium and zinc.
• Beans contain phytochemicals, which may help prevent cancer.
• Beans average only 109-120 calories per half cup (cooked). That half cup also provides 3-6 grams of fiber.
•Dry beans can cost only pennies per pound. What a bargain!

Activity 1 - Bean Trivia
After discussing the benefits of beans (listed above) and demonstrating a few recipes, tell your audience that they are going to play a bean trivia game. While everyone is tasting the foods you made, ask 10 questions about beans. Have them write their answers down on a piece of paper. They can work in teams or individually. The people (or team) with the most correct answers will be declared victorious. If there are several winners, you can give them each a small prize (such as a bag of dried beans), or you can put their names in a hat and draw the final winner.
Here are 10 trivia questions:
1) What bean is also called a chick pea?
   Answer: Garbanzo
2) Name the legume that cooks in 10 minutes and doesn't require advanced soaking.
   Answer: Lentil
3) This red bean is named for its shape and is usually used in chili.
   Answer: Kidney bean
4) These 2 ingredients tend to toughen beans and shoud only be added at the end of the cooking process.
   Answer: Salt, acid
5) You should _____ dry beans before cooking. This softens the skin.
   Answer: Soak
6) Beans are an excellent source of this macronutrient, which is also a major component in meats.
   Answer: Protein
7) Beans are high in _____, which can help lower cho-

Leader Guide: Beans

lesterol.
Answer: Fiber

8) True or false? Beans are considered both a protein and a vegetable for MyPlate.
Answer: True! You get credit for both when eating them.

9) What are two things that you can do to reduce the flatulence that accompanies the consumption of beans?
Answers: Rinse beans after soaking and cooking them (or rinse canned beans). Also, start slow and eat just one serving of beans per day.

10) Name three popular dishes made with beans.
Answers: Vary, but should include at least some of the following -- Minestrone soup, chili, pasta fagioli, hummus, bean dip, 3 bean salad, baked beans, black beans and rice.

You can find more facts at
http://www.michiganbean.org/

Activity 2 - Find the Bean!

Place several numbered cups filled with different varieties of dried beans on a table. Pass out sheets with corresponding numbers. Have the audience view the beans, then fill in the type of bean next to the number on the sheet. To make it more interesting, include a few gourmet varieties of beans, or ones they might not have seen before. The person who guesses the most varieties correctly wins. You may want to put the beans in zip lock bags and allow participants to take them home.

Another alternative to this game is to place many varieties of beans on a table in labeled cups. Have participants view them for about 5 or 10 minutes. Then cover the beans and see how many varieties they can remember. At the end, you can make a list on the board and people can share their stories of how they prepare different varieties of beans. You can also discuss what to do with the beans. Soups, salads, pasta dishes, beans and rice, chili, and dip can all be made with beans.

Activity 3 - Bean Buffet

If facilities, time and budget allow, consider letting participants make bean recipes themselves. Divide the class into groups and allow each group to make a different recipe. Set up a buffet at the end and allow everyone to try each recipe.

Another idea for hands-on class participation is by encouraging audience members to come up and assist you while you are demonstrating the recipes.

Activity 4 - Hide and Go Seek

Show participants how they can prepare dishes where beans are disguised or "snuck" into the recipe. You can use the Hearty Mashed Potato recipe in this kit, or choose from the ideas listed below.

- Spaghetti sauce - place one jar of spaghetti sauce plus 1 cup of assorted chopped cooked vegetables and 1 cup canned, drained beans in a blender. Blend on high speed. No one will know that they are eating beans and veggies. Plus, the pasta sauce will be thicker and richer than plain pasta sauce.

- Add pureed white beans to soups to thicken them and provide a creamy texture. The best way to do this is to add part of the broth from the soup to the beans and puree in the blender. Use 1 cup of beans per 4 cups of soup. Be sure to drain and rinse beans before use.

- Add pureed white beans to peanut butter to increase fiber and reduce fat. Use 1/2 cup cooked, drained white beans and 1/2 cup peanut butter.

- Add kidney beans to meatloaf. You can replace up to 25% of the meat with kidney beans. Try adding a little tomato paste for an attractive color. To further reduce fat, use ground turkey instead of ground beef.

- Add mashed garbanzo beans to egg salad and deviled eggs. You can replace up to 25% of the eggs with garbanzo beans.

- Make a salad dressing with canned white beans. Add 1 can of drained and rinsed white beans to a blender jar. Add 1/4 cup water, 4 Tbsp vinegar, 1 Tbsp olive oil, 1 tsp garlic powder and 1 tsp Italian herb seasoning, then blend on high speed until smooth. This will keep well in the refrigerator for up to 5 days. Mix before using. This dressing is similar to creamy Italian dressing except it has less sodium and more fiber! You can experiment with other flavors by adding tomatoes, lemon, various herbs or honey and mustard.

Activity 5 - Big Bean Battle

Invite attendees to bring healthy dishes made with beans to a potluck class. Award participants for the most creative use of beans, the best bean dish, the healthiest bean dish, etc. Participants should bring copies of their recipes to share. You can also have participants submit solely the recipes (without the cooked food).

© Food & Health Communications www.foodandhealth.com

29

Leader Guide: Beans

Activity 6 - Bean Kitchen for Kids

This activity is recommended for kids ages 3 to 8.
You will need the following items:

Jack and the Beanstalk book

1 bag dried beans

Paper towels

Paper cups

Water

Potting soil

Plastic spoons

Blender

1 jar peanut butter

1 can white beans

Crackers

Read Jack and the Beanstalk out loud to the children. After reading the book, tell them about the benefits of eating beans. Then explain that they will make their own beanstalks. First they need to sprout the beans. They can do this by placing dried beans in a paper cup with a little bit of water and a paper towel to cover and hold in moisture. The sprouting process can take a few days, and you may need to add water in order to keep the beans moist. When beans sprout, the kids can plant them in the same cup, now filled with potting soil. If you don't have time, sprout the beans ahead of the lesson, then have the kids plant them and take them home. You can also make one of the bean recipes in this kit. Try Beanut Butter!

Beanut Butter

3/4 cup cooked white beans

1/2 cup peanut butter, no added salt

1/2 cup water

Add beans and peanut butter to food processor. Blend on high speed, adding water slowly until smooth. Use immediately or refrigerate until ready to use.

Serves 14. Each 2 Tbsp serving: 70 calories, 4.5 g fat, 0.5 g fat, 0 g saturated fat, 0 mg cholesterol, 54 mg sodium, 4.5 g carbohydrate, 1 g fiber, 3 g protein.

For More Information...

www.foodandhealth.com - Our Bean Kit provides overheads, handouts, and recipes that feature beans. Take a look at our blog for more tips and recipes.

http://www.americanbean.org/ - American Bean provides information about different varieties of beans.

http://www.indianharvest.com/ - This site offers examples of heirloom beans, which could be great in a cooking demonstration or activity.

Our favorite bean cookbook:

Lean Bean Cuisine: Over 100 Tasty Meatless Recipes from Around the World by Jay Solomon. Jay is an excellent cook and we have tried many of his recipes - all of them are excellent.

Leader Guide: Bean Recipes

Hearty Mashed Potatoes

Makes 20 sample servings

Mashed potatoes are a very popular dish - adding garbanzo beans makes them into a nutritious, high-fiber meal.

2 pounds baking potatoes, peeled and cut into chunks
15 oz can garbanzo beans, drained
1/2-3/4 cup skim milk or fortified soy milk
1/4 cup Parmesan cheese
1/2 tsp garlic powder
Black pepper to taste

Directions:

1. Place the potatoes in a large saucepan and cover them with water. Bring to a boil over high heat, then reduce to a simmer.
2. Add the garbanzo beans 10 minutes after the potatoes have started cooking. Continue cooking until potatoes are fork tender, about 20 more minutes.
3. Drain water and place the sauce pan back on the stove. Mash the beans and potatoes using a potato masher or hand beaters. Add the milk, cheese and seasonings. Reheat if necessary. Serve hot.

Equipment needed:

____ Large, 3 quart sauce pan with lid
____ Stove
____ Cutting board
____ Chef knife
____ Kitchen spoon
____ Potato masher or hand beater
____ Potato peeler
____ Fork
____ Measuring cups and spoons
____ Can opener

Shopping list:

____ 2 pounds baking potatoes (Idaho or Russet)
____ Skim milk
____ Parmesan cheese
____ Garlic powder
____ Ground black pepper
____ Napkins
____ Spoons and mini cups (for samples)
____ Disposable cups for measured ingredients

Cooking skills/nutrition lesson:

This recipe shows how to hide beans in beloved recipes. It also demonstrates how to make healthier mashed potatoes by using skim milk and a little Parmesan cheese in place of whole milk and butter.

The beans in this dish make it heartier, gives the potatoes a buttery color, and boosts fiber and nutrient content.

Demo preparation:

1. Wash your hands before you handle food.
2. Wash, peel, and cut potatoes, then place them in the pan of water before class starts.
3. Lay out premeasured ingredients in disposable cups.
4. Assemble tools and utensils within reach.
5. Place colander or dish pan in a sink or nearby (for draining the potatoes).
6. As participants arrive, start cooking the potatoes over low heat, then continue with the directions.

Make ahead options:

Make this dish ahead and refrigerate it in a shallow, glass casserole dish. To reheat for class, just microwave on high for 8-10 minutes or until heated through.

Garnish/presentation tips:

For more color, garnish these potatoes with a sprinkle of paprika or a sprig of fresh herbs like basil, parsley or rosemary.

Number of sample servings: 20

Leader Guide: Bean Recipes

Quick and Easy Bean Dip
Makes 16-20 sample servings

This dip comes together quickly, with no cooking required. You'll need...

15 ounce can pinto beans, drained and rinsed

8 oz can no-added-salt tomato sauce

1/2 teaspoon garlic powder

1/2 teaspoon chili powder

Fresh vegetable sticks

Directions:

1. Place beans, tomato sauce, garlic powder, and chili powder in a blender or food processor and puree until smooth.

2. Serve immediately or refrigerate for later use. Serve with fresh vegetable sticks. For sample servings, we recommend 2 tablespoons of bean dip with 1 or 2 pieces of vegetables per person.

Equipment:

___ Blender or food processor

___ Measuring spoons

___ Can opener

___ Bowl for presentation

___ Platter to hold vegetables

___ Spatula

Shopping list:

___ 1 can pinto beans

___ 1 can no added salt tomato sauce (8 oz)

___ Garlic powder

___ Chili powder

___ 1 platter of pre-cut vegetable sticks or broccoli, carrots, celery, etc. to make your own

___ Mini cups and napkins (for samples)

___ Disposable cups to hold premeasured ingredients

Cooking skills/nutrition lesson:

This lesson shows that it is easy to make a healthy snack using beans. It also shows how to eat more vegetables. Making bean dip from scratch as opposed to buying a premade dip lowers the sodium content significantly. According to the Dietary Guidelines more than half of the population needs to keep sodium at or below 1500 mg per day.

Demo preparation:

1. Wash your hands before you handle food.

2. Have all ingredients premeasured and next to the blender or food processor with the spatula.

3. Arrange vegetable sticks on platter in advance and keep them covered with plastic wrap so they don't dry out.

Make ahead options:

Yes - the bean dip can be made ahead and served with the fresh vegetables for class

Garnish/presentation tips:

The bean dip looks especially nice when garnished with freshly sliced pepper rings.

Number of sample servings: 16-20

Leader Guide: Bean Recipes

2 Bean Salad
Makes 12 sample servings

This colorful bean salad will enhance any meal.

15 oz can black beans, drained and rinsed
1 cup fresh French style green beans
1 tomato, diced
1 bell pepper, diced
1 Tbsp olive oil
2 Tbsp red wine vinegar
1 tsp Italian seasoning
1 Tbsp Parmesan cheese
6 cups dark green lettuce, washed and ready to serve

Directions:
1. Place all ingredients except lettuce in a medium sized mixing bowl and stir together. Chill bean salad until ready to serve.
2. To serve, divide lettuce among 4 large salad plates then spoon bean salad over the top. We recommend using 2 ounce portions for tasting samples.

Equipment:
___ cutting board
___ knife
___ large salad bowl
___ kitchen spoon
___ measuring cup and spoons
___ can opener
___ large fancy salad plate for presentation of finished dish (optional)

Shopping list:
___ 1 can black beans
___ 1 bag frozen French style green beans
___ 1 tomato
___ 1 bell pepper
___ olive oil
___ red wine vinegar
___ Italian seasoning
___ Parmesan cheese
___ 1 bag ready-to-serve mixed greens
___ mini cups, spoons and napkins (for samples)
___ disposable cups and bags to hold ingredients

Cooking skill/nutrition lesson:
This recipe is an easy, no-cook dish that goes together quick. It helps increase the consumption of vegetables and beans. It also teaches participants that you can add beans to salads

Demo preparation:
1. Wash your hands before you handle food.
2. Have all ingredients chopped, measured, and placed in disposable bags and cups.
3. Have the salad bowl and kitchen spoon ready too.

Make ahead options:
You can cut and measure ingredients ahead of time for fast assembly in the classroom. Also, you could put the bean salad together and have the lettuce ready to go for the purpose of presentation and tasting.

Garnish/presentation tips:
This salad looks great when placed on a fancy salad plate and garnished with fresh cracked black pepper.

Number of sample servings: 12

Leader Guide: Bean Recipes

Spicy Bean Soup

Makes 16-20 sample servings

This bean soups packs a ton of flavor without high sodium and fat content. Everyone wins!

15 oz can pinto beans, drained and rinsed

15 oz can diced tomatoes, no added salt

8 oz can no-salt-added tomato sauce

1 cup water

1 Tbsp minced dried onion

1 tsp garlic powder

1 tsp chili powder

1/2 tsp dried oregano

Garnish: nonfat sour cream, fresh cilantro

Directions:

1. Place all ingredients (except garnishes) in a 2-quart pan and bring to a boil over high heat. Reduce heat to a simmer and cook for 5-6 minutes.

2. Serve hot. Garnish with nonfat sour cream and fresh chopped cilantro. We recommend 2-ounce servings for tasting samples per person.

Equipment:

_____ Can opener

_____ Colander (for rinsing beans)

_____ 2-quart pan

_____ Stove

_____ Kitchen spoon

_____ Measuring cup and spoons

_____ Soup bowl (to show finished dish)

_____ Knife and cutting board (for cilantro)

Shopping list:

_____ 1 can pinto beans

_____ 1 can no-added-salt diced tomatoes

_____ Minced dried onion

_____ Garlic powder

_____ Chili powder

_____ Dried oregano

_____ Nonfat sour cream

_____ Fresh cilantro

_____ Mini cups, spoons and napkins (for samples)

_____ Disposable cups (for premeasured ingredients)

Cooking skill/nutrition lesson:

This soup recipe is easy and delicious. It shows participants how to use canned beans and to look for no-salt-added tomatoes. The USDA revealed that most Americans get too much sodium from canned and frozen goods, and they stress the importance of low-sodium options. This lesson also outlines the idea of adding beans to other soup recipes.

Demo preparation:

1. Wash your hands before you handle food.

2. Have all ingredients measured and placed in disposable bags and cups.

3. Place the pan on the stove and position the spoon within reach.

Make ahead options:

You can measure ingredients ahead of time for fast assembly in the classroom. You can also make this soup ahead of time and reheat in a microwave oven for the purpose of tasting.

Garnish/presentation tips:

Place this soup in a soup bowl and top with nonfat sour cream and a few sprigs of fresh cilantro.

Number of sample servings: 16-18

Leader Guide: Bean Recipes

Vegetarian Double Bean Chili
Makes 24-30 sample servings
Serve this chili with a large green salad.

1 tsp vegetable oil
1 cup diced onion
1 tsp minced garlic
1/2 cup diced carrot
1 zucchini, diced
15 oz. can no-added-salt diced tomatoes
15 oz. can pinto beans, drained and rinsed
15 oz can black beans, drained and rinsed
1 cup water
1 tsp oregano
1 tsp ground cumin
1 tsp chili powder
Garnish: nonfat sour cream

Directions:
1. Add oil to a large nonstick skillet and cook over medium high heat. Saute onion, garlic and carrot in oil until they're all golden brown, about 3 minutes.
2. Add the zucchini and saute for another minute. Add the rest of the ingredients and bring to a boil over high heat. Reduce heat to simmer and cook until vegetables are tender, about 8 minutes.
3. Garnish with a dollop of nonfat sour cream and serve hot. We recommend a 2-ounce serving for tasting samples.

Equipment:
____ Cutting board
____ Knife
____ Kitchen spoon
____ Measuring cup and spoons
____ Can opener
____ Large 12" nonstick skillet
____ Stove
____ Colander (for draining and rinsing beans)
____ Large soup bowl (for final presentation)

Shopping list:
____ Vegetable oil,
____ 1 onion,
____ Minced garlic in jar or 1 head of garlic,
____ 1 can no-added-salt tomatoes,
____ 1 can pinto beans
____ 1 can black beans
____ Dried oregano
____ Ground cumin
____ Chili powder

____ Nonfat sour cream
____ Mini cups, spoons and napkins (for samples)
____ Disposable cups (for premeasured ingredients)

Cooking skill/nutrition lesson:
The USDA recommends that you plan some meals to center on a vegetable main dish. This one packs tons of protein, fiber, nutrients, and minerals.

The recipe demonstates how to cut vegetables, make a delicious entree using beans instead of meat, and how to season chili. You can also suggest they make a large batch and freeze the leftovers.

Demo preparation:
1. Wash your hands before you handle food.
2. Have all ingredients chopped, measured, and placed in disposable bags and cups.
3. Make sure all utensils are within reach.
4. You may want to preheat the stove to medium as participants begin to enter the room.

Make ahead options:
You can make this chili ahead of time and heat in a microwave for the tastings.

Garnish/presentation tips:
Garnish this chili with nonfat sour cream. You can also top with rings of bell pepper or chili pepper and fresh sprigs of cilantro.

Number of sample servings: 24-30

Leader Guide: Bean Recipes

Spaghetti with Lentils

Makes 18 sample servings

Add lentils to this classic recipe for a fiber and protein kick, not to mention all the additional nutrients that are found in lentils.

1 cup dry lentils

8 oz package dry spaghetti

26 oz jar pasta sauce, preferably low sodium

1 tsp Italian seasoning

4 Tbsp Parmesan cheese

Directions:

1. Place a large soup pan filled with water over high heat and bring to a boil. Add the lentils and bring back to a boil, then lower heat to medium and cook for 4 minutes before adding spaghetti. Bring water back to a boil over high heat and cook until spaghetti is al dente and lentils are tender, about 10 minutes. Drain in colander.

2. Place the same pot back on the stove and add the pasta sauce and Italian seasoning. Bring to a boil, then add the pasta and lentils. Heat through, then serve immediately. Place one portion on a large dinner plate and top with Parmesan cheese. Use 2 ounce servings topped with a little Parmesan for the tasting samples.

Equipment:

____ Large soup pan (3 quart is perfect)

____ Kitchen spoon

____ Colander

____ Measuring cups and spoons

____ Dinner plate to show final presentation

____ Stove

Shopping list:

____ 1 package dry lentils

____ 1 package dry spaghetti

____ 1 jar pasta sauce

____ 1 bottle Italian seasoning

____ 1 container grated Parmesan cheese

____ Mini cups, spoons and napkins (for samples)

____ Disposable cups (for premeasured ingredients).

Cooking skill/nutrition lesson:

This recipe shows participants how to add more fiber and nutrients to spaghetti - a favorite dish of many Americans. It demonstrates that lentils are very easy and fast to cook and that they don't need prior soaking. Lentils are an excellent source of folate and many other vitamins and minerals.

Demo preparation:

1. Wash your hands before you handle food.

2. Measure all ingredients and have them out around the stove along with the kitchen spoon.

3. Position the colander in a sink or bucket nearby for easy draining.

4. Have the covered pot of water on the stove at a low simmer. That way you can add the lentils as soon as class starts.

Make ahead options:

You can make this dish ahead of time and reheat in the microwave for tasting purposes.

Garnish/presentation tips:

Sprinkle the Parmesan cheese over the pasta, and be sure to let it fall onto the side/rim of the plate too.

Number of sample servings: 18

Bean Recipes

Hearty Mashed Potatoes

Mashed potatoes are a very popular dish - adding garbanzo beans makes them into a nutritious, high-fiber meal.

2 pounds baking potatoes, peeled and cut in chunks

15 oz can garbanzo beans, drained

1/2-3/4 cup skim milk or fortified soy milk

1/4 cup Parmesan cheese

1/2 tsp garlic powder

Black pepper to taste

Directions:

1. Place the potatoes in a large saucepan and cover them with water. Bring to a boil over high heat, then reduce to a simmer.
2. Add the garbanzo beans 10 minutes after the potatoes have started cooking. Continue cooking until potatoes are fork tender, about 20 more minutes.
3. Drain water and place the sauce pan back on the stove. Mash the beans and potatoes using a potato masher or hand beaters. Add the milk, cheese and seasonings. Reheat if necessary. Serve hot.

Serves 6. Each 1 cup serving: 180 calories, 2 g fat, 1 g saturated fat, 3 mg cholesterol, 198 mg sodium, 32 g carbohydrate, 5 g fiber, 8.5 g protein.

Quick and Easy Bean Dip

This dip comes together quickly, with no cooking required.

15 ounce can pinto beans, drained and rinsed

8 oz can no-added-salt tomato sauce

1/2 teaspoon garlic powder

1/2 teaspoon chili powder

Fresh vegetable sticks

Directions:

1. Place beans, tomato sauce, garlic powder and chili powder in a blender or food processor and puree until smooth.
2. Serve immediately or refrigerate for later use. Serve with fresh vegetable sticks.

Serves 8. Each 1/4 cup serving: 45 calories, 0 g fat, 0 g saturated fat, 0 mg cholesterol, 98 mg sodium, 8.5 g carbohydrate, 3 g fiber, 3 g protein.

2 Bean Salad

This colorful bean salad will enhance any meal.

15 oz can black beans, drained and rinsed

1 cup fresh French style green beans

1 tomato, diced

1 bell pepper, diced

1 Tbsp olive oil

2 Tbsp red wine vinegar

1 tsp Italian seasoning

1 Tbsp Parmesan cheese

6 cups dark green lettuce, washed and ready to serve

Directions:

1. Place all ingredients, except lettuce, in a medium mixing bowl and stir together. Chill bean salad until ready to serve.
2. To serve, divide lettuce among 4 large salad plates then spoon bean salad over the top.

Serves 4. Each 2 cup serving: 142 calories, 4 g fat, 1 g saturated fat, 1 mg cholesterol, 201 mg sodium, 20 g carbohydrate, 7 g fiber, 7 g protein.

Bean Recipes

Spicy Bean Soup

15 oz can pinto beans, drained and rinsed

15 oz can diced tomatoes, no added salt

8 oz can no-salt-added tomato sauce

1 cup water

1 Tbsp minced dried onion

1 tsp garlic powder

1 tsp chili powder

1/2 tsp dried oregano

Garnish: nonfat sour cream, fresh cilantro

Directions:

1. Place all ingredients (except garnishes) in a 2-quart pan and bring to a boil over high heat. Reduce heat to a simmer and cook for 5-6 minutes.
2. Serve hot. Garnish with nonfat sour cream and fresh chopped cilantro.

Serves 4. Each 1-1/2 cup serving: 104 calories, 1 g fat, 0 g saturated fat, 0 mg cholesterol, 188 mg sodium, 20 g carbohydrate, 6 g fiber, 5.5 g protein.

Vegetarian Double Bean Chili

Serve this chili with a large green salad.

1 tsp vegetable oil

1 cup diced onion

1 tsp minced garlic

1/2 cup diced carrot

1 zucchini, diced

15 oz. can no-added-salt diced tomatoes

15 oz. can pinto beans, drained and rinsed

15 oz can black beans, drained and rinsed

1 cup water

1 tsp oregano

1 tsp ground cumin

1 tsp chili powder

Garnish: nonfat sour cream

Directions:

1. Add oil to a large nonstick skillet and heat over medium high heat. Saute onion, garlic and carrot until golden brown, about 3 minutes.
2. Add the zucchini and saute another minute Add the rest of the ingredients and bring to a boil over high heat. Reduce heat to simmer and cook until vegetables are tender, about 8 minutes.
3. Garnish with a dollop of sour cream and serve hot.

Serves 4. Each serving: 200 calories, 2 g fat, 0 g saturated fat, 0 mg cholesterol, 372 mg sodium, 37 g carbohydrate, 11 g fiber, 10 g protein.

Spaghetti with Lentils

1 cup dry lentils

8 oz package dry spaghetti

26 oz jar pasta sauce, preferably low sodium

1 tsp Italian seasoning

4 Tbsp Parmesan cheese

Directions:

1. Place a large soup pan filled with water over high heat and bring to a boil. Add the lentils and bring back to a boil, then lower heat to medium and cook for 4 minutes before adding spaghetti. Bring water back to a boil over high heat and cook until spaghetti is al dente and lentils are tender, about 10 minutes. Drain in colander.
2. Place the same pot back on the stove and add the pasta sauce and Italian seasoning. Bring to a boil, then add the pasta and lentils. Heat through, then serve immediately. Place one portion on a large dinner plate and top with Parmesan cheese. Use 2 ounce servings topped with a little Parmesan for the tasting samples.

Serves 4. Each serving; 382 calories, 2.5 g fat, 1 g saturated fat, 4 mg cholesterol, 480 mg sodium, 72 mg carbohydrate, 6 g fiber, 17 g protein.

Beans Can't Be Beat!!

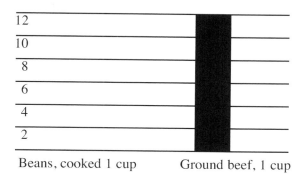

High in Fiber (grams)

12	
10	
8	
6	
4	
2	

Beans, cooked 1 cup   Ground beef, 1 cup

Low in Saturated Fat (grams)

12	
10	
8	
6	
4	
2	

Beans, cooked 1 cup   Ground beef, 1 cup

Why Should I Eat Beans?

Beans are an important part of a healthy diet. They are filling and beneficial for your heart. They help control blood sugar, ward off constipation, and may even prevent cancer as part of a more plant-based diet. Here are the facts:

• **Beans are an excellent source of fiber**. One cup of cooked beans contains around 9-13 grams of fiber, including soluble fiber. This helps lower cholesterol, control blood sugar, and aid weight loss.

• **Beans are an excellent plant-based source of protein**. Cooked beans contain an average of 14-18 grams of protein per cup. They have none of the saturated fat or cholesterol you find in animal protein.

• **Beans are a good source of iron**. One cup of cooked beans supplies over 20% of the daily value of iron for women and over 35% for men. Eating beans with vitamin C-rich foods like tomatoes further increases your body's ability to use that iron.

• **Beans supply calcium**. One cup of cooked white beans supplies around 160 mg of calcium. That's almost 20% of most people's daily goals!

• **Beans are low in sodium** when they are cooked fresh. If you are using canned beans, read labels to find ones lower in sodium. Be sure to rinse them before cooking with them.

• **Most beans are low in fat and cholesterol free**. One cup of cooked beans contains 0.5-1 gram of fat.

• **Beans contain phytochemicals**, including saponins, which may help prevent cancer.

• **Beans are an important source of folate**. One cup of boiled kidney beans supplies about 229 mg of folate that's about a half day's supply for most people. Folate reduces your risk for heart disease and can help prevent birth defects.

• **Beans contain potassium** which may reduce your risk of high blood pressure and stroke. One half cup of cooked beans contains up to 480 mg of potassium, more than found in one banana.

8 Ways to Enjoy Beans

1. **Eat beans on salads**. Throw cooked beans in tossed salads, pasta salads and 3 bean salad.

2. **Use beans in soups.** Make a pureed bean or pea soup; add them to vegetable soups.

3. **Thicken sauces**. Puree beans with a little liquid to thicken sauces.

4. **Puree them into a dip**. Puree beans with a little flavored vinegar and oregano for an easy dip. For barbecued bean dip, use no-salt-added tomato sauce and chili powder. Use as a spread on vegetables, crackers, tortilla chips and pita bread.

5. **Fill up your sandwich**. Use beans and fresh vegetables to create a pita pocket that fills you up, not out.

6. **Add beans to pasta**. Add beans for a nutritious treat. Beans and pasta make a perfect pair.

7. **Make vegetarian chili with beans**. Use cooked beans, corn, peppers, onions, tomatoes and spices for an easy chili.

8. **Add beans to mashed potatoes**. Slip a few white beans or garbanzo beans into your next batch of mashed potatoes.

How Do I Prepare Beans?

What Do I Do With Dry Beans?

1. **Sort & rinse**. Place beans in colander and remove any stones or debris. Rinse them with cold water.
2. **Soak**. Soaking reduces the cooking time and makes digestion easier. Use 3 cups of water per 1 cup of dry beans. Beans will expand to 2-3 times their dried size while soaking.
   - Best method: Place beans in large covered container and add enough water to cover the beans by a few inches. Allow them to soak in the refrigerator overnight. Note: Bringing them to a boil for one minute before soaking will cut cooking time up to 30% the next day!
   - Quick method: Place beans in large pot. Add 3 cups of water per 1 cup of beans. Bring to a boil for 2 minutes; turn stove off and allow to stand for one hour; proceed with step 3.
3. **Rinse**. Rinse and drain beans again before cooking.
4. **Add water & seasonings**. Place beans in a large pot; add 1 cup of water per cup of soaked beans.
   - For soups, add vegetables & seasonings. Increase water to 1-1/2 cups per cup beans.
   - For chili, add sauteed onions and garlic, cumin, chili powder, and oregano.
   - For general use in thigs like salads, salsas, pizza, sandwiches, pasta, bean dips, etc., season beans with a little garlic powder, a bay leaf, thyme, oregano and basil.
   - Do not add salt, vinegar, tomatoes or another type of acid. Salt and acid toughen the outer skin of the bean and increase cooking time. Wait until the beans are cooked until tender, then add those ingredients.
5. **Cook until tender**. Bring beans to a boil then reduce to a simmer. Cooking times vary, so be sure to refer to package directions. Harder water may extend cooking time.
6. **Serve immediately or chill quickly**. Store beans in a shallow, covered pan in the refrigerator for up to 5 days. You can also freeze them in small plastic bags for several months.

How Do I Prepare Canned Beans?

- Read food labels to find a brand that is low in sodium.
- Rinse and strain beans before cooking with them.
- Add broth, water or seasonings and heat them in the microwave or stovetop. You can also serve them cold in salsa, salad, or dip.

Success Tips:

- If you want to use a variety of beans, cook them separately and mix them all together at the end.
- Simmer; don't boil.
- Do not add baking soda - you lose thiamin and folate and may develop a green foam and funky flavor.
- Test doneness by tasting. Beans should be tender, but not falling apart.
- Keeping the cooking pot covered will speed up the process and help you have softer beans.

Bean Math:

1 cup dry beans = 3 cups cooked beans
1 pound of dry beans = about 2-3 cups of dry beans
1 pound of dry beans = 6-9 cups of cooked beans
1 can (15.5 oz.) beans yields 1-1/2 cups drained beans
1/2 cup cooked beans = 1 serving

Reducing Flatulence:

We all know the old song, "Beans, beans, the musical fruit, the more you eat the more you toot!" However, it should have said that the MORE you eat, the LESS you toot. Studies show that after a three week period of eating beans your body adapts and you will be in less discomfort.

- If you haven't been eating beans, start slowly and build up your consumption gradually. Flatulence will be less of a problem over time, once your digestive tract gets used to beans.
- Soaking and rinsing beans helps remove some of the oligosaccharides or sugars that cause gas. Rinse well after soaking and cooking.
- Cook beans thoroughly.

Remember, the USDA recommends that everyone consume beans and peas, either as a vegetarian protein source or as a nutrient packed vegetable dish.

Bean Glossary

What is a dry bean?

Dry beans are mature dried seeds (or legumes). They belong in the same family as split peas and lentils. Beans are left on the vine until completely mature and dry. Except for baked beans, many Americans eat only immature green beans which lack the protein and fiber content of mature dry beans.

Common Bean Guide

Let's take a look at a variety of hearty bean options.

Adzuki Beans - This bean is small and is the same size and color as red beans. Look for them in Asian markets or the Asian aisle of your grocery store. They are often found in paste form, and are delicious in ice cream and moon cakes alike.

Black Beans - These beans are also called turtle beans or frijoles negros. They have a soft texture and are often used in Latin style dishes and Caribbean soups. Did you know that black beans are an especialy great source of phytonutrients?

Black Eyed Peas - Look for these beans in the freezer section or dried bean aisle of the grocery store. As their name suggests, they have a single black spot on their skin. They are also called cowpeas or crowder peas in some areas of the country. In the summer you can find them fresh.

Cannellini - Cannellini beans are white beans that are commonly used in Italian dishes like Tuscan White Bean Soup. They are also called white kidney beans.

Chickpeas - These hazelnut shaped beans are also called garbanzo beans. They have a nutty flavor and lend themselves well to Middle Eastern cuisine, especialy hummus.

Fava Beans - These large, lima-shaped beans are also called broad beans, faba beans and horse beans. Small, young ones can be served in their pods while the older, more mature fava beans have to be shucked. Use them in Italian and Mediterranean dishes with fresh herbs.

Great Northern Beans - These large, white beans are shaped like kidney beans and taste delicious in casseroles and soups.

Heirloom Beans - These beans are now stocked in grocery stores and specialty food stores. They come in all shapes and colors and carry such names as: rattlesnake beans, Christmas beans, calypso beans, appaloosa beans, soldier beans and more. They are especially fun to mix into soups.

Kidney Beans - these beans are a deep red color and are named for their unmistakable shape. Try them in chili, soups, salads, casseroles and pasta.

Lentils - These legumes are extremely high in fiber and folate. Since they don't need to be soaked before cooking, they're pretty easy to prepare. They cook in about 20 minutes and are great in stews, pasta dishes and chili. Serve leftover cooked lentils in salads or add them to rice dishes.

Lima Beans - You can find these beans (also called butter beans) in two sizes - large and baby. They are sold frozen, canned, and dried. The dried ones make a great garlic bean soup while the green ones are wonderful in mixed veggie medleys.

Navy Beans - These small, white beans can be used in about any recipe. They make a very rich, thick soup and are named because they were a staple in the U.S. Navy.

Pigeon Peas - These small, tan beans are also called gandules and are found in grocery stores and Latin markets. They are wonderful in rice dishes, particularly with a Caribbean flair.

Pinto Beans - This mottled, tan bean is most often used in Southwestern or Mexican dishes like chili, refried beans, burritos, etc.

Red Beans - These beans are a classic in New Orleans style dishes and always team well with brown rice. They're great in chili too.

Soybeans - This bean is higher in iron and protein than most other beans. It's also higher in fat. You will most likely find it canned or dried. It is prepared in foods like tempeh, textured vegetable protein, tofu, soy milk, and nuts made from these beans.

Split Peas - These peas aremost often made into soups. They come in 2 colors, green and yellow, and when their hull is removed, they split apart naturally.

Leader Guide: Breakfast on the Go

Title:
Breakfast on the Go!

Target Audience:
This presentation kit is intended for general audiences ages 14 and up. It covers topics of wellness, heart disease, diabetes, weight loss and nutrition.

Lesson Objectives:
• Participants will learn the value of eating breakfast.
• Participants will learn how breakfast can fit with the Dietary Guidelines for Americans and MyPlate.
• Participants will learn how to prepare quick, healthy breakfasts.

Lesson Rationale:
Breakfast is an important part of a healthy diet. Most studies demonstrate improved cognitive function, better weight control and improved nutrition status among those who eat breakfast. Unfortunately, breakfast consumption is declining in the US. One article, (J Am Diet Assoc 1996 May;96(5):464-70), found that while the nutritional quality of breakfast improved from 1965 to 1991, breakfast consumption declined between 1965 and 199. The percentage of adults in the United States who ate breakfast went from 86% to 75%.

Lesson at a Glance:
This lesson introduces participants to new recipes while teaching cooking skills. It's suggestions are consistent with both MyPlate and the Dietary Guidelines for Americans.

Lesson Materials:
This lesson contains:
• Leader and activity guides
• 2 pages of copy-ready handouts and recipes

Preparation:
___ Review leader guide
___ Review handouts
___ Select activities
___ Copy and collect materials for lesson

Activity Ideas:
Introduction:
Welcome your audience and pass out the necessary handouts. Ask participants to raise their hands if they eat breakfast most days of the week. Congratulate those who do, and ask those who don't why they don't. Write a few of the more popular reasons on the board.
Ask your audience if they can name 3 different bene-

fits of eating breakfast. Here is a list of possible answers:
• Breakfast provides an excellent opportunity to increase consumption of fiber, whole grains, fruits and nonfat dairy or soy.
• Breakfast helps you break your fast from sleeping all night and provides you with energy.
• Eating breakfast can helps regulate calories and control weight.
• Breakfast can help you avoid binging on high calorie foods for morning snacks. Examples of these foods include donuts, coffee cake, muffins, vending machine snacks, etc.
Return to the audience's reasons for not eating breakfast. Ask if there is a way around those reasons, or some solution that will help them enjoy the benefits of breakfast. Here are some options:
• Not enough time - Try making breakfast the night before or develop on-the-run recipes and strategies to fit it in a tight schedule. Remember to keep the right ingredients on hand. Plus, getting up 15 minutes earlier for breakfast will give you a better start to your day than 15 more minutes of sleep.
• Not hungry - Try to wake up earlier, exercise in the morning, or take food with you so you can eat when you are actually hungry.
• Would rather sleep - Go to bed earlier. Try exercising and a healthy diet to reduce fatigue. To save on sleep, eat while you're getting ready or bring food with you.

Activity 1 - Cooking Demo
Use one or more of the recipes in this lesson to demonstrate how to make healthy, speedy breakfasts.

Activity 2 - Breakfast on the Run
Set up stations for participants to make their own breakfast on the run. Use the recipes in this lesson and multiply them as needed so you have enough food. Divide participants into as many groups as you have recipes and allow each group to make one recipe. For a fun twist, set a stop watch and time how long it takes someone to put breakfast together.

Activity 3 - Breakfast Domination
There are 2 different formats for this race to speedy breakfast success.
Team Competition
Make 2 identical stations that include ingredients and cooking supplies for one recipe from this lesson, and one larger station for a cooking demonstration. Show

Leader Guide: Breakfast on the Go

participants how to make one serving of the recipe you choose to feature, and then ask for 4 volunteers. Have volunteers come up in pairs. Each team should make one serving as fast as they possibly can. Time them, check results, and give awards the fastest cook to make a delicious meal according to the recipe. You really can throw a breakfast together fast if you have the right ingredients.

Every Man for Himself
Use the idea from above with one station and have participants come up one at a time to make breakfast. Or set up multiple stations and have everyone compete at once. Time them with a stop watch to see who is fastest, but make sure the winner followed all the steps of the recipe correctly.

Activity 4 - Breakfast Treasure Hunt
Acquire small packages and/or samples of common breakfast foods. Have participants group packages together in order to make a healthy breakfast. Alternatively, you can go through the packages and group them into a few healthy breakfast ideas. Here are a few ideas of foods you should include:

- 100% fruit juice - Make sure to include orange juice with calcium. Store brands are often less expensive.
- Bacon - Try lowfat turkey bacon
- Bagels - Use smaller bagels, like Lenders, because they are lower in calories than the larger ones found in bakeries. Be sure to pair them with fresh fruit and a light spread. Explain that bagels should be a once in a while option for breakfast because they are calorie dense and not generally made with whole grains. According to MyPlate, at least half of the grains you eat every day should be whole grains. White flour contains almost the same calories per pound as white sugar (1650 versus 1755, if you can believe it), plus it has way less fiber and nutrients than whole grain flour.
- Egg whites or egg substitute
- English muffins
- Frozen lowfat whole grain waffles - Serve with light syrup or powdered sugar.
- Fresh fruit. The USDA recommends that you purchase fresh fruit in season. That's when it is at its most delicious, yet cheapest. What a deal!
- Oatmeal - Highlight nutritional and monetary difference between flavored instant packages and bulk oatmeal. Flavored instant packages are typically higher in sugar, sodium and calories. Quick cooking oatmeal

in bulk form saves money, is lower in sodium, contains no added sugar, and cooks almost as quickly. Demonstrate how to package bulk oats in zip lock bags with some spices and dried fruit to make portable servings for anywhere.
- Pancake mixes - Arrowhead Mills has delicious whole grain mixes.
- Sausage - Try vegetarian or turkey and watch out for sodium content.
- Skim milk/fortified soymilk
- Wheatena, aka whole cream of wheat
- Wheat germ - This makes a great addition to smoothies.
- Whole grain cereals - Highlight is good to show them boxed cereals than need to be cooked (like Wheatena).
- Whole wheat bread
- Yogurt - show light and plain as being the best choices; you can also point out the new Danon Light with vitamin D. Small packages are good to eat on the go but they are more expensive than buying in bulk.

Remind participants that they should go for whole grains and fruit for breakfast. The USDA's MyPlate guidelines remind us to steer clear of fruit mixes or juices with added sugar -- these aren't as good for you. Favorites like bacon and eggs can be made healthier by choosing egg whites or nonfat egg substitute and turkey bacon.

Activity 5 - Whole Grain Cereal Sampler
This demo is great for the fall and winter, when people might be more inclined to cook whole grains. It is especially helpful to allow participants to taste these grains and see how easy it is to make them.

Make oatmeal, Wheatena and/or cooked millet. Allow participants to taste each one. Note: we strongly suggest allowing them to top their own with skim milk, fruit, honey and various spices such as cinnamon, apple pie spice or pumpkin pie spice. Follow package directions for cooking these whole grains - most can be cooked in the microwave.

Leader Guide: Breakfast Recipes

Creamy Microwave Oatmeal

Makes 10 sample servings

1/3 cup old fashioned oats
2/3 cup water
Pinch of cinnamon
1 cup skim milk or fortified soy milk
Sliced banana

Directions:

1. Place oats, water and cinnamon in a 2 quart glass or plastic microwave container with a cover. Microwave on full power for 3 to 4 minutes.
2. Stir and serve oatmeal in a large bowl with skim milk and sliced banana on top. We recommend 2 ounces of oatmeal with a dash of skim milk and a banana slice to serve as a tasting sample.

Equipment:
___ Microwave
___ Measuring cup
___ Bowl (for presentation)
___ Kitchen spoon
___ 2 quart microwave container with cover
___ Knife (to cut banana)

Shopping list:
___ Old fashioned oats
___ Cinnamon
___ skim milk or fortified soy milk
___ Banana
___ Mini cups, spoons and napkins (for samples)
___ Disposable cups to hold premeasured ingredients

Cooking skills/nutrition lesson:
This lesson shows how to make oatmeal in the microwave. It also shows how to lay out a balanced plate in accordance to some MyPlate guidelines. Cooked grain cereal can also help with weight loss. Oatmeal and other cooked grains are lower in calorie density than processed dry cereals. Prepared oatmeal contains 281 calories per pound while a dry whole grain cereal contains around 1660 calories per pound.

Demo preparation:
1. Wash your hands before you handle food.
2. Have all ingredients premeasured and next to microwave.

Make ahead options:
You can make the oatmeal ahead of time and reheat it in the microwave for tasting purposes.

Garnish/presentation tips:
Place bananas and skim milk atop the oatmeal, then add a dash of ground cinnamon.

Number of sample servings: 10

Leader Guide: Breakfast Recipes

Sunrise Smoothie
Makes 10-12 sample servings
1 cup of orange juice
1 cup of skim milk or fortified soy milk
3 Tbsp wheat germ
1 cup of fresh or frozen fruit like strawberries, blueberries, bananas, peaches, etc.
Pinch of cinnamon
Directions:
1. Place all ingredients in a blender and puree on high speed until smooth. Serve immediately. We recommend a 2 ounce serving for tasting samples.
Equipment:
___ Blender
___ Measuring cup and measuring spoons
___ Glass for presentation
___ Spatula
___ Knife (to cut fruit)
___ Cutting board
Shopping list:
___ Wheat germ
___ Cinnamon
___ Skim milk or fortified soy milk
___ Orange juice
___ 1 cup of fresh or frozen fruit
___ Mini cups, spoons and napkins (for samples)
___ Disposable cups for premeasured ingredients
Cooking skills/nutrition lesson:
This lesson shows how to make a nutritious smoothie that you can drink on the go. It highlights the importance of using fruit without added sugar, and
Demo preparation:
1. Wash your hands before you handle food.
2. Have all ingredients premeasured and next to blender.
Make ahead options:
You can make the smoothie ahead of time. We recommend giving it a final blend in the blender before serving.
Garnish/presentation tips:
Top the smoothie with ground cinnamon.
Number of sample servings: 10-12

Muesli
Makes 15 sample servings
1/2 cup oatmeal
1/4 cup skim milk or fortified soy milk
1 cup of nonfat light vanilla yogurt
2 cups of assorted fresh cut fruit
2 Tbsp chopped almonds, pecans, or walnuts
Pinch of ground cinnamon
Directions:
1. Mix all ingredients in a medium-sized mixing bowl.
2. Serve immediately. Use 2 ounce serving samples.
Equipment:
___ Measuring cup and measuring spoons
___ Bowl (for presentation)
___ Spatula
___ Knife (to cut fruit)
___ Cutting board
___ Medium-sized mixing bowl
Shopping list:
___ Oatmeal
___ Cinnamon
___ Skim milk or fortified soy milk
___ 2 cups fresh or frozen fruit
___ 1 container of light vanilla yogurt
___ Chopped nuts (almonds, pecans, or walnuts)
___ Mini cups, spoons and napkins (for samples)
___ Disposable cups for premeasured ingredients
Cooking skills/nutrition lesson:
This lesson shows a breakfast that uses 4 groups from MyPlate: grains, dairy, fruit and nuts. According to the USDA, it's important to eat reasonable servings of a wide variety of foods. This presentation demonstrates how to do just that, and quickly too.
Demo preparation:
1. Wash your hands before you handle food.
2. Have all ingredients premeasured and arranged next to the bowl.
Make ahead options:
You can make the muesli ahead of time.
Garnish/presentation tips:
Top the muesli with a sprinkle of ground cinnamon and a few pieces of fresh fruit.
Number of sample servings: 15 (1/4 cup each)

Leader Guide: Breakfast Recipes

Faster Muesli
Makes 8 sample servings

1/2 cup whole grain cereal or oatmeal
1/2 cup nonfat light vanilla yogurt
1 cup fresh fruit

Directions:
1. Mix all ingredients in a medium-sized mixing bowl.
2. Serve immediately or refrigerate for up to 12 hours for later use. We recommend a 2-ounce serving for tasting sample.

Equipment:
___ Measuring cup
___ Cup and plastic spoon (for presentation)
___ Spatula
___ Knife (to cut fruit)
___ Cutting board
___ Medium-sized mixing bowl

Shopping list:
___ Whole grain cereal or oatmeal
___ 1 cup of fresh fruit
___ 1 container of light vanilla yogurt
___ Mini cups, spoons and napkins (for samples)
___ Disposable cups for premeasured ingredients

Cooking skills/nutrition lesson:
This lesson highlights a nutritious breakfast while following many of the USDA's MyPlate recommendations. The fruit and oatmeal provide fiber, which reduces blood cholesterol and lowers the risk of heart disease, while the lowfat yogurt follows MyPlate's call for lowfat/nonfat dairy options while still offering plenty of calcium.

Demo preparation:
1. Wash your hands before you handle food.
2. Have all ingredients premeasured and next to mixing bowl.

Make ahead options:
You can make the muesli ahead of time and serve tasting samples in class.

Garnish/presentation tips:
The final dish should go in a plastic cup with a plastic spoon to emphasize this is breakfast to go!

Number of sample servings: 8

Breakfast Pizza
Makes 8 sample servings

1 English muffin, split in half
2 Tbsp peanut butter
1 Tbsp jam (or all fruit preserves)
1/2 cup assorted fresh sliced fruit

Directions:
1. Toast both English muffin halves.
2. Spread each half with 1 tablespoon peanut butter and a half tablespoon of jam or all fruit preserves.
3. Top each one with 1/4 cup fresh sliced fruit.
4. Cut pizzas into quarters for tasting samples.

Equipment:
___ Measuring cups and spoons
___ Small plate (for presentation)
___ Kitchen knife (to spread ricotta and jam)
___ Paring knife (to cut fruit)
___ Cutting board
___ Toaster or toaster oven
___ Optional: colorful napkin to go under the plate

Shopping list:
___ English muffin
___ 1/2 cup fresh fruit
___ 1 container of peanut butter
___ 1 container of jam or light fruit preserves
___ Napkins (for samples)
___ Disposable cups (to hold premeasured ingredients)

Cooking skills/nutrition lesson:
This lesson highlights a nutritious breakfast while following many of the USDA's MyPlate recommendations. It demonstrates reasonable portions and flavorful, yet healthy, combinations of foods.

Demo preparation:
1. Wash your hands before you handle food.
2. Have all ingredients premeasured.

Make ahead options:
Partially toast the English muffins before class starts.

Garnish/presentation tips:
Place the breakfast pizzas on a small salad plate. Use additional fruit to garnish the plate. You can use a colorful napkin to go underneath the salad plate to further enhance the visual, if you'd like.

Number of sample servings: 8

Leader Guide: Breakfast Recipes

Granola Cup

Makes 9 sample servings

1 cup of nonfat, light vanilla or fruit yogurt

1 cup of diced fresh fruit (berries, bananas, etc.)

1/3 cup of lowfat granola

Directions:

1. Place the yogurt in the bottom of the cup, followed by the fruit, then the granola.

2. Add a plastic spoon and go!

Equipment:

___ Knife (for cutting fruit)

___ Cutting board

Shopping list:

___ Light, nonfat vanilla or fruit flavored yogurt

___ 1 cup of fresh fruit

___ Lowfat granola

___ Plastic cup and spoon (for final presentation)

___ Mini cups and spoons (for samples)

Cooking skills/nutrition lesson:

This lesson highlights a nutritious breakfast while following many of the USDA's MyPlate recommendations. It also demonstrates proper fruit-cutting techniques, if you opt for larger fruits than berries.

Demo Preparation:

1. Wash your hands before handling food

2. Measure ingredients

Garnish/presentation tips:

Top the granola cup with a piece or slice of fresh fruit. Serve 1/4 cup of this mix to each person for tasting samples.

Number of sample servings: 9

Breakfast On The Go

Creamy Microwave Oatmeal

1/3 cup of old fashioned oats
2/3 cup of water
Pinch of cinnamon
1 cup of skim milk or fortified soy milk
Sliced banana

Place oats, water and cinnamon in a 2 quart glass or plastic microwave container. Cover it, then microwave on full power for 3 to 4 minutes. Stir and serve with skim milk and a sliced banana.

Serves 1. Each serving: 292 calories, 3 g fat, 0.5 g saturated fat, 4 mg cholesterol, 133 mg sodium, 57 g carbohydrate, 5.5 g fiber, 13 g protein.

Sunrise Smoothie

1 cup of orange juice
1 cup of skim milk or fortified soy milk
3 Tbsp of wheat germ
1 cup of fresh or frozen fruit (strawberries, blueberries, bananas, peaches, etc.)
Pinch of cinnamon

Place all ingredients in a blender and puree on high speed until smooth. Serve immediately, or refrigerate for later use (up to 6-8 hours). If you are making this the night before, we recommend that you store it in the blender jar and blend it again it quickly before you serve it.

Serves 2. Each 1-1/4 cup serving: 160 calories, 1.8 g fat, 0 g saturated fat, 2 mg cholesterol, 65 mg sodium, 20 g carbohydrate, 3 g fiber, 8.5 g protein.

Muesli - (means "mix")

1/2 cup of oatmeal
1/4 cup of skim milk or fortified soy milk
1 cup of nonfat, light vanilla yogurt
2 cups of assorted fresh fruit, sliced
2 Tbsp of chopped almonds, pecans or walnuts
Pinch of ground cinnamon

Mix all the ingredients in a medium-sized mixing bowl. Serve immediately, or refrigerate for up to 12 hours if you prefer to serve it later.

Serves 2. Each 1-1/2 cup serving: 239 calories, 6 g fat, 0.5 g saturated fat, 4 mg cholesterol, 68 mg sodium, 37 g carbohydrate, 6 g fiber, 10 g protein.

Faster Muesli

1/3 cup of whole grain cereal or oatmeal
1/2 cup of nonfat, light vanilla yogurt
1 cup of fresh fruit

Mix all the ingredients in a medium-sized mixing bowl. Serve immediately, or refrigerate up to 12 hours for later use.

Serves 1. Each serving: 201 calories, 2.5 g fat, 0 g saturated fat, 3 mg cholesterol, 52 mg sodium, 38 g cholesterol, 7 g protein, 6 g fiber.

Breakfast Pizza

1 English muffin, split in half
2 Tbsp peanut butter
1 Tbsp jam (or all fruit preserves)
1/2 cup assorted fresh sliced fruit

Toast both English muffin halves. Spread each half with 1 tablespoon of peanut butter and a half tablespoon of jam (or all fruit preserves). Top each one with 1/4 cup fresh sliced fruit.

Serves 1. Each serving: 297 calories, 9 g fat, 1.5 g saturated fat, 0 mg cholesterol, 263 mg sodium, 45 g carbohydrate, 4 g fiber, 8 g protein.

Granola Go Cup

1/3 cup lowfat granola
1 cup of nonfat, light vanilla or fruit yogurt
1 cup of diced fresh fruit (berries, bananas, melons, oranges, grapes, etc.)

Place yogurt, fruit, and granola in a plastic cup (in that order, starting with yogurt on the bottom). Add a plastic spoon and go!

Serves 1. Each serving: 293 calories, 2.5 g fat, 0 g saturated fat, 6 mg cholesterol, 143 mg sodium, 57 g carbohydrate, 5 g fiber, 10 g protein.

Start Your Day With MyPlate!

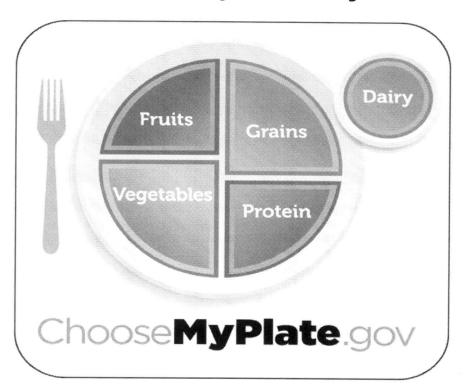

Eat Breakfast!

- **Grains** – Eat about 6 ounces of grains per day with at least half of those being whole grains. Grains include wheat, oats, corn, barley, bulgur and rye.

One ounce is the same as...
- 1 slice of bread
- 1/2 cup of cooked pasta, rice, or cereal
- 1 cup of ready-to-eat cereal

- **Vegetables** – Most people should eat 2.5 to 3 cups of vegetables per day. Be sure to get a variety of the five sub-groups: dark green, orange and red, legumes, starches, and others.

One cup is equivalent to...
- 1 cup of vegetables (fresh, frozen, raw, cooked)
- 2 cups of leafy greens

- **Fruit** – Eat about 1.5 to 2 cups of fruit per day.

One cup is the same as...
- 1 cup of fruit (raw, cooked, fresh, canned, frozen)
- 1 cup of 100% juice
- 1/2 of cup dried fruit

- **Dairy** – Get 3 cup servings of lowfat or nonfat dairy each day.

One cup is equivalent to...
- 1 cup milk (preferably skim or low-fat)
- 1.5 ounces of natural cheese
- 2 ounces of processed cheese
- 1 cup of yogurt

- **Protein** – Most people should eat between 5 and 6 ounces of protein foods per day. This group includes meat, poultry, eggs, beans and peas, nuts and seeds, and seafood.

One ounce is the same as...
- 1 ounce of meat, poultry, or fish
- ¼ cup cooked beans
- 1 egg
- ½ ounce of nuts or seeds

- How much of each of these foods that you actually need will vary based on age, gender, and activity level. Check out **www.choosemyplate.gov** for personalized recommendations.

Leader Guide: Brown Bag Lunches

Title:
Brown Bag Lunches

Target Audience:
This presentation kit is intended for general audiences age 14 and up. It covers topics of wellness, heart disease, diabetes, weight loss and nutrition.

Lesson Objectives:
• Participants will explore the substantial cost savings and nutrition improvements that accompany reducing restaurant meals and packing their own lunches.
• Participants will learn how lunch fits into MyPlate.
• Participants will learn how to prepare delicious, healthy brown bag lunches.

Lesson Rationale:
Health authorities have indicated that good nutrition is one of the most important factors in determining long-term health. Poor diet plays a major role in the development of four of the top seven killers in the United States: heart disease, cancer, stroke, and diabetes. Students who have the skills to select and prepare nutritious foods can positively impact their present and future health.

Lesson at a Glance:
This lesson introduces participants to new recipes and teaches cooking skill. It also prevents nutritional guidance that corresponds to MyPlate and the Dietary Guidelines for Americans.

Lesson Materials:
This lesson contains:
• Leader and Activity Guide
• 2 pages of copy-ready handouts and recipes

Preparation:
___ Review leader guide
___ Review handouts
___ Select activities
___ Copy and collect materials for lesson

Activity Ideas:
Introduction:
Ask your audience members to raise their hands if they pack their own lunch. Ask those that do if they usually pack the same thing on most days. Now ask if they make "planned overs," also known as extra portions of dinner the night before, which can be reheated and eaten for lunch the next day.

Activity 1 - Cooking/Food Demos
Show participants how to make a few of the lunches given in this program. Allow them to sample servings and take recipes/handouts home so that they can try some new items. Remember, according to the USDA's MyPlate, small servings of a variety of foods help you on the road to healthy eating.

Activity 2 - Quick Money Saving Tips
Use a calculator to show how much money you can save by bringing your own lunch versus eating out. We found that you can bring a lunch to work that costs only $1.50 per day versus $5 per day on eating out. That means you will save $875 over the course of a year, which includes an investment yield of 10.5%. For five years, you would save over $5000! Ask your audience to share what they do to save money with brown bag lunches. Here are some ideas you can share to get the ball rolling:
• Make your own "mini-packages" from favorite bulk items. Instead of buying smaller lunch portions of raisins, drinks, chips, pretzels, crackers, and other items, buy them in bulk and package them in small bags or containers. This can often be done at the beginning of the week to save time when things get rushed later. It could be also be protductive to demonstrate how this practice can add up to significant savings. Here are a few examples we used with prices in our area at publication time:
  • **Raisins -** A 1.5 ounce package of raisins cost .22 per ounce while a 24 ounce can cost only .15 per ounce
  • **Spoonless yogurt** (Gogurt, Expresse) - This costs almost .25 cents per unit or .125 cents per ounce. Bulk yogurt costs .06 per ounce (that's 50% less!). You can package yogurt in small, resealable containers. In addition to money, you will save fat and calories and get more calcium because spoonless yogurts contain more fat and sugar than light or nonfat bulk yogurt.
  • **Cookies -** A 1.5 ounce bag of cookies (Oreos®) costs .31 per ounce, while a 15 ounce bag costs .22 per ounce.
  • **Juice boxes** - A 2 quart container of store brand orange juice with calcium costs .049 per ounce while a brand name package of boxes of orange juice with calcium costs .63 each or .09 per ounce.
• Make large batches of soups and stews. These usually use inexpensive, healthy ingredients such as beans, potatoes and vegetables. You can freeze them in indi-

Leader Guide: Brown Bag Lunches

vidually sized containers and reheat them in the office microwave.

- Bake a whole chicken or turkey and use it for several meals - roasted chicken, soup, sandwiches, salad, etc. You will save money and consume less salt than you will find in processed deli meats. Deli chicken costs .42 per ounce, while a whole roasted chicken costs .08 per ounce. Even with a 42% yield on the roasted chicken (.18 per pound of cooked meat without the bone) you would save more than 100%. Deli chicken contains 285 mg of sodium per ounce while roasted chicken only contains 23 mg per ounce!
- Buy store brands to save money, and use unit pricing guides instead of buying brand names. A brand name orange juice with calcium in our store costs $2.99 for 2 quarts while the store brand with calcium costs just $1.99 for the same quantity.
- Take advantage of store specials.
- Buy what you need in quantities you can use.
- Have the deli clerk shave deli meat thin so that you can fill your sandwich with more vegetables.
- Bake your own healthy treats .
- Buy produce in season to take advantage of higher quality items at lower prices.
- Buy produce at local farmers markets to save money and get a generally more flavorful fresh food.

Activity 3 - Bag Lunch: Makeover Edition

Ask participants what they usually put in their lunch-box. Make a list that is visible to the audience. After receiving a few examples, show them how to modify their favorites so that they are lower in fat.

Another fun idea is to have some (or all) participants bring their bag lunch to class. Do a "makeover" for each person to show how you can improve the nutrition outcome of their lunch each day.

Use our handout, "Lighter Lunches" to help highlight how to modify what goes in the bag so that participants can eat less fat, saturated fat and sodium.

Consider awarding the healthiest lunches with a new lunchbox or gift certificate to a local food market.

Activity 4 - MyPlate, My Lunchbox, Myself

Assemble packages, samples and food items on a table according to the food groups of MyPlate. Show your audience what you have selected from each group. Ask participants to come up and make their own brown bag lunches using these items, in the proportions advocated by the USDA. Getting participants involved and letting them participate in hands-on activities will help

them remember and use what you are showing them. Here are some ideas for each group:

Grains:
- 100% whole grain bread
- Cooked brown rice
- Whole grain crackers, preferably lowfat like WASA
- Whole grain pita pockets
- Whole grain tortillas
- Tortilla chips
- Whole wheat pasta (Can be in salad form or leftovers from dinner the night before)

Fruits:
- A variety of fresh, seasonal fruit
- 100% fruit juice
- Dried fruit

Vegetables:
- Assorted raw veggies
- Vegetable juice
- Light potato chips or dried vegetable chips
- Baked potato
- Baked sweet potato

Dairy:
- Skim milk
- Yogurt (get some that is low in sugar and fat)
- Cheese sticks or slices
- Fortified soy milk
- Soy yogurt (Silk brand now contains 50% of the daily value for calcium)
- Light cheese
- Smoothies made with skim milk and fruit
- Nonfat sour cream or greek yogurt for baked potato

Protein:
- Lean cuts of meat
- Tuna fish/tuna salad
- Fish
- Shellfish
- Poultry
- Nuts or nut butter
- Beans and peas
- Seeds

Important food storage note
- You may want to include brown bags, thermoses, insulated lunchboxes, freezable gel packs, etc to ensure that these foods are stored in a safe way that will not promote bacteria growth.

See activity 5 below.

Leader Guide: Brown Bag Lunches

Activity 5 - Food Safety

You may want to include this information with any of the other activities you choose. The number one site for everyone to visit is www.fightbac.org. Here are some basic tips:

- Keep surfaces where you will handle food clean. Wash your hands. Check food preparation areas and utensils to make sure that they are clean before you start to work.
- Maintain proper temperatures while preparing and storing food for lunch bags and boxes.
- Keep hot foods hot. Use an insulated bottle for soups or chili. Make sure the food is very hot before putting it in the thermos. You should bring soups and chilis to a full boil if you're reheating them.
- Keep cold foods cold. Using a frozen gel pack or frozen box of juice is very effective if you also use an insulated pack.
- Discard perishable leftovers after lunch unless you have a way of keeping them at the correct temperature.
- Use a refrigerator if one is available. Keep portable meals out of direct sunlight and away from other heat sources.

For More Information

http://www.fightbac.org - Learn about food safety
http://www.eatright.org - Search for lunch tips
http://www.foodandhealth.com - See our blog for more recipes and tips
http://www.cspinet.org - Check out their lunch tips.

Leader Guide: Brown Bag Recipes

Garden Pita
Makes 4 sample servings

1 whole wheat pita pocket, cut in half
1 cup shredded romaine or other dark lettuce
1/4 cup sliced carrots
1 small tomato, diced
1/4 cup garbanzo beans
1 tsp olive oil
2 tsp vinegar

Toss lettuce, carrots, tomato, beans, oil, and vinegar in medium-sized bowl. Stuff pita. Wrap it in plastic and refrigerate or keep cold until you're ready to eat.

Equipment:
___ Knife (for vegetables)
___ Cutting board
___ Medium mixing bowl
___ Measuring cups and spoons
___ Kitchen spoon
___ Can opener
___ Plate (for final presentation)

Shopping list:
___ Plastic wrap
___ Romaine lettuce
___ Whole wheat pita pockets
___ Carrots
___ Tomato
___ Canned garbanzo beans
___ Olive oil
___ Vinegar (red wine, balsamic, or cider)
___ Napkins (for sample servings)

Cooking skills/nutrition lesson:
This recipe uses foods from three groups of MyPlate : grains, protein, and vegetables. It demonstrates how to properly prepare a pita, and since pita pockets are usually lower in sodium than bread and hold more fruits, vegetables, beans, and whole grains in them than a conventional sandwich, they can be considered a healthier choice.

Demo Preparation:
1. Wash your hands before handling food
2. Cut vegetables and measure ingredients

Garnish/presentation tips:
Wrap the pita in plastic wrap when finished

Number of sample servings: 4

Turkey Apple Pita
Makes 4 sample servings

2 slices of turkey
1 apple, cored and sliced
2 Tbsp nonfat, light vanilla yogurt
1/2 cup shredded romaine or other dark lettuce
1 whole wheat pita pocket, cut in half

Place one slice of turkey, 1/2 the apple, 1 tablespoon yogurt and 1/4 cup lettuce in each pita half. Wrap in plastic and refrigerate or keep cold until ready to eat.

Equipment:
___ Knife (to cut fruit)
___ Cutting board
___ Soup spoon
___ Measuring cups and spoons

Shopping list:
___ Light, nonfat vanilla yogurt
___ Sliced turkey breast
___ 1 apple (prefer granny smith, gala, jonagold)
___ Romaine
___ Whole wheat pita pocket
___ Napkins (for sample servings)

Cooking skills/nutrition lesson:
This recipe uses four groups from MyPlate: grains, fruit, protein, and dairy. It demonstrates how to properly prepare a pita, and since pita pockets are usually lower in sodium than bread and hold more fruits, vegetables, beans, and whole grains in them than a conventional sandwich, they can be considered a healthier choice.

Demo Preparation:
1. Wash your hands before you handle food.
2. Cut and measure ingredients.

Garnish/presentation tips:
Wrap the pita with plastic wrap when finished

Number of sample servings: 4

Leader Guide: Brown Bag Recipes

Black Bean Pasta Salad

Makes 10 sample servings

8 oz dry macaroni
1 cup cooked or canned black beans
2 cups pasta sauce

Cook macaroni according to package directions. Drain in colander and rinse well. Mix the macaroni with the beans and sauce and divide into lunch portions (1-1/2 cups). Keep refrigerated or chilled until ready to eat. Use 2 ounce servings for tastings.

Equipment:
___ Pan (for boiling pasta*)
___ Stove*
___ Mixing bowl
___ Kitchen spoon

Shopping list:
___ Macaroni
___ Canned black beans
___ Pasta sauce - 1 jar
___ Can opener
___ Portable container (for final presentation)
___ Mini cups and spoons (for samples)

Cooking skills/nutrition lesson:
This recipe uses three groups from MyPlate: grains, proteins, and vegetables. It outlines how a cooked pasta dish can be used for lunch the next day. It also highlights the versatility of plan overs, since this recipe is good whether it's served hot or cold.

Demo Preparation:
1. Wash your hands before you handle food
2. Measure all your ingredients
*Note: We recommend cooking the pasta before the presentation in order to save time. In this case, you would not need the stove or the pan.

Garnish/presentation tips:
Place the finished salad in a portable container. Discuss how to keep it cold - either in a refrigerator, next to a frozen juice/water container, or by a gel pack.

Number of sample servings: 10

Rabbit Bag

Makes 6 sample servings

1 apple, cored and cut in wedges
1 orange, cut in wedges
1/2 cup baby carrots or carrot sticks
1/2 cup broccoli florets

Place apple and orange wedges in a plastic bag and place the carrots and broccoli in another. Seal and shake both bags well. Keep refrigerated or chilled until ready to eat.

Equipment:
___ Knife
___ Cutting board

Shopping list:
___ Apple
___ Orange
___ Baby carrots, or carrot sticks
___ Broccoli florets
___ Ziploc bag
___ Napkins (for samples)

Cooking skills/nutrition lesson:
This recipe uses two groups from MyPlate: fruits and vegetables. Remember that half your plate should be full of fruits and vegetables at each meal. This lesson demonstrates a fun and delicious easy way to prepare fruits and vegetables for portability. Plus, the orange helps keep the apples from turning brown and will impart a nice flavor to this snack.

Demo Preparation:
1. Wash your hands before you handle food
2. Measure and cut ingredients

Garnish/presentation tips:
Place everything in 2 Ziploc bags

Number of sample servings: 6

Leader Guide: Brown Bag Recipes

10 Minute Chili Soup
Makes 16 sample servings

1 tsp oil
1 cup diced onions
1 cup diced carrots
1 can (15 ounces) diced tomatoes
1 cup water
1 can (15 ounces) kidney beans
1 tsp chili powder
1 tsp dried oregano

Heat a large, nonstick skillet over medium-high heat. Add oil and saute the onions and carrots until golden, about 3 minutes. Add the rest of the ingredients and bring to a boil. Simmer until vegetables are tender, about 4-5 minutes. Pour into thermos or refrigerate until ready to heat and serve. Use 2 ounce servings for tastings.

Equipment:
____ Knife
____ Peeler
____ Cutting board
____ Stove
____ Can opener
____ Kitchen spoon
____ Ladle
____ 12" nonstick skillet
____ Thermos
____ Measuring cups and spoons

Shopping list:
____ Onion
____ Carrots
____ 15 oz can diced, no-salt-added tomatoes
____ 15 oz can kidney beans
____ Water
____ Chili powder
____ Dried oregano
____ Vegetable oil
____ Mini cups and spoons (for samples)

Cooking skills/nutrition lesson:
This recipe uses two groups from MyPlate: proteins and vegetables. It also demonstrates basic cooking skills like dicing, sauteeing, boiling, etc. Further, this recipe shows how to make a hearty, healthy soup in just ten minutes. Homemade soups tend to have less sodium than canned soups, which makes them popular with MyPlate. Many Americans need to reduce their sodium intake, and this recipe offers a way to do just that.

Demo Preparation:
1. Wash your hands before you handle food
2. Cut and measure ingredients
3. Place skillet over stove and heat on low while participants are coming into the room.
4. Have all ingredients organized around the skillet/stove in the order you will add them.

Garnish/presentation tips:
Place the soup into a thermos when finished. You can add whole grain crackers for garnish too.

Number of sample servings: 16

Sandwich Makeover

Make a Better Tuna Sandwich!

Better Tuna Sandwich:	Difference from classic:
Calories	-54.0
Fat	-16.0
Saturated Fat	-1.5
Sodium	-162.0
Fiber	+4.4

How are they made?

Classic:	Better:
2 slices white bread	100% whole wheat bread
2 Tbsp regular mayo	Light mayo
3 oz. tuna in water	Low-sodium tuna
1/4 cup iceberg lettuce	Romaine lettuce
No tomato	1/3 tomato

The *better* tuna sandwich is tastier & more nutritious!

• It provides almost triple the amount of magnesium
• It has more than double the amount of potassium
• It also has more than double the amount of vitamin E
• Plus, it contains three B vitamins: thiamin, niacin and folate

If you made a better tuna sandwich instead of a classic, every week, you would save _____ per year:

-2808 calories
-832 g fat
-78 g saturated fat
-8424 mg sodium

Make A Better Peanut Butter Sandwich!

Better Peanut Sandwich:	Difference from classic:
Calories	-10
Fat	-5.0
Saturated Fat	-1.2
Sodium	-58.0
Fiber	+4.5

How are they made?

Classic:	Better:
2 slices white bread	100% whole wheat bread
2 Tbsp peanut butter	1 Tbsp natural peanut butter
No banana	1/2 banana
1 Tbsp grape jelly	No grape jelly

The *better* peanut butter sandwich is tastier and more nutritious!

• It provides almost double the amount of potassium
• It has a third more magnesium
• It also has almost triple the amount of vitamin E
• Plus, it contains more B vitamins: B6 and niacin

If you made a better peanut butter sandwich every week you would save _____ per year:

-1040 calories
-260 g fat
-62.4 g saturated fat
-3016 mg sodium

Make A BETTER Sandwich!

• Use 1/2 the amount of meat and replace it with more lettuce and tomato.
• Use roasted turkey breast or chicken in place of high-fat deli meats like bologna, pastrami, roast beef, ham, etc.
• Use light mayo instead of regular mayonnaise.
• Use 100% whole wheat bread instead of white bread.
• Include tuna or another fish a few times per week. Remember, according to the USDA, you should eat at least 8 ounces of seafood per week.
• Use cheese sparingly.
• Add more vegetables. Some options include red onion, carrots, tomatoes, lettuce, cucumbers, and spinach.
• Use frozen bread so you can spread peanut butter more thinly.

Delicious Brown Bag Recipes

Garden Pita
1 whole wheat pita pocket, cut in half
1 cup shredded romaine or other dark lettuce
1/4 cup sliced carrots
1 small tomato, diced
1/4 cup garbanzo beans
1 tsp olive oil
2 tsp vinegar
Directions:
1. Toss lettuce, carrots, tomato, beans, oil, and vinegar in a medium bowl.
2. Stuff the pita with salad, wrap it in plastic, and refrigerate or keep cold until ready to eat.
Serves 1. Each serving (1 pita): 289 calories, 65 g fat, 0.5 g saturated fat, 0 mg cholesterol, 515 mg sodium, 52 g carbohyrdrate, 10 g fiber, 12 g protein.

Turkey Apple Pita
2 slices of turkey
1 apple, cored and sliced
2 Tbsp nonfat light vanilla yogurt
1/2 cup shredded romaine or other dark lettuce
1 whole wheat pita pocket, cut in half
Directions:
1. Place one slice of turkey, 1/2 the apple, 1 tablespoon yogurt and 1/4 cup lettuce in each pita half.
2. Wrap in plastic and refrigerate or keep cold.
Serves 1. Each serving: 275 calories, 2.5 g fat, 0 g saturated fat, 20 mg cholesterol, 350 mg sodium, 52 g carbohydrate, 9 g fiber, 17 g protein.

Black Bean Pasta Salad
8 oz dry macaroni
1 cup cooked black beans
2 cups pasta sauce
Directions:
1. Cook macaroni according to package directions. Drain in colander and rinse well.
2. Mix the macaroni with the beans and sauce and divide into lunch portions (1-1/2 cups each). Keep refrigerated or chilled until ready to eat.
Serves 4. Each serving (about 1-1/4 cups): 307 calories,
1 g fat, 0 g saturated fat, 0 mg cholesterol, 394 mg sodium, 61 g carbohydrate, 7 g fiber, 13 g protein.

Rabbit Bag
1 apple, cored and cut in wedges
1 orange, cut in wedges
1/2 cup baby carrots or carrot sticks
1/2 cup broccoli florets
Directions:
1. Divide ingredients between 2 plastic bags and shake well.
2. Keep refrigerated or chilled until ready to eat.
Serves 1. Each 3 cup serving: 185 calories, 1 g fat, 0 g saturated fat, 0 mg cholesterol, 39 mg sodium, 45 g carbohydrate, 9.5 g fiber, 3 g protein.

10 Minute Chili Soup
1 tsp oil
1 cup diced onions
1 cup diced carrots
1 can diced tomatoes
1 cup water
1 can kidney beans
1 tsp chili powder
1 tsp dried oregano
Directions:
1. Heat a large, nonstick skillet over medium-high heat. Add oil and saute onions and carrots until golden, about 3 minutes.
2. Add the rest of the ingredients and bring to a boil. Simmer until vegetables are tender, about 4-5 minutes.
3. Pour into thermos or refrigerate until ready to heat and serve.
Serves 4. Each 1-1/4 cup serving: 130 calories, 1.5 g fat, 0 g saturated fat, 0 mg cholesterol, 339 mg sodium, 24 g carbohydrate, 8.5 g fiber, 6 g protein.

Your Own Lunch Success

Tips for variety, flavor, and good nutrition:

- **Plan** your meals a week in advance or at least the night before. This will help you utilize dinner leftovers for lunch. A roasted chicken or turkey breast can double for sandwiches, and pasta dishes hold up very well too.
- **Cut fruits and vegetables at the start of the week**. Filling half your plate with fruits and vegetables is easier when these items are ready for you.
- **Keep the right ingredients on hand** using MyPlate. Choose whole grain breads, crackers and rolls. Buy nonfat, low-sugar dairy products with lots of calcium. Keep lots of fruits and vegetables on hand. Purchase tuna, turkey or chicken breast, lean ham and other lean cuts of meat, looking for low-sodium options when possible. Remember that beans (which count as protein or vegetable) can be used in soups, salads and chilis.
- **Include soups**, chili, baked sweet potatoes or baked potatoes in lunches, especially in the winter.
- Consider drinking **low-sodium vegetable juice**.
- Instead of chips, pack a small bag of **light popcorn**. Popcorn is a whole grain!
- Pack smart! Half your plate should be filled with fruits and vegetables, protein should take up an additional quarter, and grains should finish the round. Include a side of dairy for a complete and healthy meal. **Use MyPlate guinelines** to balance your meal.

Save money!

Bringing a lunch to work for $1.50 per day versus spending $5 per day at restaurants will save you $875 for one year - this includes an investment yield of 10.5%. Here are some more tips to help you save money:

- **Make your own "mini-packages"** from favorite bulk items. Instead of buying smaller lunch portions of raisins, drinks, chips, pretzels, crackers and other items, buy these in bulk and package them in small bags or containers. This can often be done at the beginning of the week to save time.
- **Make large batches of soups and stews**. These usually use inexpensive, healthy ingredients such as beans, potatoes and vegetables. You can freeze them in small containers and reheat them in the office microwave.
- **Bake a whole chicken or turkey** and use it for several meals - roasted chicken, soup, sandwiches, salad, etc. You will save money and consume less salt than

you would if you ate processed deli meats.
- **Buy store brands** to save money. You can use unit pricing guides instead of buying brand names.
- Take advantage of store specials
- Buy what you need in **quantitities** you can use.
- Have the deli clerk shave deli meat thin and **fill your sandwich with more vegetables**.
- **Bake** your own healthy treats.
- Buy **produce in season** to take advantage of higher quality items at lower prices.
- Buy produce at **local farmers markets** to save money and get a more flavorful, fresh product

Keep it safe:

- Keep food surfaces **clean**. Wash your hands. Check food preparation areas and utensils to make sure they are clean before you start to work.
- Maintain proper **temperatures** while preparing and storing food for lunch bags and boxes. Don't let food sit out any longer than actual preparation time.
- Keep hot foods hot. Use an **insulated** bottle for soups or chili. Make sure the food is very hot before putting it in the thermos. You should bring soups and chilis to a full boil if you're reheating them.
- Keep cold foods cold. Using a **frozen gel pack** or frozen box of juice is very effective if you also use an insulated lunchbox.
- **Discard** perishable leftovers after lunch unless you have a way of keeping them at the correct temperature.
- Use a **refrigerator** if one is available. Keep portable meals out of direct sunlight or away from other heat sources.
- For more tips on food safety **visit** www.fightbac.org.

A Balanced Lunch

Grains -- Think whole, not processed
- 100% whole grain bread
- Cooked brown rice
- Whole grain crackers, preferably lowfat like WASA
- Whole grain pita pockets
- Whole grain tortillas
- Tortilla chips
- Whole wheat pasta (Can be in salad form or leftovers from dinner the night before)

Fruits -- Buy in season
- Try variety of fresh, seasonal fruit
- 100% fruit juice
- Dried fruit

Vegetables -- Try veggies in salads and sandwiches
- Assorted raw veggies
- Vegetable juice
- Light potato chips or dried vegetable chips
- Baked potato
- Baked sweet potato

Dairy -- Put dairy in portable containers
- Skim milk
- Yogurt (get some that is low in sugar and fat)
- Cheese sticks or slices
- Fortified soy milk
- Soy yogurt (Silk brand now contains 50% of the daily value for calcium)
- Light cheese
- Smoothies made with skim milk and fruit
- Nonfat sour cream or greek yogurt for baked potato

Protein -- Get a lean variety
- Lean cuts of meat
- Tuna fish/tuna salad
- Fish
- Shellfish
- Poultry
- Nuts or nut butter
- Beans and peas
- Seeds

MyPlate Guidelines and Tips
- Avoid oversized portions of foods and drinks.
- Choose low-sodium foods.
- Avoid sugary drinks like soda, artificially flavored juice, and sport drinks.
- Drink plenty of water.
- Eat a variety of fruits and vegetables. Be sure to eat a bunch of different colors every day.
- Eat varied, small portions of protein every day. Most of it should be lean, and some of it should be seafood.
- Stick to lowfat, low sugar dairy products.
- Make at least half of the grains you eat whole grains.
- Half your plate should be full of fruits and veggies at every meal.

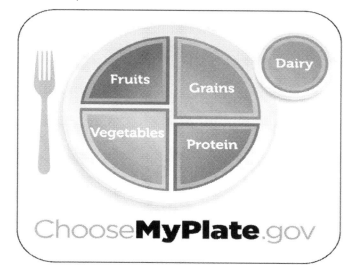

Leader Guide: Calcium

Title:
Calcium

Target Audience:
This presentation kit is intended for general audiences age 14 and up. It covers topics of wellness, heart disease, diabetes, weight loss and nutrition.

Lesson Objectives:
• Participants will learn the importance of calcium and why they should get this nutrient from food sources.
• Participants will identify food sources of calcium
• Participants will learn how to prepare three calcium-rich recipes

Lesson Rationale:
Data from the CDC shows that calcium intake increased from 1988-94 to 2003-04, but still the majority of people did not have intakes above Adequate Intake values. Female adolescents have the lowest calcium intakes compared to recommendations. You can find details at
http://www.cdc.gov/nchs/ppt/hp2010/focus_areas/fa19_2_ppt/fa19_nutrition2_ppt.htm

Lesson at a Glance:
This lesson introduces participants to new recipes and teaches cooking skills. The content and advice is consistent with MyPlate and the Dietary Guidelines for Americans.

Lesson Materials:
This lesson contains:
1) Leader/Activity guide
2) Copy-ready handouts and recipes
3) Leader guide for recipes and food demos

Leader and Activity Guide:
3 pages of copy-ready handouts and recipes
Preparation:
___ Review leader guide
___ Review handouts
___ Select activities
___ Copy and collect materials for lesson

Activity Ideas:
Introduction
Ask if anyone knows how much calcium they get on a daily basis. Have participants write down their answers. From here, we strongly recommend that you proceed to activity one.

Activity 1 – Putting the "Yum" in Calcium
Use the calcium assessment sheet, "Are You Getting Enough Calcium?" to help participants figure out their calcium intake.

Discuss ways to incorporate more calcium into their diets. We've listed a few tips and suggestions below...
• Subsitute nonfat yogurt for mayonnaise and sour cream in recipes that don't require cooking. These types of recipes include potato salad, tuna sandwiches, dips, etc.
• Include yogurt as a dessert or snack on most days of the week. Be sure to read labels and find products that have >25% of the daily value for calcium.
• Purchase calcium-fortified orange juice.
• Eat more beans, whole grains, fruits and vegetables - not only do they contain some calcium, but they also contain nutrients that are essential to bone health.
• Make smoothies with skim milk.
• Fortified skim milk may be useful, though expensive. It contains up to 500 mg of calcium.
• Make lasagna with lowfat or fat free ricotta cheese - 1/4 cup has 268 mg of calcium.
• Sprinkle almonds on top of cereal and yogurt.
• Make a stir fry dish once a week using broccoli, carrots and kale. Top it with sesame seeds
• Use plain, nonfat yogurt to top a baked potato.

Activity 2 - A Calcium Fortified Display
Assemble foods that are high in calcium. Use the foods listed on the sheet, "Are You Getting Enough Calcium?" for ideas. Also include foods that are popular with your region/population. It is helpful to assemble these in the same way as MyPlate.

We would recommend using a few of the new calcium-fortified foods like sweetened cereals, frozen waffles, etc that are also high in sugar and made mostly with refined products to show them what NOT to buy or to only buy in small quantities.

Activity 3 - Food Tasting
You might want to consider giving your audience samples of these foods so that they can try them. We would recommend letting them taste the following:

Leader Guide: Calcium

- New Silk soy "yogurt" because it is now reformulated and tastes very good - it also contains 500 mg of calcium.

- Skim Plus - most people don't realize there is such a thing as fortified skim milk - this milk is thick like whole milk and usually contains a significant amount of calcium (around 500-600 depending on the brand).

-Fortified soy milk - now is the time to let your audience try soy milk to see if they like it. You may want to bring different flavors

-Fortified orange juice - bring the store brand as well as popular brands like Tropicana. Many people are reluctant to buy this product because they don't know how it tastes, so this is a great way to find out!

-Calcium fortified frozen yogurt - when you indulge, make it high in calcium and low in fat! Remind your audience about portion control with this product. After all, MyPlate insists that people enjoy food, but eat less of it and stick to reasonable portions.

Activity 4 - Cooking Demo

Use the recipes in this section to demonstrate how to prepare meals and dishes that are high in calcium.

It is always a good idea to talk about the ingredients you are using while you are waiting for something to cook.

Further reading/info/links

• http://www.foodandhealth.com - Search for articles on bone health, calcium, and osteoporosis. You can also check out the Diet and Osteoporosis presentation kit. For More Information, call 800-462-2352.

• http://www.fda.gov - Follow the links from food to consumers, then explore their resources about calcium and osteoporosiss.

• Take a look at the article by Reed Mangels, PhD, RD about calcium in the Vegan Diet. You can find it via the Vegetarian Resource Group at *http://www.vrg.org/nutrition/calcium.htm*.

• *http://www.calciuminfo.com* - From the makers of Tums, this site has basic information and a calcium calculator.

Leader Guide: Calcium Recipes

Stuffed Shells

Makes 16 sample servings

Pasta shells are stuffed with a creamy ricotta filling and baked in tomato sauce.

8 large pasta shells, dry

Filling:

1 tub nonfat ricotta (16 ounces)

1/2 tsp garlic powder

1/2 tsp Italian Seasoning

Sauce:

1 can diced tomatoes, no salt added

1 cup pasta sauce

Topping:

1/2 cup shredded lowfat mozzarella

Directions:

1. Preheat oven to 350 degrees. Cook shells according to directions on box then drain and rinse.
2. Combine filling ingredients in a medium bowl.
3. Place all ingredients for sauce in large casserole pan and stir well.
4. Place filling in shells; use about 1/4 cup per shell.
5. Place the shells in a casserole dish and baste with sauce. Cover this casserole dish and bake until heated through (about 30 minutes).
6. Sprinkle cheese over the top and allow to melt (about 1 minute). Serve hot.

Microwave directions: Proceed as above through step five and omitting the first part of step one. Instead of the oven, place the covered casserole pan in a microwave and zap on full power for 10-15 minutes (or until shells are heated through). Top with cheese and allow to melt for one minute, then serve hot.

Cut each shell in half for tasting samples.

Equipment:

___ Medium mixing bowl

___ 2 quart glass casserole dish with cover

___ Oven or microwave

___ Stove

___ Can opener

___ 2 quart pan (to cook shells)

___ Colander (to drain shells)

___ Kitchen spoon (to mix sauce and serve shells)

___ Spatula (to mix ricotta)

___ Measuring cups and spoons

___ Dinner plate (for final presentation)

Shopping list:

___ 1 box large pasta shells

___ 1 jar (low sodium, lowfat) pasta sauce

___ 1 can no-salt-added diced tomatoes

___ 1 tub (16 ounces) nonfat ricotta

___ Garlic powder

___ Italian seasoning mix

___ 1 bag shredded lowfat Mozzarella cheese

___ Cups and spoons and napkins (for samples)

Cooking skills/nutrition lesson:

This recipe demonstrates an easy way to use nonfat ricotta cheese. Ricotta is an excellent source of calcium and it is also low in sodium. By using canned, no-salt-added tomatoes and pasta sauce you can reduce the sodium and have a chunkier, better tasting sauce. This recipe also highlights one of the best ways to use lowfat cheese - you have to add it at the end. If you add it at the beginning, it will get tough and chewy.

Demo Preparation:

1. Wash your hands before you handle food.
2. Measure ingredients and organize them so they are placed on your work table in the order you will use them.

Make ahead tips:

We recommend that you cook the shells ahead of time for this demo. The ricotta cheese should be softened slightly - allow it to sit out briefly or put it in the microwave for about half a minute.

Garnish/presentation tips:

Place 2 shells on a large dinner plate and spoon sauce around them.

Number of sample servings: 16

Leader Guide: Calcium Recipes

Broccoli Peanut Stir Fry

Makes 12 sample servings

Peanuts add crunch and protein to this delicious dish.

2 cups cooked brown rice

2 tsp oil

1 cup sliced green onion

1 cup sliced carrots

2 cups chopped kale, prewashed

1 cup chopped broccoli

1/2 tsp garlic powder

4 Tbsp light soy sauce

1/4 tsp ground ginger (or 1 Tbsp fresh ground ginger)

1/2 cup dry roasted peanuts, no salt added

Optional garnish: 4 tsp sesame seeds

Directions:

1. Cook brown rice in microwave according to package directions

2. Heat a large nonstick skillet over medium high heat and add oil. Add the vegetables in the order they appear above. Cover pan and allow to cook for a few minutes before stirring.

3. Saute until vegetables are almost tender, then add seasonings and peanuts. Serve over cooked brown rice.

We recommend a 2 ounce portion for sample servings.

Serves 4 (in regular portions) about 1-1/2 cup each

Equipment:

___ Knife (for cutting vegetables)

___ Cutting board

___ Stove

___ Large, 12-inch, nonstick skillet

___ Plastic spoon for sauteing vegetables

___ Kitchen spoon (for serving vegetables and rice)

___ Casserole dish for cooking rice (we recommend cooking it in the microwave or a rice cooker)

___ Microwave oven (for rice)

___ Measuring cups and spoons

___ Disposable cups for holding measured ingredients

Shopping list:

___ Vegetable oil

___ Sesame seeds (optional garnish)

___ Green onion

___ Carrots

___ Fresh kale

___ Broccoli

___ Garlic powder

___ Light soy sauce

___ Ground ginger (or fresh ground ginger)

___ Dry roasted peanuts, no salt added

___ Brown rice

___ Cups, spoons and napkins (for samples)

Cooking skills/nutrition lesson:

Stir fry dishes make excellent meals. They utilize a lot of vegetables, are easy to prepare, and taste great. This dish uses three groups from MyPlate: grains, protein, and vegetables. People always wonder how to use kale and this is an excellent example. One thing you might want to point out is that you don't need a lot of oil to saute vegetables and that measuring is a great way to avoid a lot of empty calories to your meals.

Demo preparation:

1. Wash your hands before you handle food.

2. Cut and measure ingredients. Organize them around the skillet in the order you will be adding them.

Make ahead options:

We recommend that you cook the brown rice ahead of time for this recipe.

Garnish/presentation tips:

Place the brown rice on a large dinner plate and top with the stir fry. One option for garnishing might be to sprinkle this dish with sesame seeds because they taste good, go well with Asian style dishes and are high in calcium.

Number of sample servings: 12

10 Minute Corn Chowder

Makes 20 sample servings

This tasty corn chowder is easily made in a skillet.

1 tsp oil

1/2 onion, chopped

1 tsp minced garlic

4 tbsp all purpose flour

3 cups skim milk

2 tsp prepared mustard

1/4 tsp dried thyme

Black pepper (to taste)

2 cups frozen corn kernels

4 Tbsp shredded reduced fat cheddar cheese

Heat a large, nonstick skillet over medium-high heat. Add the oil and saute the onion and garlic until golden, about 2 minutes. Meanwhile, place the milk, flour,

Leader Guide: Calcium Recipes

mustard, and seasonings in a small bowl and mix well. Add the milk mixture to the skillet followed by the corn and mix until the mixture comes to a boil and thickens, about 3 minutes. Stir frequently to keep the mixture from burning. Divide into four bowls and top each with 1 tablespoon of shredded cheese. We recommend a 2 ounce serving for tasting samples.

Equipment:
___ Knife (for chopping the onion)
___ Cutting board
___ 12 inch, nonstick skillet
___ Stove
___ Small bowl to mix flour and milk
___ Ladle
___ Large soup bowl to show final presentation
___ measuring cups and spoons

Shopping list:
___ Oil
___ Onion
___ Jar of minced garlic
___ All purpose flour
___ Skim milk
___ Prepared mustard
___ Dried thyme
___ Black pepper
___ Frozen corn kernels
___ Shredded reduced fat cheddar cheese
___ Spoons, cups and napkins (for samples)

Cooking skills/nutrition lesson:
This recipe outlines a healthy, easy way to make cream soups in a skillet. Many of the prepared cream soups on the market are very high in sodium. You may want to bring in a can of cream soup to show that a one cup serving often contains around 800-1200 mg of sodium. That's a half day's supply! According to the USDA, Americans should stick to low-sodium options whenever possible.

Demo Preparation:
1. Wash your hands before you handle food.
2. Cut and measure ingredients.
3. Organize ingredients around the stove and skillet in the order you will add them.

Garnish/presentation tips:
Place a serving of the soup in a large soup bowl and top with cheddar cheese to show final serving.

Number of sample servings: 20

Leader Guide: Calcium Recipes

Cappuccino

Makes 4-5 sample servings

3/4 cup strong brewed decaf coffee
1/2 cup skim milk
Cocoa powder
Ground cinnamon

Pour coffee into a large, 12-ounce mug. Place skim milk into a large, covered container and warm in microwave for a few seconds (about 10-20). Shake milk vigorously in a covered container until froth forms (30 seconds). Pour milk gently into the coffee. Top with a little cocoa powder and cinnamon. We recommend 2 ounce portions for sample servings.

Equipment:
___ Coffee maker (or thermos to carry brewed coffee)
___ Can opener for coffee
___ Large covered container to heat and shake milk
___ Coffee mug (for final presentation)
___ Measuring cups and spoons

Shopping list:
___ Brewed, decaf coffee (or filter and coffee to brew it in the coffee maker)
___ Skim milk
___ Cocoa powder
___ Ground cinnamon
___ Cups and napkins (for samples)

Cooking skills/nutrition lesson:
This recipe shows how to add more calcium to everyone's favorite beverage -- coffee. Shaking the milk produces a nice foam, just like the one steamed with an expensive cappuccino machine.

Demo Preparation:
1. Wash your hands before you handle food.
2. Measure ingredients.
3. Brew coffee and have it ready in a thermos (or set up a coffee maker and brew it just as your attendees are arriving).

Garnish/presentation tips:
Place the coffee in the mug, add the foamed milk and top with ground cinnamon and cocoa.

Number of sample servings: 4-5

Chocolate Almond Latte

Makes 4 sample servings

1/4 tsp almond extract
1 Tbsp chocolate syrup
1 tsp instant decaf coffee
1 cup skim milk
2 Tbsp fat free whipped cream
1/2 tsp toasted almonds

Combine extract, chocolate syrup and instant coffee in a large mug. Add the milk and microwave on high until hot, about 2 minutes. Place whipped cream and toasted almonds on top. Serve immediately. We recommend 2 ounce portions for sample servings.

Equipment:
___ Large coffee mug
___ Microwave
___ Can opener (for coffee)
___ Toaster oven and pan for almonds (or toast ahead)
___ Measuring cups and spoons

Shopping list:
___ Almond extract
___ Chocolate syrup
___ Instant decaf coffee
___ Skim milk
___ 1 can of fat-free whipped cream
___ Toasted almonds
___ Cups and napkins (for samples)

Cooking skills/nutrition lesson:
This recipe demonstrates how to make a delicious beverage that is high in calcium. Most people do not like to drink skim milk or milk by itself, but they do like coffee drinks, so it all works out. According to ChooseMyPlate.gov, consuming dairy products is linked to better bone health and may even reduce the risk of osteoporosis.

Demo Preparation:
1. Wash your hands before you handle food.
2. Measure ingredients. Organize them in the order you will use them.

Garnish/presentation tips:
Place the beverage in the mug. Shake the can of whipped cream and top everything with the fat free whipped cream. Top *that* with toasted almonds.

Number of sample servings: 4

Leader Guide: Calcium Recipes

Waldorf Salad
Makes 20 sample servings
3 apples, cored and diced
1 cup nonfat, light vanilla yogurt
1/4 cup diced celery
1/4 cup walnut pieces
Green, leafy lettuce (for garnish)
Mix all ingredients in a medium-sized mixing bowl. Refrigerate until ready to serve. This salad looks nice if it is served on a bed of green lettuce. Garnish with a pinch of ground cinnamon. We recommend a 2 ounce serving for tasting samples

Equipment:
___ Large knife
___ Small knife (to core and cut apples). You can also use an apple corer if that would make you more comfortable.
___ Cutting board
___ Mixing bowl
___ Kitchen spoon
___ Salad plate (for final presentation)
___ measuring cups

Shopping list:
___ 3 apples
___ Nonfat, light vanilla yogurt
___ Celery
___ Walnut pieces
___ Lettuce for garnish
___ Cups, spoons, and napkins (for samples)

Cooking skills/nutrition lesson:
This recipe outlines how to make a salad using nonfat, light vanilla yogurt instead of mayonnaise. Tell your audience to look for light yogurt because it is lower in calories, but still a fantastic source of calcium.

Demo preparation:
1. Wash your hands before you handle food.
2. Measure ingredients.

Garnish/presentation tips:
Place the green, leafy lettuce on the salad plate. Top with one serving of waldorf salad. Garnish with a few walnut pieces or ground cinnamon.
Number of sample servings: 20

Calcium Muesli
Makes 6 sample servings
Eat this delicious dish for breakfast to increase your calcium intake. It is very convenient to eat on the go.
1/4 cup rolled oats, dry
1/4 cup skim milk
1/2 cup vanilla light nonfat yogurt
1 cup diced fresh fruit
Pinch of cinnamon
Mix the rolled oats and milk; allow to soak for a few minutes or overnight. Fold in the rest of the ingredients. Eat immediately or refrigerate for up to one day or until ready to serve.

Equipment:
___ Knife (for cutting fruit)
___ Cutting board
___ Soup spoon
___ Mixing bowl
___ Cup or bowl (for final presentation)
___ Measuring cups and spoons

Shopping list:
___ Rolled oats, dry
___ Skim milk
___ Vanilla nonfat light yogurt
___ Fresh fruit
___ Ground cinnamon
___ Cups, spoons, and napkins (for samples)

Cooking skills/nutrition lesson:
This recipe uses three groups from MyPlate: grains, fruit and dairy. It highlights how to make a delicious, nutrient dense breakfast on the go using yogurt and milk, which are both high in calcium. This is an excellent opportunity to teach your audience how to purchase yogurt and read the label for calcium content and sugar/calories.

Demo preparation:
1. Wash your hands before you handle food.
2. Cut and measure ingredients.
3. Place the muesli in a cup or bowl

Garnish/presentation tips:
Top with a few pieces of fresh fruit and a pinch of ground cinnamon.
Number of sample servings: 6

Calcium Recipes

Stuffed Shells

Pasta shells are stuffed with a cream ricotta filling and baked in tomato sauce.

8 large pasta shells, dry

Filling:

1 tub nonfat ricotta (16 ounces)

1/2 tsp garlic powder

1/2 tsp Italian Seasoning

Sauce:

1 can diced tomatoes, no salt added

1 cup pasta sauce

Topping:

1/2 cup shredded lowfat mozzarella

Directions:

1. Preheat oven to 350 degrees. Cook shells according to directions on box; drain and rinse in colander until ready to use.
2. Combine filling ingredients in a medium-sized bowl.
3. Place all ingredients for sauce in large casserole pan and stir well.
4. Place filling in shells; use about 1/4 cup per shell.
5. Place the shells in a casserole dish and baste with sauce. Cover this casserole dish and bake until heated through (about 30 minutes).
6. Sprinkle cheese over the top, and allow to melt (about 1 minute). Serve hot.

Microwave directions: Proceed through step 5, omitting oven instructions. Place the covered casserole pan in a microwave and zap on full power for 10-15 minutes, or until shells are heated through. Top with cheese and allow to melt for one more minute; serve hot.

Serves 4. Each serving (2 shells): 374 calories, 4 g fat, 2 g saturated fat, 18 mg cholesterol, 509 mg sodium, 55 g carbohydrate, 3 g fiber, 27 g protein. 600 mg calcium.

Broccoli Peanut Stir Fry

Peanuts add crunch and protein to this delicious stir fry dish.

2 cups cooked brown rice

2 tsp oil

1 cup sliced green onion

1 cup sliced carrots

2 cups chopped kale, prewashed

1 cup chopped broccoli

1/2 tsp garlic powder

4 Tbsp light soy sauce

1/4 tsp ground ginger (or 1 Tbsp fresh ground ginger)

1/2 cup dry roasted peanuts, no salt added

Optional garnish: 4 tsp sesame seeds

Directions:

1. Cook brown rice in a microwave according to package directions
2. Heat a large, nonstick skillet over medium high heat and add oil. Add the vegetables in the order they appear above. Cover pan and allow to cook for a few minutes before stirring.
3. Saute until vegetables are almost tender, then add seasonings and peanuts. Serve over cooked brown rice.

Serves 4. Each 1-1/2 cup serving: 287 calories, 12 g fat, 1.5 f saturated fat, 0 mg cholesterol, 543 mg sodium, 36 g carbohydrate, 5.5 g fiber, 10 g calcium. 92 mg calcium.

Calcium Recipes

10 Minute Corn Chowder

1 tsp oil
1/2 onion, chopped
1 tsp minced garlic
4 tbsp all purpose flour
3 cups skim milk
2 tsp prepared mustard
1/4 tsp dried thyme
black pepper to taste
2 cups frozen corn kernels
4 Tbsp shredded reduced fat cheddar cheese

Heat a large, nonstick skillet over medium-high heat. Add the oil and saute the onion and garlic until golden, about 2 minutes. Meanwhile, place the milk, flour, mustard, and seasonings in a small bowl and mix well. Add the milk mixture to the skillet followed by the corn and mix until the mixture comes to a boil and thickens, about 3 minutes. Stir frequently to keep the mixture from burning. Divide into four bowls and top each with 1 tablespoon of shredded cheese.

Serves 4. Each 1-1/4 cup serving: 232 calories, 5 g fat, 2.5 g saturated fat, 13 mg cholesterol, 251 mg sodium, 35 g carbohydrate, 3 g fiber, 14 g protein. 342 mg calcium.

Cappuccino

3/4 cup strong brewed decaf coffee
1/2 cup skim milk
Cocoa powder
Ground cinnamon

Pour coffee into a large, 12-ounce mug. Place skim milk into a large, covered container and warm in microwave for a few seconds (about 10-20). Shake milk vigorously in a covered container until froth forms (30 seconds). Pour milk gently into the coffee. Top with a little cocoa powder and cinnamon.

Serves 1. Each 1-1/4 cup serving: 42 calories, 0 fat, 2 mg cholesterol, 63 mg sodium, 6 g carbohydrate, 0 fiber, 4 g protein. 151 mg calcium.

Chocolate Almond Latte

1/4 tsp almond extract
1 Tbsp chocolate syrup
1 tsp instant decaf coffee
1 cup skim milk
2 Tbsp fat free whipped cream
1/2 tsp toasted almonds

Combine extract, chocolate syrup and instant coffee in a large mug. Add the milk and microwave on high until hot, about 2 minutes. Place whipped cream and toasted almonds on top. Serve immediately.

Serves 1. Each 1 cup serving: 145 calories, 2 g fat, 1 g saturated fat, 10 mg cholesterol, 153 mg sodium, 24 g carbohydrate, 0 g fiber, 9 g protein. 312 mg calcium.

Waldorf Salad

3 apples, cored and diced
1 cup nonfat light vanilla yogurt
1/4 cup diced celery
1/4 cup walnut pieces
Green, leafy lettuce for garnish

Mix all ingredients in a medium-sized mixing bowl. Refrigerate until ready to serve. This salad looks nice if it is served on a bed of green lettuce. Garnish with a pinch of ground cinnamon.

Serves 4. Each 1 cup serving: 142 calories, 5 g fat, 0 g saturated fat, 1 mg cholesterol, 43 mg sodium, 23 g carbohydrate, 3.5 g fiber, 3 g protein. 90 mg calcium.

Calcium Muesli

1/4 cup rolled oats, dry
1/4 cup skim plus milk
1/2 cup vanilla light nonfat yogurt
1 cup diced fresh fruit
Pinch of cinnamon

Mix the rolled oats and milk; allow to soak for a few minutes or overnight. Fold in the rest of the ingredients. Eat immediately or refrigerate for up to one day or until ready to serve.

Serves 1. Each 2 cup serving: 219 calories, 2.5 g fat, 0 g saturated fat, 4 mg cholesterol, 83 mg sodium, 40 g carbohydrate, 6 g fiber, 9 g protein. 241 mg calcium.

Calcium Facts

We think of calcium for building strong bones and teeth, but calcium also plays an important role in sending messages through the nervous system, helping muscles contract, and maintaining the proper acid/base balance in the blood. When there is not enough calcium in the bloodstream for these vital functions, the body takes it from our bones, which are constantly being rebuilt. Poor calcium intake is one of many factors that can weaken bones and lead to osteoporosis.

❖Recommended calcium intake

The Food and Nutrition Board recommends an Adequate Intake (AI) for calcium of:

1 - 3 years	500 mg/day
4 - 8 years	800 mg/day
9 - 18 years	1,300 mg/day
19 - 50 years	1,000 mg/day
51+ years	1,200 mg/day

- There is no additional requirement during pregnancy and lactation because calcium absorption is increased at those times.
- The Upper Limit (UL) for calcium intake is 2,500 mg/day. This prevents calcium from interfering with zinc, magnesium and iron absorption. Be sure not to overuse calcium supplements.
- A Daily Value of 1,000 mg calcium is generally used on food labels.

❖More than just milk

Dairy products are an excellent source of calcium. In fact, according to the USDA, dairy products are the primary source of calcium in American diets. However, most people don't realize that many plant foods also contain calcium. Although most plant foods do not contain as much calcium as a glass of milk, a diet that includes many calcium-rich vegetables, fruits, grains, nuts, seeds and legumes (including soy) can add up to a lot of calcium over the course of a day. These foods also provide fiber, vitamins, and other minerals, as well as a wide range of health-promoting antioxidants. Foods that will add calcium to your diet include:

- *Legumes* (1/2 cup cooked) – baked beans (75 mg), black beans (23 mg), navy beans (63 mg)
- *Soyfoods* – 1 cup fortified soymilk (up to 400 mg) Soymilk has so much calcium when fortified that it is a part of MyPlate's dairy group.
- *Vegetables* (1/2 cup cooked) – collard greens (113 mg), kale (90 mg), broccoli (20 mg)
- *Fruits* – 5 dried figs (134 mg), 1 navel orange (56 mg), 1 cup fortified orange juice (100-300 mg)
- *Nuts & seeds* – 1 oz sesame seeds (276 mg), 2 Tbsp almonds (46 mg)
- *Grains* – 1 (6") corn tortilla (45 mg), 1 slice whole wheat bread (20 mg)
- *Fish* – 2 sardines (92 mg), 3 oz canned salmon with bones (181 mg)
- *Skim milk products* (1 cup) – milk (300 mg), plain nonfat yogurt (488 mg)

❖More ways to protect your bones

- Do weight-bearing exercise. The added stress of weight bearing exercise (like walking or running) helps build bone mass.
- Don't drink heavily or smoke. Excessive alcohol intake and smoking are associated with an increased risk for osteoporosis.
- Limit your salt intake. Salt increases the amount of calcium lost in urine.
- Eat more fruits and vegetables. These contain many nutrients that help maintain bone health and also help keep the proper acid/base balance in the blood stream. That means that less calcium from bones will be used for that purpose.
- Get enough vitamin D. This helps the body absorb calcium.

❖Calcium facts

- Recommended calcium intakes in some parts of the world are much lower than in the U.S., but lifestyle and other factors that influence bone health are different in those countries.
- About half the calcium in broccoli is absorbed from our digestive tract, compared to about a third of the calcium in milk.
- Even though spinach, Swiss chard and beet greens are rich in calcium, their high oxalate content keeps the calcium from being absorbed.

By Cheryl Sullivan, MA, RD.

Are You Getting Enough Calcium

Calculate your total calcium consumption per day using the list of foods below, then check out the chart to see if you are getting enough calcium. Numbers shown here are rounded to nearest 25 from USDA & manufacturer data.

500 mg:
___ Calcium fortified skim milk — 1 cup
___ Silk soy "yogurt" — 1 cup

450 mg:
___ Plain, nonfat yogurt — 1 cup

300 mg:
___ Milk, all types — 1 cup
___ Soy milk, fortified — 1 cup

250 mg:
___ Yogurt, fruit-flavored — 1 cup
___ Ricotta cheese — 1/4 cup
___ Swiss cheese — 1 ounce
___ Total cereal — 3/4 cup

200 mg:
___ Cheese, hard — 1 ounce
___ Cream soup prepared with milk — 1 cup
___ Salmon, canned with bones — 3 ounces
___ Sardines, canned with bones — 2 ounces

100 mg:
___ Bok choy — 1/2 cup
___ Calcium fortified juice — 1 cup
___ Calcium-fortified products (most) — 1 serving
___ Cheese pizza — 1 slice
___ Custard or pudding — 1/2 cup
___ Ice cream or frozen yogurt — 1/2 cup
___ Tofu, processed with calcium — 1/2 cup
___ Turnip greens, cooked — 1/2 cup

75 mg:
___ Almonds — 1/4 cup
___ Baked beans, cooked — 1/2 cup
___ Cottage cheese — 1/2 cup
___ Navy beans, cooked — 1/2 cup
___ Sour cream, fat free — 1/4 cup

50 mg:
___ Broccoli, cooked — 1/2 cup
___ Corn chips — 1 ounce
___ Corn tortilla — 1

___ Figs, dried — 2 figs
___ Kale, cooked — 1/2 cup
___ Orange — 1 medium
___ Shrimp, peeled & cooked — 1/2 cup

25 mg:
___ Dried beans, boiled — 1/2 cup
___ Bread made with milk — 1 slice/roll
___ Carrots, cooked — 1/2 cup
___ Dates — 10 dried
___ Eggs — 1 large
___ Lentils, cooked — 1/2 cup
___ Orange juice — 1 cup
___ Pecans — 1/4 cup
___ Raisins — 1/3 cup
___ Sesame seeds — 1 tsp
___ Sweet potato, cooked — 1/2 cup
___ Whole wheat bread — 1 slice

___ **Total mg of calcium per day**

You might be closer to your daily value than you think. Take a look at the recommendations below:

Know Your Numbers:

Babies:

0-6 months	210 mg
6-12 months	270 mg

Children:

1-3 years	500 mg
4-8 years	800 mg
9-18 years	1,300 mg

Adults:

19-30 years	1,000 mg
31-50 years	1,000 mg
51-70 years	1,200 mg
70+ years	1,200 mg

Pregnant women:

14-18	1,300 mg
19-50 years	1,000 mg

Nursing mothers:

14-18 years	1,300 mg
19-30 years	1,000 mg
31-50 years	1,000 mg

Source: U.S. National Academy of Science, Dietary Reference Intakes for Calcium, Phosphorus, Magnesium, Vitamin D, and Fluoride (2004 - iom.edu)

Leader Guide: Cooking for One

Title: Cooking For One

Target Audience:
This presentation is intended for seniors, singles and others who live alone and prepare their own meals.

Lesson Objectives:
• Participants will learn how to prepare healthy, easy meals for one person.
• Participants will learn tips for meal planning for one person.

Lesson Rationale:
Health authorities have indicated that good nutrition is one of the most important factors in determining long-term health. Poor diet plays a major role in the development of four of the top seven killers in the United States: heart disease, cancer, stroke and diabetes. Students who have the skills to select and prepare nutritious foods can positively impact their present and future health.

Lesson at a Glance:
This lesson introduces participants to new recipes and teaches cooking skills. It also provides nutrition and dietary information that is consistent with the Dietary Guidelines for Americans and MyPlate.

Lesson Materials:
This lesson contains:
• Leader and activity guide
• Leader guide for recipes
• 4 pages of copy-ready handouts and recipes

Preparation:
___ Review leader guide
___ Review handouts
___ Select activities
___ Copy and collect materials for lesson

Activity Ideas:

Introduction -
Ask participants how often they cook their own meals. Ask them to share stories about what they make for dinner. This lesson will include meal planning strategies to help participants spend less time in the kitchen and put together a working food budget.

Activity 1 - Plan it!
Use the sample meal planner handout in this lesson to show participants how to make their own meals and how to get more than one meal out of a cooked item.

Activity 2 - Cooking Demo
Use the recipes in this lesson to show participants how to prepare meals for one person.

Recipe Leader Guide: Cooking for One

Title: One Chicken Equals 3 Meals

Demonstrate how to make 3 healthy meals for one person from one roasted chicken. We do have an additional demo for making 3 additional meals, though these won't feature the same chicken. Details are in the pages following this lesson.

How to do this demo:

1. Wash your hands before you handle food.
2. Cut and measure all ingredients for all 3 recipes.
3. Show audience how to make Roasted Chicken Dinner. Serve tasting samples for this meal.
4. Outline how to make chicken broth. Allow the broth to cook while you move on to the next recipes. You can use prepared broth in the Chili Soup to save time.
5. Make Chili Soup - allow it to simmer while you make the salad.
6. Serve soup and salad in tasting samples.
7. Demonstrate how to finish preparing the broth (strain off bones, remove fat). Save the broth for future use or discard.
8. You should be able to make these 3 meals in 1 hour:
• Chicken Dinner: 15 minutes
• Broth demo: 5 minutes
• Soup and Salad: 15 minutes
• Finish broth: 5 minutes
• Discussion: 20 minutes
Total time: 60 minutes

Equipment List:

___ Microwave oven
___ Stove
___ Cutting board
___ Knife
___ Measuring cups and spoons
___ Kitchen spoons (3)
___ Ladle
___ Can opener
___ Plates and bowl (for final presentation)
___ Fork
___ Pot and steamer basket (or microwave steamer)
___ 2 quart pot
___ Gravy straining cup (for removing fat from broth)
___ Salad bowls (2)
___ Dutch oven pan

Shopping List:

___ 1 whole roasted chicken (buy premade)
___ 1 potato
___ Broccoli florets
___ Nonfat sour cream
___ 100% whole wheat bread, toasted
___ Olive oil
___ Chopped onion
___ Chicken broth
___ 1 can black beans
___ Instant brown rice
___ 1 can diced no-added-salt tomatoes
___ Dried oregano
___ Garlic powder
___ Cumin
___ Chili powder
___ Water
___ Plates, cups, spoons, forks and napkins
___ Disposable cups (for premeasured ingredients)
___ Ready to serve romaine or spring salad mix
___ 1 small tomato
___ 1 carrot
___ Red wine vinegar
___ Italian seasoning
___ Black pepper

Make ahead options:

1. You can make everything for the roasted chicken dinner ahead of time. Demonstrate how to make the soup and salad using the leftovers.
2. You can make all items ahead of time, assemble and let the audience simply sample servings.

Cooking/Nutrition Lessons:

This class will outline how to plan nutritious meals for one. It will encourage them to maximize time spent in the kitchen by cooking ahead and freezing leftovers in single portions. It shows how it is possible to make 8 meals out of a single roasted chicken.

Garnishing/Finishing Tips:

Roasted Chicken Dinner: Serve the chicken, potato and broccoli on a large dinner plate. Top the potato with sour cream and sprinkle with fresh cracked black pepper

Tossed Salad with Chicken: Place the salad on a large dinner plate, cut the toast in diagonal triangles and set them on the outer edges of the salad.

Chili Soup: Put the chili in a large soup bowl. If it has a rim, dust it lightly with chili powder.

Number of sample servings: approximately 12

Recipe Leader Guide: Cooking for One

Day 1 - Roasted Chicken Dinner

1 whole roasted chicken (buy premade)
1 potato
1 cup broccoli florets
1/4 cup nonfat sour cream

Directions:

1. Wash potato and pierce several times with a fork. Microwave on high for 3 minutes, turn over and microwave until done, about 1-2 more minutes. When finished, cut potato in half and fluff with a fork. Fill with 1/4 cup nonfat sour cream.
2. Remove skin from roasted chicken and discard. Cut chicken into quarters (2 breasts, 2 thighs with drum sticks). Individually wrap and freeze 1 breast and 1 thigh/drumstick. Refrigerate one thigh/drumstick and keep remaining chicken breast warm in the oven.
3. Steam broccoli on the stovetop or in the microwave.
4. Serve warm chicken breast alonside the baked potato and steamed broccoli.
5. (Make broth while you are eating so you have it ready for day three).

Chicken Broth

Bones from roasted chicken (from Day One)
4 cups water

1. Place water and bones in large soup pan. Bring water and bones to a boil; reduce to simmer and cook for 45 minutes. Discard bones and strain out fat. Refrigerate broth up to one week or freeze for later use.

Day 2 - Tossed Salad with Chicken

1 or 2 slices 100% whole wheat bread, toasted
Olive oil
Salad:
1-1/2 cups ready to serve romaine or spring salad mix
1 small tomato, cored and diced
1 carrot, peeled and sliced
1 cup roasted chicken meat, boneless, skinless (left-over from day one)
1 tsp olive oil
2 Tbsp red wine vinegar
Italian seasoning
Black pepper to taste

Directions:

1. Combine all ingredients in a large mixing bowl or salad bowl.
2. Toast bread and dab or mist with olive oil.
3. Serve salad with 100% whole wheat toast (1 or 2 slices depending on calorie needs).
4. Serve immediately or refrigerate for up to one hour.

TIP: Cut lettuce and veggies for the rest of the week while you are preparing this salad.

Recipe Leader Guide: Cooking for One

Day 3 - Chili Soup and Salad

Chili Soup:

1 tsp olive oil

1/2 cup chopped onion

3 cups chicken broth (from day one)

1 can black beans, drained and rinsed

1 cup instant brown rice

1 can diced no-added-salt tomatoes

1 tsp oregano

1 tsp garlic powder

1/2 tsp cumin

1/2 tsp chili powder

Directions:

1. Heat a Dutch oven pan over medium high and add oil. Add onion and saute until golden, about 3 minutes. Add the rest of the ingredients and bring to a boil. Simmer until rice is done, about 8-10 minutes.

2. Serve one serving of soup hot. Refrigerate the rest in a shallow pan immediately. When cool, freeze the remainder of the soup in 1.5 cup servings in ziploc bags. Be sure to label the bags for later identification.

Salad:

1 cup dark green lettuce (preferably prepped on day 1)

1 cup assorted vegetables (preferably from day 2)

1 tsp olive oil

1 Tbsp vinegar

Directions:

1. Combine all ingredients for salad in a medium-sized mixing bowl. Serve immediately or refrigerate for up to one hour.

Recipe Leader Guide: Cooking for One

How to do this demo for days 4, 5, and 6:

Makes about 12 sample servings

1. Wash your hands before you handle food.
2. Cook pasta ahead of time. Make pasta dish and serve samples to guests.
3. While they are eating the pasta, show them how to make the tuna salad and the tuna pita pocket.
4. Serve samples of the tuna salad and pita pocket.
5. While they are eating discuss how to plan meals and talk about the ingredients you used for these meals. They are good examples of how keeping the right ingredients on hand can enable you to whip out healthy, delicious meals.
6. You should be able to make these three meals in 30 minutes provided all ingredients are prepared and organized:

- Pasta with Black Bean Sauce: 15 minutes (includes time to serve samples)
- Tuna Tossed Salad: 5 minutes
- Tuna Garden Pita Pocket: 5 minutes
- Serve samples for tuna salad and pocket and discuss: 5 minutes
- If you have an hour to fill, we recommend starting or finishing the class using the meal planning handout and discussing the points made on "Keeping the Solo Cook Happy" in this section.

Shopping List:

- ___ 1 box spaghetti
- ___ 1 jar healthy pasta sauce (low sodium, etc)
- ___ 1 can black beans
- ___ Parmesan cheese (optional garnish)
- ___ 1 can tuna in water (low sodium preferred)
- ___ 1 jar lowfat mayonnaise
- ___ Celery
- ___ 1 bag ready-to-serve romaine or spring salad mix
- ___ Lowfat salad dressing
- ___ Lowfat whole grain crackers (like WASA)
- ___ 100% whole wheat pita pocket
- ___ 2 tomatoes
- ___ Baby carrots
- ___ Cucumber
- ___ Plates, forks and napkins (for sample servings)
- ___ Disposable bags and cups for ingredients and for highlighting how to freeze extra portions
- ___ Plastic wrap

Equipment:

- ___ Stove
- ___ Toaster (optional)
- ___ 3 quart pan
- ___ Large pot
- ___ Can opener
- ___ Knife
- ___ Cutting board
- ___ Colander
- ___ 2 kitchen spoons
- ___ Small bowl (for tuna salad)
- ___ Fork (for mixing tuna salad)
- ___ 3 plates (to present all three recipes)

Make ahead options:

1. We recommend that you cook the pasta before this demonstration.
2. You can also make all 3 dishes ahead of time and offer sample servings.

Cooking skill/Nutrition lesson:

This lesson shows people who have to cook for one how to plan ahead and maximize efforts in the kitchen. It also shows them how to make quick and healthy meals using fish, whole grains, vegetables and beans.

Garnish/finishing tips:

Spaghetti - Top the spaghetti with a sprinkle of Parmesan cheese

Tuna Salad - Arrange vegetables on top of plate. Drizzle dressing around the plate in a fine stream. Top with a round scoop of tuna and place the cracker to the side of the salad.

Pita pocket - Place 2 pocket halves on a plate and garnish with lettuce and more vegetables.

Number of sample servings: about 12

Recipe Leader Guide: Cooking for One

Day 4 - Pasta with Black Bean Sauce

8 ounces spaghetti, dry

1 26-ounce jar of healthy pasta sauce

1 can black beans, drained and rinsed

Optional garnish: Parmesan cheese

Directions:

1. Cook spaghetti according to package directions in large pot. Rinse and drain in colander.
2. Heat the sauce and beans together in a 3 quart sauce pan. Add the spaghetti and stir well.
3. Serve spaghetti hot. Freeze what remains in three individual portions for future meals.
4. We recommend serving this dish with a tossed salad, which you could garnish with Parmesan cheese

Day 5 - Tuna Tossed Salad

1 can tuna in water (low sodium preferred), drained

1/4 cup lowfat mayonnaise

1/4 cup chopped celery

1-1/2 cups ready-to serve romaine or spring salad mix

1 small tomato, sliced

1 carrot, peeled and sliced

1 tsp olive oil

2 Tbsp red wine vinegar

1 large lowfat whole grain cracker

Directions:

1. Prepare tuna salad by mixing drained tuna, mayonnaise and celery in small bowl.
2. Place greens and vegetables on a plate. Top with oil and vinegar followed by half of the tuna salad. Refrigerate the rest of the tuna salad for tomorrow.
3. Top with a whole grain, lowfat cracker.

Day 6 - Tuna Garden Pita

1 cup ready-to-serve romaine or spring salad mix

1/2 batch tuna salad (from day 5)

1 sliced tomato

1/4 cup sliced cucumber

1 100% whole wheat pita pocket

Directions:

1. Warm pita pocket in a toaster or toaster oven.
2. Cut in half and stuff with lettuce, tuna, tomato and cucumber.
3. Add a small dollop of lowfat mayonnaise if desired.
4. Serve immediately or wrap and refrigerate for later use (up to one day).

Recipes: Cooking for One

You can make at least 3 healthy meals for one from a single chicken!

Day 1 - Roasted Chicken Dinner

1 whole, roasted chicken (buy premade or roast yourself)
1 potato
1 cup broccoli florets
1/4 cup nonfat sour cream
Directions:

1. Wash potato and pierce several times with a fork. Microwave on high for 3 minutes, turn over and microwave until done, about 1-2 more minutes. When finished, cut potato in half and fluff with a fork. Fill with 1/4 cup nonfat sour cream.
2. Remove skin from roasted chicken and discard. Cut chicken into quarters (2 breasts, 2 thighs with drum sticks). Individually wrap and freeze 1 breast and 1 thigh/drumstick. Refrigerate one thigh/drumstick and keep remaining chicken breast warm in the oven.
3. Steam broccoli on the stovetop or in the microwave.
4. Serve warm chicken breast alonside the baked potato and steamed broccoli.
5. (Make broth while you are eating so you have it ready for day three).

Serves 1. Each serving: 367 calories, 4 g fat, 1 g saturated fat, 81 mg cholesterol, 151 mg sodium, 43 g carbohydrate, 4.5 g fiber, 39 g protein.

Chicken Broth

Bones from roasted chicken (from Day One)
4 cups water

1. Place water and bones in large soup pan. Bring water and bones to a boil; reduce to simmer and cook for 45 minutes. Discard bones and strain out fat. Refrigerate broth up to one week or freeze for later use.

Day 2 - Tossed Salad with Chicken

1 or 2 slices 100% whole wheat bread, toasted
olive oil
Salad:
1-1/2 cups ready to serve romaine or spring salad mix
1 small tomato, cored and diced
1 carrot, peeled and sliced
3/4 cup roasted chicken breast, boneless, skinless
1 tsp olive oil
2 Tbsp red wine vinegar

Italian seasoning, Black pepper to taste
Directions:

1. Combine all ingredients in a large mixing bowl or salad bowl.
2. Toast bread and dab or mist with olive oil.
3. Serve salad with 100% whole wheat toast (1 or 2 slices depending on calorie needs).
4. Serve immediately or refrigerate for up to one hour.

Serves 1. Each 2 cup serving: 375 calories, 11 g fat, 2 g saturated fat, 72 mg cholesterol, 400 mg sodium, 39 g carbohydrate, 8 g fiber, 33 g protein.

Day 3 - Chili Soup and Salad

Chili
1 tsp olive oil
1/2 cup chopped onion
3 cups chicken broth (from day one)
1 can black beans, drained and rinsed
1 cup instant brown rice
1 can diced no-added-salt tomatoes
1 tsp oregano
1 tsp garlic powder
1/2 tsp cumin
1/2 tsp chili powder
Directions:

1. Heat a Dutch oven pan over medium high and add oil. Add onion and saute until golden, about 3 minutes. Add the rest of the ingredients and bring to a boil. Simmer until rice is done, about 8-10 minutes.
2. Serve one serving of soup hot. Refrigerate the rest in a shallow pan immediately. When cool, freeze the remainder of the soup in 1.5 cup servings in ziploc bags. Be sure to label the bags for later identification.

Tossed Salad:
1 cup dark green lettuce (preferably prepped on day 1)
1 cup assorted vegetables (preferably from day 2)
1 tsp olive oil
1 Tbsp vinegar
Directions:

1. Combine all ingredients for salad in a medium bowl. Serve immediately or refrigerate for up to one hour.

Serves 4. Each serving (1-1/2 cups of chili soup plus 2 cups of salad): 315 calories, 7.5 g fat, 1 g saturated fat, 18 mg cholesterol, 283 mg sodium, 46 g carbohydrate, 16 g fiber, 18 g protein.

Recipes: Cooking for One

Day 4 - Pasta with Black Bean Sauce

8 ounces spaghetti, dry

1 26-ounce jar healthy pasta sauce

1 can black beans, drained and rinsed

Parmesan cheese (optional)

Directions:

1. Cook spaghetti according to package directions in large pot. Rinse and drain in colander.
2. Heat the sauce and beans together in a 3 quart sauce pan. Add the spaghetti and stir well.
3. Serve spaghetti hot. Freeze what remains in three individual portions for future meals.
4. We recommend serving this dish with a tossed salad, which you could garnish with Parmesan cheese

Serves 4. Each 2 cup serving: 337 calories, 2 g fat, 0.5 g saturated fat, 2 mg cholesterol, 625 mg sodium, 66 g carbohydrate, 8 g fiber, 15 g protein.

Day 5 - Tuna Tossed Salad

6 oz can tuna in water (low sodium), drained

2 Tbsp lowfat mayonnaise

1/4 cup chopped celery

1-1/2 cups ready-to serve romaine or spring salad mix

1 small tomato, sliced

1 carrot, peeled and sliced

1 tsp olive oil

2 tsp red wine vinegar

1 large, lowfat, whole grain cracker

Directions:

1. Prepare tuna salad by mixing drained tuna, mayonnaise and celery in small bowl.
2. Place greens and vegetables on a plate. Top with oil and vinegar followed by **half** of the tuna salad. Refrigerate the rest of the tuna salad for tomorrow.
3. Top with a whole grain, lowfat cracker.

Serves 1. Each serving (1/2 cup tuna plus 2 cups salad): 316 calories, 8.5 g fat, 0.5 g saturated fat, 45 mg cholesterol, 445 mg sodium, 38 g carbohydrate, 7.5 g fiber, 26 g protein.

Day 6 - Tuna Garden Pita

1 cup ready-to-serve romaine or spring salad mix

1/2 batch tuna salad (from day 5)

1 sliced tomato

1/4 cup sliced cucumber

1 100% whole wheat pita pocket

Directions:

1. Warm pita pocket in a toaster or toaster oven.
2. Cut in half and stuff with lettuce, tuna, tomato and cucumber.
3. Add a small dollop of lowfat mayonnaise if desired.
4. Serve immediately or wrap and refrigerate for later use (up to one day).

Serves 1. Each serving (1 pita): 326 calories, 4.5 g fat, 0 g saturated fat, 45 mg cholesterol, 671 mg sodium, 48 g carbohydrate, 9 g fiber, 31 g protein.

Cooking for One: Shopping List

Produce:
1 baking potato
1 cup broccoli florets
1 small tomato
1 pound bag carrots
1 onion
1 bag ready to serve romaine or spring salad mix
1 bunch celery
3 tomatoes
1 cucumber
1 green pepper (for salads)

Poultry:
1 whole roasted chicken (premade or roast yourself)

Dry goods:
1 small bottle olive oil
1 bottle red wine vinegar
2 cans black beans, drained and rinsed
1 box instant brown rice
15-ounce can diced no-added-salt tomatoes
8 ounce box dry spaghetti
1 26-ounce jar healthy pasta sauce
6 ounce can tuna in water (low sodium)
1 jar lowfat mayonnaise
Lowfat, whole grain crackers
Dried oregano
Garlic powder
Cumin
Chili powder
Italian seasoning
Ground black pepper

Dairy:
1 small container of nonfat sour cream

Bakery:
100% whole wheat bread, toasted - 1 bag
100% whole wheat pita pockets - 1 bag

Notes:
This shopping list is for making all dinners on days one through six for Cooking for One. You should also purchase items for breakfast and lunch.
Here are some ideas:

Breakfast:
Oatmeal with skim milk
Bananas
Orange juice
Whole grain cereal
Marmalade
Yogurt
*You will have extra whole grain bread for toast

Lunch:
Baked potatoes
Turkey sandwich
Tuna sandwich/salad
Snacks:
Assorted raw fruits
Assorted veggies
Peanut butter
*You will have extra whole grain crackers, carrots and celery

Planning Saves You Time and Money

Sample Menu:
Day 1 - Roasted Chicken Dinner
Buy a roasted chicken in your grocery store. Cut it into quarters and freeze half of it for next week.
Day 2 - Chicken Tossed Salad
Use the leftover chicken from day one. Wash and cut veggies and lettuce for the week.
Day 3 - Chili Soup and Salad
Make a batch of Chili Soup. Eat one serving tonight and freeze the rest for future meals.
Day 4 - Pasta with Black Bean Sauce
Make a batch of this recipe and freeze leftovers for future meals.
Day 5 - Tuna Tossed Salad
Use the lettuce and veggies from day 2. Save half of the tuna salad for a sandwich on day 6.
Day 6 - Tuna Pita
Use the lettuce and veggies from day 2. Use the tuna salad from day 5.
Day 7 - Your choice:
Reheat one of the foods you froze for later, Pasta with Black Bean Sauce, Chili Soup or Roasted Chicken.

Here are more ideas and tips:
- Try to balance your plate according to MyPlate directions. Add fruits and veggies to help set up every meal.
- Get baked potatoes or sweet potatoes for easy microwave meals and cook 2 at a time. Save the second one to use another day.
- Cook a large batch of rice or pasta and freeze single portions - use them for salad, soup, stir fry fry, etc.
- Use leftovers from tonight's dinner for lunch the next day.
- Try a veggie burger - these can be made in 5 minutes. Serve with lowfat baked French fries, a bit of wholegrain bread, fruit, and slaw.
- Try breakfast for dinner.
- Stock up on healthy soups. Serve them with salad and whole grain toast.
- Planning meals saves you money, since you'll eat at restaurants less often. Making and freezing meals ahead of time helps you spend less on convenience items too!

	Monday	Tuesday	Wednesday	Thursday	Friday	Saturday	Sunday
Breakfast							
Snack							
Lunch							
Snack							
Dinner							

Keeping the Solo Cook Happy

Challenge: Scaling recipes for one is time consuming and not always successful

Answer: In most cases, you can prepare a recipe for 4 and then freeze the other three portions for future meals. Or at the very least cut it in half and have a meal for the next day. For example, you can make a batch of spaghetti for four, eat one serving for dinner and then freeze the other three for future meals.

TIP: Make sure you follow food safety rules - keep hot foods hot and cold foods cold. Do not allow left-overs to sit at room temperature for any length of time. For best results, allow items to cool in the refrigerator and then freeze them in individual portions for later use.

Challenge: Eating alone is lonely

Answer: If weather permits, consider taking your meal to a park or other public area. Being outdoors and around other people may help you feel less lonely. Another option is to eat dinner at home and then go out for coffee or take a trip to the library or local bookstore.

TIP: When you are feeling lonely or tired of eating alone, treat yourself to a nicer meal by creating a fancier ambience. This can be accomplished with candles, tableclothes, flowers, etc.

Challenge: Fruits and vegetables go bad before I can eat them all

Answer: There are a few things you can do to combat this problem. The first is to ask the produce manager or clerk in your grocery store to sell you fewer items, i.e.: a package of four ears of corn can be separated so you are only buying one; a large watermelon can be cut in quarters, you can buy salad items from a salad bar in your grocery store, etc. Second, you can purchase frozen vegetables and use just what you need. Third, you can find someone else who lives alone to share groceries with you.

TIP: Plan your meals and make a list so that you don't buy more than what you can eat in a week. Some items can be frozen for later use. Buy items that you can use now *and* ones that last a little longer. For example, you can buy both green and ripe bananas - eat the ripe ones now and the green ones will be ready by the end of the week. When buying fruits and vegetables, eat the more fragile ones immediately and the more stable ones at the end of the week. For example, when buying fruit, buy melon, berries, apples, oranges and grapes. Eat the melon and berries at the beginning of the week, followed by the grapes, and then the apples and oranges toward the end of the week.

Challenge: I get bored eating the same thing over and over

Answer: Instead of trying to eat a large batch of soup or other dish over a few days or a week, try freezing it in portion sized batches. Eat these over a longer period of time so that you don't get bored by eating the same thing over and over. You might be cooking more to start, but after a week you will have a nice selection in your freezer.

TIP: Label and date items in your freezer so they will be more appealing and easier to use in a reasonable amount of time.

Challenge: I don't feel like cooking

Answer: That is why you should make meals ahead of time and freeze the leftovers. Also, keeping ready-to-eat, healthy foods on hand like fruits, vegetables, whole grain crackers, peanut butter, canned soups, whole grain cereals, etc. will help you put together a quick healthy meal with little effort.

TIP: Organize your pantry and freezer so you can store and find the right items easily.

Leader Guide: Cooking on a Budget

Title:
Cooking on a Budget

Target Audience:
This presentation kit is intended for general audiences age 14 and up. It covers topics of wellness, heart disease, diabetes, weight loss and nutrition.

Lesson Objectives:
• Participants will learn ways to save money when grocery shopping.
• Participants will see that healthy foods and cost savings go hand in hand.
• Most participants will be able to cut their food costs by over 20% by following of the tip in this lesson.

Lesson Rationale:
Health authorities have indicated that good nutrition is one of the most important factors in determining long-term health. Poor diet plays a major role in the development of four of the top seven killers in the United States: heart disease, cancer, stroke and diabetes. Consumers who have the skills to select and prepare nutritious foods can positively impact their present and future health. By showing participants that they can eat healthier food at a lower cost, they may be more motivated to improve their diets.

Lesson at a Glance:
This lesson introduces participants to new recipes and also teaches cooking skills. It gives nutritional advice that is consistent with MyPlate and the Dietary Guidelines for Americans. Additionally, it will highlight ways to lower food costs.

Lesson Materials:
This lesson contains:
• Leader and Activity Guide
• Leader and Activity Guide for Recipes
• 4 pages of recipes and copy-ready handouts

Preparation:
____ Review leader guides
____ Review handouts
____ Select activities
____ Copy and collect materials for lesson

Activity Ideas:
Introduction:
Ask for a show of hands of people who think that eating healthier costs more money. Explain that this is not the case and that you are going to demonstrate how to lower a food budget while still eating foods that are nutritious and heart healthy.

Activity 1 - Cooking Demo
Use one or more of the recipes in this lesson to show participants how to make a healthy meal using low-cost, healthy ingredients.

Activity 2 - Healthy Cart Contest
If participants are willing, you can collect sample grocery receipts for one week's worth of food. Give prizes to people who managed to get...
-Least amount of saturated fat
-Most fruits and vegetables
-Most whole grains
-Most beans
-Lowest food cost per person
-Fewest frozen meals
Once again, if participants are willing, announce the winners on a flyer or poster and show the items they bought to help them win that prize. See if you can get a local grocery store to donate a gift certificate or healthy food items for each winner.

Activity 3 - Shopping Cart Makeover
Have participants send you a grocery receipt for about a week's supply of groceries prior to class. Pick one or two receipts and show how to improve them. Here are some common ways:
-More fruits and vegetables
-Less meat
-Less refined carbohydrates
-Watch unit pricing
-Omit or limit soda
-Add beans and rice in place of meat
-Make your own treats
-Use oatmeal or grits in place of processed cereals
-Use less bread and more rice or pasta
-Make your own frozen meals by cooking meals ahead of time and freezing them.

Activity 4 - Cut Cost, Not Taste
Show participants how to select low-cost items from each portion of MyPlate. For instance, buying fresh fruit in season is easier on your wallet than buying fruit out of season. Plus, it just tastes better. Buying whole foods instead of packaged mixes or processed items is often cheaper too. For protein, this equates to beans, poultry, canned tuna and peanut butter. For the dairy category, pick up milk (skim is best!), yogurt and cottage cheese - the hard and gourmet cheeses are more expensive.

Leader Guide: Cooking on a Budget

Fruits and vegetables, along with whole grains and beans are by far the most inexpensive healthy items in the store. They contain more fiber and less saturated fat and sodium than processed, refined foods like baked goods, processed cereals, crackers, cookies, chips and desserts. One item we did not show in these charts was soup, since it spans more than one category. Soup is usually only .08 cents per ounce - this number would be even less if the soup was made from scratch. Frozen foods are not really listed here - they are very expensive per ounce, ringing in at around .25-.50 per ounce for most items. Frozen foods often contain far more fat, saturated fat, cholesterol and sodium than healthier versions made at home.

Grains	Per ounce	Prepared
Rice, bulk	0.017	0.01
Grits	0.022	0.01
Rolled oats (bulk, store brand)	0.05	0.01
Barley	0.05	0.02
Corn meal	0.05	0.02
Pancake mix	0.05	0.02
Pasta	0.05	0.03
Brown rice, bulk	0.05	0.01
Rolled oats (bulk, brand name)	0.08	0.02
Bread	0.08	
Cream of wheat, bulk	0.12	0.03

Most expensive grain foods:	Per ounce
Waffles	0.13
Bagels	0.14
Instant oats, bulk	0.16
Packaged instant oats	0.20
Boxed pasta mix	0.20
Boxed rice mix	0.21
Packaged cereal (average)	0.22
Crackers	0.25
Cereal bars	0.28
Frozen rice mix	0.29

Vegetables:	Per ounce
Cabbage	0.02
Baking potatoes	0.02
Creamer potato	0.03
Romaine	0.04
Cauliflower	0.04
Carrots	0.04
Cucumber	0.04
Corn	0.04
Green beans	0.05
Sweet potatoes	0.05
Frozen French fries	0.06
Canned vegetables (average)	0.07
Broccoli	0.07
Tomatoes	0.07
Frozen vegetables (store brand)	0.07
Yellow squash	0.08

Most expensive vegetables:	Per ounce
Frozen mashed potatoes	0.10
Frozen vegetables (brand name)	0.12
Potato chips	0.19
Instant mashed potatoes	0.21
Ready lettuce	0.65

Fruits	Per ounce
Bananas	0.03
Watermelon	0.03
Oranges	0.03
Cantaloupe	0.05
Apples	0.05
Canned fruit & apple sauce	0.06
Strawberries	0.12
Dried fruit	0.13
Peaches	0.15

Dairy	Per ounce
Skim milk	0.04
Yogurt	0.07
Cottage cheese	0.13

Most expensive dairy:	Per ounce
Cheddar cheese & hard cheese	0.23
Gourmet (average)	.50

Protein	Per ounce
Beans, dried (average)	0.04
Eggs	0.05
Turkey drumstick	0.07
Whole turkey	0.08
Whole chicken	0.08
Peanut butter	0.09

Leader Guide: Cooking on a Budget

	per ounce
Whole chicken, cut up	0.10
Ground turkey	0.12
Tofu	0.14
Raw turkey breast	0.16
Peanuts	0.16
Boneless, skinless chicken breast (store)	0.16
Tuna, canned	0.16

Most expensive protein:	**per ounce**
Ground beef	0.17
Bologna	0.17
Pork chops	0.19
Round roast, beef	0.19
Bacon	0.19
Hot dogs	0.19
Beef loin steak	0.21
Beef stew meat	0.24
Boneless skinless chicken breast (brand)	0.27
Ham	0.29
Sirloin steak	0.35
Fish, fresh (average)	0.44
Lamb (average)	0.44
Deli meat (average)	0.57
Beef tenderloin	0.75

An effective visual presentation is to use real foods and put prices on them (per ounce) so participants can see how a small box of rice mix is far higher in price than a whole bag of rice or how beef sirloin is far more expensive than beans. See the handout that shows the cost savings for whole, unprocessed foods for more details. You can also outline the amount of fat and sodium they will save by learning how to cook their own meals from scratch versus using frozen meals.

Note: Actual prices may vary depending on the locale and time of year. We believe they are accurate enough to prove our point that whole foods are less expensive than their processed counterparts, which are often higher in sugar, salt, fat, saturated fat and calories and lower in fiber and nutrients.

Conclusion:

Remind participants that buying fresh, whole foods will often save them 4 to 5 times the price per ounce. Using price per unit information will also help them spend less - usually buying a store brand will save a significant amount of money over buying a brand name.

Ask participants to name three ways that they are going to change their shopping habits to start saving more money. Encourage them to report their stories back to you so you can use them as testimonials for your next class or for a newsletter you produce.

Further reading/info/links

www.foodandhealth.com
www.thesimpledollar.com

Leader Guide: Budget Recipes

Turkey Stew

Makes 16 sample servings

This recipe uses turkey thighs, which are less expensive than beef. It also uses more potatoes and veggies and less meat. The cost per serving is only 71 cents!

1 Tbsp oil
1 onion, cut in chunks
3 carrots, peeled and cut into chunks
2 stalks celery, cut into chunks
4 cups low sodium beef or chicken broth
2 turkey thighs
3 large potatoes, cut in chunks (leave peel on)
1 bay leaf
1 tsp garlic powder
Black pepper (to taste)

Directions:

1. Heat a large Dutch oven style pan over medium high heat. Add the oil, then the onion, and saute until golden, about 2-3 minutes.
2. Add the carrots and celery and cook briefly.
3. Add the broth along with the turkey thighs, potatoes and seasonings. Bring to a boil then lower to a simmer.
4. Cook this stew on low heat, keeping covered and at a simmer, until potatoes and turkey are cooked through and tender, about 25-35 minutes. Stir occasionally.
5. Take the turkey thighs out of the stew; remove their skin and bones and cut the meat into small pieces. Add this meat back to the stew. Discard bones & skin.
6. Serve the stew hot or refrigerate/freeze for later use. We recommend a half cup serving for sample servings

Approximate cost per recipe: $2.84 or .71 per person.

Equipment:
___ Stove
___ Dutch oven style pan with lid
___ Kitchen spoon
___ Knife
___ Can opener
___ Cutting board
___ Measuring cups and spoons
___ Large soup bowl (for final presentation)

Shopping list:
___ Vegetable oil
___ 1 onion
___ 3 carrots
___ Celery
___ 32 oz beef or chicken broth, low sodium
___ 2 turkey thighs
___ 3 large potatoes
___ Bay leaf
___ Garlic powder
___ Black pepper
___ Cups, spoons and napkins
___ Disposable cups for premeasured ingredients

Cooking skill/nutrition lesson:
This recipe demonstratess how to make a healthy, delicious stew using turkey thigh meat. Using more potatoes and veggies not only cuts down on the cost, but also increases fiber and nutrients. Using less meat lowers the cost and the saturated fat. All these efforts bring the meal closer to MyPlate proportion guidelines.

Demo preparation:
1. Wash your hands before you handle food.
2. Have all ingredients chopped, measured, and placed in disposable bags and cups.
3. Make sure all utensils are within reach.
4. Preheat stove to medium-high heat as participants come into the room.

Make ahead options:
You can make this stew ahead of time and reheat during class. Outline how to remove skin and bones from turkey thighs.

Garnish/presentation tips:
Place the stew in a large soup bowl. Sprinkle a little black pepper over the top.

Number of sample servings: 16 (1/2 cup each)

Leader Guide: Budget Recipes

Budget Tossed Salad

Makes 16-20 sample servings

Using this recipe instead of fancy store mixes will save you around .61 cents per ounce! Cabbage is one of the least expensive vegetables and it adds a lot of nutrients (and a nice crunch!) to your salads.

1 head romaine
½ head cabbage
2 grated carrots
Cucumbers
Tomatoes
Oil
Vinegar
Directions:
1. Remove damaged/blemished leaves from romaine and cabbage.
2. Cut romaine into small pieces; finely shred cabbage. Wash lettuce and cabbage in large bowl or clean sink with cold water. Drain in colander.
3. Place drained lettuce and cabbage in bag; add grated carrots. Keep cold until ready to serve, up to 5 days. Toss this mixture with tomatoes, cucumbers, oil and vinegar, etc just before you are ready to serve.
4. Place this salad in a large salad bowl and toss with a little oil and vinegar for tasting purposes. We recommend using a 1/2 cup serving for sample servings.

TIP: Use leftover cabbage for slaw, soup or the stir fry recipe below.

Approximate cost per recipe: $1.29 or .10 per serving.

Equipment:
___ Colander
___ Knife
___ Cutting board
___ Large salad bowl
___ Spoons and/or tongs (to toss and serve salad)

Shopping list*:
___ 1 head romaine lettuce
___ 1 head cabbage
___ 2 carrots
___ Cucumbers
___ Tomatoes
___ Large zip lock bag to put salad mix
___ Oil
___ Vinegar
___ Forks, plates and napkins (to serve sample serv-
ings)
*See optional garnish tip

Cooking skill/nutrition lesson
This lesson allows participants to taste romaine and cabbage. It shows them that you can add flavor, variety and crunch to a salad with cabbage. Cabbage is one of the cheapest vegetables and it is a nutrient powerhouse.

Demo preparation:
1. Wash your hands before handling food.
2. If you don't have access to a sink (or water) to clean the lettuce, clean it in advance and have it in separate containers so that you can show participants how to mix it and put it in a bag.
3. Arrange a large salad bowl in the center of your table with oil, vinegar and utensils nearby.

Make ahead options:
You can prepare the salad ahead of time and serve samples when participants arrive. We recommend adding oil and vinegar at the last minute.

Garnish/presentation tips:
Optional garnish ideas: you can add all sorts of garden vegetables to this salad!

Number of sample servings: approximately 16-20.

Leader Guide: Budget Recipes

Beef Barley Soup

Makes 32 sample servings

This recipe stretches ground beef by adding lentils and using less beef. You end up giving your family more nutrients and fiber while saving money on groceries.

1/2 pound ground beef
1 onion
1 cup lentils
1/2 cup barley
3 cups mixed frozen vegetables
1 can diced tomatoes
6 tsp low-sodium beef bouillon granules
3 cups water
1 tsp garlic powder
black pepper to taste

Directions:

1. Heat a large soup pot over medium high heat. Add ground beef, breaking it into small pieces and cooking until brown, about 5 minutes. Drain off extra grease.
2. Add onion and saute until tender, about 2 minutes.
3. Add the rest of the ingredients, bring to a boil then reduce to a simmer. Cook on low until barley is tender, about 45 minutes.
4. Serve soup hot or refrigerate/freeze for later use. We recommend using a 2 ounce portion for sample servings.

Approximate cost: $4.74 or $1.18 per person.

Equipment:

___ Large soup pan
___ Stove
___ Knife
___ Cutting board
___ Can opener
___ Kitchen spoon and ladle
___ Measuring cups and spoons
___ Soup bowl (for final presentation)

Shopping list*:

___ 1/2 pound ground beef
___ 1 onion
___ 1 bag dry lentils
___ Barley
___ 1 bag mixed frozen vegetables
___ 1 can diced tomatoes
___ Low-sodium beef bouillon granules
___ Water
___ Garlic powder
___ Black pepper
___ Disposable cups (for premeasured ingredients)
___ Cups, spoons and napkins (for samples)

Cooking skill/nutrition lesson

This lesson shows how to make a healthy, economical soup using barley and vegetables, plus a little beef. It also highlights ways to add more vegetables to a meal, which is consistent with MyPlate recommendations.

Demo preparation:

1. Wash hands before handling food.
2. Cut and measure all ingredients.
3. Arrange pan and all ingredients around stove in the order they will be used.
4. Preheat stove as participants are coming into the room.

Make ahead options:

You can make the soup ahead of time and then reheat and serve for class.

Garnish/presentation tips:

Serve the soup with a sprinkle of black pepper on top.

Number of sample servings: approximately 32.

Leader Guide: Budget Recipes

Red Beans and Rice

Makes about 18 sample servings

This dish is very filling. We suggest serving it with the Budget Tossed Salad. The cost per serving is about .26!

2 cups brown rice
5 cups water
5 tsp low sodium beef bouillon granules
2 cups cooked or canned kidney beans
1/4 cup dried onion
1 tsp oregano
1 tsp paprika
1 tsp garlic powder
Pinch of cayenne pepper
Black pepper (to taste)

Directions:

1. Place all ingredients in large soup pot and bring to a boil.
2. Lower heat to simmer, cover pot and cook on low until rice is done, about 30 minutes.
3. Serve Red Beans and Rice hot or refrigerate or freeze for later use.

Approximate cost per recipe: $1.03 or .26 per serving.

Equipment:

____ Large soup pot
____ Stove
____ Knife
____ Can opener
____ Cutting board
____ Kitchen spoon
____ Ladle
____ Measuring cups and spoons
____ Soup bowl (for final presentation)

Shopping list*:

____ 2 cups of brown rice
____ Water
____ Low sodium beef bouillon granules
____ 2 cups cooked kidney beans
____ Dried onion
____ Oregano
____ Paprika
____ Garlic powder
____ Cayenne pepper
____ Black pepper
____ Disposable cups
____ Cups, spoons and napkins

Cooking skill/nutrition lesson

This lesson shows how to make a healthy, economical dish using beans and rice. It uses three groups from MyPlate: grains, protein and vegetables, so be sure to highlight the importance of including portions of dairy and fruit on the side as well.

Demo preparation:

1. Wash your hands before handling food.
2. Cut and measure all ingredients.
3. Arrange pan and all ingredients around stove in the order in which they will be used.
4. Preheat stove as participants are coming into the room.

Make ahead options:

You can make this dish ahead of time and reheat for class or serving samples.

Garnish/presentation tips:

Serve red beans and rice on an attractive platter and top with dried oregano.

Number of sample servings: approximately 18.

Leader Guide: Budget Recipes

Vegetables with Fried Egg and Rice

Makes approximately 8 sample servings

Eggs are an inexpensive source of protein. This delicious recipe will taste wonderful and only costs .78 per serving.

3 cups cooked brown rice
1 Tbsp oil
1 tsp minced garlic
1 pound bag stir fry vegetables
1 cup shredded cabbage
6 eggs, separated
3 Tbsp soy sauce

Directions:

1. Cook rice according to package directions.
2. Heat oil in a large, nonstick skillet over medium-high heat. Add garlic and saute until golden, about 1-2 minutes.
3. Add stir fry vegetables and cabbage and continue cooking until vegetables are crisp tender, about 4 more minutes. Stir frequently.
4. Meanwhile, separate eggs - use 1 egg yolk and 6 egg whites, whipping them in a small bowl (discard yolks or save for future use). Remove vegetables from skillet, add eggs and scramble briefly until done, about 3 minutes.
5. Add vegetables and soy sauce to skillet with eggs and stir well. Serve this stir fry mixture on top of the cooked rice. Serve hot or refrigerate or freeze for later use. Use a 2 ounce portion for tasting samples.

Approximate cost per recipe: $3.13 or .78 per serving.

Equipment:

___ Large, 12 inch, nonstick skillet
___ Stove
___ Knife
___ Cutting board
___ Kitchen spoon
___ Measuring cups and spoons
___ Plate (for final presentation)

Shopping list*:

___ Brown rice
___ Vegetable oil
___ Minced garlic
___ 1 pound bag stir fry vegetables
___ Cabbage
___ 6 eggs
___ Soy sauce (light is preferred)
___ Disposable cups ((for premeasured ingredients))
___ Cups, spoons and napkins

Cooking skill/nutrition lesson

This lesson shows how to use mostly egg whites instead of whole eggs. It gives participants a healthy, Asian-style meal using eggs, a low cost source of protein. It also highlights the use of eggs as a protein source. This is important because MyPlate strongly recommends consuming a wide variety of protein foods in small servings.

Demo preparation:

1. Wash your hands before you handle food.
2. Cut and measure all ingredients.
3. Arrange pan and all ingredients around stove in the order in which they will be used.
4. Preheat stove as participants are coming into the room.

Make ahead options:

You can make the stir fry ahead of time and just reheat and serve for class.

Garnish/presentation tips:

Serve the stir fry with a dash of soy sauce over the top.

Number of sample servings: approximately 8.

30 Ways to Save Food Dollars

1. **Plan your meals** and make a shopping list. Remember to keep MyPlate proportions in mind and pick up extra veggies and fruit.

2. **Reduce shopping time** to reduce impulse buys:
   -Shop when the store is not busy (if possible)
   -Shop once a week or less

3. **Follow your list.** Buy only the items on the list. Buy only what you need, with the exception of non-perishable items that are offered at substantial savings.

4. **Take advantage of store specials.** Stock up on non-perishable items. Know prices on your favorite items so you can tell if these are really a good deal.

5. **Pay attention to unit pricing.** Usually items that are at eye level or carry brand names are more expensive. Larger does not always mean less pennies per unit/ounce! (See #28.)

6. **Only buy larger items** if they are less expensive per unit and you will use them quickly.

7. **Buy fresh produce in season** to save money and get a higher quality product.

8. **Try to lessen your use of packaged cereals** and use oatmeal, grits or cream of wheat instead.

9. **Try to use less bread** and more whole grains like brown rice, barley or whole grain pasta.

10. **Plan several meals a week using dried beans** instead of meat.

11. **Only use coupons for items that you need** and will use. Coupons are often given for expensive items that you wouldn't use anyway.

12. **Buy whole chickens** and cut them up yourself instead of buying more expensive parts.

13. **Serve smaller portions of meat** and larger portions of potatoes, rice or veggies.

14. **Bake treats yourself** instead of buying expensive packaged mixes and goods from the bakery.

15. **Instead of buying expensive frozen meals**, start making recipes from scratch in larger batches and freezing the leftovers for your own frozen meals.

16. **Put off grocery shopping for a day or two** once in a while. This will force you to use up what you have.

17. **Clean and organize your pantry and freezer**. It helps to know what you already have on hand. You will also make more efficient use of your freezer.

18. **Try to use up all the items in your freezer** from time to time.

19. **Make your own salad dressings**. Use vegetable or olive oil and a dash of flavored vinegar to dress salads.

20. **Make your own soups**. Freeze what you don't eat in single portion units for later.

21. **Evaluate your shopping habits**. If you are easily swayed by store specials, shop in fewer stores. Picking one store for everything might make you spend more on a few items but you will end up spending less overall because you will be exposed to fewer "specials." On the other hand, if you have a large family to feed and are good at sticking to a list, you can often save money by taking advantage of specials in multiple stores.

22. **Cut down on refined foods** such as bagels, crackers, candies, soda, chips, etc. These add to your waist line and they increase the amount of money you spend on food dollars. If your family is used to eating these. the USDA recommends that you begin serving smaller and smaller portions. Eventually, you can replace refined foods with fresh produce and home made items.

23. **Eat out less often**. Take a look at how much you pay at a restaurant versus what this food costs if you buy it in the grocery store. You may be surprised at teh difference. Eat dinner at home and go out for ice cream or coffee.

24. **Plan for leftovers**. A roasted chicken one day becomes chicken soup or salad tomorrow. Maximize your efforts in the kitchen by planning to make leftovers.

25. **Take water and snacks with you** while you are running errands so you are not tempted to buy extra food.

26. **Pack your own lunch**.

27. **Take advantage of local farmer's markets.** Produce found at these markets is often higher quality and less expensive than local grocery stores.

28. **Pay attention to store prices** so you won't fall for marketing tricks such as "buy one get one free."

29. **Keep your refrigerator clean** and at the proper temperature so you have less food waste.

30. **Purchase lettuce by the head** instead of the ready-to-use bags. The difference in price is around .60 per ounce!!

FMI

For a fun blog on this topic, visit
http://simpledollar.com

Less Processed = Lower Price

Grains	Per ounce
Rice, bulk	0.02
Grits	0.02
Rolled oats (bulk, store brand)	0.05
Barley	0.05
Corn meal	0.05
Pancake mix	0.05
Pasta	0.05
Brown rice, bulk	0.05
Rolled oats (bulk, brand name)	0.08
Bread	0.08
Cream of wheat, bulk	0.12
Waffles	0.13
Bagels	0.14
Instant oats, bulk	0.16
Packaged instant oats	0.20
Boxed pasta mix	0.20
Boxed rice mix	0.21
Packaged cereal (average)	0.22
Crackers	0.25
Cereal bars	0.28
Frozen rice mix	0.29

Vegetables:	Per ounce
Cabbage	0.02
Baking potatoes	0.02
Romaine	0.04
Cauliflower	0.04
Carrots	0.04
Cucumber	0.04
Corn	0.04
Green beans	0.05
Sweet potatoes	0.05
Frozen french fries	0.06
Canned vegetables (average)	0.07
Broccoli	0.07
Tomatoes	0.07
Frozen vegetables (store brand)	0.07
Yellow squash	0.08
Frozen mashed potatoes	0.10
Frozen vegetables (brand name)	0.12
Potato chips	0.19
Instant mashed potatoes	0.21
Ready lettuce	0.65

Fruits	Per ounce
Bananas	0.03
Watermelon	0.03
Oranges	0.03
Cantaloupe	0.05
Apples	0.05
Canned fruit & apple sauce	0.06
Strawberries	0.12
Dried fruit	0.13
Peaches	0.15

Milk	Per ounce
Skim milk	0.04
Yogurt	0.07
Cottage cheese	0.13
Cheddar cheese & hard cheese	0.23

Meat/Beans	Per ounce
Beans, dried (average)	0.04
Eggs	0.05
Turkey drumstick	0.07
Whole turkey	0.08
Whole chicken	0.08
Peanut butter	0.09
Whole chicken, cut up	0.10
Ground turkey	0.12
Tofu	0.14
Raw turkey breast	0.16
Peanuts	0.16
Boneless skinless chicken breast (store)	0.16
Tuna, canned	0.16
Ground beef	0.17
Bologna	0.17
Pork chops	0.19
Round roast, beef	0.19
Bacon	0.19
Hot dogs	0.19
Beef loin steak	0.21
Boneless skinless chix breast (brand)	0.27
Ham	0.29
Fish, fresh (average)	0.44
Lamb (average)	0.44
Deli meat (average)	0.57
Beef tenderloin	0.75

Healthy Cooking on a Budget

Turkey Stew

This recipe uses turkey thighs, which are economical and flavorful. The cost per serving is only 71 cents!

1 Tbsp oil
1 onion, cut in chunks
3 carrots, peeled and cut in chunks
2 stalks celery, cut in chunks
4 cups beef or chicken broth, low sodium
2 turkey thighs
3 large potatoes, cut in chunks (leave peel on)
1 bay leaf
1 tsp garlic powder
Black pepper to taste

Directions:

1. Heat a large Dutch oven style pan over medium high heat. Add the oil, then the onion, and saute until golden, about 2-3 minutes.
2. Add the carrots and celery and cook briefly.
3. Add the broth along with the turkey thighs, potatoes and seasonings. Bring to a boil then lower to a simmer.
4. Cook this stew on low heat, keeping covered and at a simmer, until potatoes and turkey are cooked through and tender, about 25-35 minutes. Stir occasionally.
5. Take the turkey thighs out of the stew; remove their skin and bones and cut the meat into small pieces. Add this meat back to the stew. Discard bones & skin.
6. Serve the stew hot or refrigerate/freeze for later use. We recommend a half cup serving for sample servings

Approximate cost per recipe: $2.84 or .71 per person. Serves 4. Each 2 cup serving: 254 calories, 8 g fat, 1.5 g saturated fat, 61 mg cholesterol, 320 mg sodium, 22 g carbohydrate, 4 g fiber, 22 g protein.

Budget Tossed Salad

Using this recipe instead of the fancy store mixes will save you around .61 cents per ounce! Cabbage is one of the least expensive vegetables and it adds a lot of nutrients (and a nice crunch!) to your salads.

1 head romaine
½ head cabbage
2 grated carrots

Directions:

1. Remove damaged/blemished leaves from romaine and cabbage.
2. Cut romaine into small pieces; finely shred cabbage. Wash lettuce and cabbage in large bowl or clean sink with cold water. Drain in colander.
3. Place drained lettuce and cabbage in bag; add grated carrots. Keep cold until ready to serve, up to 5 days. Toss this mixture with tomatoes, cucumbers, oil and vinegar, etc just before you are ready to serve.
4. Place this salad in a large salad bowl and toss with a little oil and vinegar.

TIP: Use leftover cabbage for slaw, soup or the stir fry recipe below.

Approximate cost per recipe: $1.29 or .13 per serving. Serves 10. Each 1 cup serving: 21 calories, 0 fat, 0 cholesterol, 15 mg sodium, 4 g carbohydrate, 1.5 g protein, 2 g fiber.

Beef Barley Soup

This recipe stretches ground beef by adding lentils and using less beef. You end up giving your family more nutrients and fiber while saving money on groceries.

1/2 pound extra lean ground beef
1 onion
1 cup dry lentils
1/2 cup pearled barley
3 cups mixed frozen vegetables
1 can diced tomatoes
6 tsp low-sodium beef bouillon granules
6 cups water
1 tsp garlic powder
Black pepper to taste

Directions:

1. Heat a large soup pot over medium high heat. Add ground beef, breaking it into small pieces and cooking until brown, about 5 minutes. Drain off extra grease.
2. Add onion and saute until tender, about 2 minutes.
3. Add the rest of the ingredients, bring to a boil then reduce to a simmer. Cook on low until barley is tender, about 45 minutes.
4. Serve soup hot or refrigerate/freeze for later use.

Approximate cost per recipe: $4.74 or $.79 per person. Serves 6. Each serving: 303 calories, 6.5 g fat, 2.5 g saturated fat, 31 mg cholesterol, 111 mg sodium, 43 g carbohydrate, 9 g fiber, 18 g protein.

Healthy Cooking on a Budget

Vegetables with Fried Egg and Rice

Eggs are an inexpensive source of protein. This delicious recipe tastes wonderful and only costs .78 per serving.

3 cups cooked brown rice
1 Tbsp oil
1 tsp minced garlic
1 pound bag stir fry vegetables
1 cup shredded cabbage
6 eggs, separated
3 Tbsp light soy sauce

Directions:

1. Cook rice according to package directions.
2. Heat oil in a large, nonstick skillet over medium-high heat. Add garlic and saute until golden, about 1-2 minutes.
3. Add stir fry vegetables and cabbage and continue cooking until vegetables are crisp tender, about 4 more minutes. Stir frequently.
4. Meanwhile, separate eggs - use 1 egg yolk and 6 egg whites, whipping them in a small bowl (discard yolks or save for future use). Remove vegetables from skillet, add eggs and scramble briefly until done, about 3 minutes.
5. Add vegetables and soy sauce to skillet with eggs and stir well. Serve this stir fry mixture on top of the cooked rice. Serve hot or refrigerate or freeze for later use.

Approximate cost per recipe: $3.13 or .78 per serving.

Serves 4. Each 2 cup serving: 285 calories, 6 g fat, 1 g saturated fat, 53 mg cholesterol, 529 mg sodium, 44 g carbohydrate, 6 g fiber, 12 g protein.

Red Beans and Rice

This dish is very filling. We suggest serving it with the Budget Tossed Salad. The cost per serving is about .26!

2 cups brown rice
5 cups water
5 tsp low sodium beef bouillon granules
2 cups cooked kidney beans
1/4 cup dried onion
1 tsp oregano
1 tsp paprika
1 tsp garlic powder
pinch cayenne pepper
black pepper to taste

Directions:

1. Place all ingredients in large soup pot and bring to a boil.
2. Lower heat to simmer, cover pot and cook on low until rice is done, about 30 minutes.
3. Serve Red Beans and Rice hot or refrigerate or freeze for later use.

Approximate cost per recipe: $1.03 or .17 per serving.

Serves 6. Each 1-1/2 cup serving: 323 calories, 2 g fat, 0.5 g saturated fat, 0 mg cholesterol, 12 mg sodium, 65 g carbohydrate, 6 g fiber, 10 g protein.

Leader Guide: Cooking on the Run

Title:
Cooking on the Run

Target Audience:
This presentation kit is intended for general audiences age 14 and up. It covers topics of wellness, heart disease, diabetes, weight loss and nutrition.

Lesson Objectives:
• Participants will learn how to make healthy, simple, portable meals.
• Participants will understand that healthy meals do not have to take a lot of time to prepare.

Lesson Rationale:
Health authorities have indicated that good nutrition is one of the most important factors in determining long-term health. Poor diet plays a major role in the development of four of the top seven killers in the United States: heart disease, cancer, stroke and diabetes. Consumers who have the skills to select and prepare nutritious foods can positively impact their present and future health. This class shows participants that they can still eat healthy when they're very busy. Speed in the kitchen is important for today's consumer, who generally has less time for the kitchen and fewer cooking skills than past generations.

Lesson at a Glance:
This lesson introduces participants to new recipes and teaches cooking balance which are both consistent with MyPlate and Dietary Guidelines for Americans. It will teach the skills that are necessary for making healthy meals, even when schedules get tight.

Lesson Materials:
This lesson contains:
• Leader and Activity Guide
• Leader and Activity Guide for Recipes
• 1 copy-ready recipe page, 1 copy-ready handout

Preparation:
_____ Review leader guides
_____ Review handouts
_____ Select activities
_____ Copy and collect materials for lesson

Activity Ideas:

Introduction:
Ask participants to raise their hands if they think that eating healthier takes too much time. Tell them they have come to the right class, because you will show them how to eat healthy on the run.

Activity 1 - Cooking Demo
Use one or more of the recipes in this lesson to demonstrate how to make a healthy meal using healthy ingredients.

Activity 2 - Fast Plate
Make an On-the-Run MyPlate using milk crates. Arrange four into a larger square, then position a fifth off to one side. One crate in the square should be veggies, another fruit, a third protein, and a fourth grains. The outlying square should be dairy. Fill each section with foods, food packages, and models of foods that your participants can keep on hand to make fast meals on the go.
Here are some ideas for each section:
• **Grains**: Tortillas (for wrap sandwiches), whole wheat bread, whole wheat pita pockets, microwavable soups that contain pasta, angel hair pasta, lowfat whole wheat crackers, whole grain cereal, and instant brown rice.
• **Fruits**: Apples, pears, bananas, peaches, nectarines, etc. Focus on fruits that you can take with you and eat on the go.
• **Vegetables**: Baby carrots, precut vegetables, salad from the grocery store salad bar, baked potatoes, and frozen vegetables.
• **Protein**: Canned tuna, nuts, microwavable soups with beans, roasted chicken and turkey, and peanut or other nut butters.
• **Dairy**: Spoonless yogurt, individual containers of yogurt, skim milk, light string cheese.
See the accompanying handout in this section titled "MyPlate on the Run."

For More Information:
www.foodandhealth.com

Leader Guide: Recipes on the Run

Bean Burrito Wrap
Makes about 4 sample servings

1 flour tortilla (about 8 inches in diameter)
1/2 cup canned lowfat refried beans, no salt added
1 small ripe tomato, chopped
1 dollop of nonfat sour cream
Dash of hot pepper sauce

Directions:
1. Heat refried beans in a microwave. While those are heating, core and chop the tomato.
2. Spread the refried beans on the tortilla, top with tomato, nonfat sour cream and hot pepper sauce. Roll up and wrap, for eating on the go.

Equipment:
____ Microwave
____ Microwave container for beans
____ Cutting board
____ Knife
____ Can opener

Shopping list:
____ Flour tortillas
____ Lowfat refried beans
____ Tomato
____ Nonfat sour cream
____ Hot pepper sauce
____ Aluminum foil
____ Plates, napkins, and forks

Cooking skill/nutrition lesson:
This recipe outlines an easy way to make and eat food from three groups of MyPlate: grains, beans and vegetables. The product is portable enough to pack up and eat whil on the go.

Demo preparation:
1. Wash your hands before you handle food.
2. Measure refried beans into a microwaveable container.
3. Measure all ingredients.
4. Organize your work area.

Make ahead options:
1. Chop the tomato and heat the refried beans.
2. Assemble everything in front of the class.

On the go tips:
Wrap the tortilla in foil to make it more portable.

Number of sample servings: Approximately 4

Stuffed and Packed Potato
Makes about 4 sample servings

1 baking potato
1/4 cup nonfat sour cream
1 cup steamed, mixed, frozen veggies

Directions:
1. Wash potato under cold running water to remove dirt. Prick with a fork and then bake in the microwave until done, about 5 minutes. Cut in half and fluff with a fork.
2. Meanwhile, heat the veggies in the microwave or in a steamer on top of the stove.
3. Top potato with veggies and sour cream. You can also use herb mixes and or black pepper for seasoning. Wrap in foil and go.

Equipment:
____ Microwave
____ Microwave container (or pot with steamer basket) for vegetables
____ Stove for steaming vegetables (not needed if you microwave them)
____ Measuring cups

Shopping list:
____ Baking potato
____ Frozen mixed vegetables
____ Nonfat sour cream
____ Aluminum foil
____ Plates, napkins and forks

Cooking skill/nutrition lesson:
This recipe demonstrates an easy way to make and eat a variety of vegetables on the run.

Demo preparation:
1. Wash your hands before you handle food.
2. Measure all ingredients.
3. Organize your work area.

Make ahead options:
1. Bake the potato ahead of time and just show the group how to top it and prepare it for traveling.

On the go tips:
Wrap the tortilla in foil to make it more portable.

Number of sample servings: Approximately 4

Leader Guide: Recipes on the Run

Veggie Burger in a Pocket

Makes about 4 sample servings

1 frozen veggie burger
1 whole wheat pita pocket
1 cup lettuce
1 tomato
No-salt-added ketchup

Directions:

1. Heat a veggie burger for 1-2 minutes in the microwave. Toast the pita bread.
2. Cut the top off the pita bread. Stuff it with the hot burger, lettuce, tomato, and ketchup. Wrap in foil and go.

Equipment:

____ Microwave
____ Microwave-safe container
____ Knife
____ Cutting board
____ Measuring cups

Shopping list:

____ Vegetarian burger
____ Whole wheat pita pockets
____ Lettuce
____ Tomato
____ No-salt-added ketchup
____ Aluminum foil
____ Plates, napkins and forks

Cooking skill/nutrition lesson:

This recipe explores an easy way to make and eat a vegetarian burger on the run.

Demo preparation:

1. Wash your hands before you handle food.
2. Measure all ingredients.
3. Organize your work area.

On the go tips:

Wrap the pita pocket with the burger in foil.

Number of sample servings: Approximately 4.

Salad and Crackers to Go

Makes about 4 sample servings

2 cups tossed salad with veggies
2 Tbsp lowfat dressing
1/2 can tuna
1 whole grain cracker, wrapped in plastic wrap

Directions:

1. Place the tossed salad in a disposable container.
2. Pour the dressing into a corner of the container.
3. Top the salad with tuna and the cracker. Pack to go with a fork and napkin.

Equipment:

____ Mixing bowl
____ Knife
____ Cutting board
____ Can opener
____ Measuring cups and spoons

Shopping list:

____ Lettuce
____ Vegetables for salad
____ 1 can tuna
____ Whole grain crackers
____ Disposable container for salad
____ Plates, napkins and forks

Cooking skill/nutrition lesson:

This recipe demonstrates an easy way to make and eat a salad with whole grain crackers on the run. It highlights foods from the protein, vegetable, and grain groups of MyPlate.

Demo preparation:

1. Wash your hands before you handle food.
2. Measure all ingredients.
3. Organize your work area.

Make ahead options:

You can make the tuna salad ahead of time.

On the go tips:

Place all in a to-go container and set next to a fork and napkin.

Number of sample servings: Approximately 4.

Leader Guide: Recipes for Cooking on the Run

Super Soup

Makes about 4 sample servings

1 cup of frozen, mixed vegetables
1 cup of canned, healthy soup (low sodium, etc)
Directions:
1. Combine veggies and soup in a microwaveable container.
2. Microwave on high until soup comes to a full boil.
3. Pour into insulated thermos and go. We suggest you accompany this meal with lowfat, whole grain crackers.

Equipment:

____ Microwave
____ Microwave-safe container
____ Spoon (to stir soup)
____ Can opener
____ Insulated thermos
____ Measuring cups

Shopping list:

____ Frozen mixed vegetables
____ 1 can of healthy soup
____ Plates, napkins and forks

Cooking skill/nutrition lesson:

This recipe shows an easy way to make and eat vegetable soup. It highlights the importance of vegetables and finds a way to make sure they are consumed, even in the face of a busy schedule.

Demo preparation:

1. Wash your hands before you handle food.
2. Measure all ingredients.
3. Organize your work area so everything is easily accessible.

On the go tips:

Pour the soup into the thermos.

Number of sample servings: Approximately 4.

Angel Hair Pasta

Makes about 4 sample servings

8 ounces angel hair pasta
1 jar healthy pasta sauce
1 bag frozen mixed veggies
Directions:
1. Cook angel hair pasta according to package directions.
2. Heat sauce and veggies in a 2 quart pan.
3. Combine pasta and sauce. Place in an insulated thermos and go.

Equipment:

____ Stove
____ 3 quart pot (for cooking pasta)
____ 2 quart pan (for heating sauce and veggies)
____ Kitchen spoon
____ Colander
____ Insulated thermos
____ Measuring cups

Shopping list:

____ 1 box angel hair pasta
____ Frozen mixed vegetables
____ Healthy pasta sauce
____ Plates, napkins and forks

Cooking skill/nutrition lesson:

This recipe shows an easy way to make and eat angel hair pasta with veggies.

Demo preparation:

1. Wash your hands before you handle food.
2. Measure all ingredients.
3. Organize ingredients and work area.
4. Start pasta water boiling before participants enter the room.

Make ahead options:

1. Cook pasta ahead of time. Heat sauce and veggies in class and toss with cooked pasta

Garnish/presentation tips:

Place the pasta in the thermos.

Number of sample servings: Approximately 4.

Note: If you would like to reduce the sodium in this recipe, use the healthy pasta sauce recipe in the hypertension lesson.

Recipes: Cooking on the Run

Bean Burrito Wrap

1 flour tortilla (about 8 inches in diameter)
1/2 cup canned lowfat refried beans, no salt added
1 small ripe tomato, chopped
1 dollop of nonfat sour cream
dash hot pepper sauce

Directions:

1. Heat refried beans in a microwave. While those are heating, core and chop the tomato.
2. Spread the refried beans on the tortilla, top with tomato, nonfat sour cream and hot pepper sauce. Roll up and wrap, for eating on the go.

Serves 1. Each serving (1 burrito): 220 calories. 3 g fat, 0 g saturated fat, 228 g sodium, 0 mg cholesterol, 41 g carbohydrate, 13 g fiber, 11 g protein.

Stuffed and Packed Potato

1 baking potato
1/4 cup nonfat sour cream
1 cup steamed mixed frozen veggies

Directions:

1. Wash potato under cold, running water to remove dirt. Prick with a fork and then bake in the microwave until done, about 5 minutes. Cut in half and fluff with a fork.
2. Meanwhile, heat the veggies in the microwave or in a steamer on top of the stove.
3. Top potato with veggies and sour cream. You can also use herb mixes and or black pepper for seasoning. Wrap in foil and go.

Serves 1. Each serving (1 potato): 197 calories, 0 g fat, 0 mg cholesterol, 98 mg sodium, 37 g carbohydrate, 5 g fiber, 8 g protein.

Veggie Burger in a Pocket

1 frozen veggie burger
1 whole wheat pita pocket
1 cup lettuce
1 tomato
no-salt-added ketchup

Directions:

1. Heat a veggie burger for 1-2 minutes in the microwave. Toast the pita bread.
2. Cut the top off the pita bread. Stuff it with the hot burger, lettuce, tomato, and ketchup. Wrap in foil and go.

Serves 1. Each serving: 240 calories, 3.5 g fat, 0.5 g saturated fat, 600 mg sodium, 0 mg cholesterol, 40 g carbohydrate, 8 g fiber, 17 g protein.

Salad and Crackers to Go

2 cups tossed salad with veggies
1 Tbsp lowfat dressing
1/2 can tuna, low sodium
1 whole grain cracker, wrapped in plastic wrap

Directions:

1. Place the tossed salad in a disposable container.
2. Pour the dressing into a corner of the container.
3. Top the salad with tuna and the cracker. Pack to go with a fork and napkin.

Serves 1. Each serving (2-1/3 cups): 193 calories, 2 g fat, 0 g saturated fat, 45 mg cholesterol, 422 mg sodium, 22 g carbohydrate, 4 g fiber, 25 g protein.

Super Soup

1 cup frozen mixed vegetables
1 cup canned healthy soup

Directions:

1. Combine veggies and soup in a microwaveable container.
2. Microwave on high until soup comes to a full boil.
3. Pour into insulated thermos and go. We suggest you accompany this meal with lowfat, whole grain crackers.

Serves 1. Each serving (2 cups): 145 calories, 0.5 g fat, 0 g saturated fat, 0 mg cholesterol, 475 mg sodium, 20 g carbohydrate, 8 g fiber, 6.5 g protein.

Angel Hair Pasta

8 ounces angel hair pasta
1 jar healthy pasta sauce
1 bag frozen mixed veggies

Directions:

1. Cook angel hair pasta according to package directions.
2. Heat sauce and veggies in a 2 quart pan.
3. Combine pasta and sauce. Place in an insulated thermos and go.

Serves 4. Each serving (1-1/2 cups): 324 calories, 1 g fat, 0 g saturated fat, 0 mg cholesterol, 614 mg sodium, 65 g carbohydrate, 7 g fiber, 11 g protein.

Keeping Healthy On the Run

Cooking and eating on the run doesn't have to mean giving up a healthy diet. Prior planning can help, if have the right foods on hand to whip up a healthy meal. Follow MyPlate and use this list of ideas to stock your kitchen:

• Grains:
Tortillas for wrap sandwiches, whole wheat bread, whole wheat pita pockets, microwavable soups with pasta, angel hair pasta, lowfat whole wheat crackers, whole grain cereal, and instant brown rice

• Vegetables:
Baby carrots, precut vegetables, salad from the grocery store salad bar, baked potato, and frozen vegetables.

• Fruits:
Apples, pears, bananas, peaches, nectarines, etc. Get fruits that you can take with you and eat on the go.

• Milk:
Individual containers of yogurt, skim milk, light string cheese, and smoothies made with yogurt or milk.

• Meat/Beans:
Canned tuna, nuts, microwave soups with beans or

poultry, roasted chicken or turkey, and nut butters.

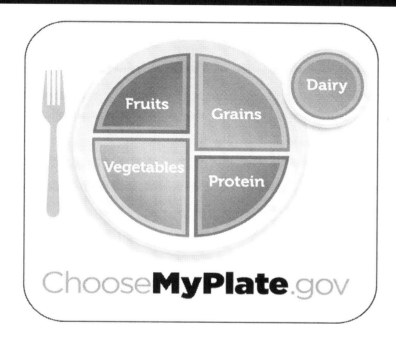

Leader Guide: Desserts

Title:
Healthy Desserts

Target Audience:
This presentation kit is intended for general audiences age 14 and up. It covers topics of wellness, heart disease, diabetes, weight loss, and nutrition.

Lesson Objectives:
• Participants will learn how to make healthy desserts with lots of fruit.
• Participants will explore how to modify their favorite baking recipes so that they will contain less fat, saturated fat, trans-fatty acids, and sugar.

Lesson Rationale:
Health authorities have indicated that good nutrition is one of the most important factors in determining long-term health. Poor diet plays a major role in the development of four of the top seven killers in the United States: heart disease, cancer, stroke and diabetes. Consumers who have the skills to select and prepare nutritious foods can positively impact their present and future health.

Everyone loves dessert. This class is designed as a positive way to teach the principles of good nutrition and exploring tasty desserts without endorsing eating large portions of unhealthy treats.

Lesson at a Glance:
This lesson introduces participants to new recipes and teaches cooking skills. It outlines rules about food which are consistent with MyPlate and the Dietary Guidelines for Americans.

Lesson Materials:
This lesson contains:
• Leader and Activity Guide
• Leader and Activity Guide for Recipes
• 1 copy-ready recipe page, 1 copy-ready handout

Preparation:
_____ Review leader guides
_____ Review handouts
_____ Select activities
_____ Copy and collect materials for lesson

Activity Ideas:

Introduction:
Ask participants if they like dessert. Tell them they have come to the right class and that you are going to show them and feed them some delicious, yet healthy desserts.

Activity 1 - Cooking Demo
Use one or more of the recipes in this lesson to show participants how to make fun and healthy desserts.

Activity 2 - Lighten Up
Use the handout "Lighten Your Baking" to show participants how make their favorite recipes less calorically dense. You can even choose a traditional recipe that is popular in your area and show them how to make it lighter. It is a good idea to bring along some of the items outlined on the handout. Here is a list of our favorites:

-**Fat free whipped cream** - You can find cans of this near the regular whipped cream.

-**Nonfat dairy topping** - Look in the freezer case.

-**Apple sauce** - This can be used to replace half the oil in most recipes.

-**Baby food prunes** - These can also be used to replace half the oil or butter in most recipes, though they're better in dark baked goods.

-**Margarine** - Choose some that doesn't contain trans-fatty acids and stick margarine for baking.

-**Splenda** - This sweetener can be used to replace half (or more) of the sugar in puddings, pie fillings, sauces, and some baked goods. For tips and more information, see www.splenda.com.

-**Fresh fruit** - Emphasize that participants should always put fruit at the center of the plate for their dessert and then accompany it with a small portion of frozen yogurt, cookies or cake. This will help them eat more fruit and lower their calorie intake. Of course fruit on its own can also be a fantastic

-**Egg whites or nonfat egg substitute** - Use 1/4 cup in place of 1 whole egg.

-**Evaporated skim milk** - Use this in place of whole milk or heavy cream.

-**Fat free half and half** - This is an excellent product that you can use to cook or bake.

FOR MORE INFORMATION:
www.foodandhealth.com

Recipe Leader Guide: Desserts

Banana Split

Makes 8-12 sample servings

4 bananas
8 small scoops of frozen vanilla yogurt (1/2 cup per person)
Drizzle of light chocolate syrup
4 tsp chopped pecans or peanuts

Directions:

1. Peel bananas and cut in half lengthwise. Place two halves on each of 4 salad plates.
2. Scoop frozen vanilla yogurt (1/2 cup portion) using a small ice cream scoop (#20) and place between the banana slices.
3. Drizzle with chocolate syrup and top each serving with 1 tsp of chopped nuts.

Equipment:

____ Cutting board
____ Knife
____ Ice cream scoop (#20, if possible)
____ Measuring spoon and cup
____ 4 large plates

Shopping list:

____ 4 ripe bananas
____ 1 pint nonfat vanilla frozen yogurt
____ Light chocolate syrup (reduced calorie)
____ Pecan pieces or peanut pieces
____ Plates, napkins and spoons
____ Disposable cups and bags
____ Optional: cocoa powder for garnish

Cooking skill/nutrition lesson:

This recipe demonstrates how to make a healthy dessert using fruit. It points out that portion control is important with frozen yogurt, it highlights fruit as the main part of the dessert, and explains that light chocolate syrup is only half the calories of regular syrup.

Demo preparation:

1. Wash your hands before you handle food.
2. Organize your work area. Have all ingredients and utensils within reach.
3. Consider asking for helpers to make the other three Banana Splits while you show them how to make one.

Garnish/presentation tips:

Place the bananas on the plate so they form an oval-shaped nest in which to put the yogurt. Drizzle the chocolate syrup slowly in a fine stream all around the plate. Sprinkle the pecan pieces so they fall haphazard-ly around the plate, including on the rim. It helps to have an attractive, large dinner plate for this presentation. As a final option, you can sprinkle the plate with cocoa powder - put it in a sieve and tap it lightly while holding it over the plate.

Number of sample servings: Approximately 8-12.

We recommend splitting one dessert between 2 or 3 people.

Recipe Leader Guide: Desserts

Strawberry Tortilla

Makes 8-12 sample servings

4 corn tortillas
Cinnamon sugar (1 cup sugar, 1 Tbsp cinnamon)
Vegetable oil cooking spray
2 cups strawberries
2 cups sorbet (chocolate, berry, mango, etc)
2 jars of peach baby food

Directions:

1. Preheat oven (or toaster oven) to 350 degrees. Lightly spray the corn tortillas with vegetable cooking spray on both sides. Dip them into cinnamon sugar.
2. Place corn tortillas on baking sheet and bake until crisp, about 8-10 minutes on each side.
3. Put each tortilla on a dinner plate. Top each one with 1/2 cup strawberries. Shave sorbet using a tablespoon and place 1/2 cup sorbet on each plate, right on top of the strawberries.
4. Mix the baby food in a small bowl until it becomes smooth, then drizzle over the top of each tortilla. Optional garnish: a sprinkle of powdered sugar.

NOTE: You can bake the corn tortillas ahead of time and keep them in a covered container for up to a week. Re-crisp in the oven if necessary.

Equipment:

____ Toaster oven or oven (you can omit this one if you bake the tortillas at home and bring them to your class)
____ Baking sheet (for corn tortillas)
____ Cutting board
____ Knife
____ 4 large dinner plates (for presentation)
____ Small bowl
____ Tablespoons
____ Medium bowl for cinnamon sugar
____ Optional: sieve for powdered sugar or cocoa powder
____ Measuring cups and spoons

Shopping List:

____ 4 corn tortillas
____ Sugar
____ Cinnamon
____ Vegetable oil cooking spray
____ 1 quart fresh strawberries
____ 1 pint sorbet (chocolate, berry, mango, etc)
____ 2 jars peach baby food
____ Plates, forks and napkins (for samples)
____ Disposable cups ((for premeasured ingredients))
____ Optional: Powdered sugar or cocoa powder for garnish

Cooking skill/nutrition lesson:

This recipe shows how to make a healthy dessert that features fruit. It points out that portion control is important with frozen sorbet and reveals that baby food can be a great dessert sauce. If baby food doesn't appeal, try pureed canned fruit.

Demo preparation:

1. Wash your hands before you handle food.
2. Measure all ingredients.
3. Organize your work area so everything is easily accessible.

Make ahead options:

We suggest that you bake the tortillas ahead of time and take them to class in a sealed container. You can show the class how to spray and dip the tortilla in the cinnamon sugar and then proceed right to assembling the dessert with the prebaked tortillas.

We suggest that you ask for audience volunteers to help you assemble three of the tortillas after you've shown everyone how to assemble one.

Garnish/presentation tips:

This is a very pretty dessert. The tortilla will curl slightly while it is baking. Place the tortilla in the center of the plate. It should look like it is spilling strawberries and sorbet onto the plate. Drizzle the baby food sauce all around the plate in a fine stream, then dust with cocoa powder or powdered sugar. Consider using two kinds of sorbet or more than one kind of berry for more color.

Number of sample servings: approximately 8-12.

We recommend serving 2 or 3 people with each tortilla.

Recipe Leader Guide: Desserts

Fruit Yogurt Parfait

Makes 12 sample servings

2 jars pear baby food
2 cups assorted fresh fruits in season
4 cups light nonfat yogurt
1/2 cup lowfat granola

Directions:

1. Place baby food in a small bowl and mix until it gets a sauce-like consistency. Divide between four tall, stemmed glasses.
2. Place 1/2 cup of fruit in each glass, right on top of the pear baby food.
3. Place 1 cup of yogurt on top of the fruit in each glass.
4. Sprinkle each parfait with 2 tablespoons of lowfat granola. Serve immediately or chill up to 2 hours before serving.

Equipment:

____ Knife
____ Cutting board
____ Measuring cups and spoons
____ Tablespoons
____ 4 elegant, tall, stemmed glasses

Shopping list:

____ 2 jars pear baby food
____ Assorted fruits in season
____ 1 quart light nonfat vanilla yogurt
____ 1 box lowfat granola cereal
____ Cups, spoons and napkins (for samples)
____ Disposable cups for premeasured ingredients

Cooking skill/nutrition lesson:

This recipe outlines how to make a healthy dessert by using fruit and nonfat, light yogurt. It also reveals that baby food can be a great dessert sauce.

Demo preparation:

1. Wash your hands before you handle food.
2. Measure all ingredients.
3. Organize your work area so everything is easily accessible.

Make ahead options:

Make three of the parfaits ahead of time and just demonstrate how to assemble one. You could also ask for three volunteers to come and help you assemble three of the parfaits while you show how to make one. You can also make these ahead of time and just sprinkle on the granola for the demo and tasting.

Garnish/presentation tips:

Layer the sauce, fruit and yogurt neatly. It helps to have a tall, thin glass so you can really see the layers. You can also make these in clear, plastic cups for kids - consider showing one made this way too.

Number of sample servings: 12

We suggest splitting each dessert between 3 people.

Recipe Leader Guide: Desserts

Chocolate Mousse with Berries

Makes 8-12 sample servings

1 box (12 ounces) silken tofu
1/3 cup sugar
1/4 cup cocoa powder
2 cups assorted berries (sliced strawberries, raspberries, blueberries, etc).
Nonfat whipped cream

Directions:

1. Puree tofu, sugar, and cocoa powder in a food processor. Divide between four tall, stemmed glasses. Refrigerate until ready to serve or proceed to the next step right away.
2. Mash berries in a bowl and divide among four glasses, placing the berry mixture on top of the chocolate mousse.
3. Top each glass with about 2 tablespoons of nonfat whipped cream.
4. Optional garnish: dust the top of the whipped cream with cocoa powder.

Equipment:
____ Food processor
____ Knife
____ Cutting board
____ Sieve (for cocoa powder)
____ Four tall stemmed glasses
____ Measuring cups and spoons

Shopping list:
____ 12 ounce box of silken tofu (we strongly recommend Mori-Nu Firm)
____ Sugar
____ Cocoa powder
____ Fresh berries
____ 1 can fat free whipped cream
____ Cups, spoons and napkins (for samples)
____ Disposable cups ((for premeasured ingredients))

Cooking skill/nutrition lesson:
This creative recipe will introduce soy to your participants. They will be surprised at how good a mousse/pudding can taste when it's made from tofu. The recipe also features fresh fruit and nonfat whipped cream.

Demo preparation:
1. Wash your hands before you handle food.
2. Measure all ingredients (except for whipped cream - that should be used at the last minute).
3. Organize your work are so everything is easily accessible.

Make ahead options:
You can make the mousse ahead of time and bring it to class. We recommend you ask for audience volunteers to help you assemble the final desserts.

Garnish/presentation tips:
Put this mousse in a tall, elegant glass. Layer the mousse, berries, and whipped cream neatly. Top the whipped cream with a light dusting of cocoa powder. It is best if you place the cocoa powder in a sieve and lightly tap it with a spoon or knife so just a little falls down on the whipped cream.

Number of sample servings: approximately 8-12.
We recommend that you split one dessert between 2 or 3 people.

Recipes: Healthy Desserts

Banana Split

4 bananas

8 small scoops frozen vanilla yogurt (1/2 cup per person)

Light chocolate syrup

4 tsp chopped pecans or peanuts

Directions:

1. Peel bananas and cut in half lengthwise. Place two halves on each of 4 salad plates.
2. Scoop frozen vanilla yogurt (1/2 cup portion) using a small ice cream scoop (#20) and place between the banana slices.
3. Drizzle with chocolate syrup and top each serving with 1 tsp of chopped nuts.

Serves 4. Each 1 cup serving: 236 calories, 4.5 g fat, 2 g saturated fat, 10 mg cholesterol, 39 mg sodium, 47 g carbohydrate, 3 g fiber, 3.5 g protein.

Strawberry Tortilla

4 corn tortillas

cinnamon sugar

vegetable oil cooking spray

2 cups strawberries

2 cups sorbet (chocolate, berry, mango, etc)

2 jars peach baby food

Directions:

1. Preheat oven (or toaster oven) to 350 degrees. Lightly spray the corn tortillas with vegetable cooking spray on both sides. Dip them into cinnamon sugar.
2. Place corn tortillas on baking sheet and bake until crisp, about 8-10 minutes on each side.
3. Put each tortilla on a dinner plate. Top each one with 1/2 cup strawberries. Shave sorbet using a tablespoon and place 1/2 cup sorbet on each plate, right on top of the strawberries.
4. Mix the baby food in a small bowl until it becomes smooth, then drizzle over the top of each tortilla. Optional garnish: a sprinkle of powdered sugar.

NOTE: You can bake the corn tortillas ahead of time and keep them in a covered container for up to a week. Re-crisp in the oven if necessary.

Serves 4. Each serving (1 cup plus 1 tortilla): 236 calories, 1 g fat, 0 g saturated fat, 0 mg cholesterol, 48 mg sodium, 55 g carbohydrate, 5 g fiber, 2 g protein.

Fruit Yogurt Parfait

2 jars pear baby food

2 cups assorted fresh fruits in season (be colorful!)

4 cups light nonfat yogurt

1/2 cup lowfat granola

Directions:

1. Place baby food in a small bowl and mix until it gets a sauce-like consistency. Divide between four tall, stemmed glasses.
2. Place 1/2 cup of fruit in each glass, right on top of the pear baby food.
3. Place 1 cup of yogurt on top of the fruit in each glass.
4. Sprinkle each parfait with 2 tablespoons of lowfat granola. Serve immediately or chill up to 2 hours before serving.

Serves 4. Each 1-1/2 cup serving: 226 calories, 1 g fat, 0 g saturated fat, 9 mg cholesterol, 19 mg sodium, 44 g carbohyrdrate, 4.5 g fiber, 9 g protein.

Chocolate Mousse with Berries

1 box (12 ounces) silken tofu

1/3 cup sugar

1/4 cup cocoa powder

2 cups assorted berries: sliced strawberries, raspberries, blueberries, etc.

Nonfat whipped cream

Directions:

1. Puree tofu, sugar, and cocoa powder in a food processor. Divide between four tall, stemmed glasses. Refrigerate until ready to serve or proceed to the next step right away.
2. Mash berries in a bowl and divide among four glasses, placing the berry mixture on top of the chocolate mousse.
3. Top each glass with about 2 tablespoons of nonfat whipped cream.
4. Optional garnish: dust the top of the whipped cream with cocoa powder.

Serves 4. Each 3/4 cup serving: 159 calories, 3.5 g fat, 1 g saturated fat, 1 mg cholesterol, 25 g carbohydrate, 3 g fiber, 7.5 g protein.

Lighten Your Baking & Desserts

Replace the Eggs
When a recipe calls for whole eggs, use egg whites instead. Here is a general guide:
- 2 egg whites = 1 whole egg
- 1/4 cup egg white or nonfat egg substitute = 1 whole egg

TIP: This substitution does not work with recipes that are cooked on top of the stove, such as egg nog, custard or Anglaise sauce.

Whole Milk Can be Replaced
For most recipes, you can easily substitute evaporated skim milk or skim milk for whole milk.

Look for Lighter Options with Cream
If a recipe for a cake, pudding, sauce or drink calls for heavy cream, use fat free half-and-half, or evaporated skim milk.

TIP: If the cream has to be whipped, use fat free non-dairy whipped topping or a spray can of fat free whipped cream.

Reduce Sugar
- Recipes for pudding, sauce, icing ,and pie filling can have the sugar reduced by 25%.
- Try the Splenda brand sweetener and use it to replace up to 50% of the sugar in most recipes.

TIP: Experiment with small reductions first.

Butter Be Gone
- Substitute the butter in most recipes with stick margarine that doesn't contain trans fatty acids.
- For baking, you will have to use the regular stick margarine because light and low-cal spreads are not meant for cooking and baking.

TIP: When you substitute margarine in place of butter, make sure you omit the salt in a recipe.

Oil Goes Down
In many recipes for cakes, quick breads or muffins, you can replace half or all of the oil with pureed prunes/apples or baby food. There are also commercial products like Lighter Bake that contain prunes and apples. Check the baking aisle in your grocery store for resources.
- For the first time you try this in a recipe, replace just half of the oil with one of these ingredients.
- If all goes well, you can increase the substituted amount of fruit the next time. Make sure you write down what you did!

TIP: Use apple sauce on lighter colored recipes and pureed or baby food prunes on chocolate or darker colored recipes. This will also reduce baking time by around 25%.

Frosting: Use Less
In many recipes, you can omit the frosting or use less.
- An easy way to use less frosting is to freeze the item first. By freezing a cake, the frosting will spread much easier without crumbs. This is what the pros do!
- Consider making cake in a bundt pan and dusting it with powdered sugar instead of frosting.
- Another option is to heat the frosting in your microwave (about 30 seconds) and drizzle it across the cake.

Make Smaller Portions
- The next time you bake brownies, bars, or blondies, use a bigger pan so that you can spread the mix thinner. Just make sure you reduce the baking time. When your item is finished, cut it into smaller portions.
- Consider baking cake mix in small muffin pans. You can freeze them and thaw as needed.
- Make a cake in 2 pans. Freeze one for later and use one for now. Cut the cake in small wedges and garnish each one with fruit. This will result in fewer calories than to bake and to ice two layers. You will save money too.
- Make cookies smaller. Freeze them and just bake them as you want to eat them - you will be less tempted to eat the whole batch in one sitting.

Lighten that Pie
- When baking pies, omit the crust on the bottom and use one layer of crust on the top. Your pie will still look beautiful, you will cut down on fat and calories and there is no way for the bottom crust to get soggy.
- Use less sugar in the filling ,or fold canned fruit filling with fresh fruit to further reduce calories.

Serve It with Fruit
Instead of piling up a big bowl of frozen yogurt for dessert, pile up fruit and top it with just a little frozen yogurt. Serve fruit as the main item and garnish it with cookies, cake or frozen yogurt. This way you are heading to a more balanced plate, reducing your calories and having your cake too!

Leader Guide: Fiber

Title:
Increase Your Fiber Intake and Improve Your Health

Target Audience:
This presentation kit is intended for general audiences age 14 and up. It covers topics of wellness, heart disease, diabetes, weight loss, and nutrition.

Lesson Objectives:
• Participants will learn the importance of getting enough fiber in their diets.
• Participants will be able to name three important benefits of fiber.
• Participants will learn some new high fiber recipes; they will see that high fiber foods taste great.

Lesson Rationale:
According to the 1988-1991 NHANES survey, the average man consumes only 17 grams of fiber per day, while women average only 13 grams per day. The National Cancer Institute has recommended that adults get 20-30 grams of fiber daily. Therefore, American consumers generally need to increase their fiber consumption. This lesson will emphasize foods that are higher in fiber, while outlining ways for the consumer to modify their eating plan in order to add more fiber to their diet.

Lesson at a Glance:
This lesson introduces participants to new recipes and teaches cooking skills. It also imparts information which is consistent with MyPlate and the Dietary Guidelines for Americans. The recipes demonstrate how to add more fiber to well-loved foods like potato salad and macaroni and cheese.

Lesson Materials:
This lesson contains:
• Leader and Activity Guide
• Leader and Activity Guide for Recipes
• 2 copy-ready recipe pages, 2 copy-ready handouts

Preparation:
____ Review leader guides
____ Review handouts
____ Select activities
____ Copy and collect materials for lesson

Activity Ideas:
Introduction:
Ask your class to guess how much fiber they eat in a day. Write down their answers. Explain that the average American's fiber intake is only around 14 grams

per day, while the recommendation is 25-33. In Africa, where people eat a high fiber, plant-based diet, the average consumption is often 70-80 grams per day.

Activity 1 - Cooking Demo
Use one or more of the recipes in this lesson to show participants how to make delicious, high-fiber meals.

Activity 2 - Fill up with Fast Fiber Facts
Use the handout "Fiber Facts" to show participants the importance of fiber.
Follow up with a trivia quiz to test their knowledge. Here are some questions you can use:
1. Name three health benefits of fiber.
   Answer: (Responses will vary but may include any of the following). Fiber improves the health of your digestive tract, prevents cardiovascular disease, helps prevent cancer, aids weight control, and lowers your risk of diabetes.
2. How much fiber should you eat in a day?
   Answer: There is no RDA for fiber, but experts recommend around 25-33 grams per day.
3. Is it difficult to get 25-33 grams of fiber per day?
   Answer: If you base your diet around plant foods like whole grains, beans, fruits, and vegetables, it is easy to consume that amount of fiber in a day. Remember, according to MyPlate, half of your plate should be fruits and veggies at every meal, and at least half the grains you eat should be whole grains.
4. What is the best source of soluble fiber?
   Answer: Beans (legumes, not green beans).
5. Name the two types of fiber.
   Answer: Soluble fiber and insoluble fiber. Soluble fiber forms gels that slow digestion and help keep levels of glucose and insulin steady. Insoluble fiber absorbs water and acts like a broom in your intestines.
6. Name at least three foods that are good sources of fiber.
   Answer: (Responses will vary but may include any food from the following MyPlate food groups) Beans, whole grains, fruits, vegetables.

For More Information:
"Dietary Fiber" This fact sheet lays out information about fiber in a very straightforward way.
www.ext.colostate.edu/pubs/foodnut/09333.html

Leader Guide: High Fiber Recipes

Country-Style Potato Salad

Makes about 10 sample servings

3 medium baking potatoes
1 cup celery
1/2 cup minced onion
1 cup frozen peas
1 Tbsp prepared mustard
1/2 cup lowfat mayonnaise
1/2 cup nonfat plain yogurt
Fresh cracked black pepper (to taste)
Garnish: lettuce and tomato

Directions:
1. Wash potatoes, leave skin on, and cut into bite-size chunks.
2. Place chunks in a pan and cover them with water. Bring to a boil, then lower to simmer and cook (uncovered) until potatoes are tender, about 20 minutes.
3. Drain in colander and sprinkle lightly with cold water.
4. In the meantime, put the rest of the ingredients in a large mixing bowl.
5. Drain potatoes well and add to the bowl. Mix well and refrigerate until ready to use.

Equipment:

____ Stove
____ 3 quart pan
____ Colander
____ Kitchen spoon
____ Knife
____ Cutting board
____ Measuring cups and spoons
____ Large mixing bowl

Shopping list:

____ 3 medium sized baking potatoes
____ Celery
____ Onion
____ Frozen peas
____ Tomato and lettuce (for garnish)
____ Prepared mustard
____ Lowfat mayonnaise
____ Nonfat, plain yogurt
____ Plates, forks, napkins (for samples)
____ plastic cups (for premeasured ingredients)

Cooking skill/nutrition lesson:

This demonstrates how to make a favorite recipe high-er in fiber. By leaving the peels on the potatoes, you increase your intake of fiber. It also adds a nice country-style look to a potato salad. By adding plain, non-fat yogurt to this recipe, you use less sodium than if you used all mayonnaise. Frozen peas add even more color and fiber.

Demo preparation:

1. Wash your hands before you handle food.
2. Measure all ingredients.
3. Organize your work area.
4. Start cooking potatoes before class begins.

Garnish/presentation tips:

Top the potato salad with fresh cracked black pepper and a large, sliced tomato. Place on a bed of lettuce

Number of sample servings: Approximately 10

(Use a 1/2 cup portion for tastings).

Leader Guide: High Fiber Recipes

Skillet Chili

Makes about 10 sample servings

1 tsp oil
1 onion, chopped
1/2 pound ground turkey breast
2 15-ounce cans of kidney beans, drained and rinsed
1 15-ounce can of no-salt-added tomatoes
1 8-ounce can of tomato sauce
1/4 cup tomato paste
1 tsp chili powder
1 tsp garlic powder

Directions:

1. Heat a 12" nonstick skillet over high heat. Add the oil, then the onion, and saute until golden brown, about 3 minutes.
2. Crumble the turkey into the skillet and continue cooking until turkey is almost done.
3. Add the rest of the ingredients, bring to a boil and reduce to a simmer. Cook until sauce is thick.
4. Serve over cooked brown rice, a baked potato or 100% whole wheat toast.

Equipment:

_____ Stove
_____ Skillet
_____ Colander (to drain beans)
_____ Can opener
_____ Kitchen spoon
_____ Knife
_____ Cutting board
_____ Measuring cups and spoons
_____ Plate or bowl (for final presentation)

Shopping list:

_____ 1 tsp oil
_____ 1 onion
_____ 1/2 pound ground turkey breast
_____ 2 cans (15 oz) kidney beans
_____ 1 can (15 oz) no-salt-added tomatoes
_____ 1 can (8 oz) tomato sauce
_____ 1 can (6 oz) tomato paste
_____ Chili powder
_____ Garlic powder
_____ Plates, forks, napkins (for samples)
_____ Plastic cups ((for premeasured ingredients))

Cooking skill/nutrition lesson:

This recipe shows everyone how to make a favorite recipe, but add more fiber. By reducing the amount of meat and adding beans, you will increase the fiber content while lowering saturated fat. This recipe uses ground turkey in place of ground beef, so be sure to bring that switch to your audience's attention.

Demo preparation:

1. Wash your hands before you handle food.
2. Measure all ingredients.
3. Organize your work area and place your supplies within reach.

Garnish/presentation tips:

Serve the chili over brown rice, a baked potato or toasted 100% whole wheat bread. Arrange everything on an attractive plate

Number of sample servings: Approximately 10
(Use a 1/2 cup portion for tastings).

Leader Guide: High Fiber Recipes

Garlic White Bean Soup

Makes about 10 sample servings

1 tsp olive oil
1 Tbsp minced garlic
1 15-ounce can white beans, drained and rinsed
1-1/2 cups chicken broth
1 tsp Italian seasoning
3 diced tomatoes
Garnish: Fresh cracked black pepper
4 Tbsp grated Parmesan cheese
Directions:

1. Heat a Dutch Oven pan over medium high heat. Add the oil and garlic and saute until golden brown.

2. Add the beans, broth, and Italian seasoning and bring to a boil. Reduce heat to simmer and cook until liquid starts to thicken, about 5 minutes.

3. Puree the soup with a hand mixer or in a blender in small batches - be careful, it's hot!

4. Put back on the stove and add the diced tomatoes. Reheat and serve in bowls. Garnish each serving with a sprinkle of fresh cracked black pepper and grated Parmesan cheese.

Equipment:

_____ Stove
_____ Skillet
_____ Colander (to drain beans)
_____ Can opener
_____ Kitchen spoon
_____ Knife
_____ Cutting board
_____ Measuring cups and spoons
_____ Plate or bowl (for final presentation)

Shopping list:

_____ 1 tsp olive oil
_____ Minced garlic
_____ 1 can white beans, drained and rinsed
_____ 1 can chicken broth
_____ Water
_____ Italian seasoning
_____ 3 tomatoes
_____ Black pepper
_____ Grated Parmesan cheese
_____ Plates, forks, napkins (for samples)
_____ Plastic cups ((for premeasured ingredients))

Cooking skill/nutrition lesson:

This recipe highlights how to make a favorite recipe higher in fiber. Accoring to the Dietary Guidelines for Americans, fiber is a nutrient of concern for Americans, because most people simply don't get enough in their diets. Simple changes like the ones outlined in this recipe may have a significant impact on overall health.

Demo preparation:

1. Wash your hands before you handle food.
2. Measure all ingredients.
3. Organize your work area.

Garnish/presentation tips:

Place the soup in an attractive bowl and garnish the top with Italian seasoning.

Number of sample servings: Approximately 10

(Use a 1/2 cup portion for tastings.)

 # Leader Guide: High Fiber Recipes

Fiber-Up Salad
Makes about 10 sample servings

4 cups romaine
1 cup cabbage
1 orange
1 tomato
1/2 cup chopped green onion
1 cup cooked kidney beans, drained and rinsed
2 Tbsp olive oil
3 Tbsp flavored vinegar
1 tsp Italian seasoning

Directions:
1. Place all ingredients in large salad bowl. Toss well and serve immediately, or chill for up to one hour for later use.

Equipment:
____ Stove
____ Skillet
____ Colander to drain beans
____ Can opener
____ Mixing bowl
____ Kitchen spoon
____ Knife
____ Cutting board
____ Measuring cups and spoons
____ Plate or bowl (for final presentation)

Shopping list:
____ 4 cups romaine
____ Cabbage
____ 1 orange
____ 1 tomato
____ Green onion
____ 1 can kidney beans
____ Olive oil
____ Flavored vinegar
____ Italian seasoning
____ Plates, forks, napkins (for samples)
____ Plastic cups ((for premeasured ingredients))

Cooking skill/nutrition lesson:
This recipe demonstrates how to make a better salad that is higher in fiber by adding beans. Using vinegar and oil instead of bottled salad dressing helps lower sodium content, too. MyPlate insists that people should choose low-sodium options whenever possible. This salad offers ways to do just that.

Demo preparation:
1. Wash your hands before you handle food.
2. Measure all ingredients.
3. Organize your work area.

Garnish presentation tips:
Top the salad with fresh cracked black pepper

Number of sample servings: Approximately 10
(Use a 1/2 cup portion for tastings).

Leader Guide: High Fiber Recipes

Quick Brown Rice Pilaf

Makes about 12 sample servings

1 tsp olive oil
1 onion chopped
Pinch of cayenne pepper
1 tsp oregano
2 cups instant brown rice
2 cups chicken broth
1 cup frozen peas

Directions:

1. Heat a large skillet over medium high heat. Add the oil, then the onion, and saute until golden, about 3 minutes.
2. Add the rice, broth and seasonings and bring to a boil. Lower the heat to simmer and cook (covered) until the rice is tender and absorbs all of the liquid, about 8-10 minutes. Allow to stand for a few minutes then fluff with a fork. Serve hot.

Equipment:
_____ Stove
_____ Skillet
_____ Can opener
_____ Kitchen spoon
_____ Knife
_____ Cutting board
_____ Measuring cups and spoons
_____ Plate or bowl (final presentation)

Shopping list:
_____ Olive oil
_____ 1 onion
_____ Cayenne pepper
_____ 1 15-ounce can of kidney beans
_____ Oregano
_____ Instant brown rice
_____ Chicken broth
_____ Plates, forks, napkins (for samples)
_____ Plastic cups (for premeasured ingredients)

Cooking skill/nutrition lesson:
This recipe outlines a simple way to prepare beans and rice pilaf. Instant brown rice cooks in the same amount of time as white rice and it contains 2 grams of fiber per 1/2 cup serving. If you prefer to use regular brown rice, cut the amount of rice in half and increase the cooking time to 35 minutes. Remember, MyPlate recommends that everyone make at least half of their grains whole grains.

Demo preparation:
1. Wash your hands before you handle food.
2. Measure all ingredients.
3. Organize your work area.

Garnish presentation tips:
Top this pilaf with a sprinkle of paprika.

Number of sample servings: Approximately 12
(Use a 1/2 cup portion for tastings).

Leader Guide: High Fiber Recipes

Better Macaroni & Cheese
Makes about 10 sample servings
1 box macaroni and cheese mix
2 cups mixed frozen vegetables, steamed
1/2 cup skim milk
1/2 packet cheese mix
Garnish: Sliced tomato, baby carrots
Directions:
1. Cook the macaroni according to package directions and drain in colander. Meanwhile, steam the vegetables.
2. Make the sauce: Combine the skim milk and cheese mix. Bring to a boil.
3. Add the vegetables and the macaroni. Serve hot.

Equipment:
____ Stove
____ Skillet
____ Colander (to drain macaroni)
____ Kitchen spoon
____ Measuring cups and spoons
____ Plate or bowl (for final presentation)

Shopping list:
____ 1 box macaroni and cheese mix
____ Mixed frozen vegetables
____ Skim milk
____ Baby carrots
____ Ripe tomato
____ Plates, forks, napkins (for samples)
____ Plastic cups (for premeasured ingredients)

Cooking skill/nutrition lesson:
This recipe shows everyone how to make a favorite recipe with extra fiber. By adding vegetables and omitting the margarine, you are making macaroni and cheese that is higher in fiber and lower in fat. If you only use half the packet of cheese mix, you will further reduce sodium. You can use the cheese mix for another batch of macaroni. For even more fiber and a thicker sauce, add 1/2 cup of garbanzo beans to the milk and puree before continuing as directed with the cheese mix, vegetables and pasta.

Demo preparation:
1. Wash your hands before you handle food.
2. Measure all ingredients.
3. Organize your work area.

Garnish presentation tips:
Place the macaroni and cheese on a plate and garnish with fresh tomato slices and baby carrots.

Number of sample servings: Approximately 10

High Fiber Recipes

Country Style Potato Salad

3 medium sized baking potatoes
1 cup celery
1/2 cup minced onion
1 cup frozen peas
1 Tbsp prepared mustard
1/2 cup lowfat mayonnaise
1/2 cup nonfat plain yogurt
Fresh cracked black pepper to taste
Garnish: lettuce and tomato

Directions:
1. Wash potatoes, leave skin on and cut in bite-size chunks. Place in pan and cover with water. Bring to a boil, lower to simmer and cook uncovered until potatoes are tender, about 20 minutes. Drain in colander and sprinkle lightly with cold water.
2. In the meantime, put the rest of the ingredients in a large mixing bowl. Drain potatoes well and add to the bowl. Mix well and refrigerate until ready to use. Garnish with fresh lettuce and sliced tomatoes.

Serves 4. Each 1 cup serving: 176 calories, 2.5 g fat, 0 g saturated fat, 0 mg cholesterol, 414 mg sodium, 32 mg carbohydrate, 4.5 g fiber, 6 g protein.

Skillet Chili

1 tsp oil
1 onion, chopped
1/2 pound ground turkey breast
2 15-ounce cans kidney beans, drained and rinsed
1 15-ounce can no-salt-added tomatoes
1 8-ounce can tomato sauce
1/4 cup tomato paste
1 tsp chili powder
1 tsp garlic powder

Directions:
1. Heat a 12" nonstick skillet over high heat. Add the oil, then the onion, and saute until golden brown, about 3 minutes.
2. Crumble the turkey into the skillet and continue cooking until turkey is almost done.
3. Add the rest of the ingredients, bring to a boil and reduce to a simmer. Cook until sauce is thick.
4. Serve over cooked brown rice, a baked potato or 100% whole wheat toast.

Serves 4. Each serving: 259 calories, 2 g fat, 0 g saturated fat, 47 g carbohydrate, 408 mg sodium, 32 g carbohydrate, 10.5 g fiber, 27 g protein.

Garlic White Bean Soup

1 tsp olive oil
1 Tbsp minced garlic
15 ounce can white beans, drained and rinsed
1-1/2 cups chicken broth
1 tsp Italian seasoning
3 diced tomatoes
Garnish: Fresh cracked black pepper
4 Tbsp grated Parmesan cheese

Directions:
1. Heat a Dutch Oven pan over medium high heat. Add the oil and garlic and saute until golden brown.
2. Add the beans, broth, and Italian seasoning and bring to a boil. Reduce heat to simmer and cook until liquid starts to thicken, about 5 minutes.
3. Puree the soup with a hand mixer or in a blender in small batches - be careful, it's hot!
4. Put back on the stove and add the diced tomatoes. Reheat and serve in bowls. Garnish each serving with a sprinkle of fresh cracked black pepper and grated Parmesan cheese.

Serves 3. Each 1 cup serving: 206 calories, 4 g fat, 1 g saturated fat, 17 mg cholesterol, 226 mg sodium, 28 g carbohydrate, 7 g fiber, 15 g protein.

Fiber-Up Salad

4 cups romaine
1 cup cabbage
1 orange
1 tomato
1/2 cup chopped green onion
1 cup cooked kidney beans, drained and rinsed
2 Tbsp olive oil
3 Tbsp flavored vinegar
1 tsp Italian seasoning

Directions:
1. Place all ingredients in large salad bowl. Toss well and serve immediately, or chill for up to one hour for later use.

Serves 1. Each serving: 153 calories, 7 g fat, 1 g saturated fat, 0 mg cholesterol, 121 mg sodium, 18 g carbohydrate, 6 g fiber, 5 g protein.

High Fiber Recipes

Quick Brown Rice Pilaf

1 tsp olive oil
1 onion chopped
Pinch of cayenne pepper
1 tsp oregano
2 cups instant brown rice
2 cups chicken broth
1 cup frozen peas

Directions:

1. Heat a large skillet over medium high heat. Add the oil, then the onion, and saute until golden, about 3 minutes.
2. Add the rice, broth and seasonings and bring to a boil. Lower the heat to simmer and cook (covered) until the rice is tender and absorbs all of the liquid, about 8-10 minutes. Allow to stand for a few minutes then fluff with a fork. Serve hot.

Serves 4. Each serving: 228 calories, 3 g fat, 0 g saturated fat, 12 mg cholesterol, 166 mg sodium, 42 g carbohydrate, 5 g fiber, 10 g protein.

Better Macaroni & Cheese

1 box macaroni and cheese mix
2 cups mixed frozen vegetables, steamed
1/2 cup skim milk
1/2 packet cheese mix
Garnish: Sliced tomato, baby carrots

Directions:

1. Cook the macaroni according to package directions and drain in colander. Meanwhile, steam the vegetables.
2. Make the sauce: Combine the skim milk and cheese mix. Bring to a boil.
3. Add the vegetables and the macaroni. Serve hot.

Serves 4. Each 1 cup serving: 204 calories, 4.5 g fat, 1 g saturated fat, 3 mg cholesterol, 258 mg sodium, 32 g carbohydrate, 3 g fiber, 8 g protein.

Easy Tips for More Fiber:

- Eat fresh fruit instead of drinking fruit juice or fruit punch (2-3 g).
- Keep fresh, raw veggies like broccoli, carrots, cauliflower, and celery on hand for snacking (4g per cup).
- Leave edible peels on your fruits and potatoes (1-3 g per serving).
- Choose high-fiber cereal in place of breakfast pastries or eggs (3-10 g per serving).
- Look for bread that uses only 100% whole wheat flour. Make sure you compare the fiber content between brands, since they vary between 2 to 6 grams of fiber per slice.
- Try baked beans, chili, bean soup, bean salsa, beans and greens, or another bean dish at least once a week. Keeping canned beans or frozen, cooked beans on hand will keep you one step closer to using these high-fiber legumes on a regular basis (5-8 g per 1/2 cup).
- Serve fresh fruit instead of dessert after dinner. You will be surprised at how much your family will try if you have it already prepared (3 -5 g per cup).
- MyPlate recommends that half your plate should be fruits and veggies. Add a whole grain to that and you'll be on the right track for fiber consumption.

Fiber Facts

Have you neglected your fiber intake because of headlines that say it won't prevent colon cancer? Think again! Fiber offers a wide range health benefits.

What is fiber?

Fiber is nondigestible matter that is found only in plants. There are many kinds of fiber, but they fall into roughly two groups: soluble fibers and insoluble fibers. In the digestive tract, soluble fibers form gels that slow digestion and help keep levels of glucose and insulin steady. These gels also decrease your absorption of cholesterol. In addition, fermentation of soluble fibers in the colon creates byproducts that may keep the colon healthy. Insoluble fibers absorb water, thereby diluting the concentration of carcinogens. They also have a laxative effect.

Health benefits

- **Digestive tract**. Insoluble fiber helps prevent or treat constipation, hemorrhoids, and diverticular disease.
- **Cardiovascular disease**. Soluble fiber helps reduce cholesterol levels and may also protect the heart by reducing insulin levels. Diets higher in fiber are linked to lower LDL (bad) cholesterol and to increased HDL (good) cholesterol.
- **Diabetes**. People whose diets are higher in fiber decrease their risk of developing diabetes. For people who already have diabetes, soluble fiber can help delay or prevent complications (like blindness) by decreasing blood sugar levels.
- **Cancer**. Some studies link a long term, high-fiber diet with lower rates of colon, prostate, and breast cancers. It may be that other factors in high fiber foods are responsible for this link rather than fiber itself, but that's just another reason to choose whole foods over supplements!
- **Weight control**. High fiber foods are bulky and help keep blood sugar levels in check, which can make you feel full for longer and stave off hunger pangs.

How much fiber?

There is no RDA for fiber, but experts recommend 25 to 35 grams a day. For children younger than 18, the rule is usually their age plus 5 (so a 10-year-old should get around 15 grams of fiber a day). On food labels, the Daily Value is 25 g for a 2000 calorie diet. Very high fiber intakes (above 50 g) may interfere with the absorption of some minerals.

Get your fiber from foods

Good news! Fiber-rich foods are also sources of many other nutrients and health-promoting substances. Adding legumes, fruits, vegetables, nuts, seeds, and whole grains is the best way to increase your fiber intake. Each fiber-rich food is a mixture of soluble and insoluble fibers, so choose a variety of whole plant foods. Cooked dried beans, oats, citrus fruits, and apples are especially rich in soluble fibers, while whole grains and bran (wheat, corn, rice) are richer in insoluble fibers. Try these simple ways to add fiber to your diet:

- Start the day with a high-fiber breakfast cereal. Top it with fresh fruit or eat an orange instead of drinking orange juice.
- Choose high-fiber snacks like popcorn or fruit.
- Don't peel fruits and vegetables -- most of the fiber can be in the peel. Scrub them well!
- Add legumes to soups, stews, salads and casseroles. Add more vegetables, too.
- When baking, substitute whole wheat flour for half the white flour. Replace some of the oil with prune puree or applesauce.
- Sprinkle wheat germ or wheat bran on top of casseroles, or stir them into yogurt.
- In general, choose whole foods over processed ones. Remember, MyPlate says at least half the grains you eat should be whole grains.

Start slowly

Suddenly increasing your fiber intake may make you feel bloated and gassy. Increase your intake slowly so your body can adapt, and be sure to drink plenty of liquids.

Fiber fun facts

- Average fiber consumption in the U.S. is only 14 grams a day, but in some parts of Africa it is 70 to 80 grams per day!
- Recommended fiber intake refers for dietary fiber, not crude fiber. Crude fiber values are different.
- Pureeing a food does not significantly lower its fiber content.

For more information

"Bulking Up Fiber's Healthful Reputation" This website discusses many benefits of fiber. http://findarticles.com/p/articles/mi_m1370/is_n5_v31/ai_19629295
"Dietary Fiber" This fact sheet lays out information about fiber in a very straightforward way. www.ext.colostate.edu/pubs/foodnut/09333.html

By Cheryl Sullivan, MA, RD.

3 Weeks to More Fiber

Week 1:
Build a Better Breakfast With Fiber!

Day 1: Starting today, drink eight cups of water daily. You need to drink plenty of fluids when you add fiber to your diet. Begin your morning with a cup of refreshing ice water or hot herb tea.

Day 2: Choose a high-fiber cereal for breakfast. Look for one with at least 5 grams of fiber per serving (like Shredded Wheat, Raisin Bran, Grape Nuts, All Bran, oatmeal, etc).

Day 3: Add 1/4 cup raisins (2 g fiber) to your high fiber cereal.

Day 4: Choose whole wheat bread instead of white bread for your toast (2-5 g fiber/slice). Spread on 1 tablespoon crunchy peanut butter (1 g fiber).

Day 5: Add a sliced medium banana to your high fiber cereal (2 g fiber).

Day 6: Mix 1/4 cup dry oatmeal with 1/2 cup nonfat plain yogurt and some fruit. Stir and enjoy those 7 grams of fiber.

Day 7: Grab an orange as a mid-morning pick-me-up (3 g fiber).

Week 2:
Join the High Fiber Lunch Bunch!

Day 1: Add a cup of black bean soup to your lunch (10 g fiber).

Day 2: Choose a baked potato (including the skin) instead of French fries (3 g fiber per 3 oz. potato).

Day 3: Add a sliced carrot (2 g fiber) and 1/2 cup chick-peas (3 g fiber) to your green salad.

Day 4: Heat up 1/2 cup vegetarian baked beans to go with your lunch (6 g fiber).

Day 5: Choose a green vegetable as a side dish, such as broccoli (2 g fiber per 1/2 cup) or Brussels sprouts (3 g fiber per 1/2 cup).

Day 6: Skip the vending machines for your afternoon snack. Instead, bring a medium apple from home (3 g fiber with skin).

Day 7: For a quick after-school snack, mix 3/4 cup bran flakes (5 g fiber), 1/4 cup dried apricots (2 g fiber), and 1/4 cup sunflower seeds (2 g fiber). Eat it plain or mix it with fat free yogurt.

Week 3:
Supper is Super When You Add Fiber!

Day 1: Eat 1/2 cup peas with your evening meal (5 g fiber).

Day 2: Warm up with a cup of turkey chili with beans (5 g fiber). Add whole grain bread and a side salad to complete the meal.

Day 3: Wrap 1/2 cup fat-free refried beans (6 g fiber), chopped tomatoes, scallions, low-fat cheese, and shredded lettuce in a tortilla.

Day 4: Serve stir-fried chicken and vegetables over brown rice instead of white rice (2 g fiber per 1/2 cup cooked rice).

Day 5: Order a cup of minestrone soup as an appetizer (5 g fiber).

Day 6: Choose a medium pear for a sweet dessert (4 g fiber).

Day 7: Stir 1/2 cup frozen raspberries (3 g fiber) or blackberries (2.5 g fiber) into low fat yogurt or ice cream.

It's easy to see what kind of foods you need to add in order to increase your fiber intake: fruits, vegetables, beans, and whole grains. These also provide the vitamins, minerals, and phytochemicals required for good health. Stick to MyPlate's recommendations and make half your plate fruits and veggies, and half the grains you eat should be whole grains.

By Hollis Bass, MEd, RD.

Substitute For More Fiber:

• Use whole wheat bread instead of white (1 slice)	2g
• Use whole wheat pasta instead of white (2 oz)	3g
• Make brown rice instead of white rice (1 cup)	3g
• Eat the potato with the skin (1)	2g
• Replace orange juice with an orange	3g
• Replace apple juice with an apple	4g
• Substitute beans for ground beef (1 cup)	11g
• Eat split pea soup & a salad instead of a sandwich	14g
• Order or make a baked potato in place of fries	4g
• Whole grain cereal in place of refined cereal	4g
Total fiber added:	**50g**

Leader Guide: Fish Twice Per Week

Title:
Fish Twice Per Week

Target Audience:
This presentation is intended for general audiences.

Lesson Objectives:
• Participants will learn the health benefits of fish
• Participants will learn how to buy, store and prepare fish in a delicious and healthy way.

Lesson Rationale:
The Dietary Guidelines for Americans and the American Heart Association recommend that people eat at least 2 servings of baked or grilled fish each week. MyPlate recommends at least 8 ounces of seafood per week.

Health authorities have indicated that good nutrition is one of the most important factors in determining long-term health. Poor diet plays a major role in the development of four of the top seven killers in the United States: heart disease, cancer, stroke and diabetes. Individuals who have the skills to select and prepare nutritious foods can positively impact their present and future health.

Lesson at a Glance:
This lesson introduces participants to new recipes and teaches cooking skills. It also provides nutrition and diet information that is consistent with the Dietary Guidelines for Americans and MyPlate.

Lesson Materials:
This lesson contains:
• Leader and Activity Guides
• 2 pages of copy-ready recipes and handouts

Preparation:
___ Review leader guide
___ Review handouts
___ Select activities
___ Copy and collect materials for lesson

Activity Ideas:

Activity 1 – Cooking Demo
Use the recipes in this lesson to plan a cooking demonstration. These recipes are designed to show participants how to prepare and serve fish.

Activity 2 - Fishing for Compliments
Buy and prepare several varieties of fish from your local grocery store. Allow participants to try them and evaluate the different flavors and characteristics.

For More Information:
"Omega Three Fatty Acids and Cardiovascular Disease" - This article tackles the the cardioprotective effects of omega-3 fatty acids.
http://www.foodandhealth.com/cpecourses/omega3.shtml
Seafood Twice A Week - This book by Evie Hansen and Cindy Snyder, outlines great ways to get your weekly dose of fish and other seafood. IBSN 0-9616426-4-5
"Seafood" - Take a look at the FDA advisory page about seafood at http://www.cfsan.fda.gov/seafood1.html

Leader Guide: Fish Twice Per Week

Baked Salmon with Fresh Salsa
Makes 8 sample servings

4 4-ounce fillets of salmon, fresh or frozen/thawed
2 tomatoes
1/2 cup green or red onion
1/2 cup green bell pepper, chopped
1 tsp hot pepper sauce
1 Tbsp fresh chopped cilantro
4 wedges fresh lemon

Directions:

1. Preheat oven to 350 degrees. Place salmon fillets in a large baking pan with about a 1/2 inch of water in the bottom. Cover the pan with foil and bake in the oven. Bake until fish is opaque and flakes easily with a fork, about 20 minutes.
2. Make the salsa by combining chopped tomatoes, onion, pepper, pepper sauce, and cilantro in a small mixing bowl.
3. Serve the salmon fillets with a side of salsa and a wedge of fresh lemon.

Equipment:
_____ Oven
_____ Mixing bowl
_____ Large baking pan
_____ Knife
_____ Cutting board
_____ Fork (to test doneness)
_____ Spoon
_____ Plate (for final presentation)

Shopping list:
_____ 4 4-ounce fillets of salmon, fresh or frozen/thawed
_____ 2 tomatoes
_____ Green or red onion
_____ Green bell pepper
_____ Hot pepper sauce
_____ Cilantro
_____ 1 fresh lemon
_____ Disposable cups (for premeasured ingredients)
_____ Paper plates, forks and napkins (for samples)

Cooking skill/nutrition lesson:
This recipe shows participants how to prepare salmon in a heart healthy way. Salmon is high in omega-3s, and the American Heart Association recommends 2 servings of omega 3 fatty acid fish per week.

Demo preparation:

1. Wash your hands before you handle food.
2. Prepare and measure all ingredients.
3. Organize your ingredients and work area.
4. Preheat oven.

Make ahead options:
You can bake the fish ahead of time and serve it either hot or cold, with salsa alongside.

Garnish/presentation tips:
Place the fish on an attractive dinner plate. Spoon the salsa over one corner of the fish. Garnish with a wedge of fresh lemon.

Number of sample servings: 8 (2 ounces each).

Leader Guide: Fish Twice Per Week

Tuna Salad on Whole Grain Bread

Makes 8 sample servings

1 can albacore tuna (low sodium version is preferred)
1/4 cup nonfat or lowfat mayonnaise
1/2 cup chopped cucumber
1/4 cup chopped red onion
1/4 cup chopped celery
Pinch of dried oregano
2 slices 100% whole wheat bread, toasted
1/2 cup ready-to-serve lettuce
1 sliced tomato

Directions:

1. Mix tuna with mayonnaise, cucumber, onion, celery and oregano in a medium mixing bowl. Spread over whole wheat bread and top with lettuce and tomato.
2. Serve open-faced sandwiches immediately or wrap and refrigerate until ready to serve.

Equipment:

_____ Mixing bowl
_____ Knife
_____ Cutting board
_____ Spoon
_____ Can opener
_____ Plate (for final presentation)

Shopping list:

_____ 1 can albacore tuna (low sodium if possible)
_____ Nonfat or lowfat mayonnaise
_____ Cucumber
_____ Red onion
_____ Celery
_____ Dried oregano
_____ 2 slices 100% whole wheat bread
_____ Ready-to-serve lettuce
_____ Tomato
_____ Disposable cups (for premeasured ingredients)
_____ Paper plates, forks and napkins (for samples)

Cooking skill/nutrition lesson:

This recipe shows participants how to prepare tuna using lowfat mayonnaise and lots of vegetables. Tuna is high in omega-3s. According to MyPlate, people should consume at least 8 ounces of seafood per week.

Demo preparation:

1. Wash your hands before you handle food.
2. Prepare and measure all ingredients.
3. Organize ingredients and work area.

Make ahead options:

You can make the salad ahead of time and assemble and serve the actual sandwiches in class.

Garnish/presentation tips:

Place the sandwich on an attractive salad plate. Garnish with additional lettuce and tomato.

Number of sample servings: 8 (1/4 sandwich each)

Leader Guide: Fish Twice Per Week

Sardine Spread

Makes 7 sample servings

Lowfat whole grain crackers

Spread:

2 cans sardines without salt, drained and mashed

Juice of 2 lemons

1/2 tsp hot pepper sauce

1/2 cup no-added-salt ketchup

Directions:

1. Mix ingredients for spread in a small bowl. Serve on whole grain crackers (we recommend 100% whole grain, lowfat crackers like WASA).

Equipment:

____ Mixing bowl

____ Knife

____ Cutting board

____ Fork (to mash sardines and mix spread)

____ Can opener

____ Butter knife (to put spread on crackers)

____ Plate (for final presentation)

Shopping list:

____ 2 cans (3-3/4 ounce) sardines

____ 3 lemons

____ Hot pepper sauce

____ No-added-salt ketchup

____ WASA or another whole grain, lowfat cracker

____ Disposable cups for premeasured ingredients

____ Paper plates, forks and napkins (for samples).

Cooking skill/nutrition lesson:

This recipe shows participants how to prepare sardines, which are high in omega-3s. The American Heart Association now recommends 2 servings of fish that contain omega 3 fatty acids per week.

Demo preparation:

1. Wash your hands before you handle food.

2. Prepare and measure all ingredients.

3. Organize ingredients and work area.

Make ahead options:

You can make the sardine spread ahead of time and serve on crackers for class.

Garnish/presentation tips:

Place a cracker with sardine spread on an attractive platter. Garnish with a lemon wheel.

Number of sample servings: 7

(1 ounce of spread each).

Leader Guide: Fish Twice Per Week

Lemon Baked Trout

Makes 8 sample servings

1 pound of fresh or frozen/thawed trout fillets

2 lemons, cut in half

1 cup thinly sliced onion

Black pepper to taste

Directions:

1. Preheat oven to 350 degrees. Place trout filets in a 9 by 12 inch baking pan. Sprinkle the juice of 1/2 a lemon over each fillet. Layer onions on top of each fish. Sprinkle black pepper over the top of each fillet.

2. Cover pan of trout with foil and bake until done, about 20-30 minutes. Fish is done when it is opaque and flakes easily with a fork.

Equipment:

____ Oven

____ Large baking pan

____ Knife

____ Cutting board

____ Fork (to test doneness)

____ Spatula

____ Plate (for final presentation)

Shopping list:

____ 4 4-ounce trout fillets

____ 3 lemons

____ 1 onion

____ Black pepper

____ Disposable cups (for premeasured ingredients)

____ Paper plates, forks, and napkins (for samples)

Cooking skill/nutrition lesson:

This recipe shows participants how to prepare trout using heart healthy cooking methods. Trout is high in omega-3s, and the USDA insists that people should get at least 8 ounces of seafood per week.

Demo preparation:

1. Wash your hands before you handle food.

2. Prepare and measure all ingredients.

3. Organize ingredients and work area.

4. Preheat oven.

Make ahead options:

You can bake the fish ahead of time and serve hot or cold for class.

Garnish/presentation tips:

Place the fish on an attractive dinner plate. Garnish with a wedge of fresh lemon.

Number of sample servings: 8 (2 ounces each).

Fish Twice Per Week

Baked Salmon with Fresh Salsa

4 4-ounce fillets of salmon, fresh or frozen/thawed
2 tomatoes
1/2 cup green or red onion
1/2 cup green bell pepper, chopped
1 tsp hot pepper sauce
1 Tbsp fresh chopped cilantro
4 wedges fresh lemon
Directions:

1. Preheat oven to 350 degrees. Place salmon fillets in a large baking pan with about a 1/2 inch of water in the bottom. Cover the pan with foil and bake in the oven. Bake until fish is opaque and flakes easily with a fork, about 20 minutes.
2. Make the salsa by combining chopped tomatoes, onion, pepper, pepper sauce, and cilantro in a small mixing bowl.
3. Serve the salmon fillets with a side of salsa and a wedge of fresh lemon.

Serves 4. Each serving (1 fish fillet plus 1/2 cup salsa): 186 calories, 7.5 g fat, 1 g saturated fat, 62 mg cholesterol, 65 mg sodium, 5 g carbohydrate, 1.5 g fiber, 12 g protein.

Sardine Spread

Lowfat whole grain crackers
Spread:
2 cans sardines without salt, drained and mashed
juice of 2 lemons
1/2 tsp hot pepper sauce
1/2 cup no-added-salt ketchup
Directions:

1. Mix ingredients for spread in a small bowl. Serve on whole grain crackers (we recommend 100% whole grain, lowfat crackers like WASA).

Serves 2. Each 1/4 cup serving: 107 calories, 5 g fat, 1 g saturated fat, 25 mg cholesterol, 192 mg sodium, 7 g carbohydrate, 0 g fiber, 7 g protein.

Tuna Salad on
Whole Grain Bread

1 can albacore tuna (low sodium if possible)
1/4 cup nonfat or lowfat mayonnaise
1/2 cup chopped cucumber
1/4 cup chopped red onion
1/4 cup chopped celery
Pinch of dried oregano
2 slices 100% whole wheat bread, toasted
1/2 cup ready-to-serve lettuce
1 sliced tomato
Directions:

1. Mix tuna with mayonnaise, cucumber, onion, celery and oregano in a medium mixing bowl. Spread over whole wheat bread and top with lettuce and tomato.
2. Serve open-faced sandwiches immediately or wrap and refrigerate until ready to serve.

Serves 2. Each serving: 257 calories, 4 g fat, 1 g saturated fat, 46 mg cholesterol, 315 mg sodium, 5 g fiber, 26 g protein.

Lemon Baked Trout

1 pound of fresh or frozen/thawed trout fillets
2 lemons, halved
1 cup of thinly sliced onion
Black pepper to taste
Directions:

1. Preheat oven to 350 degrees. Place trout filets in a 9 by 12 inch baking pan. Sprinkle the juice of 1/2 a lemon over each fillet. Layer onions on top of each fish. Sprinkle black pepper over the top of each fillet.
2. Cover pan of trout with foil and bake until done, about 20-30 minutes. Fish is done when it is opaque and flakes easily with a fork.

Serves 4. Each serving: 172 calories, 6 g fat, 1.5 g saturated fat, 66 mg cholesterol, 40 mg sodium, 4 g carbohydrate, 0 g fiber, 24 g protein.

Fish Twice Per Week

Why should I eat fish twice per week?

The Dietary Guidelines for Americans advise people to eat a variety of seafood and sub in seafood for meat or poultry at several meals. The American Heart Association recommends that people eat at least 2 servings of baked or grilled fish each week in order to obtain a rich diet of omega-3 fatty acids found in high-fat fish like salmon and tuna. Plus, MyPlate calls for at least 8 ounces of seafood per week.

Omega 3 fatty acids, particularly those found in high-fat fish, have been found to lower blood pressure, improve blood lipids and insulin resistance, reduce the tendency of blood to clot, and reduce the risk of abnormal heart rhythms.

How much should I eat?

Eat 2-3 servings of fish per week. One serving of fish is about 3 ounces. Here are 3 ways you can measure a serving of fish:

- By eye - A 3-ounce fillet or steak is about the size of a deck of playing cards.
- 3/4 cup of flaked fish - Measure the fish loosely
- 1/2 a can - Most cans of tuna are around 6 ounces. If you use half the can, you will be using 3 ounces.

What kind of fish should I buy?

Fish that are high in omega-3 fatty acids include: mackerel, lake trout, herring, sardines, albacore tuna, and salmon.

What are easy ways to include fish in my diet?

- **Make tuna fish salad** using canned albacore tuna in water and lowfat mayonnaise. Serve it on whole grain bread or over salad.
- **Serve salmon** once a week for dinner. Replace chicken or steak with a salmon steak. Since you only need a 3 ounce serving, buying 9 ounces or a little over half a pound should serve 3 people. At average market prices, this can be as little as $1 each. Watch for store specials and stock up - thanks to its higher fat content, salmon freezes very well.
- **Make salmon salad** instead of tuna salad. For best nutritional value, purchase canned salmon with bones and no added salt - that way you will be getting extra calcium with no added sodium. Salmon salad is delicious when served over whole grain rye or wheat bread or on top of a big tossed salad.
- **Herring** can be mixed with nonfat sour cream and served over a bed of fresh lettuce.
- **Add sardines to dip**, salads, and seafood chowder.

Sardines are good sources of calcium and vitamin D, both of which are important for healthy bones.

- **Serve baked trout** once in a while for a nice treat. Watch for store specials and stock up. Serve baked trout with baked potatoes and fresh veggies.

How should I prepare my fish?

Grilling, baking or poaching are the most heart healthy methods of cooking fish because they do not add a lot of fat to the final product. Deep-frying adds a significant amount of trans-fatty acids and calories to a finished dish, so it should be avoided.

- **Grill** - Heat a barbecue grill or oven broiler to medium-high. Lightly brush the fish with oil, and grill on both sides until done. Fish is done when it's opaque and flakes easily when prodded with a fork.
- **Bake** - Preheat your oven to 350 degrees. Place fish fillets in a baking pan with a little water in the bottom. Cover with foil and bake until done.
- **Poaching** - Place a nonstick skillet over medium-high heat and add a few cups of water. Bring to a boil, then lower to a simmer. Add citrus, dill, or other seasonings. Simmer briefly, then add fish and cover pan. Keep heat to a simmer and cook until done. Do not let the water boil while the fish is in it.

How should I store my fish?

Fresh fish should be kept on ice or in your refrigerator. It usually stays fresh for about 3 days. If you are buying from a fish counter, ask the store personnel to let you smell it first - it should be fresh, succulent, and not at all fishy. If you want to keep fish longer than 3 days, you should freeze it, but do not refreeze fish that has already been frozen and thawed. The best way to thaw fish is in the refrigerator. You can also thaw it in the microwave using about 30% power.

Leader Guide: 5 Ingredient Meals

Title:
Fast & Healthy Meals with 5 Ingredients or Less

Target Audience:
This presentation kit is intended for general audiences age 14 and up. It covers topics of wellness, heart disease, diabetes, weight loss, and nutrition.

Lesson Objectives:
• Participants will learn how to make healthy meals that need only 5 ingredients (or even fewer!).
• Participants will learn how to stock their kitchen with the right ingredients so that they can throw healthy meals together quickly.

Lesson Rationale:
Health authorities have indicated that good nutrition is one of the most important factors in determining long-term health. Poor diet plays a major role in the development of four of the top seven killers in the United States: heart disease, cancer, stroke and diabetes. Consumers who have the skills to select and prepare nutritious foods can positively impact their present and future health.

Lesson at a Glance:
This lesson introduces participants to new recipes and teaches cooking skills. It also provides nutrition and diet information that is consistent with the Dietary Guidelines for Americans and MyPlate.

Lesson Materials:
This lesson contains:
• Leader and Activity Guide
• Leader and Activity Guide for Recipes
• 1 copy-ready recipe page, 1 copy-ready handout

Preparation:
____ Review leader guides
____ Review handouts
____ Select activities
____ Copy and collect materials for lesson

Activity Ideas:
Introduction:
Tell participants that the purpose of your class is to help them make healthier meals that use 5 (or fewer) ingredients. Supermarkets are full of combinations and items that really simplify this endeavor.

Activity 1 - Cooking Demo
Use one or more of the recipes in this lesson to show participants how to make easy, quick meals.

Activity 2 - What's in Your Pantry?
Use the handout "Secrets to a Fast & Healthy Kitchen" to outline how to properly stock kitchens for fast and healthy meals.
It would be wise to bring along some of the items on that sheet. Here is a list of our favorites:
• **Flavored tomatoes** - You can find diced, canned tomatoes that also have onions, peppers, garlic, and seasonings. The advantage of these is that you only need one in order to add a lot of ingredients and a flavor kick!
• **Healthy soups** - Watch sodium content here. A healthy soup contains less than 3 g and no more than 400 mg of sodium per serving. You can add more vegetables, beans, rice, and pasta to these in order to further lower the sodium content, make them more nutritious, and increase the number of possible servings.
• **Italian seasoning** - This spice blend typically features basil, oregano and marjoram. It tastes great in chili, soup, pasta, salads, etc.
• **Stir fry medley** - This one is a must have for making stir fry dishes. You can add fresh bean sprouts or mushrooms to spruce them up a bit. Season with light soy sauce and a little sesame oil.
• **Minced garlic** - Minced garlic is a true time saver. Use it to add nice flavor to many of your meals. You can even buy it pre-roasted!
• **Vegetarian burgers** - These burgers are already cooked, so all you have to do is heat them in the microwave for a minute or two.
• **Baking potatoes** -These aren't really prepared, but they do make a fast microwave meal.

For More Information:
www.foodandhealth.com - Check out our Best Quick and Easy Healthy Meals Kit. Go to Food Links and click on Recipes for a list of sites on the internet with even more healthy options.

Leader Guide: 5 Ingredient Meals

Chili Rice Pot

Makes 10 sample servings

1 cup instant brown rice
1 can diced no-salt-added tomatoes
1 can of pinto beans, drained and rinsed
1/2 cup water
1 tsp chili powder

Directions:

1. Place all ingredients into a 2 quart microwave container. Cover and microwave on high until rice is done, about 8-10 minutes. Stir well and serve hot.

Equipment:

____ Microwave
____ 2 quart microwave container
____ Kitchen spoon
____ Can opener
____ Measuring cups and spoons
____ Plate (for final presentation)

Shopping list:

____ 1 box instant brown rice
____ 1 can (15 oz) diced Mexican style tomatoes
____ 1 can (15 oz) pinto beans
____ Water
____ Garlic powder
____ Plates, forks, and napkins (for samples)
____ Plastic cups (for premeasured ingredients)

Cooking skill/nutrition lesson:

This recipe only contains 5 ingredients but it uses 3 groups from MyPlate: grains, protein, and veggies. (Remember, beans can count as either a protein food or a vegetable -- convenient, huh?). It features instant brown rice and can be made in one pot in the microwave.

Demo preparation:

1. Wash your hands before you handle food.
2. Measure all ingredients and open cans.
3. Organize your work area.

Garnish presentation tips:

Optional garnish: Top with nonfat sour cream.

Number of sample servings: Approximately 10

(Use a 1/2 cup portion for tastings).

Tuna Tomato Casserole

Makes 10 sample servings

2-1/2 cups water
2 cups dry macaroni
1 can low-sodium tuna in water, drained
1 can diced Italian tomatoes
1 cup light shredded cheddar cheese

Directions:

1. Boil water in a 2 quart microwave container. Add macaroni and cook until done (8-10 minutes).
2. Drain and rinse macaroni before putting it back in the 2-quart container. Stir in tuna, tomatoes and cheddar. Microwave until heated through, about 5 minutes.

Equipment:

____ Microwave
____ 2 quart microwave container
____ Kitchen spoon
____ Can opener
____ Colander
____ Measuring cups and spoons
____ Plate (for final presentation)

Shopping list:

____ Macaroni
____ 1 can tuna
____ 1 15-oz can of diced Italian-flavored tomatoes
____ 1 bag shredded cheddar cheese
____ Plates, forks, napkins (for samples)
____ Plastic cups (for premeasured ingredients)

Cooking skill/nutrition lesson:

This recipe only contains 5 ingredients but it uses 3 groups from MyPlate: grains, protein and veggies. By using a tuna fish, this recipe also brings people closer to getting their recommended 8 ounces of seafood per week, which brings it in line with MyPlate guidelines.

Demo preparation:

1. Wash your hands before you handle food.
2. Measure all ingredients and open cans.
3. Organize your work area.

Garnish presentation tips:

Place on a large plate and top with a bit more cheese.

Make ahead options:

Cook the macaroni ahead of time and assemble the whole dish in class.

Number of sample servings: Approximately 10

# Leader Guide: 5 Ingredient Meals

Chicken with Rice
Makes 10 sample servings

2 cups cooked chicken meat, skinless
1 cup white rice
2 cups chicken broth
1 cup frozen mixed vegetables
1 tsp Italian seasoning

Directions:
1. Place all ingredients in 2-quart microwave container. Cover and cook on medium power until rice is done, about 20-25 minutes. Stir occasionally. Serve hot.

Equipment:
____ Microwave
____ 2-quart microwave container
____ Kitchen spoon
____ Can opener
____ Measuring cups and spoons
____ Plate (for final presentation)

Shopping list:
____ Cooked chicken (we suggest buying a roasted chicken at your grocery store)
____ White rice
____ 1 large can chicken broth
____ 1 bag frozen mixed vegetables
____ Italian seasoning
____ Plates, forks, napkins (for samples)
____ Plastic cups (for premeasured ingredients)

Cooking skill/nutrition lesson:
This recipe only contains 5 ingredients but it uses 3 groups from MyPlate: grains, protein and veggies. Be sure to select low-sodium frozen vegetables and chicken broth, in accordance with USDA guidelines.

Demo preparation:
1. Wash your hands before you handle food.
2. Measure all ingredients, open cans.
3. Organize your work area.

Garnish presentation tips:
Serve Chicken and Rice in a large bowl or dinner plate. Top with freshly cracked black pepper.

Make ahead options:
You should buy and cut the chicken ahead of time. You can also make this recipe before class and simply reheat before serving.

Number of sample servings: Approximately 10

Pasta Primavera
Makes 10 sample servings

8 ounces dry spaghetti
1 jar of healthy pasta sauce (low sodium, low fat etc)
2 cups of frozen mixed vegetables
1 tsp oregano
2 Tbsp Parmesan cheese

Directions:
1. Cook spaghetti according to package directions. Drain in colander.
2. Heat sauce, frozen veggies, and oregano in a 2-quart pan and cook until done. Mix sauce with spaghetti and top with Parmesan cheese.

Equipment:
____ Pot (to cook spaghetti)
____ Stove
____ 2-quart pan for sauce
____ Kitchen spoon
____ Colander
____ Measuring cups and spoons
____ Plate (for final presentation)

Shopping list:
____ Spaghetti
____ Pasta sauce
____ 1 pound bag frozen mixed vegetables
____ Dried oregano
____ Grated Parmesan cheese
____ Plates, forks, napkins (for samples)
____ Plastic cups (for premeasured ingredients)

Cooking skill/nutrition lesson:
This recipe sets up the beginning of a healthy meal that follows MyPlate ratios and guidelines.

Demo preparation:
1. Wash your hands before you handle food.
2. Measure all ingredients.
3. Organize your work area. Start boiling your water.

Garnish presentation tips:
Place the spaghetti in the center of the plate. Top with grated Parmesan cheese.

Make ahead options:
You can cook the spaghetti ahead of time and assemble everything else, heating the spaghetti at the last minute.

Number of sample servings: Approximately 10

Leader Guide: 5 Ingredient Meals

Baked Potato Pizza
Makes 10 sample servings

4 medium Idaho potatoes
2 cups low sodium pasta sauce, heated
1 cup nonfat sour cream
4 cups mixed frozen veggies, steamed
1 cup lowfat shredded mozzarella

Directions:

1. Wash potatoes in cold water to remove dirt, then prick with a fork. Place potatoes in the microwave and bake on full power until done, about 5 minutes per potato. Turn them over once during cooking, and, if possible, keep them from touching.
2. Meanwhile, heat pasta sauce and steam veggies.
3. Split potatoes in half lengthwise and place on a dinner plate. Fluff with a fork, then fill each one with 1/2 cup heated pasta sauce, 1/4 cup nonfat sour cream and 1 cup steamed veggies. Top each with 1/4 cup of lowfat shredded mozzarella cheese. Serve hot.

Equipment:
____ Microwave
____ Stove
____ Pan (to heat pasta sauce)
____ Pan with steamer basket (to steam veggies)
____ Fork
____ Tablespoon
____ Kitchen spoon
____ Knife
____ Measuring cups and spoons
____ Plate (for final presentation)

Shopping list:
____ 4 medium Idaho potatoes
____ Pasta sauce
____ Nonfat sour cream
____ Mixed frozen veggies
____ Lowfat shredded mozzarella
____ Plates, forks, napkins (for samples)
____ Plastic cups (for premeasured ingredients)

Cooking skill/nutrition lesson:
This recipe only contains 5 ingredients but it uses groups from MyPlate: grains, protein and veggies. If you substitute plain, nonfat yogurt for the sour cream, you'll also include the dairy group.

Demo preparation:
1. Wash your hands before you handle food.
2. Measure all ingredients.
3. Organize your work area.
4. Place the pasta sauce in a pan on the stove and turn the heat to low.
5. Place a pan with water and a steamer basket on the stove and turn the heat to low. Cover the pan.

Garnish presentation tips:
Slice the potato in half lengthwise and use a fork to fluff it. Top with sauce and sour cream, then veggies. Sprinkle the cheese over the top of the potato, allowing it to fall around the plate too.

Make ahead options:
You can bake the potato ahead of time and assemble everything at the last minute.

Number of sample servings: Approximately 10

Leader Guide: 5 Ingredient Meals

Chicken Teriyaki Stir Fry

Makes 10 sample servings

1 pound bag of frozen stir fry vegetables
1 cup cooked chicken meat
4 Tbsp light soy sauce
1 Tbsp sesame oil
3 cups cooked hot brown rice

Directions:

1. Lightly spray a large, nonstick skillet with vegetable cooking spray and heat over medium high heat. Saute the vegetables until crisp tender and heated through, about 5 minutes. Season the vegetables with soy sauce and sesame oil and then add the chicken. Heat through.
2. Serve the vegetables over cooked, hot rice.

Equipment:

_____ Stove
_____ 12-inch, nonstick skillet
_____ Kitchen spoon
_____ Knife
_____ Measuring cups and spoons
_____ Plate (for final presentation)

Shopping list:

_____ 1 pound bag of frozen stir fry vegetables
_____ 1 cup cooked chicken meat (we recommend buying a roasted chicken from your grocery store)
_____ Light soy sauce
_____ Sesame oil
_____ Brown rice
_____ Water (for cooking rice)
_____ Plates, forks, napkins (for samples)
_____ Plastic cups (for premeasured ingredients)

Cooking skill/nutrition lesson:

This recipe only contains 5 ingredients but it uses 3 groups from MyPlate: grains, protein and veggies.

Demo preparation:

1. Wash your hands before you handle food.
2. Measure all ingredients and open cans.
3. Organize your work area.
4. Cook rice ahead of time
5. Pick and cut chicken. Remove skin, bones, and gristle, then cut into bite size pieces.

Garnish presentation tips:

Place the stir fry on a large dinner plate. Dot the top with sesame oil and a little soy sauce.

Make ahead options:

You can cook this recipe ahead of time and reheat for sample servings.

Number of sample servings: Approximately 10

Recipes: 5 Ingredient Meals

Chili Rice Pot

1 cup instant brown rice
1 can diced, Mexican style tomatoes
1 can pinto beans, drained and rinsed
1/2 cup water
1 tsp chili powder

Place all ingredients into a 2 quart microwave container. Cover and microwave on high until rice is done, about 8-10 minutes. Stir well and serve hot.

Serves 4. Each serving: 181 calories, 1 g fat, 0 g saturated fat, 0 mg cholesterol, 237 mg sodium, 37 g carbohydrate, 7 g fiber, 7.5 g protein.

Tuna Tomato Casserole

2-1/2 cups water
2 cups dry macaroni
1 can tuna in water (low sodium), drained
1 can diced Italian tomatoes
1 cup light shredded cheddar cheese

Directions:

1. Boil water in a 2 quart microwave container. Add macaroni and cook until done (8-10 minutes).
2. Drain and rinse macaroni before putting it back in the 2-quart container. Stir in tuna, tomatoes and cheddar. Microwave until heated through, about 5 minutes.

Serves 4. Each serving: 330 calories, 5.5 g fat, 3 g saturated fat, 32 mg cholesterol, 430 mg sodium, 42 g carbohydrate, 2 g fiber, 26 g protein.

Chicken with Rice

2 cups cooked chicken meat, skinless
1 cup white rice
2 cups chicken broth
1 cup frozen mixed vegetables
1 tsp Italian seasoning

Place all ingredients in a 2-quart microwave container. Cover and cook on medium power until rice is done, about 20-25 minutes. Stir occasionally. Serve hot.

Serves 4. Each serving: 318 calories, 3.5 g fat, 0.5 g saturated fat, 72 mg cholesterol, 190 mg sodium, 38 g carbohydrate, 2 g fiber, 28 g protein.

Pasta Primavera

8 ounces dry spaghetti
1 jar healthy pasta sauce
2 cups frozen mixed vegetables
1 tsp oregano
2 Tbsp Parmesan cheese

Directions:

1. Cook spaghetti according to package directions. Drain in colander.
2. Heat sauce, frozen veggies, and oregano in a 2-quart pan and cook until done. Mix sauce with spaghetti and top with Parmesan cheese.

Serves 4. Each 1-1/2 cup serving: 317 calories, 1.5 g fat, 0.5 g saturated fat, 2 mg cholesterol, 625 mg sodium, 62 g carbohydrate, 6 g fiber, 11 g protein.

Baked Potato Pizza

4 medium sized baking potatoes, washed
2 cups heated pasta sauce, low sodium
1 cup nonfat sour cream
4 cups steamed veggies
1 cup lowfat shredded mozzarella

Directions:

1. Wash potatoes in cold water to remove dirt, then prick with a fork. Place potatoes in the microwave and bake on full power until done, about 5 minutes per potato. Turn them over once during cooking, and, if possible, keep them from touching.
2. Meanwhile, heat pasta sauce and steam veggies.
3. Split potatoes in half lengthwise and place on a dinner plate. Fluff with a fork, then fill each one with 1/2 cup heated pasta sauce, 1/4 cup nonfat sour cream and 1 cup steamed veggies. Top each with 1/4 cup of lowfat shredded mozzarella cheese.

Serves 4. Each serving: 312 calories, 3.5 g fat, 2 g saturated fat, 10 mg cholesterol, 263 mg sodium, 43 g carbohydrate, 7 g fiber, 18 g protein.

Chicken Teriyaki Stir Fry

1 pound bag frozen stir fry vegetables
1 cup cooked chicken meat
4 Tbsp light soy sauce
1 Tbsp sesame oil
3 cups cooked brown rice

Directions:

1. Lightly spray a large, nonstick skillet with vegetable cooking spray and heat over medium high heat. Saute the vegetables until crisp tender and heated through, about 5 minutes. Season the vegetables with soy sauce and sesame oil and then add the chicken. Heat through.
2. Serve the vegetables over cooked, hot rice.

Serves 4. Each 2 cup serving: 306 calories, 6 g fat, 1 g saturated fat, 29 mg cholesterol, 540 mg sodium, 43 g carbohydrate, 4 g fiber, 20 g protein.

Secrets To A Fast & Healthy Kitchen

Do you want to spend less time in the kitchen? From most people, the answer is a resounding "yes." Spending less time in the kitchen doesn't mean having to sacrifice good nutrition and health. The secret to having more time and healthier meals is to shop smart and have the right ingredients on hand. Here is a list of our favorite strategies to save time and increase the nutritional value of your meals.

Pick canned goods that save time:
Your grocery store is filled with canned items that make cooking a healthy meal very easy. Canned goods can be high in sodium, so be sure to follow MyPlate's suggestion and read the label, choosing a low sodium option. Try to find items that contain 10-15% of your daily value for sodium. Some of our favorite time-saving items include...

• **Flavored tomatoes** - You can find diced, canned tomatoes that also have onions, peppers, garlic, and seasonings. The advantage of these is that you only need one in order to add a lot of ingredients and a flavor kick!

• **Beans** - Canned beans can save you a significant amount of time, especially since you won't have to soak and cook them! Be sure to rinse and drain them first, and read labels to find the brands that are lower in sodium.

• **Healthy soups** - Watch sodium content here. A healthy soup contains less than 3 g and no more than 400 mg of sodium per serving. You can add more vegetables, beans, rice, and pasta to these in order to further lower the sodium content, make them more nutritious, and increase the number of possible servings.

Buy seasonings mixes:
Seasoning mixes save a lot of time -- you can you add more than one herb or spice with just one scoop. Having premixed spices takes the guesswork out of seasoning your favorite recipe. Here is a list of our favorites:

• **Italian seasoning** - Usually composed of basil, oregano and marjoram, this seasoning tastes great in chili, soup, pasta, salads, etc.

• **Lemon pepper** - Find a variety that is salt free. This seasoning mix tastes great on poultry, fish, veggies, salads, and baked potatoes.

• **Cajun seasoning** - Again, try to find a variety that is salt-free. Try it on poultry, fish, or baked fries.

• **Garlic parsley** - This seasoning adds new life to

beans, rice, pasta, chicken, fish, and salads.

• **Chili powder** - This mix usually contains ground chili peppers, cumin, and garlic. Find one without salt and use it to spice up rice, chicken, and soups.

• **Apple pie spice** - Add this mix to baked apples, yogurt, fruit salad, apple sauce, and even coffee.

• **Pumpkin pie spice** - Use it to season winter squash, apples, pears, muffins, and other baked goods.

Find helpers in the freezer:
The grocery store freezer is loaded with different fruits and vegetables. Vegetable mixes like stir fry blends make meal assembly quick and easy. Keep them on hand for the end of the week, when your fresh produce supply is starting to get low. Frozen meals tend to be very high in sodium and fat, so read the label to be sure of what you are buying. We recommend...

• **Stir-fry Medley** - This one is a must-have for making stir fry dishes. You can add fresh bean sprouts or mushrooms to spruce them up a bit. Season with light soy sauce and a little sesame oil.

• **Festive medley** - usually this frozen mix contains kidney beans, which count as either a protein food or a veggie. Choose what you need to balance your plate like MyPlate.

• **Frozen chopped onions** - These totally save time.

• **Frozen mixed peppers** - usually a great way to add color to soups, chili mixes and pasta.

• **Lowfat french fries** - These are easy to bake and can be served with grilled chicken, fish, sandwiches, or veggie burgers.

• **Vegetarian burgers** - tThese burgers are already cooked, so all you have to do is heat them in the microwave for a minute or two.

Buy prepared produce:
The produce aisle is filled with prepared produce. Here is just a sampling of what you might find...

• **Stir Fry medley** - This has fresh veggies ready cut and already mixed for a stir fry.

• **Salad mixes** - You can find prewashed and mixed salad mixes - just pour, dress and serve.

• **Salad bar** - Here you can find items that are already washed and cut.

• **Baby carrots** - Eat these right out of the bag! They also make a nice garnish for simple meals.

• **Minced garlic** - Minced garlic is a true time saver. Use it to add nice flavor to many of your meals. You can even buy it pre-roasted!

• **Baking potatoes** - These aren't really prepared, but

Leader Guide: Flax

Title:
Flax Seeds

Target Audience:
This presentation kit is intended for general audiences age 14 and up. It covers topics of wellness, heart disease, diabetes, weight loss, and nutrition.

Lesson Objectives:
• Participants will learn the health benefits of flax.
• Participants will explore ways to use flax in their own kitchens.
• Participants will try some new recipes using flax so they are encouraged to try them at home.

Lesson Rationale:
Health authorities have indicated that good nutrition is one of the most important factors in determining long-term health. Poor diet plays a major role in the development of four of the top seven killers in the United States: heart disease, cancer, stroke and diabetes. Consumers who have the skills to select and prepare nutritious foods can positively impact their present and future health.

Lesson at a Glance:
This lesson introduces participants to new recipes and teaches cooking skills. It also provides nutrition and dietary information that is consistent with the Dietary Guidelines for Americans and MyPlate.

Lesson Materials:
This lesson contains:
• Leader and Activity Guide
• Leader and Activity Guide for Recipes
• 1 copy-ready recipe page, 1 copy-ready handout

Preparation:
____ Review leader guides
____ Review handouts
____ Select activities
____ Copy and collect materials for lesson

Activity Ideas:

Introduction:
Ask the people in your group to raise their hands if they have ever tried flax seeds. Encourage people who raised their hands to share stories of how they use flax.

Activity 1 - Cooking Demo
Use one (or more) of the recipes in this lesson to introduce participants to the delicious, nutty flavor of flax. You may want to consider making some items ahead of time and bringing them to class so participants can have a wider variety of foods to try. For example, you might want to make pancakes and muffins ahead of time and then show them how to grind flax and use it in a smoothie. That means pancakes, muffins, and smoothies for all!

Activity 2 - Grind Baby, Grind!
Show participants how to grind flax using a coffee grinder, blender, or food processor. (By the way, the coffee grinder works best).
Use the "Flax Facts" handout to explain the benefits and uses of flax.

Activity 3 - Just the Flax Ma'am
Show participants a few commercial foods made with flax. Some of our favorite examples can be found at natural food stores. They include:
-**Grain breads** made with flax
-**Whole grain cereals** made with flax
-**Toaster waffles** made with flax
-**Pancake mixes** that contain flax
We suggest bringing in samples of whole and milled flax seeds for participants to compare.

For More Information:
http://www.flaxcouncil.ca/ - Check out the Flax Council of Canada.
http://www.dakotaflax.com/ - The Dakota Flax Council has a great homepage too!
http://www.heintzmanfarms.com/default.htm - You'll find all kinds of flax facts at Heintzman Farms. The site even features pictures of how flax is harvested.
http://www.foodandhealth.com/cpecourses/omega3.shtml -- Here you'll learn about the omega-3s that flax seeds contain. You can also explore exactly why you should eat them.
http://www.goldenflax.com -- This site features flax facts, seeds for sale, and even starter kits.
www.flaxcouncil.ca/english/index.jsp?p=food2&mp=food - This link takes you right to an extensive list of commercial foods that are made with flax

Recipe Leader Guide: Flax

Strawberry Flax Smoothie

Makes 6 tasting samples

1 cup fresh or defrosted frozen sliced strawberries

1/2 cup nonfat light vanilla yogurt

1/2 cup skim milk

3 Tbsp ground flax seeds

1/2 tsp ground cinnamon

Directions:

1. Place all ingredients in a blender and blend on high speed until smooth. Pour into a glass with a straw and enjoy. Consume immediately, or refrigerate for up to 2 hours before serving.

Equipment:

____ Blender

____ Measuring cups and spoons

____ Tall, elegant glass (for final presentation)

____ Knife (to cut tops off strawberries)

Shopping List:

____ Fresh or frozen strawberries

____ Nonfat light vanilla yogurt

____ Skim milk

____ Flax seeds (ground)

____ Cinnamon

____ Cups and napkins (for samples)

____ Disposable cups (to hold premeasured ingredients)

Cooking/nutrition lesson:

This recipe outlines an easy way to consume more flax. The smoothie it presents is full of healthy, nutritious ingredients. The recipe also highlights one of MyPlate's favorite bits of advice by about choosing lowfat dairy options that are also light in sugar.

Demo preparation:

1. Wash your hands before you handle food.

2. Measure all ingredients. Cut the tops off the strawberries.

3. Organize work area.

Make ahead options:

1. Cut the strawberries ahead of time. If there are a lot of students in the group, you might want to make a few batches ahead of time.

Garnish/presentation tips:

Garnish the finished smoothie with a fresh, slitted strawberry on the edge of the glass.

Approximate number of sample servings: 6

Recipe Leader Guide: Flax

Banana Flax Loaf

Makes 20 tasting samples

Wet Ingredients:
4 ripe bananas
1/2 cup sugar
3/4 cup skim milk
1 tsp vanilla

Dry Ingredients:
2 cups all purpose flour
1/2 cup ground flax
1/3 cup oat bran
1/4 cup chopped pecans
2 tsp baking soda
1 tsp cinnamon

Directions:

1. Preheat oven to 350 degrees. Mash bananas and sugar in a medium mixing bowl using a fork or handbeaters. Add the milk and vanilla. Add the dry ingredients and mix smooth.
2. Lightly spray a 2 pound nonstick loaf pan with vegetable cooking oil spray. Pour batter into pan and bake until loaf is done - when it springs back to the touch and a toothpick inserted in the center comes out clean, about 45-50 minutes.

Equipment:

____ Mixing bowl
____ Fork or handbeaters (to mash bananas)
____ Kitchen spoon
____ Measuring cups and spoons
____ Oven
____ 2 pound loaf pan
____ Spatula
____ Knife (to cut loaf)
____ Cutting board
____ Disposable cups (to hold premeasured ingredients)
____ Platter (for final presentation)

Shopping List:

____ 4 bananas
____ Sugar
____ Skim milk
____ Vanilla
____ All purpose flour
____ Ground flax
____ Oat bran
____ Chopped pecans
____ Baking soda
____ Cinnamon

Cooking/nutrition lesson:

This recipe shows participants how to make banana bread using flax seeds.

Demo preparation:

1. Wash your hands before you handle food.
2. Measure all ingredients.
3. Organize work area

Make ahead options:

Bake a few loaves ahead of time and allow participants to taste sample.

Garnish/presentation tips:

Cut the loaf in thin slices and arrange them on an attractive platter. Place additional ground flax in a bowl beside the platter.

Approximate number of sample servings: 20

Recipe Leader Guide: Flax

Blueberry Flax Pancakes
Makes 24 tasting samples
1 cup whole wheat flour
1/2 cup all purpose flour
1/2 cup oatmeal
1/4 cup ground flax seeds
2 tsp baking powder
1/4 tsp baking soda
1/2 tsp ground cinnamon
2 cups skim milk
1 cup fresh or frozen blueberries
Garnish: Powdered sugar and low-cal syrup
Directions:
1. Combine dry ingredients in a large mixing bowl. Add milk and stir until smooth. Fold blueberries in by hand (gently!).
2. Lightly spray a large 12" nonstick pan with cooking oil spray. Heat pan over medium-high heat. Spoon 1/4 cup of pancake batter in the pan for each pancake. Cook until the batter bubbles, then flip the pancake over with a spatula. Cook until golden brown and firm in the center. Serve with powdered sugar and low-cal syrup.

Equipment:
_____ Mixing bowl
_____ Kitchen spoon
_____ Measuring cups and spoons
_____ Stove
_____ Nonstick skillet
_____ Plastic spatula
_____ Large plate (for final presentation)
_____ Sieve or shaker (for powdered sugar)

Shopping list:
_____ Whole wheat flour
_____ All purpose flour
_____ Oatmeal
_____ Flax seeds (ground)
_____ Baking powder
_____ Baking soda
_____ Cinnamon
_____ Skim milk
_____ Fresh or frozen blueberries
_____ Reduced calorie syrup
_____ Powdered sugar
_____ Disposable cups (to hold premeasured ingredients)
_____ Plates, forks, and napkins (for samples)

Cooking/nutrition lesson:
This recipe introduces flax pancakes to the audience. They can replace 1-2 tablespoons for every cup of flour in their own recipes. Plus, these pancakes feature whole grains in addition to processed grains, which brings participants one step closer to fulfilling MyPlate's call for half of all grains consumed to be whole grains.

Demo preparation:
1. Wash your hands before you handle food.
2. Measure all ingredients.
3. We suggest you make most pancakes ahead of time and just show participants how to mix the batter and make a few pancakes.
4. Have stove heating on low as participants are coming into the room.

Make ahead options:
We strongly suggest making a batch of pancakes ahead of time and just demonstrating how to make 4 in a skillet. You could also ask for a volunteer to come up and watch them cook while you demo another recipe or go on to explain how to use flax and its benefits.

Garnish/presentation tips:
Place pancakes on a large plate. Dust with powdered sugar and drizzle with low-calorie syrup.

Approximate number of tastes: 24 - use a half pancake per person.

Recipe Leader Guide: Flax

Chocolate Chip Cookies

Makes about 18 tasting samples

1 stick trans-free margarine
1/3 cup brown sugar
1/3 cup granulated sugar
1 egg white
1 tsp vanilla extract
1 cup all purpose flour
1/2 cup oatmeal
1/2 cup ground flaxseeds
1 tsp apple pie spice
1 cup mini chocolate chips

Directions:

1. Cream margarine and sugar together in a large mixing bowl. Add egg white and mix until smooth.
2. Add the rest of the ingredients. Scrape the bowl and mix until the cookie dough forms a ball.
3. Preheat oven to 350 degrees. Scoop cookies using small #30 scoop or tablespoon onto nonstick cookie tray. Bake in the oven until done, around 10 minutes. Remove from pan and allow to cool at room temperature. Store in bags or sealed container.

Equipment:

____ Oven
____ Cookie pans
____ #30 cookie/ice cream scoop (or tablespoon)
____ Measuring cups and spoons
____ Hand beaters or commercial mixer
____ Rubber spatula
____ Spatula (to remove cookies from pan)
____ Platter (for final presentation)

Shopping list:

____ Promise margarine (stick)
____ Brown sugar
____ Granulated sugar
____ 1 egg white or nonfat egg substitute
____ Vanilla extract
____ All purpose flour
____ Oatmeal
____ Ground flaxseeds
____ Apple pie spice
____ Mini chocolate chip morsels
____ Disposable cups (to hold premeasured ingredients)
____ Napkins (for samples)

Cooking/nutrition lesson:

Participants will see a classic cookie recipe made a little healthier. We use trans-fat free margarine instead of butter and we use less sugar. Plus, this recipe adds oatmeal and flax seeds.

Demo preparation:

1. Wash your hands before you handle food.
2. Measure all ingredients.
3. Organize work station

Make ahead options:

Make cookies ahead of time and just show the audience how to mix and scoop the dough.

Garnish/presentation tips:

Assemble the cookies on an attractive platter.

Sample servings: approximately 18 (1 cookie per person).

Flax Recipes

Banana Flax Loaf

Wet Ingredients:

4 ripe bananas

1/2 cup sugar

3/4 cup skim milk

1 tsp vanilla

Dry Ingredients:

2 cups all purpose flour

1/2 cup ground flax

1/3 cup oat bran

1/4 cup chopped pecans

2 tsp baking soda

1 tsp cinnamon

Directions:

1. Preheat oven to 350 degrees. Mash bananas and sugar in a medium mixing bowl using a fork or handbeaters. Add the milk and vanilla. Add the dry ingredients and mix smooth.

2. Lightly spray a 2 pound nonstick loaf pan with vegetable cooking oil spray. Pour batter into pan and bake until loaf is done - when it springs back to the touch and a toothpick inserted in the center comes out clean, about 45-50 minutes.

Serves 10. Each slice: 196 calories, 4.5 g fat, 0.5 g saturated fat, 0 mg cholesterol, 266 mg sodium, 35 g carbohydrate, 3.5 g fiber, 5 g protein.

Blueberry Flax Pancakes

1 cup whole wheat flour

1/2 cup all purpose flour

1/2 cup oatmeal

1/4 cup ground flax seeds

2 tsp baking powder

1/4 tsp baking soda

1/2 tsp ground cinnamon

2 cups skim milk

1 cup fresh or frozen blueberries

Garnish: Powdered sugar and low-cal syrup

Directions:

1. Combine dry ingredients in a large mixing bowl. Add milk and stir until smooth. Fold blueberries in by hand (gently!).

2. Lightly spray a large 12" nonstick pan with cooking oil spray. Heat pan over medium-high heat. Spoon 1/4 cup of pancake batter in the pan for each pancake. Cook until the batter bubbles, then flip the pancake over with a spatula. Cook until golden brown and firm in the center. Serve with powdered sugar and low-cal syrup.

Serves 6. Each serving (2 pancakes): 203 calories, 3 g fat, 0.5 g saturated fat, 1 mg cholesterol, 221 mg sodium, 38 g carbohydrate, 5 g fiber, 9 g protein.

Chocolate Chip Cookies

1 stick trans-free margarine

1/3 cup brown sugar

1/3 cup granulated sugar

1 egg white

1 tsp vanilla extract

1 cup all purpose flour

1/2 cup oatmeal

1/2 cup ground flaxseeds

1 tsp apple pie spice

1 cup mini chocolate chips

Directions:

1. Cream margarine and sugar together in a large mixing bowl. Add egg white and mix until smooth.

2. Add the rest of the ingredients. Scrape the bowl and mix until the cookie dough forms a ball.

3. Preheat oven to 350 degrees. Scoop cookies using small #30 scoop or tablespoon onto nonstick cookie tray. Bake in the oven until done, around 10 minutes. Remove from pan and allow to cool at room temperature. Store in bags or sealed container.

Makes 18 cookies. Each cookie: 167 calories, 9 g fat, 2.5 g saturated fat, 0 mg cholesterol, 66 mg sodium, 20 g carbohydrate, 1.5 g fiber, 2 g protein.

Strawberry Flax Smoothie

1 cup fresh or defrosted frozen sliced strawberries

1/2 cup nonfat light vanilla yogurt

1/2 cup skim milk

3 Tbsp ground flax seeds

1/2 tsp ground cinnamon

Directions:

1. Place all ingredients in blender and blend on high speed until smooth. Pour into glass with straw and enjoy. Consume immediately or refrigerate up to 2 hours before serving.

Serves 2. Each 1 cup serving: 145 calories, 5 g fat, 0.5 g saturated fat, 3 mg cholesterol, 66 mg sodium, 18 mg carbohydrate, 4 g fiber, 7 g protein.

Flax Facts

What is flax?
L. usitatissimum, a.k.a commercial flax, is of two types - one is grown for its fiber and the other is grown for its oily seeds. Flax plants grow about four feet high and bear white or blue flowers that mature into pods that hold ten seeds each. It appears to have been cultivated since 3000 BC. Uses for flax seed in breads and other baked goods tripled in the 1990s.

Why is it good for me?
There are 3 main reasons why you should consider giving flax seed a try:

1. Omega 3 fatty acids
   Flax is the richest plant source of the alpha-linolenic acid (ALA), an omega 3 fatty acid. It is considered essential for human health.
   Here is a profile of the fatty acids found in flax:
   • 57% Omega 3 fatty acids
   • 18% Monounsaturated fatty acids
   • 16% Omega 6 fatty acids
   • 9% Saturated fatty acids

2. Lignans
   Flax is the richest source of plant lignans, a type of phytoestrogen similar to the isoflavones found in soy. Animal trials, lab research, and population studies strongly suggest that lignans may inhibit the growth of certain types of cancer, especially hormone-related types such as breast or prostate cancer, and perhaps even colon cancer.

3. Fiber
   Flaxseed is high in fiber (2.5 grams per tablespoon) with a 60:40 mix of both insoluble and soluble types. Soluble fiber lowers LDL cholesterol, while insoluble fiber aids digetsion.

Nutritional Content of Flaxseed
(1 tablespoon/8 grams of ground seed)

39 calories
2.7 g fat
1800 mg ALA (an Omega 3 fatty acid)
2.7 g carbohydrate
2.5 g fiber
1.5 g protein
41% fat, 28% fiber, 20% protein, 7% Moisture, 4% Ash
Source: USDA & Flax Council

How do I use flax?
Whole flaxseed is poorly digested, so you shoud generally grind it before trying it. This is easily accomplished by placing the seeds in a blender, coffee grinder, or food processor. Whole seeds store for 6-12 months at room temperature, but ground ones should be refrigerated and eaten within a couple weeks. We suggest that you buy a bag of flax seed at a natural food store, grind it up, freeze it, and keep it in a plastic bag for easy storage and use.

What do I make with flax?
Unlike pure flaxseed oil, ground flax seed is heat-stable and can be used in baking breads, muffins, and cookies. When you bake with it, use it to replace part of the flour OR some of the fat in most recipes.
Here is a guide for baking with flaxseeds:
- Ground flaxseed can replace up to 10-15% of the flour in a recipe. If a recipe calls for 1 cup of flour replace 1-2 tablespoons of the flour with ground flax seed.
- Ground flaxseed can also replace up to 50% of the butter, shortening, or oil in a recipe. Use a 3:1 ratio. For example, 3 tablespoons of ground flax seed can replace 1 tablespoon of oil. Browning occurs more rapidly when flaxseed replaces oil, so you may want to lower the oven temperature or reduce baking time. The end result will include a nutty flavor and golden color. This substitution works best in recipes with a dark color like bran muffins or carrot cake. You may also need to reduce the amount of flour slightly or increase the amount of liquid.

Cooking with Flaxseed
Whether used as a topping or in baked goods, flaxseed's agreeable nutty taste and texture is a welcome addition. Here are some delicious ideas:
• Sprinkle raw flaxseed on cereal, yogurt or fruit.
• Replace 10-15% of the flour in muffin, pancake or quick bread recipes with ground flax.
• Make a smoothie with skim milk, yogurt, fruit, and ground flax!
• Put some flax in your next batch of chocolate chip cookies or brownies for. Remember to replace part of the flour with the flax - we recommend 10%.
• Add ground flax to your next batch of rice pilaf. It enhances the flavor of brown rice and goes great with a vegetable stir fry.

Leader Guide: Folate

Title:
Folate

Target Audience:
This presentation kit is intended for general audiences age 14 and up. It covers topics of pregnancy, wellness, heart disease, and nutrition.

Lesson Objectives:
- Participants will understand the importance of getting enough folate.
- Participants will learn which foods are good sources of folate.
- Participants will see and taste recipes that are rich in folate.

Lesson Rationale:
In 1992, the U.S. Public Health Service recommended that women of child-bearing age increase consumption of the vitamin folic acid to reduce spina bifida and anencephaly (neural tube defects) cases. Since then, national efforts have been implemented to increase the use of dietary supplements containing folic acid. In 1996, the U.S. Food and Drug Administration mandated that all enriched cereal grain products be fortified with folic acid. If all women of childbearing age followed the PHS recommendation of daily folic acid consumption, the number of pregnancies affected by NTD would be reduced by half.

Of several substances in the blood that are now thought to predict odds for vascular disease, the amino acid, homocysteine, is the one for which the case is strongest. Homocysteine levels can be lowered by taking folic acid. In a 1995 review of work exploring the relationships among homocysteine levels, folic acid and blood vessel disease (JAMA, vol. 274, pp.1049-1057), University of Washington researchers proposed that increasing folic acid intake might prevent as many as 50,000 heart attack deaths a year.

Lesson at a Glance:
This lesson introduces participants to new recipes and teaches cooking skills. It also provides nutrition and dietary information that is consistent with the Dietary Guidelines for Americans and MyPlate.

Lesson Materials:
This lesson contains:
- Leader and Activity Guide
- Leader and Activity Guide for Recipes
- 1 copy-ready recipe page, 1 copy-ready handout

Preparation:
____ Review leader guides
____ Review handouts
____ Select activities
____ Copy and collect materials for lesson

Activity Ideas:
Introduction:
Ask your class if they are getting enough folate. Chances are most people will not know whether they are or not. Ask if they know how much they are supposed to get, and whether they know how to read a food label to determine if a food is a good source of folate.

Activity 1 - Cooking Demo
Use one or more of the recipes in this lesson to introduce participants to foods that are rich in folate. You may want to consider making some items ahead of time and bringing them to class so participants can have a wider variety of items to try.

Activity 2 - Folate for Everyone!
Bring in packages and samples of foods that are high in folate. Put stickers on the bottom (or create a master list) to show how much folate is in each item. Throw in some samples of foods that do not contain significant amounts of folate. Ask participants to make a meal or dish that is high in folate using the food samples. Whoever makes a meal with the most folate wins. (Note, meal must be tasty). Highlight a few combinations of foods can help them meet their daily requirements.

Activity 3 - Folate Display
Set up milk crates containing folate rich foods from each MyPlate food group. Use food models, produce, and food packages.

For More Information:
www.foodandhealth.com - Check out folate rich recipes and articles (no, the articles don't have actual folate... just fantastic folate facts!).

http://ods.od.nih.gov/factsheets/Folate/ - Read up on sources of folate, recommended daily amounts of folate, and folate deficiencies.

http://www.womenshealth.gov/publications/our-publications/fact-sheet/folic-acid.cfm - This fact sheet is full of information about folate.

Leader Guide: High-Folate Recipes

Spinach Salad
Makes 12 sample servings

1/4 cup chopped walnuts
2 cups cooked kidney beans, drained and rinsed
6 cups ready-to-eat spinach leaves
1 Tbsp olive oil
1 Tbsp flavored vinegar
Juice of one lemon
1/8 cup sliced red onion
2 Tbsp crumbled feta cheese
Fresh ground black pepper

Directions:
1. Combine all ingredients in a large mixing bowl. Serve immediately.

Equipment:
____ Knife and cutting board
____ Can opener
____ Large mixing bowl
____ 2 spoons to toss and serve salad
____ Plate for presentation
____ Measuring cups and spoons

Shopping list
____ Walnuts
____ Ready-to-serve spinach (1 bag)
____ 2 cans (15-ounces each) kidney beans
____ Olive oil
____ Flavored vinegar (balsamic, red wine, etc)
____ 1 lemon
____ Red onion
____ Feta cheese
____ Black pepper
____ Plates, napkins and forks (for samples)
____ Disposable cups (for premeasured ingredients)

Cooking/nutrition lesson:
This recipe uses spinach and walnuts, which are fantastic sources of folate from two separate MyPlate food groups.

Demo preparation:
1. Wash your hands before you handle food.
2. Measure and chop all ingredients.
3. Organize your work station.

Garnish/presentation tips:
Place the salad on a large plate. Top with fresh cracked black pepper.

Number of sample servings (1/2 cup): 12

Leader Guide: High-Folate Recipes

Macaroni with Lentils

Makes 14 sample servings

2 cups enriched macaroni, dry
1 cup lentils
1 jar healthy pasta sauce
1 cup frozen chopped spinach leaves
1 tsp dried oregano
1/4 cup Parmesan cheese

Directions:

1. Boil water in a large pot on the stove. Add lentils and boil for 10 minutes. Add the macaroni and cook until macaroni is tender, about 10 more minutes. Drain the lentils and macaroni in a colander.

2. Put the same pot back on the stove and add the pasta sauce, spinach and oregano. Bring to a boil, then add the lentils and macaroni. Serve hot, topping each portion with 2 tablespoons of Parmesan cheese.

Equipment:

____ 3 quart pot
____ Stove
____ Colander
____ Measuring cups and spoons
____ Kitchen spoon
____ Plate (for final presentation)

Shopping list:

____ 1 pound box macaroni
____ 1 bag lentils
____ 1 jar (26 oz) healthy pasta sauce
____ 1 bag frozen chopped spinach leaves
____ 1 jar dried oregano
____ 1 can grated Parmesan cheese

Cooking/nutrition lesson:

This recipe uses 3 ingredients that are high in folate: lentils, spinach and enriched macaroni. It also shows the audience how to make a simple pasta meal in a single pot. It even features four MyPlate food groups.

Demo preparation:

1. Wash your hands before you handle food.
2. Measure all ingredients.
3. Organize work area.
4. Start boiling water and cooking lentils just before class arrives - that way all you have to do is add the pasta when you start your demo.

Make ahead options:

You can cook this recipe ahead of time and reheat it for class. Another option would be to cook the lentils and pasta ahead of time, then assemble and reheat for class.

Garnish/presentation tips:

Serve this dish on a large platter or bowl. Top with grated Parmesan and a sprinkle of dried oregano. We suggest pairing this recipe with one of the salads in this lesson.

Number of sample servings (1/2 cup each): 14

Leader Guide: High-Folate Recipes

Folate Up Smoothie
Makes 10 sample servings

1 cup orange juice
1/2 cup skim milk
1 banana
1/2 cup strawberries
2 Tbsp wheat germ

Directions:
1. Place all ingredients in a blender. Blend on high speed until smooth. Pour into a large glass and enjoy.

Equipment:
____ Blender
____ Tall glass (for final presentation)
____ Knife
____ Cutting board
____ Measuring cups and spoons

Shopping list:
____ 1 quart orange juice
____ 1 quart skim milk
____ 1 banana
____ 1 pint strawberries
____ 1 jar wheat germ
____ Cups and napkins (for samples)
____ Straw
____ Disposable cups (for premeasured ingredients)

Cooking/nutrition lesson:
This recipe features orange juice, bananas, strawberries and wheat germ, all of which are excellent sources of folate. Plus, it uses a small serving of lowfat dairy, a practice heartily endorsed by the USDA's MyPlate.

Demo preparation:
1. Wash your hands before you handle food.
2. Measure all ingredients.
3. Organize work area.

Garnish/presentation tips:
Pour smoothie into tall glass. Garnish with a sliced berry and add a straw.

Number of sample servings (1/4 cup): 10

Broccoli Walnut Salad
Makes 10 sample servings

2 cups steamed broccoli
1/4 cup walnut pieces
1/4 cup chopped red onion
1 Tbsp olive oil
2 Tbsp red wine vinegar

Directions:
1. Mix all ingredients in a medium mixing bowl. Refrigerate until ready to serve.

Equipment:
____ Medium salad bowl
____ 2 spoons (to toss and serve salad)
____ Knife
____ Cutting board
____ Microwave and container to steam broccoli
____ Measuring cups and spoons
____ Plate (for final presentation)

Shopping list:
____ 1 head broccoli
____ 1 bag walnut pieces
____ 1 red onion
____ 1 bottle olive oil
____ 1 bottle red wine vinegar

Cooking/nutrition lesson:
This recipe shows participants how to make a delicious salad using broccoli and walnuts, which are both rich sources of folate from two separate MyPlate food groups.

Demo preparation:
1. Wash your hands before you handle food.
2. Measure all ingredients.
3. Organize work area.
4. It is a good idea to steam broccoli ahead of time. Use a microwave or the stove.

Garnish presentation/tips:
Place salad on an attractive plate. Place small drops of vinegar around the plate. Finish with a little fresh cracked black pepper.

Number of sample servings (1/4 cup): 10

Peanut Banana Sandwiches
Makes 8 sample servings
4 slices whole wheat bread
4 Tbsp natural peanut butter
2 bananas, sliced in half lengthwise
4 Tbsp wheat germ
Directions:
1. Make 4 open-faced sandwiches using 1 tablespoon of peanut butter, 1/2 banana and 1 tablespoon of wheat germ per sandwich. Cut each sandwich in half. Eat immediately or cover and refrigerate for up to one hour until ready to serve.

Equipment:
____ Cutting board
____ Table knife
____ Larger knife (to cut sandwiches)
____ Tablespoons (to measure peanut butter and wheat germ)

Shopping list:
____ 1 loaf whole wheat bread
____ 1 jar natural peanut butter
____ 2 bananas
____ 1 jar wheat germ
____ Napkins (for samples)

Cooking/nutrition lesson:
This lesson outlines an easy snack made with four folate-rich ingredients. It also combines foods from three separate MyPlate food groups. Add a tossed salad and a glass of skim milk for a healthy, balanced MyPlate of your very own.

Demo preparation:
1. Wash your hands before you handle food.
2. Organize your work area

Garnish/presentation tips:
Cut sandwiches in attractive triangles and place on a pretty plate.

Number of sample servings (1/4 sandwich): 8

High-Folate Recipes

Spinach Salad

1/4 cup chopped walnut halves or pieces
2 cups cooked kidney beans, drained and rinsed
6 cups spinach leaves, ready-to-serve
1 Tbsp olive oil
1 Tbsp flavored vinegar
1 Tbsp lemon juice
1/8 cup sliced red onion
2 Tbsp crumbled feta cheese
fresh ground black pepper

Directions:

1. Combine all ingredients in a large mixing bowl. Serve immediately or refrigerate for up to 2 hours before serving.

Serves 4. Each serving: 218 calories, 10 g fat, 2 g saturated fat, 6 mg cholesterol, 136 mg sodium, 23 g carbohydrate, 10 g fiber, 11 g protein. 124 mcg or 31% daily value for folate.

Macaroni Lentil Casserole

2 cups macaroni, dry
1 cup lentils
1 jar healthy pasta sauce
1 cup frozen chopped spinach leaves
1 tsp dried oregano
1/4 cup Parmesan cheese

Directions:

1. Boil water in a large pot on the stove. Add lentils and boil for 10 minutes. Add the macaroni and cook until macaroni is tender, about 10 more minutes. Drain the lentils and macaroni in a colander.

2. Put the same pot back on the stove and add the pasta sauce, spinach and oregano. Bring to a boil, then add the lentils and macaroni. Serve hot, topping each portion with 2 tablespoons of Parmesan cheese.

Serves 5. Each 1-1/2 cup serving: 308 calories, 2 g fat, 1 g saturated fat, 4 mg cholesterol, 545 mg sodium, 57 g carbohydrate, 6 g fiber, 15 g protein. 177 mcg or 44% daily value for folate.

Folate Up Smoothie

1 cup orange juice
1/2 cup skim milk
1 banana
1/2 cup strawberries
2 Tbsp wheat germ

Directions:

1. Place all ingredients in a blender. Blend on high speed until smooth. Pour into 2 large glasses and enjoy.

Serves 2. Each 1 cup serving: 169 calories, 1.5 g fat, 0 g saturated fat, 1 mg cholesterol, 34 mg sodium, 35 g carbohydrate, 3.5 g fiber, 6 g protein. 83 mcg or 21% daily value for folate.

Broccoli Walnut Salad

2 cups steamed broccoli
1/4 cup chopped walnuts
1/4 cup chopped red onion
1 Tbsp olive oil
2 Tbsp red wine vinegar

Directions:

1. Mix all ingredients in a medium mixing bowl. Refrigerate until ready to serve.

Serves 4. Each 1/2 cup serving: 95 calories, 8 g fat, 1 g saturated fat, 0 mg cholesterol, 13 mg sodium, 5 g carbohydrate, 2 g fiber, 2 g protein. 40 mcg or 10% daily value for folate.

Peanut Banana Finger Sandwiches

4 slices whole wheat bread
4 Tbsp natural peanut butter
2 bananas, sliced in half lengthwise
4 Tbsp wheat germ

Directions:

1. Make 4 open-faced sandwiches using 1 tablespoon of peanut butter, 1/2 banana and 1 tablespoon of wheat germ per sandwich. Cut each sandwich in half. Eat immediately or cover and refrigerate for up to one hour until ready to serve.

Serves 4. Each serving (1 open faced sandwich or two halves): 286 calories, 11 g fat, 2 g saturated fat, 0 mg cholesterol, 295 mg sodium, 40 g carbohydrate, 6 g fiber, 8 g protein. 50 mch or 13% daily value for folate.

Folate Facts

Folate (folic acid, folacin) is a B vitamin that is crucial to the formation of DNA and RNA. A deficiency of folate can lead to megaloblastic anemia, which occurs when red blood cells become very large because they are unable to divide and form new cells.

What are the health benefits of folate?

- **Fewer birth defects**. Insufficient folate intake increases a woman's risk of giving birth to a child with a neural tube defect (NTD). All women of childbearing age should consume the recommended amount of folate every day. The damage that leads to NTDs often occurs before most women even know they are pregnant.
- **Healthy hearts**. Adequate folate intake lowers blood levels of homocysteine. High levels of homocysteine are associated with increased risk for coronary vascular disease.
- **Less risk for colon cancer**. In the Nurses' Health Study, women whose long-term folate intake was greater than 400 mcg a day had a significantly reduced risk of colon cancer.
- **Maintaining the brain**. Some studies have shown an association between poor folate status in the elderly and higher rates of depression and dementia, as well as poorer cognitive function.

What is my folate requirement?

1-3 years	150 mcg
4-8 years	200 mcg
9-13 years	300 mcg
14 years and older	400 mcg
Pregnancy	600 mcg
Lactation	500 mcg

Talk to your physician if you are taking anticonvulsants, methotrexate, triamterene, metformin or sulfasalazine, as these medications may increase your need for folate. Do not self-prescribe folic acid supplements!

There is little chance of toxicity from food folate, but taking 1000 mcg or more of folic acid can hide the symptoms of a vitamin B12 deficiency, which can lead to irreversible neurological damage. Anyone over age 50 is at risk for B12 deficiency.

How do I get enough folate?

- **Eat fortified grains**. Since 1998, enriched cereal grains in the U.S. have been fortified with folate. Each serving of fortified grain foods (such as bread, rolls, cereal, pasta, rice, flour) provides about 40 mcg of folate. Some breakfast cereals contain as much as 400 mcg folate. These fortified foods are now the largest source of folate in the American diet.
- **Eat heart-healthy foods that are naturally high in folate**. These include:
  - **Legumes** – Chick peas, black-eyed peas, pinto beans, lima beans, and peanuts
  - **Leafy greens** – Spinach, collard greens, turnip greens, and romaine lettuce
  - **Other vegetables** – Asparagus, broccoli, and green peas
  - **Fruit** – Orange juice, citrus fruits and juices, avocado, berries, and bananas
  - **Grain products** - Wheat germ, wheat bran, and whole grain wheat products
- **Read food labels**. The Daily Value (DV) for folate is 400 mcg. Packaged foods that contain at least 20% of the DV for folate can claim to be "high in folate" or "high in folic acid." The label can say the food is a "good source" of the vitamin if it contains 10-19% of the DV.

Add more folate in your diet:

- Start the day with fortified breakfast cereal topped with berries or bananas and drink a glass of orange juice.
- Use dark, leafy greens in salads.
- Add legumes to soups, salads, and casseroles.
- Use wheat germ or wheat bran when baking, or use them to top casseroles.
- Have a peanut butter sandwich on whole grain or enriched bread.

Did you know?

- Folate got its name from folium, the Latin word for leaf, because it was extracted from spinach leaves shortly after its discovery.
- Before 1980 it was difficult to measure the folate content of food. That means that nutrient charts printed prior to that date may be inaccurate.
- Folate is found in a variety of foods. Folic acid is a synthetic form of folate that is added to many vitamin and mineral supplements.

For further information:

http://ods.od.nih.gov/factsheets/Folate/ - Read up on sources of folate and recommended amounts of folate.
http://www.womenshealth.gov/publications/our-publications/fact-sheet/folic-acid.cfm - This fact sheet is full of even more information about folate.
By Cheryl Sullivan, MA, RD.

Leader Guide: Food Safety

Title:
Food Safety

Target Audience:
This lesson is intended for food and nutrition professionals who give food and cooking demonstrations. It is meant to be a "train the trainer" session. The handout "Keep Your Kitchen Safe" and activities in this lesson can also be used to teach the basics of food safety to consumers.

Lesson Objectives:
- Participants will learn the basics about food safety
- Participants will be advised of the challenges of working in a cooking demo-type kitchen
- Participants will be able to plan ahead and effectively keep food safe during all stages of a cooking/food demo. That means everything from planning/prepping to serving the sample servings

Lesson Rationale:
The Center for Disease Control estimates that foodborne diseases cause approximately 76 million illnesses, 323,000 hospitalizations, and over 5,000 deaths in the United States each year. Known pathogens account for an estimated 14 million illnesses, 60,000 hospitalizations, and 1,800 deaths. Three pathogens, Salmonella, Listeria, and Toxoplasma, are responsible for 1,500 deaths each year, more than 75% of those caused by known pathogens, while unknown agents account for the remaining 62 million illnesses, 265,000 hospitalizations, and 3,200 deaths. The Dietary Guidelines for Americans emphasize the need for food safety by everyone.

Lesson at a Glance:
This lesson provides food and nutrition professionals with information on food safety in a cooking demo environment. It also provides handouts that can be used for consumers.

Lesson Materials:
This lesson contains:
- Leader and Activity Guide
- 1 copy-ready handout

Preparation:
____ Review leader guides
____ Review handouts
____ Select activities
____ Copy and collect materials for lesson

Activity Ideas:
Introduction:
Read the statistics given on this page under Lesson Rationale.

Activity 1 - Keep Your Demo Kitchen Safe
Use the handout titled, "Food Safety Tips for Cooking Demos" to explain special considerations for keeping food safe during a cooking demonstration. Consider quizzing participants afterward. Here are some good questions that deal with what is explored in that handout:

1. Name three ways to keep food cold during a food demo.
   Answer: Bowls of ice, a cooler with ice, refrigerator
2. What are the two things you should do before handling food?
   Answer: Wash your hands and make sure all food contact areas are clean and sanitized.
3. How would you handle food or leftovers if they become contaminated?
   Answer: Discard them after the demo - do not serve them.
4. What do you need to take with you to ensure that you will have proper handwashing supplies?
   Answer: Soap, water, and paper towels.
5. How will you know if you have reheated food to the proper temperature or kept it at the proper temperature prior to cooking?
   Answer: Use a thermometer
6. What is the best thing to do to make sure you don't cross contaminate prepared ingredients with raw ingredients?
   Answer: Keep a separate set of utensils for both and wash your hands after handling raw ingredients.
7. How will you sanitize food contact surfaces and the demo area?
   Answer: Bring a portable spray bottle and put a solution of 1 quart of water and 1 tsp of bleach into it. Make sure it is properly marked.
8. If facilities are not adequate, what can you do to ensure that people get a safe food sample?
   Answer: Prepare the food under controlled conditions and transport/maintain it at the proper temperature. Use the demo facilities to demonstrate how to do the recipe.

It is a good idea to see if people in the audience have questions or situations to share for discussion.

Leader Guide: Food Safety

Activity 2 - Guest Speaker

If possible, invite a local health department official to come in and tell your audience some stories about foodborne illness outbreaks in your area. The official can then go over the basics of food safety and answer questions related to cooking demonstrations. Ask your guest to point out the most common violations found in kitchens.

Activity 3 - Handwashing 101

Industry experts agree that poor handwashing is the most common route for transmission of disease by food handlers in restaurants and food plants. They also agree that it is the most common cause of foodborne illness in home kitchens. Infections from E-coli, salmonella, and other bacteria are most commonly attributed to poor hand hygiene.

Demonstrate the proper way to wash hands:

1. Wash your hands under warm, running water.
2. Use liquid or pump soap and lather to the elbow.
3. Wash your hands vigorously for 10-20 seconds, paying special attention to fingernails cuticles.
4. Rinse hands thoroughly and dry with paper towels

Ask participants if they know WHEN you should wash your hands.

Wash your hands:

1. Before handling any food or food contact surfaces.
2. After eating, smoking, or using the toilet.
3. After touching any raw ingredients such as meat, fish, or poultry or anything else that will contaminate your hands.
4. After touching money, blowing your nose, coughing or sneezing.

For More Information:

http://fsrio.nal.usda.gov/nal_display/index.php?info_ce nter=1&tax_level=1&tax_subject=615 - USDA foood handling safety research and information.

http://www.fightbac.org - This campaign for food safety has information for media, consumers and professionals provided by the Partnership for Food Safety. Members represent all aspects of the food and consumer industry.

http://www.fsis.usda.gov/Food_Safety_Education/index .asp - Food Safety and Inspection Service - this page offers links for educators and consumers.

http://www.fsis.usda.gov/Food_Safety_Education/Ther

my/index.asp- This site provides information about Thermy, a loveable animated food thermometer who is trying to root out unsafe food practices.

http://www.cdc.gov/ncidod/eid/vol5no5/mead.htm - This page provides statistics related to foodborne illness.

http://www.foodsafety.gov/ - This website is a gold mine of government food safety information.

http://www.glogerm.com - Glo Germ™ is a product that contains safe ingredients formulated to be the same size as bacteria (basically 5 microns in size). When combined with ultra-violet light, it simulates the spread of germs, demonstrating how quickly and broadly germs can be spread in a short period of time. *"Home Food Safety. It's in Your Hands"* by the American Dietetic Association - call 800-877-1600 X 5000 for more information on this kit.

Food Safety Tips for Cooking Demos

Food safety is especially important during cooking demos. Usually, cooking demos are done under less than ideal conditions- no sink, very little space, no refrigerator, etc...

We have assembled these tips from a range of professional experiences and have compiled them here for your convenience.

- These **four rules of food safety** are often challenged in cooking demonstration conditions:
  1- Wash hands and food contact surfaces often.
  2- Separate: don't cross contaminate.
  3- Bring food to proper temperatures fast.
  4- Keep chilled items at the proper temperature (below 45 degrees!). Combine thermometer with a cooler stocked with plenty of ice if you don't have access to a refrigerator. If you are using a refrigerator, make sure you don't open the door too frequently, overload the refrigerator or leave the door open for any length of time.
- **Don't depend on the site to have adequate facilities and supplies** for handwashing, refrigeration and cooking unless you've checked it out.
- **Bring hand soap** and fingernail brushes so you and your helpers can wash your hands at the local faucet (or bring a water carrier with a spout). Dry your hands with paper towels.
- If you are using **volunteers** from the audience, make sure they wash their hands before helping you.
- Have **a separate set of implements for raw and ready-to-eat food**: cutting boards, bowls, forks, knives, etc... This is important whether or not you have running water. With separate implements, you won't cross contaminate cooked or cold ready-to-serve food with raw food. In a cooking demo, you are moving rapidly and working to keep your audience entertained. So even if you do have running water and adequate washing/sanitizing facilities, you might not have time to keep track of all this.
- **Emphasize to your helpers** that implements for raw and ready-to-eat foods, as well as the foods themselves, are to be kept separate. Do not serve any food that gets contaminated.
- **Bring plenty of paper towels** and a couple of big trash bags. One trash bag is for trash, the other is for dirty implements. Paper towels are important for wiping your hands and cleaning up. Cloth towels are not sanitary and should not be used.
- **Bring perishable foods to the site in a cooler** filled with an adequate amount of ice. Use a thermometer to ensure that internal temperature remains below 45 degrees F.
- Judging from conditions at your demo kitchen, **you may want to serve food that you prepared off-site** under more sanitary conditions and just demo enough to show how it is done.
- **Bowls of ice water** help you keep food cold during demos and tastings. Just float smaller bowls in the ice water that the larger ones contain.
- If you're slicing and dicing fruits, vegetables, etc, it is important to wash them well before the demo and then transfer them on site in plastic bags. **It is also efficient to bring prewashed and cut produce to** the demo in zipped plastic bags.
- **Hot plates** are good for keeping hot foods hot, IF you have electricity. Propane camping stoves or butane stoves are excellent alternatives when electricity isn't part of the plan. Did you know that you can rent them?
- **Bring a portable sanitizer** for counters. A pump spray bottled (labeled "bleach water") with 1 quart of water and 1 tsp of bleach works very well.
- **Bring clean, disposable cups, plates and/or serving utensils** for serving "tastes" of your goods.
- **Plan ahead for leftovers**, particularly during warm weather. Before giving any away, ask yourself: can the recipient take it home quickly, can they cool it and keep it cool, and will they reheat it?
- **Check out your site**. If at all possible, visit the site before your presentation and figure out exactly what you'll need for a safe and successful demonstration.

Food safety necessities:

_____ Handwashing: Soap, nail brush, paper towels

_____ Trash bags for trash and dirty implements

_____ Ice for keeping items on the counter cold and for the cooler

_____ Thermometers (liquids and meat)

_____ Disposable containers for tasting and premeasured ingredients

_____ Portable sanitizer for counters

_____ Hot plate to keep foods warm

_____ Separate utensils for raw and cooked foods

Keep Your Kitchen Safe

What Is Foodborne Illness?

Foodborne illness is caused by bacteria or other pathogens in food. It often presents with flu-like symptoms like nausea, vomiting, diarrhea, or fever. The Center for Disease Control estimates that foodborne diseases cause approximately 76 million illnesses, 325,000 hospitalizations, and 5,000 deaths in the United States each year. Most of these cases can be prevented with proper cooking or processing of food. Very young children, pregnant women, the elderly, and people with compromised immune systems are at greatest risk from any pathogen. Some people may become ill after ingesting only a few harmful bacteria, while others may remain symptom-free after ingesting thousands.

How Do You Prevent Foodborne Illness?
Don't contaminate the food.

- **Wash your hands** before preparing food and after using the bathroom. Wash them after you eat, cough, sneeze, or touch anything that could contaminate your hands.
- **Don't cross-contaminate prepared food with raw meat, poultry and seafood**. You wouldn't want to cut lettuce with the same knife and cutting board that were just used to cut raw chicken, for example. Or you wouldn't want to store raw chicken or meat above a chicken salad in the refrigerator, because they could drip juice into it.
- **Make sure all food contact surfaces are clean** and sanitized.
- **Keep food covered** so it does not become contaminated with foreign objects such as chards of glass, rust or other debris.

Keep an eye on temperature:

Bacteria counts in food, especially foods high in protein and moisture content such as eggs, meat and dairy products, can increase rapidly if food is left in the danger zone (40-140 degrees F) for any length of time. Follow these tips:

- **Do not leave food at room temperature for any length of time**. Keep it refrigerated or on ice as much as possible. Most food will not be safe if left out at room temperature for more than 2 hours. This time is cumulative and starts with handling and storing.
- **If you are cooling a cooked item**, do so quickly. Use an ice bath to cool large amounts of liquids like soup or use a shallow pan for leftovers. Refrigerate as soon as possible.

- **If you are defrosting an item, do so in the refrigerator**, under cold running water, or in the microwave. Do not leave items at room temperature to defrost.
- **Reheat leftovers quickly and thoroughly**. Bring liquids to a full boil. Bake or roast meat at adequate temperatures (above 350 degrees).
- **Cook meat, poultry, fish and eggs to the proper temperature**. Here is a guideline from the USDA:

Food	°F
- Ground Meat & Meat Mixtures	
Beef, Pork, Veal, Lamb	160
Turkey, Chicken	165
- Fresh Beef, Veal, Lamb	
Medium Rare	145
Medium	160
Well Done	170
- Poultry	
Chicken & Turkey, whole	180
Poultry breasts, roast	170
Poultry thighs, wings	180
Duck & Goose	180
Stuffing (cooked alone or in bird)	165
- Fresh Pork	
Medium	160
Well Done	170
- Ham	
Fresh (raw)	160
Pre-cooked (to reheat)	140
- Eggs & Egg Dishes	
Eggs	Cook until yolk & white are firm
Egg dishes	160
Leftovers & Casseroles	165
- Fish	
Fish	Cook until fish is opaque & flakes with fork

- **Use a thermometer to confirm temperatures.**
- **Maintain proper temperature in the refrigerator**. Don't pack it with too much food or leave the door open too long. Use a thermometer to measure the inside temperature - refrigerators should be below 40 degrees F while freezers should be at 0 degrees F.

Leader Guide: Fruits & Veggies

Title:
Fruits & Vegetables

Target Audience:
This presentation kit is intended for general audiences age 14 and up. It covers topics of wellness, aging, diabetes, heart disease, family health, limited income, WIC, cancer prevention, and nutrition.

Lesson Objectives:
• Participants will learn the importance of consuming enough fruits and vegetables.
• Participants will be able to identify different types of fruits and vegetables.
• Participants will learn how to modify favorite dishes and meals so they contain more fruits and vegetables.
• Participants will learn to prepare new recipes that feature fruits and vegetables.

Lesson Rationale:
Health authorities have indicated that good nutrition is one of the most important factors in determining long-term health. Poor diet plays a major role in the development of four of the top seven killers in the United States: heart disease, cancer, stroke and diabetes. Students who have the skills to select and prepare nutritious foods can positively impact their present and future health.

Lesson at a Glance:
This lesson introduces participants to new recipes and teaches cooking skills. It also provides nutrition and dietary information that is consistent with the Dietary Guidelines for Americans and MyPlate.

Lesson Materials:
This lesson contains:
• Leader and Activity Guide
• 3 pages of copy-ready handouts and recipes

Preparation:
___ Review leader guide
___ Review handouts
___ Select activities
___ Copy and collect materials for lesson

Activity Ideas:
Introduction
Ask participants to write down everything they ate yesterday. Then ask them to count how many fruits and vegetables they ate. Ask them to share their findings with the group. Congratulate everyone who made it to MyPlate's recomended daily servings. Here is a quick guide to cup servings:
-1 piece of fruit
-1 cup of 100% fruit juice
-1/2 cup dried fruit
-1 cup of cooked or raw vegetables
-2 cups of leafy greens like lettuce

Activity 1 – Cooking Demo
Use the recipes in this lesson to give your audience a cooking demonstration. Note that we used recipes to teach basic preparation of fruits and vegetables. For example, when we want to feature fruits, we show how to make a cooked fruit dish, a simple fruit cup, a smoothie and fruit sorbet. For vegetables, we show how to make a raw platter, steamed veggies, and a great tossed salad. If possible you should try to use all the recipes provided in this section.

Activity 2 - Taste Test Treats
Make a list of the fruits and vegetables you want your audience to try. This can be based on...
• What is in season at a local farmer's market or your grocery store (MyPlate strongly recommends this type of option, as seasonal fruit is especially delicious and typically more affordable).
• One type of fruit or vegetable in multiple preparations (examples include apples, berries, peppers, tomatoes or potatoes).
• A classification of fruit or vegetable (like cruciferous or tree fruit).
Whatever fruit you choose to feature, be sure to mention the following:
- The benefits of fruits and vegetables
(see http://www.fruitsandveggiesmorematters.org/ for facts and inspiration).
- Fiber and nutrient content of the featured foods.
- How to purchase, store and prepare everything.
Provide small sample servings of each item.
Encourage attendees to comment on appearance, texture, and flavor.
If you are comparing foods of the same type (i.e. different varieties of apples), you can have participants compare and score each item on appearance, texture,

Leader Guide: Fruits & Veggies

flavor, color, etc. Get a class composite score to see which item everyone liked the best. Award those individuals who came closest to that score with a fruit basket or small kitchen tool.

Activity 3 - Pick a Color, Any Color

Make participants aware of the importance of eating a variety of fruits and vegetables by picking a color and working together to name as the fruits and veggies of that color as possible. (Red is always good and includes a lot of items. Beets, red chard, tomatoes, red cabbage, apples, watermelon, strawberries, raspberries, radishes, rhubarb and red grapes are just a few examples). Repeate with multiple colors. You can also use MyPlate to highlight the importance of eating small servings of a wide range of foods.

Activity 4 - Seeking Serving Sizes

Show participants examples of a cup serving of fruits and vegetables:

-1 individual piece of fruit, such as a banana, orange, or apple.

-1 cup of cooked or canned vegetables like peas, carrots, beans or corn.

-1 cup of canned fruit, such as canned peaches or pears.

-2 cups of raw, leafy greens like spinach, cabbage, kale or lettuce.

-1 cup of 100% juice (fruit or vegetable).

-1/2 cup dried fruit, such as dates or raisins.

After you have outlined this information, present the following stories and see if your audience can guess the number of servings:

1) Susie made a large salad for dinner. It consisted of 2 cups of salad and 1 cup of chopped vegetables. How many cup servings did Susie eat? (*Answer: 2*).

2) Jack made himself a stir fried dinner. He used raw vegetables and cooked them until they filled just 1.5 cups. He served them over brown rice. How many cup servings of vegetables did Jack eat? (*Answer: 1.5*)

3) Michael made pasta sauce using 1 cup of pasta sauce and 1 cup of assorted vegetables. He served it over spaghetti and topped it with Parmesan cheese. How many cup servings of vegetables did he eat? (*Answer: 2*)

Make a large salad to demonstrate that a salad often contains more than one serving of vegetables.

Activity 5 - The Price is Oh So Right

Use the MyPlate on a Budget guide from the Cooking on a Budget Lesson in this kit to show participants that fruits and vegetables are really a bargain. Let them see that the more processed a food, the more they pay per ounce.

You may also want to let them see the difference in calories between fruit canned in heavy juice and fresh fruit or between dried fruit and fresh fruit. Bring in some samples of frozen vegetables that contain a fatty or cream sauce and let them see how the calories, fat and sodium really climb higher.

Activity 6 - Who Am I?

Give your audience hints about different fruits and vegetables using clues about their health benefits. See if they can guess which fruit or vegetable you are referring to.

Activity 7 - Fun wiht Fruit Baskets

Show participants how to make an attractive fruit basket. Here are some tips:

-Pick a nice round basket

-Put stronger, larger fruits on the bottom - bananas, apples, oranges, etc.

-Put lighter, more delicate fruits on the top.

-Use a variety of colors - yellow, orange, green, red and purple.

Activity 8 - MyPlate Rainbow

Get a copy of the MyPlate plate graphic and display it for the class. Then, pick a color and see if they can name foods in each food group that are that color. Or choose a different color for each food group (i.e. fruits red, veggies dark green, etc). Discuss the health benefits of eating a rainbow of fruits and veggies every day.

Further reading/info/links

www.foodandhealth.com - You'll find a ton of fun recipes and tips here, along with more information about fruits and veggies than you could fit in a week's worth of lessons. Click on *What's Cooking* and see a variety of topics using Farmer's Markets, Making A Rabbit out of fruit and making a tropical fruit platter.

http://www.fruitsandveggiesmorematters.org/ - Chock out this site for for all kinds of fruit and veggie information and resources.

http://www.choosemyplate.gov/ - Visit this webpage for information on serving sizes and suggested servings per day.

Recipe Leader Guide: Fruits

Fruit with Peach Sauce

Makes 4 sample servings

1 jar of peach baby food
1 green apple, cored and sliced
1 cup fresh berries or melon
1 orange, sectioned
Optional garnish: Fresh mint and orange zest
Directions:
1. Divide peach baby food between 2 tall stemmed glasses or dessert bowls. Divide fruit and place on top. Serve immediately or chill for up to 2 hours for later use.

Equipment:
_____ Cutting board
_____ Knife
_____ 2 stemmed glasses

Shopping list:
_____ 1 jar peach baby food
_____ 1 green apple
_____ 1 pint fresh berries or 1 melon
_____ 1 orange
_____ Fresh mint (for garnish)
_____ Cups, spoons and napkins (for samples)

Cooking skill/nutrition lesson:
This recipe shows participants how to make a creative fruit dessert using peach baby food for the sauce. Pureed peaches (baby food) are very similar to expensive European coulis sauces found in the nicest hotels. They add color to dessert and save time and money.

Demo preparation:
1. Wash your hands before you handle food.
2. Organize your work area.

Garnish/presentation tips:
(For a picture of the finished product, see the PowerPoint show Modify.ppt, slide#23).

To make the orange zest, use a vegetable peeler to peel off 2-inch sections of the thin orange skin on the outside of the orange. Be careful not to get the white pith underneath. Use a sharp knife to cut the zest into very thin strips. We also used fresh mint (sprigs and finely minced slices) for garnish.

You could also arrange this dessert on a plate. If you use this approach, arrange the fruit in an elegant fashion and drizzle peach puree over the whole thing.

Number of sample servings: 4

Peach Berry Crush

Makes 4 sample servings

14.5 ounce can of peaches in juice (not syrup!)
2 cups mixed berries
1/2 tsp dried ground ginger
Optional garnish: Fresh fruit and chopped, fresh mint
Directions:
1. Slice all the fruit into small pieces. Place in a large plastic bag, flatten, and freeze overnight.
2. Grind all ingredients together in a food processor. Serve immediately or put back in the freezer to harden until ready to serve (up to 1 hour) stirring occasionally. This frozen treat looks especially nice when served in a footed bowl.

Equipment:
_____ Food processor
_____ Knife
_____ Cutting board
_____ Can opener
_____ 2 stemmed glasses or footed bowl

Shopping list:
_____ 14.5 ounce can peaches in juice
_____ Mixed berries, fresh or frozen
_____ Ground ginger
_____ Disposable bag (for fruit)
_____ Fresh fruit and mint (for garnish)
_____ Cups, spoons and napkins (for samples)

Cooking skill/nutrition lesson:
This recipe outlines how to make a fruit sorbet using frozen fruit and a food processor. It combines several different fruits with varying nutritional profiles, which means that people will get a wider range of vitamins by consuming this variety.

Demo preparation:
1. Wash your hands before you handle food.
2. At least one day prior to demo you need to cut and freeze fruit.
3. Organize your work station.

Garnish/presentation tips:
Place fruit mix in an elegant glass or bowl. Garnish with fresh fruit and chopped mint.

Number of sample servings: 4

Recipe Leader Guide: Fruits

Deep Dish Apple Rhubarb Pie
Makes 2 sample servings

1 prepared pie crust

Filling:

4 large apples, peeled, cored, and sliced

1 cup chopped rhubarb, fresh or frozen

1 cup sugar or Splenda brand sweetener

1/4 cup flour

1 tsp apple pie spice

Optional garnish: Powdered sugar

Directions:

1. Combine filling ingredients in a medium mixing bowl and place in a 10 inch deep dish pie pan. Place one pie crust on top of the fruit. Cut 3 or 4 slits to allow the steam to escape, then bake at 375 degrees for about an hour.
2. Serve warm with a slice of pie crust atop the fruit. Promptly refrigerate any leftovers.

Equipment:
_____ Oven
_____ Cutting board
_____ Knife
_____ Measuring cups and spoons
_____ 10 inch diameter deep dish pie pan
_____ Pie server
_____ Plate (for final presentation)
_____ Sieve (for powdered sugar)

Shopping list:
_____ Prepared pie crust
_____ 4 baking apples
_____ 1 bag frozen rhubarb or 1 bunch fresh
_____ Sugar or Splenda (consider using half of each)
_____ All purpose flour
_____ Apple pie spice (cinnamon, ginger, nutmeg, cloves)
_____ Powdered sugar (for garnish)
_____ Disposable cups (for premeasured ingredients)
_____ Plates, forks, and napkins (for samples)

Cooking skill/nutrition lesson:
This recipe highlights how to make a healthy fruit dessert. It also demonstrates how to use only one pie crust, which cust down on the fat and calories in the dessert.

Demo preparation:
1. Wash your hands before you handle food.
2. We suggest that you make and bake one pie ahead of time. For class, show participants how to put a pie together and then take out the finished pie to see and sample.
3. Organize work area.

Make ahead options:
See above - we suggest you make one pie ahead of time and make a second pie in class.

Garnish/presentation tips:
Serve one slice of pie on a small dessert plate or in a bowl. Garnish with a dusting of powdered sugar. (For a clearer view, see the photo on slide number 45 in the PowerPoint presentation Modify.ppt).

Number of sample servings: 2

Recipe Leader Guide: Fruits

Frosty Fruit Smoothie

Makes 4 sample servings

1 frozen banana
1 cup frozen strawberries
1 cup orange juice

Directions:

1. Place all ingredients in a blender and puree on high speed.
2. Pour into a tall glass and serve immediately.

Equipment:

____ Blender
____ Glass (for final presentation)
____ Spoon

Shopping list:

____ Banana
____ Strawberries - fresh or frozen
____ Orange juice
____ Cups and napkins (for samples)

Cooking skill/nutrition lesson:

This recipe shows participants how to make a delicious smoothie using frozen fruit. It is a great way to use up fruit that is getting too ripe, since you just store it in the freezer until you're ready to make a smoothie. This recipe is also good for ice cream cravings!

Demo preparation:

1. Wash your hands before you handle food.
2. Cut and measure all ingredients. Make sure fruit is frozen. If you are in a hurry, cut it in pieces and spread it out on a tray so it will freeze faster.
3. Organize work area.

Garnish/presentation tips:

Pour smoothie into glass and serve with a straw. You can garnish the smoothie with a strawberry placed over the side of the glass.

Number of sample servings: 4

Microwave Cinnamon Apples

Makes 4 sample servings

2 apples, cored and sliced
1/2 tsp cinnamon
1/4 cup apple juice

Directions:

1. Place all ingredients in a microwaveable container. Cover and microwave on high until apples are very tender, about 5-6 minutes. Stir well and allow to stand for 5 minutes. Serve warm.

Note: You can also use berries, pears, peaches or plums in place of the apples. This also makes a nice sauce for frozen yogurt, waffles and frozen yogurt.

Equipment:

____ Microwave
____ Cutting board
____ Knife
____ Microwaveable container with cover
____ Spoon
____ Bowl (for final presentation)

Shopping list:

____ 2 apples
____ Cinnamon
____ Apple juice

Cooking skill/nutrition lesson:

This recipe shows participants a very simple way to make and enjoy a warm fruit dessert. This food is versatile and can also be used as a pancake or waffle topping.

Demo preparation:

1. Wash your hands before you handle food.
2. Measure and chop all ingredients.
3. Organize work area.

Garnish/presentation tips:

Place baked apples in dessert bowls and top with a little more ground cinnamon.

Number of sample servings: 4

Recipe Leader Guide: Vegetables

Tossed Salad

Makes 8 sample servings

4 cups dark green lettuce, ready to serve
1 tomato, cored and chopped
1 pepper, seeded and sliced
1 carrot, peeled and sliced
1 red onion
2 Tbsp flavored vinegar
1 Tbsp olive oil
1 tsp Italian seasoning
Fresh cracked black pepper
1 Tbsp Parmesan cheese
Directions:
1. Place all ingredients in large salad bowl and toss well. Serve immediately.

Equipment:

____ Large salad bowl
____ Utensils for tossing and serving salad
____ Measuring cups and spoons
____ Knife
____ Cutting board
____ Peeler
____ Plate (for final presentation)

Shopping list:

____ 1 bag or 1 head dark green lettuce
____ 1 tomato
____ 1 pepper
____ 1 carrot
____ 1 red onion
____ Flavored vinegar (balsamic, red wine, etc)
____ Olive oil
____ Italian seasoning
____ Black pepper (we suggest whole peppercorns in a mill but you can also use ground black pepper)
____ Grated Parmesan cheese
____ Plates, napkins and forks (for samples)

Cooking skill/nutrition lesson:

This lesson shows participants how to make an elegant tossed salad using a variety of vegetables. We encourage you to add seasonal/ethnic ingredients where applicable. This recipe also outlines how to reduce sodium by using oil and vinegar instead of a commercial salad dressing.

Now is the time to introduce your audience to a variety of flavored vinegars. You can also use a spray can of olive oil to teach them to use less oil.

Demo preparation:

1. Wash your hands before you handle food.
2. Peel, cut and measure all ingredients.
3. Organize work area.

Make ahead options:

You can prepare all ingredients ahead of time and transport them to your demonstration site.

Garnish/presentation tips:

This salad looks very nice if you serve it on a large plate or interesting platter. Try to pile it high. Garnish with fresh ground black pepper and a light dusting of grated Parmesan cheese. (For an especially beautiful salad, see slide 25 of the PowerPoint presentation modify.ppt).

Number of sample servings: 8

Recipe Leader Guide: Vegetables

Raw Vegetable Platter

Makes 16 sample servings

2 cups carrot sticks
2 cups celery sticks
1 cup cherry tomatoes
1 cup broccoli florets
1 cup cauliflower florets
1 cup radishes
1 cup hummus, bean dip or fat free Ranch dressing
Directions:
1. Peel and cut all vegetables. Arrange them on an attractive platter with a bowl of dip in the center.
2. Cover and refrigerate until ready to serve.

Equipment:

____ Cutting board
____ Knife
____ Vegetable peeler
____ Platter and bowl (for veggies and dip)

Shopping list:

____ Carrots
____ Celery
____ Cherry tomatoes
____ Broccoli
____ Cauliflower
____ Radishes
____ Hummus, bean dip or fat free Ranch dressing
(see the bean lesson for a great dip recipe).

Cooking skills/nutrition lesson:

This lesson shows participants how to make an attractive vegetable platter with a wide variety of vegetables. Variety is especially important when consuming vegetables, otherwise participants may not get all the vitamins and nutrients they should. People should eat veggies all of the MyPlate veggie groups (dark green, red and orange, starchy, beans and peas, and other) every day.

Demo preparation:

1. Wash your hands before you handle food.
2. Wash and peel veggies.
3. Organize work area.

Make ahead options:

You can make this platter ahead of time and just serve sample servings in class.

Garnish/presentation tips:

Add a variety of vegetables for more color - try using different colored peppers or tomatoes and add fresh herbs. You can also make a dip using fresh herbs and nonfat sour cream. (Add 1-2 Tbsp of fresh chopped herbs per cup of sour cream). Further, you can ask for volunteers to come up to help you peel and cut the vegetables. Or buy a party platter from the grocery store and spruce it up during class. Try to feature seasonal produce whenever possible.

Number of sample servings: 16

Recipe Leader Guide: Vegetables

Microwave Steamed Vegetables

Makes 4-8 sample servings

4 cups assorted raw or frozen veggies

1 lemon, cut in wedges

Directions:

1. Place vegetables in a large, covered, microwave container. Cover and microwave on high until vegetables are crisp tender.

2. Serve hot with a lemon wedge on the side.

For **corn on the cob**: Peel ears of corn and remove silk. Wrap each ear in plastic wrap and microwave until tender, about 3 minutes each.

For **broccoli**: Rinse broccoli in water. Microwave in covered container until tender, about 3 minutes per 2 cups.

For **winter squash**: Cut winter squash in half and remove seeds. Place in cut side down in a covered container and microwave on full power until tender, about 12-15 minutes for medium-sized squash such as spaghetti squash, acorn squash or butternut squash. Serve hot with reduced calorie syrup and a sprinkle of ground cinnamon.

For **sweet potatoes**: Wash and pierce sweet potato with a fork. Microwave sweet potato until tender, about 5-7 minutes per potato. Turn sweet potatoes over about halfway during cooking. Serve hot with reduced calorie syrup and ground cinnamon.

For **baked potatoes**: Wash and pierce potato with a fork. Microwave on high until potato is fork tender, about 4-6 minutes per potato. Turn potatoes over about halfway during cooking. Serve hot with nonfat sour cream.

Equipment:

____ Microwave

____ Microwave container

____ Cutting board

____ Knife

____ Fork

____ Vegetable peeler

____ Measuring cups

____ Plates (to show finished products)

Shopping list:

____ Assorted seasonal vegetables

____ Lemon

____ Plastic wrap (if using fresh corn)

____ Plates, forks and napkins (for samples)

____ Disposable cups (to hold premeasured ingredients)

Cooking skills/nutrition lesson:

Many people do not realize that they can easily steam vegetables in the microwave. This is an efficient way to cook vegetables and ensuring that they retain flavor and nutrients. This lesson will show how to cook and finish various vegetables in the microwave.

Demo preparation:

1. Wash your hands before you handle food.

2. Peel and cut all vegetables (you may want to reserve some of the interesting ones for class in order to demonstrate proper technique).

3. Organize work area.

Make ahead options:

You may want to precook items that require longer cooking times and just reheat them in class.

Number of sample servings: 4-8

4 cups of vegetables can serve 4 to 8 people. This is an excellent time to discuss the vegetable "quota" as described in MyPlate.

Fruit Recipes

Fruit with Peach Sauce

1 jar peach baby food
1 green apple, cored and sliced
1 cup fresh berries or melon
1 orange, sectioned
Directions:
1. Divide peach baby food between 2 tall, stemmed glasses or dessert bowls.
2. Divide fruit between bowls. Serve immediately or chill for later use, up to 2 hours.

Serves 2. Each 1 cup serving: 114 calories, 0.5 g fat, 0 g saturated fat, 0 mg cholesterol, 1 mg sodium, 28 g carbohydrate, 6 g fiber, 1.5 g protein.

Peach Berry Crush

1 can peaches in juice
2 cups mixed berries
1/2 tsp dried ground ginger
Directions:
1. Slice all the fruit into small pieces. Place in a large plastic bag, flatten, and freeze overnight.
2. Grind all ingredients together in a food processor. Serve immediately or put back in the freezer to harden until ready to serve (up to 1 hour) stirring occasionally.

Serves 3. Each 1/2 cup serving: 112 calories, 0 g fat, 0 mg saturated fat, 0 mg cholesterol, 21 mg sodium, 26 mg carbohydrate, 3 g fiber, 1.5 g protein.

Frosty Fruit Smoothie

1 frozen banana
1 cup frozen strawberries
1 cup orange juice
Directions:
1. Place all ingredients in a blender and puree on high speed.
2. Pour into a tall glass and serve immediately.

Serves 2. Each 1-1/4 cup serving: 131 calories, 1 g fat, 0 g saturated fat, 0 mg cholesterol, 2 mg sodium, 31 g carbohydrate, 3.5 g fiber, 2 g protein.

Deep Dish Apple Rhubarb Pie

1 prepared pie crust
Filling:
4 large apples, peeled, cored and sliced
1 cup chopped rhubarb, fresh or frozen
1 cup sugar or Splenda brand sweetener
1/4 cup flour
1 tsp apple pie spice
Directions:
1. Combine filling ingredients in a medium mixing bowl and place in a 10 inch deep dish pie pan. Place one pie crust on top of the fruit. Cut 3 or 4 slits to allow the steam to escape, then bake at 375 degrees for about an hour.
2. Serve warm with a slice of pie crust atop the fruit. Promptly refrigerate any leftovers.

Serves 10. Each 3/4 cup serving: 201 calories, 6 g fat, 2.5 g saturated fat, 4 mg cholesterol, 86 mg sodium, 38 g carbohydrate, 3 g fiber, 1 g protein.

Microwave Cinnamon Apples

2 apples, cored and sliced
1/2 tsp cinnamon
1/4 cup apple juice
Directions:
1. Place all ingredients in a microwaveable container. Cover and microwave on high until apples are very tender, about 5-6 minutes. Stir well and allow to stand for 5 minutes. Serve warm.

Note: You can also use berries, pears, peaches or plums in place of the apples. This also makes a nice sauce for frozen yogurt, waffles and frozen yogurt.

Serves 2. Each 3/4 cup serving: 95 calories, 0.5 g fat, 0 g saturated fat, 0 mg cholesterol, 25 mg sodium, 3.5 g fiber, 0 g protein.

Vegetable Recipes

Tossed Salad

4 cups dark green lettuce, ready to serve
1 tomato, cored and chopped
1 pepper, cored and sliced
1 carrot, peeled and sliced
1 red onion
2 Tbsp flavored vinegar
1 Tbsp olive oil
1 tsp Italian seasoning
fresh cracked black pepper
1 Tbsp Parmesan cheese
Directions:
1. Place all ingredients in large salad bowl and toss well. Serve immediately.

Serves 4. Each 1-3/4 cup serving: 80 calories, 4 g fat, 1 g saturated fat, 0 mg cholesterol, 39 mg sodium, 10 g carbohydrate, 3 g fiber, 2.5 g protein.

Raw Vegetable Platter

2 cups carrot sticks
2 cups celery sticks
1 cup cherry tomatoes
1 cup broccoli florets
1 cup cauliflower florets
1 cup radishes
1 cup hummus, bean dip or fat free Ranch dressing
Directions:
1. Peel and cut all vegetables. Arrange them on an attractive platter with a bowl of dip in the center.
2. Cover and refrigerate until ready to serve.

Serves 6. Each serving: 63 calories, 2 g fat, 0 g saturated fat, 0 mg cholesterol, 87 mg sodium, 9.5 g carbohydrate, 3 g fiber, 2 g protein.

Microwave Steamed Vegetables

4 cups assorted raw or frozen veggies
1 lemon, cut in wedges
Directions:
1. Place vegetables in a large, covered microwave container. Cover and microwave on high until vegetables are crisp tender.
2. Serve hot with a lemon wedge on the side.

Serves 4. Each 1 cup serving: 49 calories, 0 fat, 0 cholesterol, 45 mg sodium, 9 g carbohydrate, 3.5 g fiber. 1.5 g protein

For **corn on the cob**: Peel ears of corn and remove silk. Wrap each ear in plastic wrap and microwave until tender, about 3 minutes each.

For **broccoli**: Rinse broccoli in water. Microwave in covered container until tender, about 3 minutes per 2 cups.

For **winter squash**: Cut winter squash in half and remove seeds. Place in cut side down in a covered container and microwave on full power until tender, about 12-15 minutes for medium-sized squash such as spaghetti squash, acorn squash or butternut squash. Serve hot with reduced calorie syrup and a sprinkle of ground cinnamon.

For **sweet potatoes**: Wash and pierce sweet potato with a fork. Microwave sweet potato until tender, about 5-7 minutes per potato. Turn sweet potatoes over about halfway during cooking. Serve hot with reduced calorie syrup and ground cinnamon.

For **baked potatoes**: Wash and pierce potato with a fork. Microwave on high until potato is fork tender, about 4-6 minutes per potato. Turn potatoes over about halfway during cooking. Serve hot with nonfat sour cream.

Produce Power Match Up

Hippocrates once said, "Let food be thy medicine." In many cases, food can be exactly that. So many plant foods have disease-fighting and health-promoting capabilities. See if you can match up these fourteen definitions with the list of fruits and veggies. After you ace this puzzle, head on over to the produce section of the grocery store and plan your meals around seasonal favorites.

1. A large group of plant substances that may help to prevent cancer and heart disease.

2. Substances that latch grab free radicals and render them harmless. They're found in most fruits and vegetables.

3. Sometimes called a spud, this vegetable contains phenols and vitamin C, both of which act as antioxidants.

4. This bulb is related to the onion. It is used for its delicious flavor and contains allicin, which has been shown to lower cholesterol and blood pressure. It may even help prevent cancer.

5. This popular green vegetable looks like a tree and contains multiple cancer-fighting properties. It is also rich in phytochemicals, which appear to offer protection against certain cancers and heart disease.

6. These small fruits come in red, blue and purple. They all contain components which may help prevent cancer and heart disease.

7. Popeye's favorite - this leafy green vegetable contains lutein, a carotenoid that protects the eye.

8. Used to make red sauce for spaghetti, this vegetable contains lycopene. Lycopene is a phytochemical that may help prevent prostate cancer.

9. This vegetable will make you cry when you cut it. It contains allyl sulfides (phytochemicals) which help fight cancer.

10. This beverage is delicious hot or iced and contains antioxidants.

11. These tiny "cabbages" are in the cruciferous family and contain many phytochemicals.

12. This orange root, a favorite of Bugs Bunny, is colored by beta-carotene and makes a great snack.

13. This herb goes well on poultry, fish, and veggies and has a pine essence. It contains oils which may inhibit the growth of cancer and has antibacterial properties.

14. Used to make wine or eaten fresh as a snack, these fruits of the vine contain resveratrol, a phytochemical that may help prevent cancer.

_____ Onions

_____ Broccoli

_____ Potato

_____ Berries

_____ Spinach

_____ Garlic

_____ Rosemary

_____ Phytochemicals

_____ Tomatoes

_____ Tea

_____ Carrots

_____ Grapes

_____ Antioxidants

_____ Brussels sprouts

Answers: 1. phytochemicals, 2. antioxidants, 3. potato, 4. garlic, 5. broccoli, 6. berries, 7. spinach, 8. tomatoes, 9. onions, 10. tea, 11. Brussels sprouts, 12. carrots, 13. rosemary, 14. grapes. By Leslie Fink, MS, RD.

Easy Ideas for Fruit:

• Add salsa to fresh diced **peaches** for a quick and easy topping on fish, poultry or grilled vegetables.

• Freeze **bananas** and serve them with light chocolate syrup for a yummy dessert. Add a little fat free whipped cream and a few pecans and you have a gourmet dessert.

• Take advantage of store specials on **berries** and buy extra. Freeze them and blend them with skim milk for delicious smoothies. This is a great treat for a sweet tooth.

• Cut **watermelon** into stick shapes and freeze them on a tray. Place them in a plastic bag and keep in freezer. It tastes like a watermelon popsicle.

• Mix **fresh fruit** with cereal and yogurt for breakfast on the run.

Produce Guide

Item	Buying Tips	How to Store	How to Use
Apples	Heavy for size, no brown spots	Refrigerate in bag	Raw, in salads, baked
Bananas	Slightly under-ripe	Room temperature	Dessert, cereal, yogurt, fruit salad
Berries	Firm, ripe, no mold	Refrigerate in ventilated container	Dessert, cereal, yogurt, fruit salad
Broccoli	Bright green and firm	Refrigerate in ventilated bag	Steam, stir frys, pasta dishes, salads
Cabbage	Firm and unblemished	Refrigerate in bag	Slaws, stir frys, salads and soups
Cantaloupe	Feel heavy for size	Refrigerate	Breakfast through dessert
Carrots	Firm, crisp	Refrigerate	Eat raw, serve steamed, use in salads
Cherries	Plump, firm	Keep cool and moist	Eat them as is for snacks or dessert
Corn	Fresh small kernels	Refrigerate in the husk	Microwave, boil, grill
Cucumbers	Firm and bright green	Refrigerate	Salads, sandwiches, snacks
Grapefruit	Heavy for size	Refrigerate	Eat as is or in fruit salad
Green Beans	Firm and bright green	Refrigerate in bag	Steamed or microwaved
Honeydew	Heavy for size	Refrigerate	Breakfast, dessert
Lettuce	Unblemished, fresh leaves	Refrigerate	Salads
Nectarines	Ripe and slightly soft	Room temperature until ripe	Eat as a snack, use in salads or salsa
Okra	Short, moist pods	Refrigerate in plastic bag	Boil or saute and use as side dish
Oranges	Heavy for size	Refrigerate	Dessert, cereal, yogurt, fruit salad
Peaches	Ripe and slightly soft	Room temperature until ripe	Snack, on cereal, in salads or salsa
Pears	Heavy for size, no brown spots	Refrigerate in bag	Raw, salads, baked
Plums	Ripe and slightly soft	Refrigerate when ripe	Eat as is or bake and eat as a dessert
Potatoes	Firm, without eyes	Keep cool and dry	Baked, boiled, roasted
Summer Squash	Large and firm	Refrigerate in bag	Kabobs, pasta, steamed as side dish
Sweet Potatoes	Firm, no blemishes	Refrigerate	Bake, microwave, boil
Tomatoes	Plump, ripe, heavy	Store at room temperature	Salads, salsa, raw, grilled
Watermelon	Yellow belly, no cracks	Refrigerate	Eat as is, in beverages and salads

What is One Cup Serving?:
- 1 piece fruit like a banana, orange, or apple
- 1 cup cooked or canned vegetables such as peas, carrots, beans or corn
- 1 cup canned fruit, such as canned peaches or pears
- 2 cups raw leafy greens, like spinach, cabbage, kale or lettuce
- 1 cup of 100% juice (fruit or vegetable)
- 1/2 cup dried fruit, such as dates or raisins (about a handful)

Leader Guide: Grains

Title:

Grains

Target Audience:

This presentation kit is intended for general audiences age 14 and up. It covers topics of wellness, aging, diabetes, heart disease, family health, limited income, WIC, cancer prevention, and nutrition.

Lesson Objectives:

• Participants will learn the importance of consuming whole grains.

• Participants will understand where grains fit into their diet by using MyPlate.

• Participants will know what constitutes one serving of grains.

• Participants will learn new recipes that feature a variety of whole grains.

Lesson Rationale:

Health authorities have indicated that good nutrition is one of the most important factors in determining long-term health. Poor diet plays a major role in the development of four of the top seven killers in the United States: heart disease, cancer, stroke and diabetes. Students who have the skills to select and prepare nutritious foods can positively impact their present and future health.

Lesson at a Glance:

This lesson introduces participants to new recipes and teaches cooking skills. It also provides nutrition and dietary information that is consistent with the Dietary Guidelines for Americans and MyPlate.

Lesson Materials:

This lesson contains:

• Leader and Activity Guide

• 2 pages of copy-ready handouts and recipes

Preparation:

___ Review leader guide

___ Review handouts

___ Select activities

___ Copy and collect materials for lesson

Activity Ideas:

Introduction

Ask participants to write down everything they ate yesterday. Then ask them to count how many grains they ate. From there, ask each person to determine how many of those grains were whole grains. MyPlate states that at least half (or about 3 ounces) of grains should be whole grains each day. Here is a guide to a one ounce serving equivalent from MyPlate:

-1 slice of bread

-1/2 cup cooked cereal, rice, or pasta

-1 ounce ready-to-eat cereal

Activity 1 – Cooking Demo

Use the recipes in this lesson to give your audience a cooking demonstration. If possible, try to demonstrate a few recipes so participants can try a variety of grains.

Activity 2 - Whole Grain, No Pain Workshop

Allow participants to compare the flavor of whole grain pasta and regular pasta. Whole grain pasta has a nutty flavor and is more filling than regular pasta. Here are some success tips for preparing delicious whole grain pasta:

-Make sure you use plenty of boiling water to cook the pasta. If the water is not actually boiling, then the pasta will sit and get soggy before it is cooked.

-Do not overcook whole grain pasta. Your pasta should be al dente, which means that it still has a slight bite to it. Remember that the heat in the pasta will cause it to continue cooking, even after it is removed from the stove.

-For best results, rinse the whole grain pasta briefly with cold water in a colander after it is cooked.

-Reduce cooking time. Often whole grain pasta cooks faster than regular pasta. Check for doneness by tasting the pasta - often the package directions can be misleading.

-Serve the whole grain pasta in a thick, red sauce. If necessary, use tomato paste to thicken and sweeten it. If you add vegetables to the pasta, it may even hide the type of pasta from picky family members.

Activity 3 - To Serve Man... I Mean Pasta

Show participants examples of a single serving of grains, then present the following stories and see if they can guess the number of servings in each meal:

1) Johnny ate 1 cup of spaghetti topped with a 1/2 cup of pasta sauce for dinner. He also had 1 slice of garlic toast. How many servings of grains did Johnny eat?

Leader Guide: Grains

(Answer: 3)

2) Evelyn made a stir fry for dinner. She served 1 cup of brown rice and 2 cups of stir fried veggies. How many grain servings did Evelyn serve for each meal? *(Answer: 2)*

3) Mark ate 1 cup of cooked oatmeal for breakfast. How many grain servings did he eat? *(Answer: 2)*

4) Susan ate 1 cup or 1 ounce of bran cereal for breakfast. How many grain servings did she consume? *(Answer: 1)*

Demonstrate how easy it is to get the proper number of servings of grains per day by using food samples and models. Emphasize that what they many may think of as a single serving is actually several servings.

Another way to get this point across is to provide several visual samples of grains and have the audience guess how many servings you are showing them. For example, you can use..

• 2 cups of spaghetti - This is 4 servings
• 1 cup of rice - This is 2 servings
• A big bowl of cereal - This is often up to 3 servings!

Activity 4 - Compare

Use the MyPlate on a budget handout to show participants that grains that are less processed are also lower in price. They are also healthier.

Further reading/info/links

www.foodandhealth.com - Food and Health features a wide variety of grain recipes and preparation tips.

http://www.choosemyplate.gov/ - Check out MyPlate's website for personalized grain recommendations and information about whole and processed grains.

Leader Guide: Grain Recipes

Tomato-Basil Spaghetti
Makes 8 sample servings

Pasta:
8 ounces whole grain spaghetti, dry
Sauce:
2 cups pasta sauce
1 Tbsp tomato paste
1 Tbsp fresh chopped basil
1/2 cup sliced green onion
1 cup diced fresh tomatoes
4 Tbsp grated Parmesan cheese

Directions:
1. Cook pasta according to package directions. Drain and rinse in colander.
2. Place all ingredients for sauce in a 3 quart sauce pan. Bring to a boil then reduce heat to a simmer. Cook for 3 minutes.
3. Mix pasta with sauce, place on plates or bowls, top with Parmesan cheese and serve hot.

Equipment:
_____ Stove
_____ Large pot (to cook spaghetti)
_____ 3 quart sauce pan for sauce
_____ Colander
_____ Can opener
_____ Spaghetti rake
_____ Spoon
_____ Measuring cups and spoons
_____ Cutting board
_____ Knife
_____ Plate (for final presentation)

Shopping list:
_____ 2 jars of pasta sauce
_____ 6-ounce can tomato paste
_____ 1 bunch fresh basil
_____ 1 bunch green onions
_____ 2 ripe tomatoes
_____ 1 container grated Parmesan cheese
_____ Disposable cups (to hold premeasured ingredients)
_____ Plates, forks and napkins (for samples)

Cooking skill/nutrition lesson:
This recipe will teach participants how to prepare whole grain pasta. It shows them how to thicken pasta sauce with tomato sauce and how to add more vegetables and flavoring agents to it. A thicker pasta sauce will help mask the fact that you made the pasta dish with whole grains, which can help acceptance by family members.

Demo preparation:
1. Wash your hands before you handle food.
2. Place a pot of water on the stove and turn the heat to low before covering the pot.
3. Chop and measure all ingredients.
4. Organize work area.

Make ahead options:
You can cook the pasta ahead of time for this demo. If you choose to do this, be extra careful not to overcook it. Drain and rinse your pasta in cold water to prevent it from cooking more than you'd like. For class, make the sauce, then add the pasta and allow it to reheat in the sauce.

Garnish/presentation tips:
Place the pasta on a large decorative plate. It looks nice if you are able to twirl the spaghetti into a knot or ball on the plate - use a large fork or spaghetti rake to do this. Top the pasta with grated Parmesan and a sprig of basil.

Number of sample servings: 8 (1/2 cup each)

Leader Guide: Grain Recipes

Mushroom Barley Soup

Makes 15 tasting samples

1 Tbsp oil
1 onion, chopped
2 stalks celery, sliced thin
2 carrots, peeled and sliced thin
2 cups sliced mushrooms
1/2 cup quick-cooking barley
1 tsp garlic powder
1/2 tsp thyme
3 cups chicken broth
2 cups water
1 Tbsp chopped fresh parsley

Directions:

1. Heat oil in large soup pot over high heat. Saute onion, celery, carrots and mushrooms until golden, about 4 minutes.
2. Add the rest of the ingredients except for the parsley and bring to a boil. Lower heat to a simmer and cook until the barley is tender, about 20 minutes.
3. Sprinkle parsley on top of the soup and serve hot.

Equipment:

____ Stove
____ Large soup pot
____ Knife
____ Cutting board
____ Vegetable peeler
____ Can opener
____ Spoon
____ Ladle
____ Measuring cups
____ Bowl (for final presentation)

Shopping list:

____ Oil
____ 1 onion
____ 1 bunch celery
____ 1 bag carrots
____ 1 pint fresh mushrooms
____ 1 box quick-cooking barley
____ Garlic powder
____ Thyme
____ 3 cups chicken broth
____ Water
____ Fresh parsley

Cooking skill/nutrition lesson:

This recipe shows participants how to prepare barley soup using quick cooking barley. If you do not have quick cooking barley in your area, use pre-cooked barley and reduce water to 1 cup.

Demo preparation:

1. Wash your hands before you handle food.
2. Chop and measure all ingredients.
3. Heat stove prior to class if you are using electric.
4. Organize work area.

Make ahead options:

You can make this soup ahead of time and reheat for sample servings.

Garnish presentation tips:

Place soup in a large soup bowl. Top with a sprig of fresh parsley.

Number of sample servings: 15 (1/2 cup each)

Leader Guide: Grain Recipes

Chicken Rice Salad

Makes 18 sample servings

4 cups lettuce
2 cups cooked brown rice
2 cups skinless roasted chicken (preferably breast)
1 tomato, cored and diced
1 green pepper, cored and diced
1 Tbsp olive oil
Juice of 1 lemon
2 Tbsp flavored vinegar
Dash of hot pepper sauce
Italian herb mix (to taste)
black pepper to taste
Directions:
1. Toss all ingredients together in a large salad bowl. Adjust seasonings to taste and serve immediately.

Equipment:
____ Knife
____ Cutting board
____ Large salad bowl
____ Measuring cups and spoons
____ Plate (for final presentation)

Shopping list:
____ 1 bag ready-to-serve lettuce
____ Brown rice
____ Roasted chicken
____ Tomato
____ Green pepper
____ Olive oil
____ Lemon
____ Flavored vinegar (balsamic, red wine, etc)
____ Hot pepper sauce
____ Italian herb mix
____ black pepper
____ Disposable cups (for premeasured ingredients)
____ Plates, forks and napkins (for samples)

Cooking skill/nutrition lesson:
This is an easy recipe that will show participants how to use brown rice. It is also an excellent way to use up leftover rice and chicken from another meal. It incorporates three groups from MyPlate: grains, protein, and vegetables.

Demo preparation:
1. Wash your hands before you handle food.
2. Prepare and measure all ingredients.
3. Organize work area.

Make ahead options:
You can premake and measure all ingredients before class and simply assemble everything once you arrive.

Garnish/presentation tips:
This salad looks great when served on a large plate with a few of the seasonings sprinkled on top. Top with the Italian herb mix and the black pepper.

Number of sample servings: 18 (1/2 cup each)

Leader Guide: Grain Recipes

Apple Almond Rice Pilaf

1 tsp oil
1/3 cup sliced almonds
1 cup chopped red apples (don't peel)
2 cups water
1 cup brown rice
1/4 tsp cinnamon
1 Tbsp parsley flakes
1/2 Tbsp chicken bouillon granules, low-sodium
Directions:

1. Heat oil in a large, nonstick skillet or Dutch Oven over medium-high heat. Swirl the almonds in the pan until golden brown and add the water and apples.
2. Cook apples briefly, then add the rest of the ingredients. Bring to a boil, then cover pan and reduce to a simmer. Cook until rice is tender and liquid is absorbed, about 45 minutes.

Microwave instructions: Toast the almonds in a toaster oven or regular oven. Place all ingredients in a large, covered microwave container and cook on full power until liquid is absorbed and rice is tender, about 33-40 minutes.

Equipment:

____ Microwave or stove
____ 3 quart pan or large microwave container
____ Measuring cups and spoons
____ Knife
____ Cutting board
____ Plate (for final presentation)
____ Spoon

Shopping list:

____ Oil
____ Almonds
____ 1 or 2 red apples
____ Water
____ Brown rice
____ Cinnamon
____ Parsley flakes
____ Chicken bouillon granules
____ Disposable cups (for premeasured ingredients)
____ Plates, forks and napkins (for samples)

Cooking skill/nutrition lesson:

This delicious recipe uses three groups from MyPlate: grains, fruit and protein. It shows participants an easy way to prepare a flavorful brown rice dish.

Demo Preparation:

1. Wash your hands before you handle food.
2. Measure and chop all ingredients.
3. Organize work area.
4. If you are using the stove, turn it on prior to class if it is electric.

Make ahead options:

You can make this dish ahead of time and reheat in a microwave prior to serving sample servings.

Garnish/presentation tips:

Place the rice on a small salad plate and garnish with a slice of apple.

Number of sample servings: 8 (1/2 cup each)

Whole Grain Recipes

Tomato-Basil Spaghetti

Pasta:

8 ounces whole grain spaghetti, dry

Sauce:

2 cups pasta sauce

1 Tbsp tomato paste

1 Tbsp fresh chopped basil

1/2 cup sliced green onion

1 cup diced fresh tomatoes

Directions:

1. Cook pasta until al dente. Drain and rinse in a colander.
2. Place all ingredients for sauce in a 3 quart sauce pan. Bring to a boil, then reduce heat to a simmer. Cook for 3 minutes.
3. Mix pasta with sauce and serve hot.

Serves 4. Each 1-1/2 cup serving: 269 calories, 1 g fat, 0 g saturated fat, 0 mg cholesterol, 404 mg sodium, 55 g carbohydrate, 4.5 g fiber, 10 g protein.

Mushroom Barley Soup

1 Tbsp oil

1 onion, chopped

2 stalks celery, sliced thin

2 carrots, peeled and sliced thin

2 cups sliced mushrooms

1/2 cup quick-cooking barley

1 tsp garlic powder

1/2 tsp thyme

3 cups chicken broth

2 cups water

1 Tbsp chopped fresh parsley

Directions:

1. Heat oil in a large soup pot over high heat. Saute onion, celery, carrots, and mushrooms until golden, about 4 minutes.
2. Add the rest of the ingredients except for the parsley and bring to a boil. Lower heat to a simmer and cook until the barley is tender, about 20 minutes.
3. Sprinkle parsley on top of the soup and serve hot.

Serves 4. Each 1-1/2 cup serving: 148 calories, 5 g fat, 0.5 g saturated fat, 0 mg cholesterol, 152 mg sodium, 21 g carbohydrate, 4 g fiber, 8 g protein.

Chicken Rice Salad

4 cups lettuce

2 cups cooked brown rice

2 cups skinless roasted chicken breast

1 tomato, cored and diced

1 green pepper, cored and diced

1 Tbsp olive oil

juice of 1 lemon

2 Tbsp flavored vinegar

dash hot pepper sauce

Italian herb mix and black pepper to taste

Directions:

1. Toss all ingredients together in a large salad bowl. Add seasonings to taste and serve immediately. This salad looks great when served on a large plate with a few of the seasonings sprinkled on top.

Serves 4. Each 2 cup serving: 389 calories, 8 g fat, 1.5 g saturated fat, 60 mg cholesterol, 69 mg sodium, 51 g carbohydrate, 5.5 g fiber, 28 g protein.

Apple Almond Rice Pilaf

1 tsp oil

1/3 cup sliced almonds

1 cup chopped red apples (don't peel)

2 cups water

1 cup brown rice

1/4 tsp cinnamon

1 Tbsp parsley flakes

1/2 Tbsp chicken bouillon granules

Directions:

1. Heat oil in large nonstick skillet or Dutch Oven over medium-high heat. Swirl the almonds in the pan until nutty and add the oil and apples. Cook apples briefly then add the rest of the ingredients.
2. Bring to a boil, then cover pan and reduce to a simmer. Cook until rice is tender and liquid is absorbed, about 45 minutes.

Microwave instructions: Toast the almonds in a toaster oven or regular oven. Place all ingredients in a large, covered microwave container and cook on full power until liquid is absorbed & rice is tender, about 33-40 minutes.

Serves 4. Each 1 cup serving: 269 calories, 8.5 g fat, 1 g saturated fat, 0 mg cholesterol, 5 mg sodium, 45 g carbohydrate, 3 g fiber, 6 g protein.

Grain Facts

What are whole grains?

Whole grains are unrefined products from various cereal plants. These plants include wheat, oats, rye, corn, rice, millet, sorghum and barley. Whole grains contain the grain's starchy endosperm, the bran, and the germ.

What are refined grains?

Refined white flour and grain products are composed of the starchy endosperm of the grain.

Why should I eat whole grains?

Whole grains are nutrient rich, and good sources of complex carbohydrates, vitamins, and minerals. They're also low in fat and high in fiber. Whole grains and their fiber appear to decrease the risk of a heart disease and cancers of the stomach, colon, rectum, endometrium, and pancreas. The USDA's MyPlate recommends that most adults eat about 5-8 ounces of grains each day (depending on age, gender, and activity level) with at least half those being whole grains. One ounce of grains is equivalent to 1 ounce of ready-to-eat cereal, a half cup of cooked cereal, rice or pasta, or 1 slice of bread.

How can I eat more whole grains?

Look for products that contain whole grains only, or at least have whole grains as a major ingredient. Remember, ingredient lists are ordered from most to least!

The Food and Drug Administration defines whole grain foods as foods that contain 51 percent or more whole grain ingredient(s) by weight, per reference amount customarily consumed. The FDA allows claims on whole grain products and health - here are a couple examples:

Heart Disease: "Diets low in saturated fat and cholesterol and rich in fruits, vegetables, and grain products that contain some types of dietary fiber, particularly soluble fiber, may reduce the risk of heart disease, a disease associated with many factors."

Cancer: "Low-fat diets rich in fiber-containing grain products, fruits, and vegetables may reduce the risk of some types of cancer, a disease associated with many factors."

Easy whole grain substitutions

- Buy 100% whole wheat bread products (check out whole grain pita pockets, bread and rolls).
- Choose whole grain breakfast cereals.
- Cook brown rice instead of white rice.
- Eat whole grain cereals, oatmeal, and cooked whole cream of wheat for breakfast.
- Choose lowfat whole grain crackers like WASA.
- Try other whole grains and foods made with them. How about giving quinoa, barley, or bulgur a spin? Did you know popcorn is a whole grain?

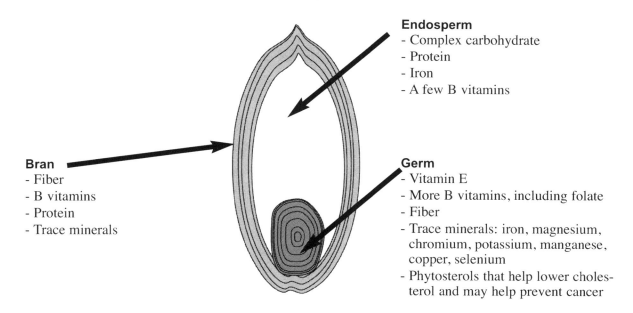

Endosperm
- Complex carbohydrate
- Protein
- Iron
- A few B vitamins

Bran
- Fiber
- B vitamins
- Protein
- Trace minerals

Germ
- Vitamin E
- More B vitamins, including folate
- Fiber
- Trace minerals: iron, magnesium, chromium, potassium, manganese, copper, selenium
- Phytosterols that help lower cholesterol and may help prevent cancer

Leader Guide: Healthy Ethnic Cooking: African American

Title:
Healthy Ethnic Cooking: African American

Target Audience:
This presentation kit is intended for general audiences age 14 and up. It covers topics of wellness, aging, diabetes, heart disease, family health, limited resources, cancer prevention, and nutrition.

Lesson Objectives:
• Participants will learn about healthy ingredients to use in African-American cooking
• Participants will learn how to modify traditional African American dishes so they contain less fat, saturated fat, and sodium

Lesson Rationale:
African Americans are more prone to diet related diseases such as hypertension, heart disease, diabetes, and stroke than many other people. The recently released Healthy Eating Index reveals that the quality of the African American diet lags behind that of other cultures. A new report by the USDA's Center for Nutrition Policy and Promotion, "Report Card on The Diet Quality of African Americans," finds that only 5 percent of African Americans (compared with 11 percent of whites), have a good diet. Twenty eight percent of African Americans and sixteen percent of whites have a poor quality diet. The report also indicates that the diet of most Americans needs improvement.

From a health perspective, diets of African Americans have both favorable and unfavorable characteristics. Among the favorable features are a relatively high intake of red and orange (sweet potatoes) and dark green vegetables (collard greens) which contain vitamins A and C. It also includes pork, which is a rich source of thiamin, as well as fish and poultry which are low fat sources of protein. In contrast, the extensive use of frying, overcooking vegetables and consuming high-sodium foods are unfavorable. (Source: Maryland Cooperative Extension).

Health authorities have indicated that good nutrition is one of the most important factors in determining long-term health. Poor diet plays a major role in the development of four of the top seven killers in the United States: heart disease, cancer, stroke and diabetes. Individuals who have the skills to select and prepare nutritious foods can positively impact their present and future health.

Lesson at a Glance:
This lesson is designed to explore the benefits of traditional African American cooking and ingredients. It focuses on using healthy ingredients that are easily found in most US grocery stores that can be made in most US kitchens. Most recipes given are modified from originals so they are healthier, yet still delicious. This lesson introduces participants to new recipes and cooking skills, while providing information that is consistent with MyPlate and the Dietary Guidelines for Americans.

Lesson Materials:
This lesson contains:
• Leader and Activity Guides; Recipe Leader Guides
• 3 pages of copy-ready handouts and recipes

Preparation:
____ Review leader guide
____ Review handouts
____ Select activities
____ Copy and collect materials for lesson

Activity Ideas:
Introduction
Ask participants what their favorite African American dishes are, and make a list of their responses. Ask them about the healthiness of each dish and whether they feel improvements are ever necessary. If they do, have them explain their changes.

Activity 1 – Cooking Demo
Use the recipes in this lesson to plan a cooking demonstration. The cooking demonstrations are designed to show individuals how to modify favorite and traditional dishes in order to make them healthier. They also focus on the healthier ingredients that are used in traditional African American cooking. Use as many recipes as possible, even if it means you have to precook some items and take them with you for sample servings. By combining all the recipes provided, you will have a hearty, colorful meal.

Activity 2 - My Soul Food Plate
Many traditional African American foods were quite healthy. Changes in traditional lifestyles and food choices have caused the increased intake of calories, salt, fat and sugar. With a few modifications, African American cuisine can be high in fiber, low in sodium and still taste delicious.

Assemble traditional African American foods. Display them by MyPlate group (fruits, vegetables, grains, protein, and dairy). Show participants the items and explain how they fit on MyPlate. Be sure to mention what a serving size in each group, and focus on the

Leader Guide: Healthy Ethnic: African American

healthier ingredients.

Grains:

Corn bread

Grits

Rice

Pasta (especially macaroni)

Comment: Discuss how to add more variety to the grains category. Use the information from the Grains lesson to help explain the importance of whole grains.

Vegetables:

Corn

Green beans

Greens (Chard, collard greens, kale, mustard greens, spinach, and turnip greens)

Lima beans

Okra

Onions

Peas

Potatoes

Pumpkins

Squash

Sweet potatoes

Tomatoes

Fruits:

Apples

Bananas

Citrus

Peaches

Strawberries

Watermelon

Protein:

Black eyed peas - You can buy these dried or frozen

Chicken - Use white meat without skin or use a little bit dark meat without skin

Fish - Especially catfish

Ham - Go for fresh or lean varieties

Peanuts, peanut butter

Red beans - You can buy these dried or canned

Sausage - Go for vegetarian or lowfat varieties

Turkey bacon - This can replace pork, ham, and bacon in many recipes. It should be a staple of healthy African American cooking. It can be diced and stored in a zip lock bag in the freezer, where it will be ready for addition to black-eyed peas, collard greens, and beans and rice.

Dairy*:

Buttermilk - Buy lowfat versions

Cheese - Reduce the amount up to 75% in your recipes

Milk - buy skim or evaporated skim milk

*Lactose intolerance is common among African Americans. Explain alternative ways to get calcium, using the calcium lesson in this kit.

Further reading/info/links

http://www.nhlbi.nih.gov/health/public/heart/other/chd black/cooking.htm - Here's a guide to healthy cooking for African Americans from the National Heart, Lung and Blood Institute.

http://ohioline.osu.edu/hyg-fact/5000/pdf/5250.pdf
This fact sheet covers African American diet and provides glimpses into the culture.

http://www.choosemyplate.gov/ - This website provides recommendations of what types of food to eat each day, why, and how much of everythign you should eat, based on gender, age, and activity level.

Credits:

We would like to thank Constance Pergeson, MS, RD, Maryland Cooperative Extension Educator, for her help and guidance with this lesson. The Delicious Greens recipe, courtesy of Maryland Coop Extension was adapted from the American Heart Assoc, Low Fat, Low Chol Cookbook.

Leader Guide: Healthy Soul Food Recipes

Healthy, Hearty Cornbread

Makes 24 sample servings

1 cup cornmeal
1 cup flour
1/2 cup sugar
2 tsp baking powder
1 tsp salt
1 cup fat-free buttermilk
1/2 cup applesauce
1/2 cup egg whites
2 Tbsp vegetable oil

Directions:

1. Preheat oven to 400° F. Lightly spray an 8-inch square pan with vegetable oil cooking spray.
2. Mix dry ingredients in a medium bowl. Add the rest of the ingredients and mix well. Pour the batter into the sprayed pan and shake until it is level.
3. Bake until a toothpick inserted in the center comes out clean, about 25 minutes. Allow to cool, then cut into 12 squares.

Equipment:

____ Oven
____ Medium mixing bowl
____ Spoon
____ Whisk
____ 8-inch square baking pan
____ Measuring cups and spoons
____ Platter (for final presentation)

Shopping list:

____ Cornmeal
____ All purpose flour
____ Sugar
____ Baking powder
____ Baking soda
____ Buttermilk
____ Apple sauce
____ Eggs (or nonfat egg substitute)
____ Vegetable oil
____ Toothpicks
____ Disposable cups (for premeasured ingredients)
____ Napkins (for samples)

Cooking skill/nutrition lesson:

This recipe shows participants how to modify a traditional corn bread recipe. We use vegetable oil instead of butter, lard, or hydrogenated shortening. We reduced the sugar and used applesauce to add sweetness. We reduced the fat and specify fat free buttermilk (or 1% buttermilk) in accordance with MyPlate guidelines.

Demo preparation:

1. Wash your hands before you handle food.
2. Measure all ingredients.
3. Organize your ingredients and work area.
4. Preheat oven.

Make ahead options:

You may want to make one or two pans of cornbread ahead of time and bring them to class. This is especially helpful if time is short or you don't have an oven. You can demonstrate how to mix this recipe and then use the finished pans for tasting.

Garnish/presentation tips:

Slice the loaf into squares and arrange them on an attractive platter.

Number of sample servings: 24

Leader Guide: Healthy Soul Food Recipes

Light and Fluffy Homestyle Biscuits
Makes 24 tasting samples

2 cups flour
2 tsp baking powder
1/2 tsp baking soda
2 Tbsp sugar
2 Tbsp apple sauce
2/3 cup fat-free buttermilk
3 Tbsp vegetable oil

Directions:

1. Preheat oven to 400° F.
2. In a medium bowl, combine flour, baking powder and baking soda. Add the rest of the ingredients and mix gently until the mixture forms a dough.
3. Turn the dough onto a lightly floured surface and pat to 1/2-inch thickness. Cut into rounds with a 2-inch biscuit cutter. Dip the cutter in flour between cuts. Place biscuits on a nonstick cookie sheet.
4. Bake the biscuits until they are golden brown, about 12 minutes. Serve warm.

Equipment:
____ Mixing bowl
____ Spoon
____ Oven
____ Measuring cups and spoons
____ Biscuit cutter (2 inch)
____ Nonstick cookie sheet
____ Spatula (to remove biscuits)
____ Platter (for final presentation)

Shopping list:
____ All purpose flour
____ Sugar
____ Baking soda
____ Baking powder
____ Apple sauce
____ Fat free buttermilk (or 1%)
____ Vegetable oil
____ Napkins (for samples)
____ Disposable cups (for premeasured ingredients)

Cooking skill/nutrition lesson:
This recipe shows participants how to modify their favorite biscuit recipe and make it healthier. We use apple sauce in place of the sugar and vegetable oil in place of lard or hydrogenated shortening. Fat free or 1% buttermilk replaces the regular buttermilk.

Demo preparation:
1. Wash your hands before you handle food.
2. Measure all ingredients.
3. Organize your ingredients and work area.
4. Preheat oven.

Make ahead options:
You can make these biscuits ahead of time and just take them to class for sample servings. Demonstrate how to make the dough in class, then pull out the finished biscuits.

Garnish/presentation tips:
Place the baked biscuits on an attractive platter or a basket with a pretty cloth.

Number of sample servings: 24

Leader Guide: Healthy Soul Food Recipes

Oven Fried Potatoes

Makes 12 sample servings

2 large baking potatoes
1 tsp garlic powder
Black pepper to taste
1/4 cup Parmesan cheese

Directions:

1. Preheat oven to 400 degrees.
2. Wash and dry potatoes, then slice into 1/4 inch thick wedges. Mix the rest of the ingredients in a small bowl and set aside.
3. Spray a large cookie sheet with vegetable oil spray. Arrange the potato wedges in rows so that none are touching. Spray the top side of the potatoes with the vegetable oil spray and place them in the oven.
4. Bake potatoes until golden brown, about 10 minutes. Flip them over and continue baking until brown on the other side, about 10 more minutes. Place potatoes in a serving bowl and toss with seasoning/cheese mixture.

Equipment:

____ Oven
____ Baking pan
____ Knife
____ Cutting board
____ Mixing bowl
____ Platter (for final presentation)

Shopping list:

____ 2 large Idaho potatoes
____ Garlic powder
____ Black pepper
____ Grated Parmesan cheese
____ Ketchup (for garnish)
____ Vegetable oil cooking spray
____ Plates and napkins (for samples)

Cooking skill/nutrition lesson:

This recipe outlines a healthier way to prepare potatoes. Participants bake them in the oven, rather than frying them in fat.

Demo preparation:

1. Wash your hands before you handle food.
2. Chop and measure all ingredients.
3. Organize your ingredients and work area while preheating the oven.

Garnish presentation tips:

Serve fries on a platter with ketchup on the side.

Number of sample servings: Approximately 12

(2 fries per person).

Leader Guide: Healthy Soul Food Recipes

Delicious Greens

Makes 16 sample servings

1 bunch (about 1/2 pound) collard greens, stemmed, rinsed and coarsely shredded
2 cups shredded cabbage
1 Tbsp olive oil
2 Tbsp minced garlic
1 onion, chopped
1 Tbsp vinegar

Directions:

1. Bring 2 quarts of water to a boil in a large soup pot. Add collard greens, return to a boil, and cook for 3 minutes. Add cabbage and cook for 1 more minute. Drain in colander.
2. Heat a large, nonstick skillet over medium high heat. Add oil and saute garlic and onion until golden brown, about 3 minutes. Add greens and vinegar and cook briefly, about 3 minutes. Serve hot.

Equipment:

____ Stove
____ Large soup pot
____ Large, nonstick skillet
____ Spoon
____ Knife
____ Cutting board
____ Colander
____ Measuring cups and spoons
____ Bowl (for final presentation)

Shopping list:

____ 1 bunch (1/2 lb) collard greens
____ Cabbage
____ Olive oil
____ Minced garlic
____ 1 onion
____ Vinegar
____ Disposable cups (for premeasured ingredients)
____ Cups, forks, and napkins (for samples)

Cooking skill/nutrition lesson:

Collard greens are an excellent source of beta carotene, some vitamin C, calcium, and iron. Like broccoli and cabbage, the antioxidants and phytochemicals in collards may help to reduce the risk of some forms of cancer and heart disease. This recipe outlines a simple way to make collard greens even healthier by adjusting cooking methods and ingredient lists.

Demo preparation:

1. Wash your hands before you handle food.
2. Chop and measure all ingredients.
3. Organize your work area.
4. If you are using an electric stove, bring the heat to medium as participants are arriving.

Make ahead tips:

You can start this recipe before class arrives, then explain how you made it. Be sure to serve sample servings. Or you can make the entire dish ahead of time and reheat it for class.

Garnish/presentation tips:

Serve these greens in a bright, colorful bowl.

Number of sample servings: 16 (1/4 cup each)

Leader Guide: Healthy Soul Food Recipes

Oven-Fried Chicken or Catfish

Makes 12 sample servings

1/2 cup fat free buttermilk
4 skinless chicken breasts, with ribs OR 1 lb catfish fillets
Breading:
1/2 cup corn flake crumbs
1 cup bread crumbs
1 Tbsp garlic powder
1 tsp ground black pepper
1 tsp poultry seasoning
1 tsp paprika
Pinch cayenne pepper
Vegetable oil cooking spray

Directions:

1. Preheat oven to 450° F.
2. Combine ingredients for breading in a shallow pan. Place buttermilk in a bowl.
3. Rinse chicken breasts in cold running water. Remove skin and excess fat, then pat dry. If using catfish, rinse fillets and pat dry.
4. Dip the meat side of the chicken into buttermilk, then dip in the breading mixture. Press down firmly so the breading sticks to the chicken.
5. Place the chicken (breaded side up) on a lightly oiled pan and spray the top of the chicken well with vegetable oil cooking spray. Bake the until done, about 30 minutes. If using fish, the cooking time should be about 20 minutes.

Equipment:

____ Oven
____ Baking pan
____ Shallow pan
____ Bowl
____ Spatula
____ Measuring cups and spoons
____ Platter (for final presentation)

Shopping list:

____ Paper towels
____ 4 skinless chicken breasts with ribs or 1 lb catfish fillets
____ Vegetable oil cooking spray
____ Corn flake crumbs
____ Plain bread crumbs
____ Garlic powder
____ Ground black pepper
____ Poultry seasoning
____ Paprika
____ Cayenne pepper
____ Disposable cups (for premeasured ingredients)
____ Plates, forks, knives, and napkins (for samples)

Cooking skill/nutrition lesson:

This recipe teaches participants how to make a healthier, baked version of fried food. It uses less fat, yet it yields a crispy crust and tender, moist chicken or fish.

Demo preparation:

1. Wash your hands before you handle food.
2. Measure all ingredients.
3. Preheat oven and organize your ingredients and work area.

Make ahead options:

You can make this recipe ahead of time and just reheat for sample servings.

Garnish/presentation tips:

Place the chicken on an attractive platter. Use kale or a leafy vegetable for a garnish.

Number of sample servings: 12

Leader Guide: Healthy Soul Food Recipes

Quick and Healthy Black Eyed Peas

Makes 16 sample servings

1/2 cup turkey bacon, chopped
2 pounds frozen black-eyed peas
2 cups water
1/4 tsp black pepper, ground
1 Tbsp sugar

Directions:

1. Place a Dutch Oven pan over medium high heat and cook bacon for 3-4 minutes.
2. Add the rest of the ingredients and bring to a boil. Reduce heat to simmer and allow to cook until the peas are tender, about 30 minutes. Serve hot.

Equipment:

____ Stove
____ Dutch Oven pan
____ Measuring cups and spoons
____ Cutting board and knife
____ Spoon

Shopping list:

____ Turkey bacon
____ Frozen black-eyed peas
____ Water
____ Black pepper
____ Sugar
____ Parsley (for garnish)
____ Disposable cups (for premeasured ingredients)
____ Cups, forks, and napkins (for samples)

Cooking skill/nutrition lesson:

This recipe highlights how to use turkey bacon instead of pork fat back (or other fatty cuts of meat) for flavor. It also demonstrates how to prepare black-eyed peas. Frozen black eyed peas take less time to cook than dried black eyed peas and, unlike their canned counterparts, they contain no added salt. The USDA advises people to consume less sodium, and this recipe explains a way to do just that.

Demo preparation:

1. Wash your hands before you handle food.
2. Measure and chop all ingredients.
3. Organize your work area. If you are using an electric stove, preheat it to low.

Make ahead options:

You can make this recipe ahead of time and simply reheat for sample servings.

Presentation/garnish tips:

Place the peas on an attractive plate. Garnish with a fresh sprig of parsley.

Number of sample servings: 16 (1/2 cup each)

Leader Guide: Healthy Soul Food Recipes

Sweet Potato Casserole
Makes 18 sample servings

1 pound sweet potatoes (about 4 medium potatoes)
3 egg whites (or 1/3 cup nonfat egg substitute)
1/2 cup sugar
1 can evaporated skim milk
1 Tbsp vanilla extract
1 tsp cinnamon
1/2 tsp nutmeg
1/2 tsp ginger

Directions:

1. Rinse sweet potatoes in cold running water and pierce with fork. Microwave on full power until tender, about 15 minutes. Flip and turn potatoes halfway through the cooking process.
2. Preheat oven to 400 degrees. Remove skin from sweet potatoes (use a spoon to scrape out the pulp) and mash with hand beaters or a food processor. Add the rest of the ingredients and mix until smooth.
3. Pour mixture in an 8-inch square baking pan. Bake until casserole is firm in the center, about 40 minutes. Remove from oven. Allow to stand for 5 minutes, then cut into 9 even squares. Serve hot and refrigerate leftovers.

Equipment:
____ Microwave oven
____ Oven
____ 8-inch square baking pan
____ Spoon
____ Food processor or hand beaters
____ Knife
____ Can opener
____ Plate (for final presentation)

Shopping list:
____ 1 pound sweet potatoes (about 4 medium ones)
____ Egg whites (or nonfat egg substitute)
____ Sugar
____ 1 can evaporated skim milk
____ Vanilla extract
____ Cinnamon
____ Nutmeg
____ Ginger
____ Disposable cups (for premeasured ingredients)
____ Plates, forks and napkins (for samples)

Cooking skill/nutrition lesson:
This recipe teaches the audience how to prepare a sweet potato dish that can be used as a side dish or dessert. When used as a dessert, it is like a crustless pie. We lightened this recipe by using evaporated skim milk, less sugar, and egg whites instead of whole eggs.

Demo preparation:
1. Wash your hands before you handle food.
2. Measure all ingredients.
3. Organize your ingredients and work area while pre-heating the oven.

Make ahead options:
Make one casserole ahead of time for sample servings. Assemble ingredients to make another one that outlines the steps of the recipe. You can also prebake the sweet potatoes and start with step 2.

Garnish/presentation tips:
Serve a square of this custard on an attractive plate. Dust the top with some of the spices that are used in the recipe.

Number of sample servings: 18

Healthy Soul Food Recipes

Healthy, Hearty Cornbread

1 cup cornmeal
1 cup all purpose flour
1/2 cup sugar
2 tsp baking powder
1/2 tsp salt
1 cup fat free buttermilk
1/2 cup applesauce, unsweetened
1/2 cup egg whites
2 Tbsp vegetable oil

Directions:

1. Preheat oven to 400° F. Lightly spray an 8-inch square pan with vegetable oil cooking spray.
2. Mix dry ingredients in a medium bowl. Add the rest of the ingredients and mix well. Pour the batter into the sprayed pan and shake until it is level.
3. Bake until a toothpick inserted in the center comes out clean, about 25 minutes. Allow to cool, then cut into 12 squares.

Makes 12 squares. Each square: 144 calories, 3 g fat, 0 g saturated fat, 0 mg cholesterol, 201 mg sodium, 26 g carbohydrate, 1 g fiber, 26 g protein.

Light and Fluffy Homestyle Biscuits

2 cups flour
2 tsp baking powder
1/2 tsp baking soda
2 Tbsp sugar
2 Tbsp apple sauce, unsweetened
2/3 cup fat free buttermilk
3 Tbsp vegetable oil

Directions:

1. Preheat oven to 400° F.
2. In a medium bowl, combine flour, baking powder and baking soda. Add the rest of the ingredients and mix gently until the mixture forms a dough.
3. Turn the dough onto a lightly floured surface and pat to 1/2-inch thickness. Cut into rounds with a 2-inch biscuit cutter. Dip the cutter in flour between cuts. Place biscuits on a nonstick cookie sheet.
4. Bake the biscuits until they are golden brown, about 12 minutes. Serve warm.

Makes 15 biscuits. Each biscuit: 96 calories, 3 g fat, 0.5 g saturated fat, 0 mg cholesterol, 101 mg sodium, 15 g carbohydrate, 0.5 g fiber, 2 g protein.

Oven Fried Potatoes

2 large baking potatoes
1 tsp garlic powder
Black pepper to taste
1/4 cup Parmesan cheese

Directions:

1. Preheat oven to 400 degrees.
2. Wash and dry potatoes, then slice into 1/4 inch thick wedges. Mix the rest of the ingredients in a small bowl and set aside.
3. Spray a large cookie sheet with vegetable oil spray. Arrange the potato wedges in rows so that none are touching. Spray the top side of the potatoes with the vegetable oil spray and place them in the oven.
4. Bake potatoes until golden brown, about 10 minutes. Flip them over and continue baking until brown on the other side, about 10 more minutes. Place potatoes in a serving bowl and toss with seasoning/cheese mixture.

Serves 4. Each serving: 69 calories, 2 g fat, 1 g saturated fat, 5 mg cholesterol, 118 mg sodium, 9 g carbohydrate, 2 g fiber, 4 g protein.

Delicious Greens

1 bunch (about 1/2 pound) collard greens, stemmed, rinsed, and coarsely shredded
2 cups shredded cabbage
1 Tbsp olive oil
2 Tbsp minced garlic
1 onion, chopped
1 Tbsp vinegar

Directions:

1. Bring 2 quarts of water to a boil in a large soup pot. Add collard greens, return to a boil, and cook for 3 minutes. Add cabbage and cook for 1 more minute. Drain in colander.
2. Heat a large, nonstick skillet over medium high heat. Add oil and saute garlic and onion until golden brown, about 3 minutes. Add greens and vinegar and cook briefly, about 3 minutes. Serve hot.

Serves 4. Each 1-1/2 cup serving: 73 calories, 3 g fat, 0.5 g saturated fat, 0 mg cholesterol, 19 mg sodium, 9 g carbohydrate, 2.5 g protein, 3.5 g fiber.

Healthy Soul Food Recipes

Oven-Fried Chicken or Catfish

1/2 cup fat free buttermilk
4 skinless chicken breasts with ribs, or 1 lb catfish fillets
Breading:
1/2 cup corn flake crumbs
1 cup bread crumbs
1 Tbsp garlic powder
1 tsp ground black pepper
1 tsp poultry seasoning
1 tsp paprika
Pinch cayenne pepper
Vegetable oil cooking spray
Directions:

1. Preheat oven to 450° F.
2. Combine ingredients for breading in a shallow pan. Place buttermilk in a bowl.
3. Rinse chicken breasts in cold running water. Remove skin and excess fat, then pat dry. If using catfish, rinse fillets and pat dry.
4. Dip the meat side of the chicken into buttermilk, then dip in the breading mixture. Press down firmly so the breading sticks to the chicken.
5. Place the chicken (breaded side up) on a lightly oiled pan and spray the top of the chicken well with vegetable oil cooking spray. Bake the until done, about 30 minutes. If using fish, the cooking time should be about 20 minutes.

Serves 4. Each serving (4 oz chicken or fish): 207 calories, 2 g fat, 0.5 g saturated fat, 66 mg cholesterol, 271 mg sodium, 16 g carbohydrate, 0 g fiber, 29 g protein.

Quick and Healthy Black-Eyed Peas

1/2 cup turkey bacon, chopped
2 pounds frozen black-eyed peas
2 cups water
1/4 tsp black pepper, ground
1 Tbsp sugar
Directions:

1. Place a Dutch Oven pan over medium high heat and cook bacon for 3-4 minutes.
2. Add the rest of the ingredients and bring to a boil. Reduce heat to simmer and allow to cook until the peas are tender, about 30 minutes. Serve hot.

Serves 6. Each 1-1/2 cup serving: 233 calories, 3.5 g fat, 0 g saturated fat, 6 mg cholesterol, 147 mg sodium, 41 g carbohydrate, 7 g fiber, 14 g protein.

Sweet Potato Casserole

1 pound sweet potatoes (about 4 medium ones)
3 egg whites (or 1/3 cup nonfat egg substitute)
1/2 cup sugar
1 can evaporated skim milk
1 Tbsp vanilla extract
1 tsp cinnamon
1/2 tsp nutmeg
1/2 tsp ginger
Directions:

1. Rinse sweet potatoes in cold running water and pierce with fork. Microwave on full power until tender, about 15 minutes. Flip and turn potatoes halfway through the cooking process.
2. Preheat oven to 400 degrees. Remove skin from sweet potatoes (use a spoon to scrape out the pulp) and mash with hand beaters or a food processor. Add the rest of the ingredients and mix until smooth.
3. Pour mixture in an 8-inch square baking pan. Bake until casserole is firm in the center, about 40 minutes. Remove from oven. Allow to stand for 5 minutes, then cut into 9 even squares. Serve hot and refrigerate leftovers.

Serves 10. Each square: 111 calories, 0 g fat, 0 g saturated fat, 1 mg cholesterol, 55 mg sodium, 24 g carbohydrate, 1.5 g fiber, 4 g protein.

Make a Healthy Soul Food Plate

Grains:
Corn bread - Modify the recipe and use vegetable oil instead of lard or hydrogenated shortening
Rice - Try brown rice instead of white rice
Pasta - Try whole wheat pasta instead of white pasta

Vegetables:
Corn
Green beans
Greens (chard, collard greens, kale, mustard greens, spinach, and turnip greens)
Lima beans
Okra
Onions
Peas
Potatoes
Pumpkins
Squash
Sweet potatoes
Tomatoes

Fruits:
Apples
Bananas
Citrus
Peaches
Strawberries
Watermelon

Protein:
Black eyed peas - You can buy these dried or frozen
Chicken - Use white meat without skin or use a little bit dark meat without skin
Fish - Especially catfish
Ham - Go for fresh or lean varieties
Peanuts, peanut butter
Red beans - You can buy these dried or canned
Sausage - Go for vegetarian or lowfat varieties
Turkey bacon - This can replace pork, ham, and bacon in many recipes. It should be a staple of healthy African American cooking. It can be diced and stored in a zip lock bag in the freezer, where it will be ready for addition to black-eyed peas, collard greens, and beans and rice.

Dairy:
Buttermilk - Buy fat free or 1% buttermilk
Cheese - Buy reduced fat versions and reduce amount you use in recipes up to 75%
Milk - Buy skim or evaporated skim milk
Yogurt - Buy fat free or light yogurt

Apply MyPlate Lessons to Soul Food
1. Enjoy your food, but eat less.
2. Avoid oversized portions.
3. Make half your plate fruits and vegetables.
4. Make at least half your grains whole grains.
5. Switch to fat-free or lowfat dairy products.
6. Choose low-sodium food options.
7. Drink water instead of sugary drinks.

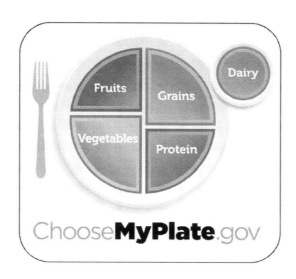

Leader Guide: Healthy Ethnic: Asian

Title:
HealthyEthnic Cooking: Asian

Target Audience:
This presentation kit is intended for general audiences age 14 and up. It covers topics of wellness, aging, diabetes, heart disease, family health, limited income, WIC, cancer prevention, and nutrition.

Lesson Objectives:
• Participants will learn about healthy ingredients used in Asian cooking. These ingredients are readily available in most U.S. grocery stores.
• Participants will learn how to make a healthy recipes using these available, healthy Asian ingredients.

Lesson Rationale:
According to researchers from Cornell and Harvard University, the traditional, plant-based Asian diet, (along with other lifestyle factors) is linked to lower rates of certain cancers, heart disease, and obesity. In some cases, it has also been linked to a lower risk of osteoporosis and other chronic, degenerative diseases. In addition, many ingredients common to traditional Asian cuisine have been recognized for their health-promoting properties. These ingredients include soy, tea, ginger, garlic, and cabbage.

Health authorities have indicated that good nutrition is one of the most important factors in determining long-term health. Poor diet plays a major role in the development of four of the top seven killers in the United States: heart disease, cancer, stroke and diabetes. Students who have the skills to select and prepare nutritious foods can positively impact their present and future health.

Lesson at a Glance:
This lesson is designed to explore the benefits of Asian cooking and ingredients. It focuses on using healthy ingredients that are easily found in most US grocery stores. Most of the featured recipes are modified from the originals to make them healthier, yet still delicious. This lesson also introduces participants to recipes and cooking skills, while providing information that is consistent with MyPlate and the Dietary Guidelines for Americans.

Lesson Materials:
This lesson contains:
• Leader and Activity Guide
• 4 pages of copy-ready handouts and recipes

Preparation:
___ Review leader guide
___ Review handouts
___ Select activities
___ Copy and collect materials for lesson

Activity Ideas:
Introduction
Ask participants to share their favorite Asian dish. For many, answers will be limited to what they would order in a restaurant.

The purpose of this lesson is to show participants a variety of Asian ingredients and condiments and then demonstrate how to make healthy, easy, Asian-style meals in their own kitchens.

Activity 1 – Cooking Demo
Use the recipes in this lesson to give your audience a cooking demonstration. The recipes are designed to outline how to make healthy, simple meals including stir fry and green tea.

Activity 2 - Make an Asian Plate
Many traditional Asian ingredients are very healthy. Introduce your audience to some or all of these below. You may want to arrange them in the same formation as MyPlate.

Grains:
Brown rice, rice noodles, other rice products, millet, corn

Vegetables:
Healthy veggie options are abundant and include cabbage, carrots, bok choy, soybeans, water chestnuts, bean sprouts, ginger, etc.

Fruits:
Healthy fruit options are abundant.

Milk:
Fortified soy milk

Meat/Beans:
Tofu, nuts, seeds, fish, poultry, lean meat, eggs.

*Lactose intolerance is common among Asians. Explain alternatives ways to get calcium, using the calcium lesson in this kit.

Common Asian Ingredient Glossary:
The list of delicious Asian ingredients seems endless, but here is a rundown of a few favorites, all of which can be found in most US grocery stores.

Adzuki beans - These are reddish brown beans with a sweet, mild flavor. Commonly purchased dried, they are used in both sweet and savory dishes in China and Japan. Adzuki beans can be made into a paste that is avaliable in many Asian markets.

Leader Guide: Healthy Ethnic Recipes: Asian

Basil - Basil is a fresh herb that is used extensively in Thai cuisine.

Bok Choy - This type of cabbage has a white stem and long green leaves. Store it in a ventilated bag inside your vegetable crisper. Slice it into thin strips for stir fry dishes.

Chinese eggplant - Similar to North American eggplant, this vegetable is longer and thinner. It usually is purple with white streaks.

Cilantro - A fresh herb used in Thai cooking, cilantro adds a nice flavor to stir fry dishes.

Cornstarch - This is used extensively to thicken sauces. Dilute it in water before adding to boiling liquid. You should usually use 1 tsp of corn starch per 1 cup of liquid.

Daikon - Daikon is a Chhinese radish that resembles a white carrot. Japanese cooks use daikon for relishes and salads, while Chinese cooks tend to feature it in soups. Daikon can withstand long periods of cooking without losing its shape.

Fish sauce - This salty sauce is made from dried fish. Use it sparingly, since it is very high in sodium.

Five spice powder - This elegant blend of spices includes cinnamon, fennel, cloves, star anise and white pepper. It adds a nice flavor to stir fry dishes

Garlic - Garlic is used extensively in many Asian cuisines and has many phytochemicals that may inhibit the growth of certain cancers or lower cholesterol.

Ginger - This is said to have beneficial digestive properties. It also adds a lot of flavor to many dishes and can be used fresh or dried.

Green tea - This tea is a product of a plant known as C. sinensis, a native of Southeast Asia. Green tea is made by drying the leaves of this plant without the fermentation (fermentation produces black tea). Scientists have identified a substance in green tea called catechins, which act as strong antioxidants and remain unchanged in green tea processing.

Hoisin sauce - This sweet and spicy sauce is usually used in barbecue dishes. Use sparingly, since it is very high in sodium.

Hot mustard - When you mix dried mustard powder with water, you'll come up with a very pungent sauce.

Mung bean sprouts - These thick, succulent bean sprouts come from Mung beans and should be cooked or steamed before use.

Mushrooms - Asian cooking uses a variety of dried mushrooms, which need to be reconstituted in very warm water for 20 minutes before use. Shitake are the most popular and are sometimes called Chinese Black Mushrooms.

Napa Cabbage - Also known as Chinese Cabbage, Napa Cabbage has curly leaves and a milder flavor than regular cabbage.

Pickled ginger - These thin, pink slices of ginger have been pickled, which gives them a whole new flavor profile.

Rice wine vinegar - This mild vinegar can be used in Asian style salads.

Sesame oil - A very flavorful oil made from pressed toasted sesame seeds, sesame oil enhances a stir fry. Remember, a little bit goes a long way.

Snow peas - These flat pea pods can be eaten whole; look for crisp, fresh-looking pods and keep them covered in the refrigerator.

Soy sauce - This sauce is very high in sodium; purchase light versions and use them sparingly.

Tofu - This can be silken, regular, and baked. See the soy section of this collection for more information. Generally speaking, you can use any of those three for stir fry dishes. The regular and baked versions are best at holding their shape.

Wasabi - This pungent green horseradish usually accompanies sushi.

Water chestnuts - This aquatic vegetable grows in marshes and adds a nice, crisp texture to stir fry dishes.

Further reading/info/links

http://www.oldwayspt.org/asian-diet-pyramid - This website provides details about many of the foods used in Asian cuisine.

http://www.ciaprochef.com/fbi/books.html - Check out the selection of Asian cookbooks from the Culinary Institute of America.

Leader Guide: Healthy Asian Recipes

Easy Stir Fry With Tofu

Makes 16 sample servings

4 cups cooked brown rice
Juice of 1 orange
1/4 cup chicken broth
1 Tbsp corn starch
4 Tbsp light soy sauce
1 Tbsp sesame oil
1 cup diced firm tofu (not silken)
1 Tbsp vegetable oil
1 Tbsp minced garlic
1 Tbsp grated fresh ginger
1 pound package of frozen stir-fry vegetables

Directions:

1. Cook the rice according to package directions.
2. Mix the orange juice, chicken broth, corn starch, soy sauce, sesame oil and tofu in a small mixing bowl. Stir well and set aside.
3. Meanwhile, heat the oil in a large nonstick skillet or wok over high heat. Saute the garlic and ginger until golden, about 3 minutes. Add the frozen veggies and cook until tender, about 6 minutes. Add sauce and cook until the mixture is heated through. Serve veggies and tofu over the cooked brown rice.

Equipment:

____ Stove
____ Wok or large nonstick skillet
____ Spoon
____ Knife
____ Cutting board
____ Measuring cups and spoons
____ Grater
____ Mixing bowls
____ Pot (to cook rice)
____ Can opener
____ Plate (for final presentation)

Shopping list:

____ Brown rice
____ 1 orange
____ Chicken broth
____ Corn starch
____ Light soy sauce
____ Sesame oil
____ Firm or extra firm tofu (not silken)
____ Vegetable Oil
____ Minced garlic
____ Fresh ginger
____ 1 pound package of frozen stir-fry vegetables
____ Disposable cups (for premeasured ingredients)
____ Plates, forks, and napkins (for samples)

Cooking skill/nutrition lesson:

This recipe teaches participants how to make a basic stir fry. It uses frozen vegetables to cut preparation time, but you can also use an assortment of fresh vegetables. This lesson outlines a way to incorporate whole grains, protein, and vegetables in a healthy meal that works with MyPlate guidelines.

Demo preparation:

1. Wash your hands before you handle food.
2. Prepare and measure all ingredients.
3. Organize your work area. If you are using an electric stove, turn it on low as participants enter the room.

Make ahead options:

Make the brown rice ahead of time and have it ready before class starts. To make 4 cups of cooked brown rice, you'll need 1-1/3 cups of rice and 2-2/3 cups of water.

Garnish/presentation tips:

Place the rice in the center of the plate and make a well for the stir fry mix. Place that in the center of the rice.

Number of sample servings: 16 (1/2 cup each)

Leader Guide: Healthy Asian Recipes

Egg Fried Vegetables with Rice
Makes 16 sample servings
4 cups cooked brown rice
1 Tbsp oil
1 Tbsp minced garlic
1 Tbsp grated fresh ginger
1 pound package of frozen stir-fry vegetables
1 cup sliced fresh mushrooms
1 cup shredded cabbage
6 egg whites or 3/4 cup nonfat egg substitute
4 Tbsp light soy sauce
1 Tbsp sesame oil
Directions:
1. Cook rice according to package directions.
2. Heat the oil in a large, nonstick skillet or wok over high heat. Add the garlic and ginger and saute until golden, about 3 minutes. Add the frozen veggies and cook until tender, about 6 minutes. Remove the vegetables from the pan.
3. Add the egg whites and scramble until done, about 1 minute. Return the vegetables to the pan and season with soy sauce and sesame oil. Serve egg fried vegetables over the brown rice.

Equipment:
____ Stove
____ Wok or large, nonstick skillet
____ Spoon
____ Cutting board and knife
____ Measuring cups and spoons
____ Grater
____ Mixing bowls
____ Pot (to cook rice)
____ Plate (for final presentation)

Shopping list:
____ Brown rice
____ Oil
____ Minced garlic
____ Fresh ginger
____ 1 pound package of frozen stir-fry vegetables
____ Fresh mushrooms
____ Cabbage
____ 6 egg whites or 3/4 cup nonfat egg substitute
____ Light soy sauce
____ Sesame oil
____ Disposable cups (for premeasured ingredients)
____ Plates, forks and napkins (for samples)

Cooking skill/nutrition lesson:
This recipe teaches participants how to make a basic stir fry. It uses frozen vegetables to cut preparation time, but you can also use an assortment of fresh vegetables. By adding egg to the vegetables, the recipe offers a low calorie protein source to help balance the grains and vegetables.

Demo preparation:
1. Wash your hands before you handle food.
2. Prepare and measure all ingredients.
3. Organize work area, if you are using an electric stove turn it on low as participants are entering the room.

Make ahead options:
Make the brown rice ahead of time and have it ready before class starts. For 4 cups of cooked brown rice, you need 1-1/3 cups of rice and 2-2/3 cups of water.

Garnish/presentation tips:
Place the rice in the center of the plate making a well for the stir fry. Place the stir fry in the center of the rice.

Number of sample servings: 16 (1/2 cup each)

Leader Guide: Healthy Asian Recipes

Cashew Stir Fry Salad

Makes 16 sample servings

4 Tbsp light soy sauce
2 Tbsp rice wine vinegar
1 tsp sesame oil
Pinch red pepper flakes
4 cups shredded Nappa cabbage
1 Tbsp vegetable oil
2 tsp minced garlic
2 Tbsp grated fresh ginger
1/2 cup sliced carrots
1 cup sliced mushrooms
1 cup mung bean sprouts
1 cup broccoli florets
1 cup roasted unsalted cashews

Directions:

1. Mix the soy sauce, vinegar, sesame oil, and red pepper flakes in a small bowl.
2. Place shredded Nappa cabbage in a large salad bowl and set aside.
3. Heat a large, nonstick skillet or wok over high heat. Add the oil, then the garlic and ginger. Saute until the garlic is nutty brown, about 1 minute. Add the rest of the veggies and nuts. Saute until vegetables are crisp-tender, about 4-5 minutes. Add the soy sauce mixture and cook briefly. Add this stir-fry mixture to the cabbage, toss together and serve warm.

Equipment:

____ Stove
____ Wok or large, nonstick skillet
____ Spoon
____ Knife
____ Cutting board
____ Measuring cups and spoons
____ Grater (for ginger)
____ Mixing bowls
____ Plate (for final presentation)

Shopping list:

____ Light soy sauce
____ Rice wine vinegar
____ Sesame oil
____ Red pepper flakes
____ Nappa cabbage
____ Vegetable oil
____ Minced garlic
____ Fresh ginger
____ Carrots
____ Mushrooms
____ Mung bean sprouts
____ Broccoli florets
____ Roasted, unsalted cashews
____ Disposable cups (for premeasured ingredients)
____ Plates, forks, and napkins (for samples)

Cooking skill/nutrition lesson:

This recipe teaches participants how to make a basic stir fry into a salad. It is a delicious way to eat more vegetables.

Demo preparation:

1. Wash your hands before you handle food.
2. Prepare and measure all ingredients.
3. Organize your work area. If you are using an electric stove, turn it on low as participants arrive.

Garnish/presentation tips:

Arrange the salad on a large, attractive platter. Dab the edges of the salad with a few drops of sesame oil.

Number of sample servings: 16 (1/2 cup each)

Leader Guide: Healthy Asian Recipes

Asian Wrap

Makes 6 sample servings

1/2 cup cubed firm tofu (not silken)
2 Tbsp light soy sauce
2 tsp honey
1 tsp sesame oil
Pinch sesame seeds
Pinch five spice seasoning
1 cup broccoli florets, rinsed with water
1/2 cup sliced carrots
1 cup sliced mushrooms
2 cups cooked brown rice
4 whole wheat tortillas

Directions:

1. Marinate the tofu in the soy sauce, honey, sesame oil, sesame seeds, and five spice seasoning in a small bowl.
2. Combine broccoli, carrots and mushrooms in a covered microwave container. Cook on full power until the veggies are almost tender, about 4 minutes.
3. Heat tortillas in the microwave until warm, about 20 seconds.
4. Combine the veggies, brown rice, and tofu mixture. Divide this filling among the warm tortillas, roll them up, and serve warm.

Equipment:

____ Microwave
____ Microwave-safe container with cover
____ Spoon
____ Knife
____ Cutting board
____ Measuring cups and spoons
____ Mixing bowls
____ Plate (for final presentation)

Shopping list:

____ 1/2 cup cubed firm tofu (not silken)
____ Light soy sauce
____ Honey
____ Sesame oil
____ Sesame seeds
____ Five spice seasoning
____ Broccoli florets
____ Carrots
____ Mushrooms
____ Brown rice
____ Whole wheat tortillas

____ Disposable cups (for premeasured ingredients)
____ Plates, forks, and napkins (for samples)

Cooking skill/nutrition lesson:

This recipe teaches participants how to make a wrap sandwich using Asian ingredients. It is healthy, delicious, and perfect for people on the go.

Demo preparation:

1. Wash your hands before you handle food.
2. Prepare and measure all ingredients.
3. Organize your work area. If you are using an electric stove, turn it on low as participants arrive.

Garnish/presentation tips:

Cut the wrap sandwich in half and place on an attractive plate. Garnish with lettuce and add some dots of sesame oil and soy sauce to the plate.

Number of sample servings: 6

Leader Guide: Healthy Asian Recipes

Oriental Slaw
Makes 16 sample servings

1/4 cup silken firm tofu
2 Tbsp sugar
1/4 cup red wine vinegar
1 Tbsp peanut butter
1 Tbsp light soy sauce
1 Tbsp water
1/4 cup water chestnuts
4 cups shredded cabbage

Directions:

1. Combine tofu, sugar, vinegar, peanut butter, soy sauce, and water in a food processor. Blend until smooth.
2. Toss the dressing with water chestnuts and cabbage in a large mixing bowl. Chill until ready to serve.

Equipment:
____ Food processor
____ Spoon
____ Knife
____ Cutting board
____ Measuring cups and spoons
____ Mixing bowls
____ Can opener
____ Plate (for final presentation)

Shopping list:
____ Silken firm tofu
____ Sugar
____ Red wine vinegar
____ Peanut butter
____ Light soy sauce
____ Water
____ Water chestnuts
____ Cabbage
____ Parsley (for garnish)
____ Disposable cups (for premeasured ingredients)
____ Plates, forks and napkins (for samples)

Cooking skill/nutrition lesson:
This recipe teaches participants how to make a basic oriental slaw. It uses silken tofu to create a creamy dressing, while incorporating new and delicious vegetables into the participants' repertoire.

Demo preparation:
1. Wash your hands before you handle food.
2. Prepare and measure all ingredients.
3. Organize your work area. If you are using an electric stove, turn it on low as participants arrive.

Garnish/presentation tips:
Arrange the slaw on a large, attractive platter. Garnish with parsley.

Number of sample servings: 16 (1/4 cup each)

Leader Guide: Healthy Asian Recipes

Hot and Sour Soup

Makes 8 sample servings

6 dried shiitake mushrooms
2 cups chicken broth
2 cups water
1 Tbsp miso
1/2 cup sliced green onions
1/2 cup cubed firm tofu (not silken)
1 Tbsp chopped fresh cilantro
1 Tbsp sesame oil
Pinch cayenne pepper

Directions:

1. Soak the shiitake mushrooms in very warm water for 15 minutes while you assemble the rest of the ingredients. Drain mushrooms and slice thinly.
2. Place the chicken broth, water, and miso in a 3 quart pan and heat over high heat until boiling. Reduce the heat to a simmer and add the rest of the ingredients. Stir well and cook briefly, about 3 minutes. Serve hot.

Equipment:

_____ Stove
_____ 3 quart sauce pan
_____ Spoon
_____ Knife
_____ Cutting board
_____ Measuring cups and spoons
_____ Mixing bowl
_____ Can opener
_____ Bowl (for final presentation)

Shopping list:

_____ 6 dried shiitake mushrooms
_____ Chicken broth
_____ Water
_____ Miso
_____ Green onions
_____ Firm tofu (not silken)
_____ Fresh cilantro
_____ Sesame oil
_____ Cayenne pepper
_____ Disposable cups (for premeasured ingredients)
_____ Cups, spoons and napkins (for samples)

Cooking skill/nutrition lesson:

This recipe teaches participants how to make hot and sour soup. It is fast and easy and can accompany any stir fry meal or salad to round out a light meal.

Demo preparation:

1. Wash your hands before you handle food.
2. Prepare and measure all ingredients.
3. Organize your work area. If you are using an electric stove, turn it on low as participants arrive.

Garnish/presentation tips:

Place the soup in an attractive bowl. Garnish with a fresh cilantro sprig.

Number of sample servings: 8 (1/2 cup each)

Healthy Asian Cooking

Easy Stir Fry With Tofu

4 cups cooked brown rice
Juice of 1 orange
1/4 cup chicken broth
1 Tbsp corn starch
4 Tbsp light soy sauce
1 Tbsp sesame oil
1 cup diced firm tofu (not silken)
1 Tbsp vegetable oil
1 Tbsp minced garlic
1 Tbsp grated fresh ginger
1 pound package of frozen stir-fry vegetables
Directions:

1. Cook the rice according to package directions.
2. Mix the orange juice, chicken broth, corn starch, soy sauce, sesame oil and tofu in a small mixing bowl. Stir well and set aside.
3. Meanwhile, heat the oil in a large nonstick skillet or wok over high heat. Saute the garlic and ginger until golden, about 3 minutes. Add the frozen veggies and cook until tender, about 6 minutes. Add sauce and cook until the mixture is heated through. Serve veggies and tofu over the cooked brown rice.

Serves 4. Each 2 cup serving: 398 calories, 11 g fat, 1.5 g saturated fat, 1 mg cholesterol, 538 mg sodium, 59 g carbohydrate, 16 g protein, 5 g fiber.

Egg Fried Vegetables with Rice

4 cups cooked brown rice
1 Tbsp oil
1 Tbsp minced garlic
1 Tbsp grated fresh ginger
1 pound package of frozen stir-fry vegetables
1 cup sliced fresh mushrooms
1 cup shredded cabbage
6 egg whites or 3/4 cup nonfat egg substitute
4 Tbsp light soy sauce
1 Tbsp sesame oil
Directions:

1. Cook rice according to package directions.
2. Heat the oil in a large, nonstick skillet or wok over high heat. Add the garlic and ginger and saute until golden, about 3 minutes. Add the frozen veggies and cook until tender, about 6 minutes. Remove the vegetables from the pan.
3. Add the egg whites and scramble until done, about 1 minute. Return the vegetables to the pan and season with soy sauce and sesame oil. Serve egg fried vegetables over the brown rice.

Serves 4. Each 2 cup serving: 372 calories, 9 g fat, 1 g saturated fat, 0 mg cholesterol, 603 mg sodium, 57 mg cholesterol, 16 g protein, 5.5 g fiber.

Healthy Asian Cooking

Cashew Stir Fry Salad

4 Tbsp light soy sauce
2 Tbsp rice wine vinegar
1 tsp sesame oil
Pinch red pepper flakes
4 cups shredded Nappa cabbage
1 Tbsp vegetable oil
2 tsp minced garlic
2 Tbsp grated fresh ginger
1/2 cup sliced carrots
1 cup sliced mushrooms
1 cup mung bean sprouts
1 cup broccoli florets
1 cup roasted unsalted cashews

Directions:

1. Mix the soy sauce, vinegar, sesame oil, and red pepper flakes in a small bowl.
2. Place shredded Nappa cabbage in a large salad bowl and set aside.
3. Heat a large, nonstick skillet or wok over high heat. Add the oil, then the garlic and ginger. Saute until the garlic is nutty brown, about 1 minute. Add the rest of the veggies and nuts. Saute until vegetables are crisp-tender, about 4-5 minutes. Add the soy sauce mixture and cook briefly. Add this stir-fry mixture to the cabbage, toss together and serve warm.

Serves 4. Each 2 cup serving: 230 calories, 14 g fat, 2 g saturated fat, 0 mg cholesterol, 535 mg sodium, 21 g carbohydrate, 9.5 g protein, 5 g fiber.

Asian Wrap

1/2 cup cubed firm tofu (not silken)
2 Tbsp light soy sauce
2 tsp honey
1 tsp sesame oil
Pinch sesame seeds
Pinch five spice seasoning
1 cup broccoli florets, rinsed with water
1/2 cup sliced carrots
1 cup sliced mushrooms
2 cups cooked brown rice
4 whole wheat tortillas

Directions:

1. Marinate tofu in soy sauce, honey, sesame oil, sesame seeds, and five spice seasoning in a small bowl.
2. Combine broccoli, carrots and mushrooms in a covered microwave container. Cook on full power until the veggies are almost tender, about 4 minutes.
3. Heat tortillas in the microwave until warm, about 20 seconds.
4. Combine the veggies, brown rice, and tofu mixture. Divide this filling among the warm tortillas, roll them up, and serve warm.

Serves 4. Each serving (1 wrap): 244 calories, 4 g fat, 0.5 g saturated fat, 0 mg cholesterol, 454 mg sodium, 43 g carbohydrate, 9.5 g protein, 12 g fiber.

Healthy Asian Cooking

Oriental Slaw

1/4 cup silken firm tofu
2 Tbsp sugar
1/4 cup red wine vinegar
1 Tbsp peanut butter
1 Tbsp light soy sauce
1 Tbsp water
1/4 cup water chestnuts
4 cups shredded cabbage
Directions:

1. Combine tofu, sugar, vinegar, peanut butter, soy sauce, and water in a food processor. Blend until smooth.
2. Toss the dressing with water chestnuts and cabbage in a large mixing bowl. Chill until ready to serve.

Serves 4. Each 1 cup serving: 87 calories, 2.5 g fat, 0 g saturated fat, 0 mg cholesterol, 145 mg sodium, 14 g carbohydrate, 2 g fiber, 3 g protein.

Hot and Sour Soup

6 dried shiitake mushrooms
2 cups chicken broth
2 cups water
1 Tbsp miso
1/2 cup sliced green onions
1/2 cup cubed firm tofu (not silken)
1 Tbsp chopped fresh cilantro
1 Tbsp sesame oil
Pinch cayenne pepper
Directions:

1. Soak the shiitake mushrooms in very warm water for 15 minutes while you assemble the rest of the ingredients. Drain mushrooms and slice thinly.
2. Place the chicken broth, water, and miso in a 3 quart pan and heat over high heat until boiling. Reduce the heat to a simmer and add the rest of the ingredients. Stir well and cook briefly, about 3 minutes. Serve hot.

Serves 4. Each 1 cup serving: 60 calories, 2.5 g fat, 0 g saturated fat, 12 mg cholesterol, 289 mg sodium, 3 g carbohydrate, 6 g protein, 0.5 g fiber.

Perfect Brown Rice

1 cup brown rice
2 cups water
Stove Top Directions:

1. Place water in 2 quart pot and bring to a boil. Add the rice, bring back to a boil, then lower to a simmer.
2. Cover the pot and cook until all the water is absorbed, about 45 minutes. Do not stir during cooking or the rice will be sticky. Allow the rice to stand for a few minutes and fluff with a fork.

Microwave Directions:

1. Place the rice and water in a covered microwave container. Cook in the microwave under 80-100% power for 30 minutes or until rice has absorbed all water. Do not stir during cooking. Allow to stand for a few minutes, then fluff with a fork. Yield: 3 cups.

Serves 4. Each 3/4 cup serving: 171 calories, 1.5 g fat, 0 g saturated fat, 0 mg cholesterol, 6 mg sodium, 35 g carbohydrate, 1.5 g fiber, 3.5 g protein.

Brown Rice Success Tips:

- Use 1 part rice to 2 parts water for brown rice. Instant brown rice uses equal parts water to rice. For best results, you should measure instead of guess on the amounts.
- Time rice accurately while cooking to avoid under or over cooking your rice.
- Don't lift the lid or stir the rice while cooking.
- At the end of cooking time, if liquid is not absorbed, cook 2 to 4 minutes longer.
- If the cooked rice is still crunchy, add a little more liquid, cover tightly and cook until rice is tender, about 5-6 more minutes. This is usually the result of the pot not being covered tightly.
- When rice is done cooking, allow it to sit for a few minutes then fluff with a fork.

Asian Ingredient Glossary

Do you find yourself stumped by Asian recipes with unusual ingredients? Or would you like to know what to do with some of the Asian produce and condiments that you see in your grocery store? Here is a list of our favorite Asian foods that you can find in almost any grocery stores.

Adzuki beans - These are reddish brown beans with a sweet, mild flavor. Commonly purchased dried, they are used in both sweet and savory dishes in China and Japan. Adzuki beans can be made into a paste that is avaliable in many Asian markets.

Basil - Basil is a fresh herb that is used extensively in Thai cuisine.

Bok Choy - This type of cabbage has a white stem and long green leaves. Store it in a ventilated bag inside your vegetable crisper. Slice it into thin strips for stir fry dishes.

Chinese eggplant - Similar to North American eggplant, this vegetable is longer and thinner. It usually is purple with white streaks.

Cilantro - A fresh herb used in Thai cooking, cilantro adds a nice flavor to stir fry dishes.

Cornstarch - This is used extensively to thicken sauces. Dilute it in water before adding to boiling liquid. You should usually use 1 tsp of corn starch per 1 cup of liquid.

Daikon - Daikon is a Chhinese radish that resembles a white carrot. Japanese cooks use daikon for relishes and salads, while Chinese cooks tend to feature it in soups. Daikon can withstand long periods of cooking without losing its shape.

Fish sauce - This salty sauce is made from dried fish. Use it sparingly, since it is very high in sodium.

Five spice powder - This elegant blend of spices includes cinnamon, fennel, cloves, star anise and white pepper. It adds a nice flavor to stir fry dishes

Garlic - Garlic is used extensively in many Asian cuisines and has many phytochemicals that may inhibit the growth of certain cancers or lower cholesterol.

Ginger - This is said to have beneficial digestive properties. It also adds a lot of flavor to many dishes and can be used fresh or dried.

Green tea - This tea is a product of a plant known as C. sinensis, a native of Southeast Asia. Green tea is made by drying the leaves of this plant without the fermentation (fermentation produces black tea). Scientists have identified a substance in green tea called catechins, which act as strong antioxidants and remain unchanged in green tea processing.

Hoisin sauce - This sweet and spicy sauce is usually used in barbecue dishes. Use sparingly, since it is very high in sodium.

Hot mustard - When you mix dried mustard powder with water, you'll come up with a very pungent sauce.

Mung bean sprouts - These thick, succulent bean sprouts come from Mung beans and should be cooked or steamed before use.

Mushrooms - Asian cooking uses a variety of dried mushrooms, which need to be reconstituted in very warm water for 20 minutes before use. Shitake are the most popular and are sometimes called Chinese Black Mushrooms.

Napa Cabbage - Also known as Chinese Cabbage, Napa Cabbage has curly leaves and a milder flavor than regular cabbage.

Pickled ginger - These thin, pink slices of ginger have been pickled, which gives them a whole new flavor profile.

Rice wine vinegar - This mild vinegar can be used in Asian style salads.

Sesame oil - A very flavorful oil made from pressed toasted sesame seeds, sesame oil enhances a stir fry. Remember, a little bit goes a long way.

Snow peas - These flat pea pods can be eaten whole; look for crisp, fresh-looking pods and keep them covered in the refrigerator.

Soy sauce - This sauce is very high in sodium; purchase light versions and use them sparingly.

Tofu - This can be silken, regular, and baked. See the soy section of this collection for more information. Generally speaking, you can use any of those three for stir fry dishes. The regular and baked versions are best at holding their shape.

Wasabi - This pungent green horseradish usually accompanies sushi.

Water chestnuts - This aquatic vegetable grows in marshes and adds a nice, crisp texture to many dishes.

For More Information:
http://www.foodandhealth.com/cpecourses/msg.php - This article about MSG outlines its features and discusses ways to avoid getting MSG symptom complex. *http://www.oldwayspt.org/asian-diet-pyramid* - This website provides details about many of the foods used in Asian cuisine.

Leader Guide: Healthy Ethnic: Italian

Title:
Healthy Ethnic Cooking: Italian

Target Audience:
This presentation kit is intended for general audiences age 14 and up. It covers topics of wellness, aging, diabetes, heart disease, family health, limited resources, cancer prevention, and nutrition.

Lesson Objectives:
• Participants will learn about healthy ingredients to use in Italian cooking.
• Participants will learn how to modify traditional Italian dishes so that they contain less fat, saturated fat, and sodium.
• Participants will taste a variety of Italian foods.

Lesson Rationale:
Italian foods are often healthy and flavorful, especially when they contain whole grain pasta, fruits, vegetables, legumes, and nuts. This class is designed to show participants how to select ingredients and make healthy dishes in their own kitchen. The recipes in this lesson are all comprised of common ingredients found in grocery stores across the U.S. Many recipes modify traditional Italian recipes and make them lower in fat. For example, the lasagna in this lesson contains far less saturated fat than traditional lasagna because it is made with fat-free ricotta cheese and without meat.

Health authorities have indicated that good nutrition is one of the most important factors in determining long-term health. Poor diet plays a major role in the development of four of the top seven killers in the United States: heart disease, cancer, stroke and diabetes. Individuals who have the skills to select and prepare nutritious foods can positively impact their present and future health.

Lesson at a Glance:
This lesson is designed to explore the benefits of traditional Italian cooking and ingredients. It focuses on using healthy ingredients that are easily found in most US grocery stores that can be made in most US kitchens. Most recipes given are modified from originals so they are healthier, yet still delicious. This lesson introduces participants to new recipes and cooking skills, while providing information that is consistent with MyPlate and the Dietary Guidelines for Americans.

Lesson Materials:
This lesson contains:
• Leader and Activity Guides; Recipe Leader Guides
• 3 pages of copy-ready handouts and recipes

Preparation:
___ Review leader guide
___ Review handouts
___ Select activities
___ Copy and collect materials for lesson

Activity Ideas:
Introduction
Ask participants to name their favorite Italian dishes. Many may mention a pasta dish. List everyone's responses and ask whether they ever feel a dish could be made healthier. If anyone says yes, ask how that might be accomplished.

Activity 1 – Cooking Demo
Use the recipes in this lesson to plan a cooking demonstration. The cooking demonstrations are designed to show individuals how to modify favorite and traditional dishes to make them healthier.

Activity 2 - Focus on Healthy Italian Foods/Ingredients
Display a variety of healthy Italian ingredients. Arrange them into the categories and proportions described by MyPlate. You can also print a copy of the Mediterranean Diet Pyramid, which can be found at: http://www.oldwayspt.org/mediterranean-diet-pyramid
Here is a list of possible options to include...

Grains:
Pasta - Offer a variety of shapes and make sure to include whole grain pasta.
Rice - Feature brown rice
Risotto - Since risotto is made from Arborio (short grain) rice, you should feature this type as well. You can buy brown Arborio rice in most supermarkets
Polenta - Bring out some of this fantastic cornmeal.

Vegetables:
Asparagus
Carrots
Chard
Fennel
Eggplant
Mushrooms
Olives
Onions
Peppers

Leader Guide: Healthy Ethnic: Italian

Potatoes
Spinach
Tomatoes
Zucchini

Fruits:
Apples
Apricots
Currants
Dates
Figs
Lemon
Oranges
Peaches
Pears
Prunes
Raisins

Protein:
Beans - Try featuring lentils, fava beans, white beans, and kidney beans.
Eggs - Use only the whites of the eggs or go for nonfat egg substitute.
Fish and seafood - Remember, people should eat around 8 ounces of seafood per week, according to MyPlate.
Nuts - Bring in some hazelnuts, almonds, pinenuts, pistachios, and walnuts.
Poultry

Dairy:
Yogurt
Cheese - Include Romano, Parmesan, fat-free ricotta and fat-free mozzarella. Explain that Romano and Parmesan have strong flavors, so a little bit goes a long way. When using fat-free mozzarella cheese, put it on the top at the end of baking. Otherwise it takes on the texture of shoe leather, and nobody wants that.

Herbs & Spices/Seasonings:
Anise - Anise seeds have a slight licorice flavor.
Balsamic Vinegar - This is a thick, strong, slightly sweet aged vinegar from Italy.
Basil - Fresh basil generally has a superior flavor to dried basil.
Bay leaves - Also known as laurel, bay leaves are common ingredients in pasta sauces.
Fennel - Fennel is an aromatic herb with a licorice flavor. The bulbs are also edible, with a similar licorice taste.
Garlic - Garlic plays a huge role in Italian cooking

and can be used it fresh or in powder form.
Italian Seasoning - This excellent herb mix is made from oregano, basil, and marjoram.
Oregano - This herb is used extensively in Italian cooking and can be fresh or dried.
Parsley - Fresh parsley is much better than dried parsley (in most cases).
Red wine vinegar - This bright, flavorful vinegar often plays a starring role in salad dressings.
Rosemary - This herb is mostly used in northern Italian cuisine. It is delicious with beans and smells like a Christmas tree. If you are using dried rosemary, be sure to crumble or chop the leaves because they are very sharp.
Saffron - This one comes from from the stigma of the flower of the saffron plant. You can use tumeric, annato, or even a little yellow food coloring in its place.
Sage - This earthy herb is delcious fresh or dried.
Savory - This peppery herb is also delicious fresh or dried
Tarragon - Tarragon has a bitter, licorice flavor. Dried tarragon is especially potent
Thyme - This herb is great fresh or dried and has a delicate, earthy flavor.

Further reading/info/links
http://www.ilovepasta.org/ - This site, run by the National Pasta Association, features news about pasta and outlines a variety of recipes to try.
http://www.oldwayspt.org/mediterranean-diet-pyramid - This website gives details about the foods that make up a Mediterranean diet. It also features the Mediterranean Diet Pyramid.

Leader Guide: Healthy Ethnic: Italian Recipes

Light Lasagna

Makes 20 sample servings

8 ounce box lasagna noodles
2 26-ounce jars pasta sauce
32 ounces fat free ricotta cheese
12 ounce box silken tofu
1 Tbsp Italian seasoning
1 cup shredded mozzarella cheese

Directions:

1. Preheat oven to 350 degrees. Place ricotta, tofu and Italian seasoning in a food processor and blend on high speed until smooth.
2. Layer lasagna in a 9x12 inch pan: Start with sauce, top with noodles, then ricotta. Repeat until pan is almost full. Finish with sauce on top and sprinkle with mozzarella cheese.
3. Cover the lasagna with foil and bake for one hour or until heated through. Check to make sure the noodles are tender (since there is no need to cook the noodles). Allow lasagna to stand for 5 minutes, then cut into 10 cubes and serve hot.

Equipment:

____ Stove
____ Oven
____ Food processor
____ Spatula
____ Measuring cups and spoons
____ 9x12 inch pan
____ Plate (for final presentation)

Shopping list:

____ 8 ounce box lasagna noodles
____ 2 26-ounce jars pasta sauce
____ 32 ounces fat free ricotta cheese
____ 12 ounce box silken tofu
____ Italian seasoning
____ Shredded mozzarella cheese
____ Fresh basil for garnish
____ Aluminum foil
____ Plates, forks, and napkins (for samples)

Cooking skill/nutrition lesson:

This recipe shows participants how to lighten a traditional lasagna recipe without sacrificing flavor. The silken tofu mixed with the fat-free ricotta cheese makes a great creamy filling and adds protein.

Demo preparation:

1. Wash your hands before you handle food.
2. Measure all ingredients.
3. Organize your work area.

Make ahead options:

We recommend that you bake one pan of lasagna ahead of time and then demo another during class.

Garnish/presentation tips:

Cut the lasagna into 10 squares. Place one square on an attractive dinner plate and garnish with a sprig of fresh basil.

Number of sample servings: 20 (1/2 piece of lasagna per person)

Leader Guide: Healthy Ethnic: Italian Recipes

Pasta Primavera

Makes 16 sample servings

4 cups cooked, small pasta (like penne, wagon-wheel, bow-tie, shells, macaroni, etc).

1 Tbsp olive oil

1 Tbsp minced garlic

1 cup sliced mushrooms

3 cups assorted mixed frozen vegetables (use a blend with cauliflower, carrots and zucchini, if possible)

1 can diced no-salt-added tomatoes

1 Tbsp Italian seasoning

black pepper to taste

1 cup chicken broth

2 Tbsp grated Parmesan cheese

Directions:

1. Cook pasta according to package directions. For 4 cups of cooked pasta, you will need 3 cups of dry pasta.

2. Heat a large, nonstick skillet over medium-high heat. Add the olive oil and garlic and saute until garlic is golden brown, about 1 minute. Add the mushrooms and frozen mixed vegetables and cook until vegetables are thawed and starting to brown, about 3-5 minutes. Add the tomatoes, seasonings, broth and Parmesan. Bring to a boil; lower heat to simmer and cook briefly. Toss with pasta and serve hot.

Equipment:

_____ Large pot (to cook pasta)

_____ Stove

_____ Nonstick skillet

_____ Measuring cups and spoons

_____ Colander

_____ Knife

_____ Cutting board

_____ Can opener

_____ Plate (for final presentation)

Shopping list:

_____ 4 cups cooked, small pasta (like penne, wagon-wheel, bow-tie, shells, macaroni, etc).

_____ Olive oil

_____ Garlic

_____ Sliced mushrooms

_____ Assorted mixed frozen vegetables (use a blend with cauliflower, carrots and zucchini if possible)

_____ 1 can diced no-salt-added tomatoes

_____ Italian seasoning

_____ Black pepper

_____ Chicken broth

_____ Grated Parmesan cheese

_____ Disposable cups (for premeasured ingredients)

_____ Plates, forks and napkins (for samples)

Cooking skill/nutrition lesson

This recipe shows participants how to make a delicious pasta dish using simple ingredients and broth for sauce. You can buy the garlic already minced and the mushrooms already sliced to make this recipe even easier. Reductions in sodium content follow the guidelines laid out by MyPlate.

Demo preparation:

1. Wash your hands before you handle food.

2. Prepare and measure all ingredients.

3. Organize work area and ingredients. If you are using an electric stove, turn it on prior to participants entering the classroom.

Make ahead options:

You can make this entire recipe ahead of time and just reheat for sample servings. We do recommend that you cook the pasta ahead of time.

Garnish/presentation tips:

Serve this pasta on a large attractive dinner plate. Garnish with a little grated Parmesan cheese and black pepper.

Number of sample servings: 16 (1/2 cup per person)

Leader Guide: Healthy Ethnic: Italian Recipes

Pasta Fagioli
Makes 16 sample servings

1 tsp olive oil
2 tsp minced garlic
2 cups chicken broth
2 cups frozen Italian-style mixed vegetables
1 cup fresh-diced tomatoes
1 Tbsp Italian seasoning
1 15-ounce can white beans, drained and rinsed
1 cup dry macaroni

Directions:

1. Heat a large pan over medium-high heat. Add the olive oil and garlic and saute until garlic is golden brown, about 1 minute.
2. Add the rest of the ingredients and bring to a boil. Lower heat to a simmer and cook until macaroni is tender, about 10 minutes. Ladle into bowls and serve hot.

Equipment:
_____ Large pot
_____ Stove
_____ Measuring cups and spoons
_____ Colander
_____ Knife and cutting board
_____ Can opener
_____ Bowl (for final presentation)

Shopping list:
_____ Olive oil
_____ Minced garlic
_____ 2 cups chicken broth
_____ Frozen Italian-style mixed vegetables
_____ 2-3 fresh ripe tomatoes
_____ Italian seasoning
_____ 15-ounce can white beans, drained and rinsed
_____ Dry macaroni
_____ Parmesan cheese and fresh parsley (for optional garnish)
_____ Disposable cups (for premeasured ingredients)
_____ Cups, spoons, and napkins (for samples)

Cooking skill/nutrition lesson:
This recipe teaches participants how to make a delicious soup using vegetables, beans and pasta. Go for whole-wheat macaroni if you can find it, since MyPlate recommends that at least half of all grains consumed should be whole grains.

Demo preparation:
1. Wash your hands before you handle food.
2. Prepare and measure all ingredients.
3. Organize your ingredients and work area.
4. If you are using an electric stove, preheat it to low as participants arrive.

Make ahead options:
You can make this dish ahead of time and simply reheat it for class.

Garnish/presentation tips:
Place the soup in a large, attractive soup bowl. Garnish with fresh parsley and a sprinkle of grated Parmesan.

Number of sample servings: 16 (1/2 cup per person)

Leader Guide: Healthy Ethnic: Italian Recipes

Mushroom Risotto
Makes 16 sample servings

1 Tbsp olive oil
1 Tbsp minced garlic
2 cups sliced mushrooms
1 cup arborio or short-grained rice
5 cups chicken stock, heated
black pepper to taste
1 tsp dried oregano
1 tsp fresh chopped basil
1/4 cup grated Parmesan cheese

Directions:

1. Heat a Dutch oven pan over medium high heat. Add the olive oil and garlic and saute until garlic is golden, about 3 minutes. Add the mushrooms and cook briefly, about 2 minutes. Add the rice and stir well.
2. Add 1 cup of the stock, black pepper, and oregano. Bring this mixture to a boil then lower heat to a simmer. When almost all of the liquid is absorbed, add another cup of broth. Stir ocassionally. Continue cooking until all of the broth is used up. Add broth in one cup increments and stir until absorbed.
3. The risotto should take about 30-35 minutes. Add the fresh basil, grated Parmesan cheese and serve hot.

Equipment:
____ Dutch oven pan
____ Stove
____ Measuring cups and spoons
____ Spoon
____ Knife
____ Cutting board
____ Can opener
____ Plate (for final presentation)

Shopping list:
____ Olive oil
____ 1 Tbsp minced garlic
____ 2 cups sliced mushrooms
____ Arborio or short-grained rice
____ 5 cups chicken stock, heated
____ Black pepper to taste
____ Dried oregano
____ Fresh basil
____ Grated Parmesan cheese
____ Disposable cups (for premeasured ingredients)

____ Plates, forks and napkins (for samples)

Cooking skill/nutrition lesson:
This recipe teaches participants how to make risotto, a delicious grain-based dish. We would recommend serving this dish with a big tossed salad and a side of fresh fruit.

Demo preparation:
1. Wash your hands before you handle food.
2. Prepare and measure all ingredients.
3. Organize ingredients and work area.
4. If you are using an electric stove, preheat it to low before participants enter the room.

Make ahead options:
You can make this recipe ahead of time and reheat for sample servings. We recommend that you make a salad while the risotto is cooking.

Garnish/presentation tips:
Place the risotto on an attractive dinner plate. Garnish with a little Parmesan cheese and fresh cracked black pepper.

Number of sample servings: 16 (1/2 cup per person)

Leader Guide: Healthy Ethnic: Italian Recipes

Lemon Glazed Fruit Cup
Makes 12 sample servings

4 cups strawberries, hulled and halved
2 cups seedless red grapes
2 Tbsp sugar
2 teaspoons finely chopped fresh mint
Juice and zest of 1 lemon

Directions:
1. Combine all ingredients in large bowl; toss to coat fruit. Serve immediately or refrigerate up to 4 hours before serving.

Equipment:
_____ Knife
_____ Cutting board
_____ Grater
_____ Mixing bowl
_____ 4 dessert glasses

Ingredients:
_____ 4 cups strawberries
_____ 2 cups seedless red grapes
_____ Sugar
_____ Fresh mint
_____ 1 lemon

Cooking skill/nutrition lesson:
This lesson teaches participants how to make a delicious and light fruit salad. It also outlines how to use the zest of a citrus fruit. The zest is the thin outer skin - grate it off gently so you don't get the bitter white pith underneath.

Demo preparation:
1. Wash your hands before you handle food.
2. Prepare and measure ingredients.
3. Organize ingredients and work area.

Make ahead options:
You can prepare fruit ahead of time.

Garnish/presentation tips:
Place the fruit in an attractive stemmed glass. Finely chop mint and sprinkle it over the top of the fruit.

Variations:
You can also pair this fruit with sorbet. We suggest using small scoops of different colored sorbet. If you are going to do this, omit the lemon and sugar.

Number of sample servings: 12 (1/2 cup each)

Leader Guide: Healthy Ethnic: Italian Recipes

Grilled Portobello Mushrooms
Makes 12-16 sample servings

1/4 cup balsamic vinegar
1 Tbsp minced garlic
1/2 tsp dried thyme
2 Tbsp olive oil
1 pound Portobello mushrooms, stemmed and rinsed (be sure to get out all the dirt)

Directions:

1. Mix the vinegar, garlic, thyme, and oil together in a medium bowl. Add the mushrooms, and coat them in the marinade. Cover and refrigerate the mushrooms for 20 minutes or up to 24 hours.
2. Heat your oven broiler, grill, or non-stick grill pan to medium-high heat. Grill the mushrooms on both sides until tender, about 10 minutes. Slice mushrooms and serve hot over rice or on a whole wheat bun. These mushrooms have a beefy flavor and texture and can be served just like steak!

Equipment:
____ Broiler, grill, or stove with nonstick grill skillet
____ Knife
____ Cutting board
____ Large mixing bowl
____ Measuring spoons
____ Plate (for final presentation)

Shopping list:
____ 2 tablespoons balsamic vinegar
____ Minced garlic
____ Dried thyme
____ Olive oil
____ 1 1/2 pounds Portobello mushrooms
____ Disposable cups (for premeasured ingredients)
____ Plates, forks, knives and napkins (for samples)
____ Optional: whole wheat bun or rice
____ Optional: parsley and black pepper (for garnish)

Cooking skill/nutrition lesson:
This recipe shows participants how to use portabello mushrooms, which are becoming more popular in restaurants and grocery stores. They make an excellent replacement for steak and you can serve them on toasted whole grain bread or over brown rice.

Demo preparation:
1. Wash hands before preparing food.
2. Prepare and measure all ingredients.
3. Organize ingredients and work area.
4. Preheat broiler, grill, or grill pan to low as participants arrive.

Make ahead options:
You can grill these ahead of time, reheat for class, and then show participants how to serve them.

Garnish/presentation tips:
Serve the mushrooms on an attractive salad plate and top with fresh cracked black pepper and a sprig of parsley. You can also serve them over whole grain toast or rice.

Number of sample servings: 12-16

Healthy Ethnic Recipes: Italian

Light Lasagna

8 ounce box lasagna noodles
2 26-ounce jars pasta sauce
32 ounces fat free ricotta cheese
12 ounce box silken tofu
1 Tbsp Italian seasoning
1 cup shredded mozzarella cheese

Directions:

1. Preheat oven to 350 degrees. Place ricotta, tofu and Italian seasoning in a food processor and blend on high speed until smooth.
2. Layer lasagna in a 9x12 inch pan: Start with sauce, top with noodles, then ricotta. Repeat until pan is almost full. Finish with sauce on top and sprinkle with mozzarella cheese.
3. Cover the lasagna with foil and bake for one hour or until heated through. Check to make sure the noodles are tender (since there is no need to cook the noodles). Allow lasagna to stand for 5 minutes, then cut into 10 cubes and serve hot.

Serves 10. Each serving: 249 calories, 3 g fat, 1 g saturated fat, 12 mg cholesterol, 690 mg sodium, 45 g carbohydrate, 3 g fiber, 14 g protein.

Pasta Primavera

4 cups cooked, small pasta (like penne, wagon-wheel, bow-tie, shells, macaroni, etc).
1 Tbsp olive oil
1 Tbsp minced garlic
1 cup sliced mushrooms
3 cups assorted mixed frozen vegetables (use a blend with cauliflower, carrots and zucchini, if possible)
1 can diced no-salt-added tomatoes
1 Tbsp Italian seasoning
Black pepper to taste
1 cup chicken broth
2 Tbsp grated Parmesan cheese

Directions:

1. Cook pasta according to package directions. For 4 cups of cooked pasta, you will need 3 cups of dry pasta.
2. Heat a large, nonstick skillet over medium-high heat. Add the olive oil and garlic and saute until garlic is golden brown, about 1 minute. Add the mushrooms and frozen mixed vegetables and cook until vegetables are thawed and starting to brown, about 3-5 minutes. Add the tomatoes, seasonings, broth and Parmesan. Bring to a boil; lower heat to simmer and cook briefly. Toss with pasta and serve hot.

Serves 4. Each 1-1/2 cup serving: 302 calories, 6 g fat, 1 g saturated fat, 8 mg cholesterol, 188 mg sodium, 49 g carbohydrate, 6 g fiber, 12 g protein.

Healthy Ethnic Recipes: Italian

Pasta Fagioli

1 tsp olive oil
2 tsp minced garlic
2 cups chicken broth
2 cups frozen Italian-style mixed vegetables
1 cup fresh-diced tomatoes
1 Tbsp Italian seasoning
1 15-ounce can white beans, drained and rinsed
1 cup dry macaroni
Directions:
1. Heat a large pan over medium-high heat. Add the olive oil and garlic and saute until garlic is golden brown, about 1 minute.
2. Add the rest of the ingredients and bring to a boil. Lower heat to a simmer and cook until macaroni is tender, about 10 minutes. Ladle into bowls and serve hot.
Serves 4. Each 1-1/2 cup serving: 265 calories, 2.5 g fat, 0.5 g saturated fat, 12 mg cholesterol, 178 mg sodium, 45 g carbohydrate, 7 g fiber, 14 g protein.

Grilled Portobello Mushrooms

1/4 cup balsamic vinegar
1 Tbsp minced garlic
1/2 tsp dried thyme
2 Tbsp olive oil
1 pound Portobello mushrooms, remove stems and rinse well to remove dirt
Directions:
1. Mix the vinegar, garlic, thyme and oil together in a medium sized bowl. Add the mushrooms, turning to coat them in the marinade. Cover and refrigerate the mushrooms for 20 minutes or up to 24 hours.
2. Heat your oven broiler, grill or ridged non-stick grill pan to medium-high heat. Grill the mushrooms on both sides until tender, about 10 minutes. Slice mushrooms and serve hot over rice or on a whole wheat bun. These mushrooms have a "beefy" flavor and texture and can be served just like steak!
Serves 4. Each 1/2 cup serving: 112 calories, 9 g fat, 1 g saturated fat, 0 mg cholesterol, 7 mg sodium, 6 g carbohydrate, 1 g fiber, 5 g protein.

Mushroom Risotto

1 Tbsp olive oil
1 Tbsp minced garlic
2 cups sliced mushrooms
1 cup arborio or short-grained rice
5 cups chicken stock, heated
black pepper to taste
1 tsp dried oregano
1 tsp fresh chopped basil
1/4 cup grated Parmesan cheese
Directions:
1. Heat a Dutch oven pan over medium high heat. Add the olive oil and garlic and saute until garlic is golden, about 3 minutes. Add the mushrooms and cook briefly, about 2 minutes. Add the rice and stir well.
2. Add 1 cup of the stock, black pepper, and oregano. Bring this mixture to a boil then lower heat to a simmer. When almost all of the liquid is absorbed, add another cup of broth. Stir ocassionally. Continue cooking until all of the broth is used up. Add broth in one cup increments and stir until absorbed.
3. The risotto should take about 30-35 minutes. Add the fresh basil, grated Parmesan cheese and serve hot.
Serves 4. Each 1 cup serving: 310 calories, 8 g fat, 2 g saturated fat, 36 mg cholesterol, 431 mg sodium, 42 g carbohydrate, 2 g fiber, 16 g protein.

Lemon Glazed Fruit Cup

4 cups strawberries, hulled, cut in half
2 cups seedless red grapes
2 Tbsp sugar
2 teaspoons finely chopped fresh mint
juice and zest of 1 lemon
Directions:
1. Combine all ingredients in large bowl; toss to coat fruit. Serve immediately or refrigerate up to 4 hours before serving.
Serves 4. Each 1 cup serving: 123 calories, 1 g fat, 0 g saturated fat, 0 mg cholesterol, 3 mg sodium, 30 g carbohydrate, 4 g fiber, 1.5 g protein.

10 Tricks for Healthy Italian Food

1. Drop the fat
Measure olive oil -- don't just pour some into a pan. Although olive oil contains healthy fats, it is also extremely calorie dense. Using a nonstick skillet will also help you cut down on the amout of oil a recipe needs.

2. Lighten up the cheese
Opt for small amounts of flavorful cheese like Parmesan or Romano cheese. Try using fat-free ricotta in place of regular ricotta cheese for an even stronger health boost.

3. Go for a little bit of lean meat
Use high-fat items like sausage or ground meat very sparingly, if at all. Fish, seafood, and white poultry are better choices.

4. Emphasize whole grains, vegetables, and fruits
Use meat as a flavoring or side dish, not the main attraction. Be sure to get protein from a wide variety of sources, in accordance to MyPlate guidelines.

5. Eat whole grain pasta.
Choose whole grain pasta instead of white pasta wherever possible. Whole grain pasta contains more fiber and nutrients and is super easy to prepare.

6. Make low-sodium choices
See if you can find pasta sauce with no salt or at least less than 400 mg of sodium per serving. You can lower the sodium in prepared pasta sauce by adding no-salt-added canned tomato sauce.

7. Eat lots of tomatoes
Tomatoes are high in vitamins A & C and are a good source of potassium. They also contain lycopene, a phytochemical that may help prevent certain cancers.

8. Switch cream with broth
Broth makes an excellent pasta sauce. Add mushrooms, basil, thyme, and rosemary for more flavor.

9. Go easy on the bread
Bread is calorie dense and it is easy to eat too much of it, especially in Italian restaurants where baskets of bread tend to be bountiful.

10. Use flavorful herbs
Use herbs instead of salt to season your meals. Italian cooks use generous amounts of basil and oregano along with mushrooms, sun-dried tomatoes, fresh parsley, garlic and onions.

Pasta Tips & Facts:

- For small pasta, like elbow macaroni, shells, spirals, wagon wheels, penne, bowties, etc., 2 ounces of it uncooked comes to a 1/2 cup dry and just over 1/2 cup cooked.

- For long pastas like spaghetti, angel hair, vermicelli, linguine, etc., 2 ounces uncooked equals a 1/2 inch bunch dry and 1 cup of cooked pasta.

- The best way to tell if pasta is done is to taste it. You want a bite to it, which is how properly prepared pasta became known as "al dente."

- Use package directions to determine cooking times.

- Cook the pasta in plenty of boiling water. For 1 pound of dry pasta, you should use 4 quarts of water.

- Stir the pasta while it cooks to keep it from sticking.

- The best way to keep pasta from sticking is to use plenty of boiling water and keep an eye on it so you don't over cook it. It is not necessary to oil the pasta after cooking or use oil in the cooking water.

Leader Guide: Healthy Ethnic: Latin

Title:
Healthy Ethnic Cooking: Latin

Target Audience:
This presentation kit is intended for general audiences age 14 and up. It covers topics of wellness, aging, diabetes, heart disease, family health, limited income, WIC, cancer prevention, and nutrition.

Lesson Objectives:
• Participants will learn about healthy ingredients used in Latin cooking that are readily available in U.S. grocery stores.
• Participants will learn how to make a few healthy recipes using Latin ingredients.

Lesson Rationale:
The Hispanic-American community is the fastest growing minority population in the United States. The US census estimated the projected growth for Latinos to double between 2010 and 2050.

On average, Hispanics/Latin Americans are almost twice as likely to have diabetes as non-Hispanic whites of similar age (according to the National Institute of Health).

Health authorities have indicated that good nutrition is one of the most important factors in determining long-term health (along with limited alcohol consumption and avoidance of tobacco products). Poor diet plays a major role in the development of four of the top seven killers in the United States: heart disease, cancer, stroke and diabetes. Students who have the skills to select and prepare nutritious foods can positively impact their present and future health.

Lesson at a Glance:
This lesson is designed to explore the benefits of traditional Hispanic/Latin American cooking and ingredients. It focuses on using healthy ingredients that are easily found in most US grocery stores and can be prepared in typical US kitchens. Most recipes given are modified from originals so they are healthier, yet still delicious. This lesson introduces participants to new recipes and cooking skills, while providing information that is consistent with MyPlate and the Dietary Guidelines for Americans.

Lesson Materials:
This lesson contains:
• Leader and Activity Guide
• 4 pages of copy-ready handouts and recipes

Preparation:

___ Review leader guide
___ Review handouts
___ Select activities
___ Copy and collect materials for lesson

Activity Ideas:
Introduction
Ask participants to share their favorite dish from Latin cooking. Latin American cuisine can't be summed up easily. It's as diverse as the countries that make up Latin America, which include the Spanish-speaking Caribbean islands and South American countries, as well as Central America and Mexico. Although many dishes and foods are common throughout Latin America, each country has its own specialties and cooking styles.

The purpose of this lesson is to show participants a variety of healthy Latin ingredients and condiments, then demonstrate how to make healthy, easy, Latin-style meals in their own kitchens.

Activity 1 – Cooking Demo
Use the recipes in this lesson to give your audience a cooking demonstration. The recipes in this lesson are designed to outline how to make healthy, easy meals like chicken with rice and Cuban beans.

Activity 2 - Get to Know Latin Ingredients
Many traditional Latin ingredients are very healthy. Introduce your audience to some or all of these below. You may want to bring in samples or models for everyone to see.

Grains:
Common grain elements in Latin foods include rice, cornmeal, and tortillas. Look for whole grain options whenever possible.

Vegetables:
Latin cuisine features an abundance of healthy vegetables. Some of our favorites include chilis, tomatoes, peppers, onions, squash, corn, and sweet potatoes.

Fruits:
Latin recipes also include a ton of healthy fruits like papaya, banana, plantain, oranges, pineapple, strawberries, mango, guava, mamey, cherimoya, pomelo and passion fruit.

Protein:
Healthy Latin recipes include a wide range of protein and often feature combinations of beans, chicken, fish, seafood, eggs, ground turkey (sub it in for ground beef), or lean pork.

Dairy:

Leader Guide: Healthy Ethnic: Latin

This group includes skim milk, lowfat cheese, and nonfat sour cream

Common Seasonings:

Annatto - This spice also functions as food coloring and produces a saffron-like yellow shade.

Chili Pepper - There are a variety of chili peppers in an abundance of flavor profiles. Check the web or ask your grocer about which ones are right for your palate.

Cilantro - Cilantro is an herb with a lemony/peppery flavor. It looks very much like parsley.

Culantro - With a flavor that is similar to cilantro, this herb features large, thick leaves.

Cumin - This ground spice that imparts an earthy flavors to almost any dish.

Lemon, Lime - These fruits are often used with seafood, salsa and many other dishes.

Oregano - This herb plays a vital role in Mexican cooking.

Sazon - This one is mostly MSG and plays a role in Puerto Rican cooking.

Sofrito - This seasoning sauce is made from lean cured ham, onion, green pepper, cilantro, and garlic sauteed in oil. It is often used in Puerto Rican cooking.

Further reading/info/links

http://www.oldwayspt.org/latino-nutrition - This website features recipes and information about traditional Latin foods. It even has a Latin Diet Pyramid.

# Leader Guide: Healthy Latin Recipes

Fun with Flan

Makes 8 sample servings

1/2 cup sugar
1 cup nonfat egg substitute
1 Tbsp vanilla extract
2 cups skim milk
4 tsp caramel syrup
2 cups assorted diced fresh fruits

Directions:

1. Mix 1/4 cup sugar with nonfat egg substitute and vanilla in a medium bowl.
2. Bring the skim milk and other 1/4 cup of sugar to a boil in a small saucepan over medium-high heat. Pour the milk into the egg mixture and stir well.
3. Preheat the oven to 325 degrees. Pour the custard into 4 ramekins or custard cups. Place the cups of custard into a pan of hot water and place that in the center of the oven. Bake until the custard is firm in the center, about 45-60 minutes. Remove from oven, allow to cool, then refrigerate.
4. To remove custard from ramekins, run a knife around the edge of the custard cup and invert onto plate, tapping if necessary.
5. Serve each flan with with a half cup of fresh fruit and a teaspoon-sized drizzle of caramel syrup.

Equipment:

____ Stove
____ Oven
____ Saucepan
____ Mixing bowl
____ Whisk
____ Measuring cups and spoons
____ Knife
____ Cutting board
____ Plate (for final presentation)

Shopping list:

____ Sugar
____ Nonfat egg substitute
____ Vanilla extract
____ Skim milk
____ Caramel syrup
____ Assorted fresh fruits
____ Disposable cups (for premeasured ingredients)
____ Plates, spoons and napkins (for samples)

Cooking skill/nutrition lesson:

This recipe will teach individuals how to modify a traditional flan recipe by using skim milk in place of whole milk and nonfat egg substitute in place of whole eggs. This cuts down on saturated fat with no noticeable difference in flavor. The recipe also uses a drizzle of prepared caramel syrup instead of a large amount of caramel at bottom of the custard cup, while emphasizing the use of fresh fruit.

Demo preparation:

1. Wash your hands before you handle food.
2. Prepare and measure all ingredients.
3. Organize ingredients and work area.

Make ahead options:

We recommend that you make and bake the custard ahead of time, then show participants how to finish setting up the dessert. It might be fun to ask different members of the audience to help you garnish each one.

Garnish/presentation tips:

Place custard on an attractive plate. Garnish with colorful fruit and a drizzle of caramel syrup.

Number of sample servings: 8 (1/2 flan per person)

Leader Guide: Healthy Latin Recipes

Tutti Fruiti

Makes 12 sample servings

3 cups diced watermelon

1 cup halved and hulled strawberries

1 cup diced papaya

1 cup diced pineapple

2 oranges, peeled, seeded, and diced

Juice of 2 limes

Directions:

1. Dice all fruit and place in a large mixing bowl. Add lime juice and mix well. Refrigerate until ready to serve.

Equipment:

____ Knife

____ Cutting board

____ Measuring cups

____ Glass or bowl (for final presentation)

Shopping list:

____ Watermelon

____ Strawberries

____ Papaya

____ Pineapple

____ 2 oranges

____ 2 limes

____ Disposable cups (for premeasured ingredients)

____ Plates, forks, and napkins (for samples)

Cooking skill/nutrition lesson:

This lesson outlines a fun and healthy fruit dish with common ingredients from Latin cultures.

Demo preparation:

1. Wash your hands before you handle food.

2. Measure and prepare all ingredients.

3. Organize ingredients and work area.

Make ahead options:

You can make this dish ahead of time and just serve it in class.

Garnish presentation tips:

This recipe looks especially nice when served in a hollowed out half of a watermelon shell.

Number of sample servings: 12 (about 1/2 cup ea)

Cuban Beans and Rice

Makes 14 sample servings

1 tsp olive oil

1 Tbsp minced garlic

1 cup chopped onion

1 cup diced green bell pepper

3 cups cooked black beans

2 cups low sodium chicken broth

1 Tbsp vinegar

1/2 tsp dried oregano

Black pepper to taste

3 cups cooked brown rice

Directions:

1. Heat the olive oil in a large nonstick skillet. Saute the garlic, onion and green bell pepper until garlic and onion are golden, about 3 minutes.

2. Stir in beans, broth, vinegar, and seasoning. Bring mixture to a boil, then lower to a simmer and cook (covered) for 5 minutes. Spoon over rice and serve.

Equipment:

____ Stove

____ Large nonstick skillet

____ Measuring cups and spoons

____ Cutting board and knife

____ Kitchen spoon and can opener

____ Pan to cook the rice, plate (for final presentation)

Shopping list:

____ Olive oil

____ Minced garlic

____ Onion

____ Green bell pepper

____ Cooked black beans

____ Vinegar

____ Dried oregano

____ Black pepper

____ Brown rice

____ Plates, forks and napkins (for samples)

Demo preparation:

1. Wash your hands before you handle food.

2. Measure ingredients and organize work area.

Garnish/presentation tips:

Garnish beans with slices of fresh peppers. You can use a rainbow of bright colors, so feel free to explore.

Number of sample servings: 14 (1/2 cup each)

Leader Guide: Healthy Latin Recipes

Chicken and Rice - Arroz con Pollo

Makes 16 sample servings

1 Tbsp olive oil
1 cup chopped onion
1 cup chopped green bell pepper
1 Tbsp minced garlic
1 pound boneless, skinless chicken breasts, cut in pieces
1/2 tsp annatto
1 tsp ground coriander
1 tsp ground cumin
2 cups frozen peas and carrots
2 cups long-grain brown rice
4 cups chicken broth

Directions:

1. Heat a large Dutch oven style pan over medium high heat. Add the oil, onion, green bell pepper, and garlic and saute until onion and garlic are golden, about 3 minutes. Add the chicken breast pieces and cook for 3 more minutes.
3. Add the rest of the ingredients and bring to a boil. Lower heat to simmer and cook until the chicken is done, about 10 minutes. Serve hot.

Equipment:

____ Dutch oven style pan
____ Stove
____ Knife
____ Cutting board
____ Measuring utensils
____ Spoon
____ Can opener
____ Plate (for final presentation)

Shopping list:

____ Olive oil
____ Onion
____ Green bell pepper
____ Minced garlic
____ 1 pound boneless, skinless chicken breasts
____ Frozen peas and carrots
____ Long-grain brown rice
____ Chicken broth
____ Ground cumin
____ Black pepper

Cooking skill/nutrition lesson:

This recipe teaches participants how to make a healthy chicken and rice dish. We reduced the amount of chicken, removed the skin, and used only white meat. Also, we reduced the amount of oil and used brown rice instead of white rice. This brings the plate more in line with MyPlate recommendations.

Demo preparation:

1. Wash your hands before you handle food.
2. Measure and prepare all ingredients.
3. Organize ingredients and work area.

Make ahead options:

You can make this dish ahead of time and reheat and serve for class.

Garnish/presentation tips:

Serve this dish on an attractive platter. Garnish with fresh pepper slices.

Number of sample servings: 16 (1/2 cup each)

Leader Guide: Healthy Latin Recipes

Taco Salad
Makes 16 sample servings
1 15-ounce can pinto beans, rinsed and drained
2 cups tortilla chips
4 tablespoons nonfat sour cream
Salad:
6 cups romaine lettuce
1 cup chopped tomatoes
1 mild chili pepper, chopped
1/4 cup chopped red onion
1 cup corn kernels
2 tsp olive oil
2 Tbsp flavored vinegar
1 tsp oregano
1/2 tsp chili powder
Directions:
1. Place the beans in a small microwave container and microwave on full power until heated through, about 2 minutes.
2. Toss all ingredients for the salad in a large mixing bowl.
3. Place 1/3 cup beans on each plate, then put 1/2 cup tortilla chips on top of the beans. Follow with 2 cups of the salad. Top each one with 1 tablespoon of nonfat sour cream and serve immediately.

Equipment:
____ Knife
____ Cutting board
____ Microwave-safe container
____ Microwave oven
____ Measuring utensils
____ Mixing bowl
____ Can opener
____ 3 spoons
____ Plates (for final presentation)

Shopping list:
____ 15 ounce can pinto beans
____ Tortilla chips
____ Nonfat sour cream
____ Romaine lettuce
____ Tomatoes
____ 1 mild chili pepper
____ Red onion
____ Corn kernels
____ Olive oil
____ Flavored vinegar
____ Oregano
____ Chili powder
____ Disposable cups (for premeasured ingredients)
____ Plates, forks and napkins (for samples)

Cooking skill/nutrition lesson:
This recipe explains how to make a healthier taco salad. We reduced the amount of fried tortilla chips, used beans instead of ground beef, added more vegetables, used nonfat sour cream, and omitted the cheddar cheese.

Demo preparation:
1. Wash your hands before you handle food.
2. Measure and prepare all ingredients.
3. Organize ingredients and work area.

Garnish/presentation tips:
Place the salad on a large, attractive plate. Pile the salad on top of the tortilla chips and beans, then place the dollop of sour cream on the top. You can also add fresh chopped cilantro as a garnish.

Number of sample servings: 16 (1/2 cup each)

Leader Guide: Healthy Latin Recipes

Bean Burritos - Burritos con Frijoles

Makes 6 sample servings

2 (10-inch) flour tortillas
1 tsp vegetable oil
1 cup chopped onion
1/2 cup chopped green bell pepper
1 Tbsp minced garlic
1 tsp minced jalapeno peppers
15 ounce can pinto beans, rinsed and drained
2 Tbsp water
2 Tbsp chopped fresh cilantro

Directions:

1. Place tortillas in microwave and heat for a few seconds. This makes them warm and pliable.
2. Heat oil in a 10-inch skillet over medium heat. Saute onion, bell pepper, garlic and jalapenos for about 3 minutes.
3. Add beans, water, and chopped cilantro. Cook until heated through, about 2-3 minutes.
5. Spoon mixture evenly down the center of warmed tortilla and roll up. Serve immediately. We recommend serving alongside steamed veggies or a tossed salad.

Equipment:

____ Microwave oven
____ Stove
____ Nonstick skillet
____ Spoon
____ Can opener
____ Knife
____ Cutting board
____ Measuring utensils
____ Plate (for final presentation)

Shopping list:

____ 2 (10 inch) flour tortillas
____ Vegetable oil
____ Onion
____ Green bell pepper
____ Minced garlic
____ Jalapeno pepper
____ 15-ounce can pinto beans
____ Nonfat sour cream
____ Fresh cilantro
____ Disposable cups (for premeasured ingredients)
____ Plates, forks, and napkins (for samples)

Cooking skill/nutrition lesson:

This recipe outlines how to prepare a healthy version of bean burritos. It uses nonfat sour cream, vegetables, beans, and no cheese. It features four MyPlate food groups -- grains, protein, vegetables, and dairy.

Demo preparation:

1. Wash your hands before you handle food.
2. Measure and prepare all ingredients.
3. Organize ingredients and work area. If you are using an electric stove, turn it to low when participants arrive.

Make ahead options:

You can make the bean mixture ahead of time and reheat in the microwave. Roll up and serve. It might be fun to get volunteers from the audience to come and assemble the burritos.

Garnish/presentation tips:

Cut the burritos in half and place on attractive plates or platters. Garnish with a rainbow of sliced peppers or a sprig of fresh cilantro.

Number of sample servings: 6 (3 from each burrito)

Healthy Latin Recipes

Fun with Flan

1/2 cup sugar
1 cup nonfat egg substitute
1 Tbsp vanilla extract
2 cups skim milk
4 tsp caramel syrup
2 cups assorted diced fresh fruits
Directions:

1. Mix 1/4 cup sugar with nonfat egg substitute and vanilla in a medium bowl.
2. Bring the skim milk and other 1/4 cup of sugar to a boil in a small saucepan over medium-high heat. Pour the milk into the egg mixture and stir well.
3. Preheat the oven to 325 degrees. Pour the custard into 4 ramekins or custard cups. Place the cups of custard into a pan of hot water and place that in the center of the oven. Bake until the custard is firm in the center, about 45-60 minutes. Remove from oven, allow to cool, then refrigerate.
4. To remove custard from ramekins, run a knife around the edge of the custard cup and invert onto plate, tapping if necessary.
5. Serve each flan with with a half cup of fresh fruit

Serves 4. Each one: 187 calories, 0.5 g fat, 0 g saturated fat, 2 mg cholesterol, 163 mg sodium, 35 g carbohydrate, 1.5 g fiber, 11 g protein.

Tutti Fruiti

3 cups diced watermelon
1 cup halved and hulled strawberries
1 cup diced papaya
1 cup diced pineapple
2 oranges, peeled, seeded, and diced
Juice of 2 limes
Directions:

1. Dice all fruit and place in a large mixing bowl. Add lime juice and mix well. Refrigerate until ready to serve.
2. Pile fruit into a hollowed-out watermelon shell.

Serves 6. Each 1 cup serving: 74 calories, 0 fat, 0 cholesterol, 3 mg sodium, 17 g carbohydrate, 2.5 g fiber, 1.5 g protein.

Chicken and Rice - Arroz con Pollo

1 Tbsp olive oil
1 cup chopped onion
1 cup chopped green bell pepper
1 Tbsp minced garlic
1 pound boneless, skinless chicken breasts, cut in pieces
1/2 tsp annatto
1 tsp ground coriander
1 tsp ground cumin
2 cups frozen peas and carrots
2 cups long-grain brown rice
4 cups chicken broth
Directions:

1. Heat a large Dutch oven style pan over medium high heat. Add the oil, onion, green bell pepper, and garlic and saute until onion and garlic are golden, about 3 minutes. Add the chicken breast pieces and cook for 3 more minutes.
3. Add the rest of the ingredients and bring to a boil. Lower heat to simmer and cook until the chicken is done, about 10 minutes. Serve hot.

Serves 6. Each 1-1/2 cup serving: 242 calories, 2.5 g fat, 0.5 g saturated fat, 43 mg cholesterol, 149 mg sodium, 31 g carbohydrate, 4 g fiber, 23 g protein.

Cuban Beans and Rice - Habichuelas y Arroz Cubano

1 tsp olive oil
1 Tbsp minced garlic
1 cup chopped onion
1 cup diced green bell pepper
3 cups cooked black beans
2 cups low sodium chicken broth
1 Tbsp vinegar
1/2 tsp dried oregano
Black pepper to taste
3 cups cooked brown rice
Directions:

1. Heat the olive oil in a large nonstick skillet. Saute the garlic, onion and green bell pepper until garlic and onion are golden, about 3 minutes.
2. Stir in beans, broth, vinegar, and seasoning. Bring mixture to a boil, then lower to a simmer and cook (covered) for 5 minutes. Spoon over rice and serve.

Serves 4. Each 1-1/2 cup serving: 314 calories, 3 g fat, 0.5 g saturated fat, 0 mg cholesterol, 10 mg sodium, 60 g carbohydrate, 11.5 g fiber, 12 g protein.

Healthy Latin Recipes

Taco Salad

1 15-ounce can pinto beans, rinsed and drained
2 cups tortilla chips
4 tablespoons nonfat sour cream
Salad:
6 cups romaine lettuce
1 cup chopped tomatoes
1 mild chili pepper, chopped
1/4 cup chopped red onion
1 cup corn kernels
2 tsp olive oil
2 Tbsp flavored vinegar
1 tsp oregano
1/2 tsp chili powder
Directions:

1. Place the beans in a small microwave container and microwave on full power until heated through, about 2 minutes.
2. Toss all ingredients for the salad in a large mixing bowl.
3. Place 1/3 cup beans on each plate, then put 1/2 cup tortilla chips on top of the beans. Follow with 2 cups of the salad. Top each one with 1 tablespoon of nonfat sour cream and serve immediately.

Serves 4. Per Serving: Calories 260, Total Fat 1.5g, Saturated Fat 0g, Trans Fat 0g, Cholesterol 0mg, Sodium 330mg, Carbohydrates 41g, Dietary Fiber 7g, Sugars 6g, Protein 20g.

Bean Burritos - Burritos con Frijoles

2 (10-inch) flour tortillas
1 tsp vegetable oil
1 cup chopped onion
1/2 cup chopped green bell pepper
1 Tbsp minced garlic
1 tsp minced jalapeno peppers
15 ounce can pinto beans, rinsed and drained
2 Tbsp water
2 Tbsp chopped fresh cilantro
Directions:

1. Place tortillas in microwave and heat for a few seconds. This makes them warm and pliable.
2. Heat oil in a 10-inch skillet over medium heat. Saute onion, bell pepper, garlic and jalapenos for about 3 minutes.
3. Add beans, water, and chopped cilantro. Cook until heated through, about 2-3 minutes.
5. Spoon mixture evenly down the center of warmed tortilla and roll up. Serve immediately. We recommend serving alongside steamed veggies or a tossed salad.

Serves 4. Per serving: Calories 220, Total Fat 3g, Saturated Fat 0g, Trans Fat 0g, Cholesterol 0mg, Sodium 228mg, Carbohydrates 41g, Dietary Fiber 12g, Sugars 5.4g, Protein 11g.

Latin Choices: Make It Healthy!

Grains:

Rice - This grain is very popular in Hispanic/Latino cultures. Try brown rice instead of white rice for more fiber and nutrients, plus a pat on the back from MyPlate.

Cornmeal - This is used in corn bread and for making tamales and tortillas.

Tortillas - These round, flat, pancake-like disks that are eaten with nearly any dish, including salads, meats, seafood, beans, and veggies. Look for lowfat options.

Vegetables:

Avocado - This is the backbone of great guacamole.

Cassava - This is a starchy staple of South American foods. Its flour, called farofa, is used for to make flat breads called yuca.

Calabaza - A squash that resembles a pumpkin, calabaza is native to the West Indies.

Chilis - These hot peppers range in intensity from mild to extremely hot.

Corn

Onions - These veggies add flavor to everything from salsas to salads.

Peppers - Both hot and sweet peppers are often used.

Squash - Latin cuisine features both summer and winter squashs. It includes chayote squash, and zucchini

Sweet potatoes - Try both yellow and orange varieties

Tomatillos - These sour vegetables resemble green tomatoes.

Tomatoes - Tomatoes are used in salsa and many other dishes.

Fruits:

Papaya - Mexican papayas are much larger than the Hawaiian types and may weigh up to 10 pounds. The flesh can be yellow, orange or pink.

Banana

Plantain - Plantains are staples in many tropical countries around the world. This fruit is used in many of the same ways potatoes are used in North America.

Oranges

Pineapple

Strawberries

Mango

Guava - Guava fruits may be round, oval or pear-shaped. Their length ranges from two to four inches. Soft when ripe and creamy in texture, a guava has a rind that will soften to be fully edible.

Mamey - Mamey is a berry with a thick woody skin. The pulp ranges in color from pink to red and has a sweet, almond-like flavor.

Cherimoya - The flesh of the ripe cherimoya is most commonly eaten out of hand or scooped with a spoon.

Pomelo - This is the largest citrus fruit. It is similar to grapefruit, but is much sweeter.

Passion fruit - The round fruit has a tough rind that is smooth and waxy. It ranges in hue from dark purple with faint, fine white specks, to light yellow or orange. The cavity within is filled with an aromatic mass of double-walled, membranous sacs that contain orange, pulpy juice and as many as 250 small seeds. The unique flavor is appealing, musky, guava-like and sweet/tart.

Lean Protein:

Beans

Chicken

Eggs

Fish

Ground turkey (as ground beef substitute)

Lean pork

Peanuts

Dairy:

Skim milk, cheese (use lowfat), nonfat sour cream

Common Seasonings:

Annatto - This spice also functions as food coloring and produces a saffron-like yellow shade.

Chili Pepper - There are a variety of chili peppers in an abundance of flavor profiles. Check the web or ask your grocer about which ones are right for your palate.

Cilantro - Cilantro is an herb with a lemony/peppery flavor. It looks very much like parsley.

Culantro - With a flavor that is similar to cilantro, this herb features large, thick leaves.

Cumin - This ground spice that imparts an earthy flavors to almost any dish.

Lemon, Lime - These fruits are often used with seafood, salsa and many other dishes.

Oregano - This herb is common in Mexican cooking.

Sazon - This one is mostly MSG and plays a role in Puerto Rican cooking.

Sofrito - This seasoning sauce is made from lean cured ham, onion, green pepper, cilantro, and garlic sauteed in oil. It is often used in Puerto Rican cooking

Vanilla - This delicious extract is made from the orchid plant. It is used in flan and other baked dishes.

Leader Guide: Heart Healthy Cooking

Title:
Heart Healthy Cooking

Target Audience:
This presentation kit is intended for general audiences age 14 and up. It covers topics of wellness, aging, diabetes, heart disease, family health, limited income, and nutrition.

Lesson Objectives:
• Participants will learn risk factors for heart disease and how to lower them.
• Participants will learn how to modify favorite dishes and meals so they are better for their hearts.
• Participants will learn new, heart-healthy recipes.

Lesson Rationale:
Health authorities have indicated that good nutrition is one of the most important factors in determining long-term health. Poor diet plays a major role in the development of four of the top seven killers in the United States: heart disease, cancer, stroke and diabetes. Students who have the skills to select and prepare nutritious foods can positively impact their present and future health.

Lesson at a Glance:
This lesson introduces participants to new recipes and teaches cooking skills. It also provides nutrition and dietary information that is consistent with the Dietary Guidelines for Americans and MyPlate.

Lesson Materials:
This lesson contains:
• Leader and Activity Guide
• Recipe Leader Guide
• 4 pages of copy-ready handouts and recipes

Preparation:
___ Review leader guide
___ Review handouts
___ Select activities
___ Copy and collect materials for lesson

Activity Ideas:
Introduction
Provide the following statistics to your audience.
Over 60 million Americans have one or more types of cardiovascular disease, which causes 40% of all deaths in the US. (Source: Center for Disease Control)
Every 29 seconds, someone in the US will suffer a coronary event; every minute someone will die from one. (Source: American Heart Association)

For more information, check out http://www.american-heart.org/statistics/index.html

Activity 1 – Cooking Demo
Use the recipes in this lesson to present a cooking demonstration. Follow a healthy meal with one of the heart-healthy desserts from Cooking Demo II.

Activity 2 – There's No Accounting for Taste
Make a buffet that features skim milk, Skim Plus milk, soy milk (chocolate, vanilla, and/or plain), lactose-reduced skim milk, lowfat or reduced fat cheese, non-fat yogurt, fat free ricotta, nonfat sour cream and a few low calorie margarines. Allow participants to taste test these items, either alone or spread on a complimentary food. Consumers are often hesitant to try new things when it means spending their own money, so now they don't have to.

Explain that one cup of whole milk contains 5 grams of saturated fat. That's about the same as the saturated fat content of a serving of steak. Did you know that skim milk only contains a small amount of saturated fat (0.25 g per 1 cup serving)? 1% milk contains 1.5 g of saturated fat. That's why MyPlate insists that Americans eat mostly low fat dairy products. They put their heart at much less risk that way.

Use the handout, "10 Top Strategies for A Healthy Heart" to show the major sources of saturated fat and how to avoid them.

Activity 3 - Eat Your Heart Out
Approach heart healthy eating in a positive light by showing participants all the items they CAN eat. We suggest serving a fruit tray, a veggie tray, a few bean dishes, pasta salads, tossed salad, whole grain cereal, lowfat whole grain crackers, natural peanut butter, skim milk, nonfat yogurt, etc. All items should be low in saturated fat and sodium. Remember, according to MyPlate, people should compare sodium content and then pick the foods that have the lowest numbers.

Use the handout, "10 Top Strategies for A Healthy Heart" to explore excellent sources of soluble fiber.

Further reading/info/links
www.foodandhealth.com - This site is full of healthy cooking tips and information about the impact of your diet on your heart.
http://www.heart.org/HEARTORG/ - Information and statistics from the American Heart Association.
www.nhlbi.nih.gov - This is the homepage of the Heart, Lung and Blood Institute, for health facts and details about the heart.

Leader Guide: Heart Healthy Recipes

Lentil Chili
Makes 24 sample servings
1-1/2 tsp vegetable oil
1 Tbsp chopped garlic
2 cups chopped onion
1 lb frozen crinkle cut carrots
12 oz dry lentils (1-1/2 cups)
4 cups low-sodium V8
2 cups water
1/2 tsp chili powder
1/2 tsp cumin
1 tsp dried oregano
Garnish: 4 Tbsp nonfat sour cream, 1 Tbsp cilantro
Directions:
1. Place the vegetable oil in a large soup pot or Dutch-oven style pan. Heat over medium-high. Add the garlic and onion and saute until golden, about 2-3 minutes. Add the rest of the ingredients and mix.
2. Bring to a boil then lower to a simmer. Cook uncovered until the lentils are tender, about 15 minutes. Serve hot. You can add more or less chili powder to suit your personal taste preference.
Speed tip: Buy pre-minced garlic. You can find it in the produce or spice sections of your grocery store.

Equipment:
____ Dutch-oven style pan
____ Stove
____ Kitchen spoon
____ Knife and cutting board
____ Measuring cups and spoons
____ Bowl (for final presentation)

Shopping List:
____ Vegetable oil
____ Garlic
____ Onion
____ 1 lb frozen crinkle cut carrots
____ 1 bag dry lentils
____ Low-sodium V8
____ Water
____ Chili powder
____ Cumin
____ Dried oregano
____ Nonfat sour cream
____ Cilantro
____ Cups, spoons, and napkins (for samples)
____ Disposable cups (for premeasured ingredients)

Cooking/nutrition lesson:
This recipe shows participants how to make a quick recipe using lentils. Lentils are an excellent source of folate and soluble fiber along with other nutrients and phytochemicals that are beneficial to your heart.

Demo preparation:
1. Wash your hands before you handle food.
2. Chop and measure all ingredients.
3. Organize your work area.

Make ahead options:
Make this chili ahead of time and reheat for class. You can show participants how to make it or show them different ways to use it ,such as to top a baked potato, pasta or brown rice.

Garnish/presentation tips:
Place this chili in a large soup bowl. Garnish it with nonfat sour cream and a sprinkle of fresh chopped cilantro.

Number of sample servings (1/4 cup each): 24

Leader Guide: Heart Healthy Recipes

Easy Mild Salsa

Makes about 10 sample servings

This delicious recipe will add sodium-free flavor to grilled chicken or fish. You can use it to top salads or dip chips. This versatile salsa can also be made into Black Bean Salsa, Peach Salsa, Spicy Salsa, etc - see variations below.

1 Tbsp chopped fresh cilantro
1 small red onion, chopped
1 medium green bell pepper, chopped
2 Tbsp red wine vinegar
Juice of 1 lemon or lime
1 tsp ground cumin
6 plum tomatoes, cored and cut in chunks

Directions:

1. Place cilantro, onion, and pepper in a food processor or blender. Blend until coarsely chopped. Add the rest of the ingredients and pulse until the mixture is in small pieces.
2. Place salsa in a serving bowl and serve immediately, or cover and refrigerate until ready to use, up to 3 days.

Variations:

- Hot salsa - Add one jalapeno and a few dashes of hot pepper sauce
- Black bean salsa - Add a can of drained black beans
- Pineapple salsa - Add 1/2 cup chopped, fresh pineapple
- Peach salsa - Add 1/2 cup chopped, pitted peaches
- Mango salsa - Add 1 peeled, diced mango

Equipment:

____ Knife
____ Cutting board
____ Food processor
____ Spatula
____ Bowl (for final presentation)
____ Measuring cups and spoons

Shopping list:

____ Fresh cilantro
____ 1 small red onion
____ 1 medium green bell pepper
____ Red wine vinegar
____ 1 lemon or lime
____ Ground cumin
____ 6 plum tomatoes
____ Cups, spoons and napkins (for samples)
____ Disposable cups (for premeasured ingredients)

Cooking/nutrition lesson:

This recipe demonstrates ways to make an excellent condiment that can be used to top fish, chicken, baked potatoes, and rice. It is a fantastic appetizer when served with baked tortilla chips or pita triangles. This recipe explains how to use peppers, onions, and tomatoes, all of which are excellent sources of soluble fiber.

Demo preparation:

1. Wash your hands before you handle food.
2. Chop and measure all ingredients so they are ready to go in food processor.
3. Organize work area.

Make ahead options:

You can make this salsa in a large batch before class and then show how to make the variations.

Garnish/presentation tips:

We recommend that you make at least one or two of the variations for this recipe so participants can see how versatile it is. If time and budget allow, it would be good to show how the salsa can be used i.e. over grilled chicken or fish, pasta, rice, kabobs or baked potatoes, in addition to a wonderful baked chip dip. Place the finished salsa in a decorative bowl for final presentation. Garnish with a sprig of fresh cilantro.

Number of sample servings (1/4 cup each): approximately 10.

Leader Guide: Heart Healthy Recipes

Stir Fry Salad with Tofu

Makes about 20 sample servings

2 cups diced firm tofu (not silken)
4 Tbsp light soy sauce
2 tsp corn starch
1/2 cup orange juice
2 Tbsp vinegar
1 Tbsp sesame oil
5 ounce package prewashed spinach leaves
1 tsp vegetable oil
2 tsp minced garlic
1 Tbsp grated fresh ginger
1/2 cup sliced carrots
1 cup sliced mushrooms
1 cup broccoli florets
Pinch red pepper flakes

Directions:

1. Marinate tofu with the soy sauce, cornstarch, orange juice, vinegar, and sesame oil in a small bowl. Place fresh spinach leaves in a large salad bowl; set aside.
2. Heat a large, nonstick skillet or wok over high heat. Add the oil and then the garlic and ginger. Saute until the garlic is nutty brown, about 1 minute. Add the rest of the veggies. Saute until crisp-tender, about 4-5 minutes. Add the tofu along with the marinade and cook briefly.
3. Add the hot stir-fry mixture to the spinach, toss together and serve warm.

Equipment:

____ Knife
____ Cutting board
____ Vegetable peeler
____ Grater
____ Large, nonstick skillet
____ Stove
____ Large salad bowl
____ 3 kitchen spoons
____ Plate (for final presentation)
____ Measuring cups and spoons
____ Small bowl

Shopping list:

____ 1 pound package diced firm tofu (not silken)
____ Light soy sauce
____ Corn starch
____ Orange juice
____ Vinegar (rice wine or cider is best)
____ Sesame oil
____ 5 ounce package prewashed spinach leaves*
____ Vegetable oil
____ Minced garlic*
____ Fresh ginger
____ Carrots*
____ Sliced mushrooms*
____ Broccoli florets*
____ Red pepper flakes

*Tip: Look for pre-chopped versions of these items

Cooking/nutrition lesson:

This recipe shows participants how to increase the soy in their diets. This is a delicious way to serve a stir-fry or even use up leftovers. A stir fry packs more vegetables per serving than any other dish we feature in this lesson.

Demo preparation:

1. Wash your hands before you handle food.
2. Chop and measure all ingredients.
3. Organize work area.

Garnish/presentation tips:

Place this salad on a large decorative plate and set chopsticks on the side. You can drizzle the plate with a little additional soy sauce and sesame oil.

Number of sample servings (1/4 cup): about 20

Leader Guide: Heart Healthy Recipes

Baked Salmon with Cucumber Dill Sauce
Makes 16 sample servings
4 4-ounce salmon fillets
Juice of one lemon
2 Tbsp water
Sauce:
1 cup nonfat sour cream
2 tsp dried dill or 2 Tbsp fresh dill
1/2 cup diced cucumbers
1/4 cup minced green onion
Directions:
1. Preheat oven to 350 degrees. Rinse salmon fillets under cold, running water and place them in a large baking pan. Sprinkle the lemon juice and water over the salmon and place pan in the center of the oven. Bake until done (when the fish turns opaque and flakes easily with a fork), about 20 minutes.
2. Meanwhile, mix ingredients for sauce in small bowl.
3. Serve fish fillets hot with the sauce to the side.

Equipment:
_____ Oven
_____ Baking dish (9"x12", glass preferred)
_____ Knife and cutting board
_____ Measuring spoons and cups
_____ Spoon
_____ Spatula
_____ Plate (for final presentation)

Shopping list:
_____ 4 4-ounce salmon fillets
_____ Lemon (more for garnish)
_____ Water
_____ Nonfat sour cream
_____ Dried or fresh dill
_____ Cucumber
_____ Green onion
_____ Plates, forks, and napkins (for samples)
_____ Disposable cups (for premeasured ingredients)

Cooking/nutrition lesson
Salmon is a good source of omega-3 fatty acids. Omega 3s have been shown to be beneficial for the heart. They may reduce the risk of sudden death from a heart attack and they help to prevent arrythmia (irregular heartbeat). Fish is also a better choice than beef for many other reasons. This recipe shows participants how to bake fish and tell if it is done. It also allows them to sample it with a delicious lowfat sauce.

Demo preparation:
1. Wash hands before preparing food.
2. Measure and chop all ingredients; place them in disposable containers.
3. Organize work area and preheat oven.

Make ahead options:
You can bake the fish ahead of time and serve it cold with the sauce. If you take this approach, we recommend serving it on a bed of greens. Also, you can bake the fish ahead of time and reheat for tasting, just be careful not to overcook the fish.

Garnish/presentation tips:
Serve the fish on a decorative plate. Drizzle the sauce over one corner of the fish and garnish with wedges of lemon.

Number of sample servings: 16 (cut each fillet of fish in quarters)

Heart Healthy Recipes

Lentil Chili

1-1/2 tsp vegetable oil
1 Tbsp chopped garlic
2 cups chopped onion
1 lb frozen crinkle cut carrots
12 oz dry lentils (1-1/2 cups)
4 cups low-sodium V8
2 cups water
1/2 tsp chili powder
1/2 tsp cumin
1 tsp dried oregano
Garnish: 4 Tbsp nonfat sour cream, 1 Tbsp cilantro
Directions:

1. Place the vegetable oil in a large soup pot or Dutch-oven style pan. Heat over medium-high. Add the garlic and onion and saute until golden, about 2-3 minutes. Add the rest of the ingredients and mix.
2. Bring to a boil then lower to a simmer. Cook uncovered until the lentils are tender, about 15 minutes. Serve hot. You can add more or less chili powder to suit your personal taste preference.

Speed tip: Buy pre-minced garlic. You can find it in the produce or spice sections of your grocery store.

Serves 8. Each 1 cup serving: 229 calories, 1.5 g fat, 0 g saturated fat, 0 mg cholesterol, 116 mg sodium, 40 g carbohydrate, 16 g fiber, 12 g sugars, 14 g protein.

Easy Mild Salsa

This delicious recipe will add sodium-free flavor to grilled chicken or fish. You can use it to top salads or dip chips. This versatile salsa can also be made into Black Bean Salsa, Peach Salsa, Spicy Salsa, etc - see variations below.

1 Tbsp chopped fresh cilantro
1 small red onion, chopped
1 medium green bell pepper, chopped
2 Tbsp red wine vinegar
Juice of 1 lemon or lime
1 tsp ground cumin
6 plum tomatoes, cored and cut in chunks
Directions:

1. Place cilantro, onion, and pepper in a food processor or blender. Blend until coarsely chopped. Add the rest of the ingredients and pulse until the mixture is in small pieces.
2. Place salsa in a serving bowl and serve immediately, or cover and refrigerate until ready to use, up to 3 days.

Serves 4. Each 1/2 cup serving: 39 calories, .5 g fat, 0 g saturated fat, 0 mg cholesterol, 12 mg sodium, 8 g carbohydrate, 2 g fiber, 1.5 g protein. Diabetic exchange: 1/2 vegetable.

Variations:

• Hot salsa - Add one jalapeno and a few dashes of hot pepper sauce
• Black bean salsa - Add a can of drained black beans
• Pineapple salsa - Add 1/2 cup chopped, fresh pineapple
• Peach salsa - Add 1/2 cup chopped, pitted peaches
• Mango salsa - Add 1 peeled, diced mango

Heart Healthy Recipes

Stir Fry Salad with Tofu

2 cups diced firm tofu (not silken)
4 Tbsp light soy sauce
2 tsp corn starch
1/2 cup orange juice
2 Tbsp vinegar
1 Tbsp sesame oil
5 ounce package prewashed spinach leaves
1 tsp vegetable oil
2 tsp minced garlic
1 Tbsp grated fresh ginger
1/2 cup sliced carrots
1 cup sliced mushrooms
1 cup broccoli florets
Pinch red pepper flakes
Directions:

1. Marinate tofu with the soy sauce, cornstarch, orange juice, vinegar, and sesame oil in a small bowl. Place fresh spinach leaves in a large salad bowl; set aside.

2. Heat a large, nonstick skillet or wok over high heat. Add the oil and then the garlic and ginger. Saute until the garlic is nutty brown, about 1 minute. Add the rest of the veggies. Saute until crisp-tender, about 4-5 minutes. Add the tofu along with the marinade and cook briefly.

3. Add the hot stir-fry mixture to the spinach, toss together, and serve warm.

Serves 4. Nutrition Facts for one 2-cup serving: 153 calories, 8 g fat, 1 g saturated fat, 0 mg cholesterol, 602 mg sodium, 13 g carbohydrate, 4.5 g fiber, 7.5 g sugars, 10 g protein.

Baked Salmon Steaks with Cucumber Dill Sauce

4 4-ounce salmon fillets
juice of one lemon
2 Tbsp water
Sauce:
1 cup nonfat sour cream
2 tsp dried dill or 2 Tbsp fresh dill
1/2 cup diced cucumbers
1/4 cup minced green onion
Directions:

1. Preheat oven to 350 degrees. Rinse salmon fillets under cold running water and place them in a large baking pan. Sprinkle the lemon juice and water over the salmon and place in the center of the oven. Bake until done - when the fish turns opaque and flakes easily with a fork, about 20 minutes.

2. Meanwhile, mix ingredients for sauce in small bowl.

3. Serve salmon fillets hot with the sauce to the side.

Serves 4. Each serving: 237 calories, 7 g fat, 1 g saturated fat, 62 mg cholesterol, 101 mg sodium, 13 g carbohydrate, 0 g fiber, 26 g protein.

Heart Facts

Did you know?
- Over 60 million Americans have one or more types of cardiovascular disease. Cardiovascular disease causes 40% of all deaths in the US. (1998 National Vital Statistics Report, Center for Disease Control)
- Every 29 seconds, someone in the US suffers a coronary event. Every minute, someone will die from one. (American Heart Association)

What is cardiovascular disease?
Cardiovascular diseases (CVD) are disorders of the heart and blood vessel system. We've listed some below...

Coronary artery disease - This blood vessel disease is caused by atherosclerosis. It is likely to prompt angina and/or heart attack.

Stroke - Strokes occur during a sudden decrease or interruption in blood flow to parts of the brain

High blood pressure - Also known as hypertension, high blood pressure occurs when the force of blood against the artery walls is too great.

What are the risk factors for CVD?
Controllable (dietary/lifestyle) **Factors**:

Hypertension - Chronic high blood pressure

High cholesterol - Total cholesterol >200 mg/dl

Overweight - If your body mass index is greater than or equal to 27.8 (men) and greater than or equal to 27.3 (women), you are at risk.

Diabetes - This increases your risk of CVD by three times for women and two times for men.

Smoking - Current regular use of cigarettes by persons who smoked at least 100 cigarettes increases risk.

Sedentary lifestyle - Lack of physical activity is bad for your heart.

Uncontrollable Factors:

Age - If you are a male over 45 or a female over 55

Heredity - CVD risk is higher if your parents have heart disease or if you are African American, Mexican American, Native American or Native Hawaiian.

Gender - Males have higher risk than females.

How do I lower my risk for CVD?
- Eat a diet that is low in saturated fats, trans-fats, cholesterol, salt, and processed, refined foods.
- Eat a diet rich in whole plant foods in their natural form (whole grains, fruits, legumes and vegetables). This will increase your intake of fiber.
- Exercise or lead an active lifestyle -- even walking will help!
- Lose weight and reduce body fat (if you're at risk).
- If you smoke, quit.

Glossary of Common Terms:
Atherosclerosis - Plaque-prompted narrowing of the artery walls.

Cholesterol - Cholesterol is a soft, waxy substance found in your body. High cholesterol levels in the blood can cause plaque to form on artery walls.

Dyslipidemia - Elevation of total cholesterol, LDL and triglycerides, and a decrease in HDL cholesterol.

HDL - High-density lipoprotein is also known as "good" cholesterol, since it transports excess cholesterol away from the arteries and back to the liver.

Heart attack - Heart attacks occur when an artery that leads to the heart becomes blocked.

LDL - Low-density lipoprotein; also known as "bad" cholesterol. If too much LDL circulates in the blood, it can contribute to plaque buildup.

Lipoprotein - Lipoproteins are special carriers that transport cholesterol (and other fats) in the blood.

Lipoprotein profile - This is a measurement of LDL, total cholesterol, HDL, and triglycerides. These should be done every 5 years.

Monounsaturated fat - Fat that is liquid at room temperature. It's found in olive oil and canola oil.

Plaque - Plaque is made up of deposits of fatty substances, cholesterol, cellular waste products, calcium etc in the inner lining of an artery.

Polyunsaturated fat - This is fat that is liquid at room temperature. It is found in corn oil and safflower oil.

Saturated fat - Saturated fat is solid at room temperature (lard, butter, etc). It raises cholesterol in the blood.

Stroke - Strokes occur when blood vessels that supply blood flow to the brain are blocked or ruptured.

Syndrome X - Also known as metabolic syndrome, this is a grouping of risk factors including a high amount of fat around the abdomen (apple shape), high triglycerides, low HDL, high blood sugar and high blood pressure.

Trans-fat - These fatty acids raise cholesterol; they are found in products made with hydrogenated oil and the meat and dairy products of ruminant animals.

Triglycerides - This is the main type of fat transported by your body. Calories ingested in a meal and not used immediately by tissues are converted to triglycerides

10 Top Strategies for Lowering LDL

1. Consume foods that are naturally high in fiber, especially soluble fiber. Soluble fiber is found in legumes, fruits, root vegetables, oats, barley, and flax. For every 1 or 2 grams of soluble fiber you consume daily, you will lower your LDL by 1%. Try to consume 10-25 grams of soluble fiber per day. If you have trouble consuming a lot of soluble-fiber rich foods, talk to your physician about using psyllium husk.

2. Eat 6 to 8 small meals daily instead of 1 or 2 large ones.

3. MyPlate recommends that you substitute nonfat/lowfat dairy products for full fat options whenever possible. Regular dairy products like whole milk, butter, cheese, cream cheese and ricotta cheese are very high in saturated fat.

4. Accumulate 30 minutes of moderate intensity physical activity on most days of the week. This will help raise HDL. Alternately, try to walk at least 2-3 miles per day at least 5-6 days per week.

5. Limit the amount of saturated fat you consume from dairy products, red meat and tropical oils. Ideally, you should consume no more than 5% of your daily calories from saturated fat (around 10-11 g for most people). Base most of your meals on beans, vegetables, fruits and whole grains, with a minimum of low-saturated fat animal protein foods like nonfat dairy, fish & egg whites.

6. Avoid foods with added trans-fat. This fat comes from partially hydrogenated vegetable oils (often found in fried foods and processed foods like crackers, baked goods and desserts). Generally, the more solid the fat is, the higher the trans-fatty acid content.

7. Limit your daily cholesterol intake to no more than 100 mg.

8. If you are overweight, lose weight. This will help lower your total cholesterol and raise your HDL. The best way to lose weight and keep it off is to exercise and eat a diet that is high in fiber and low in calorie density.

9. Limit your intake of sugar and fructose. This should lower triglycerides, aid weight loss and lower LDL.

10. Consider using sterol and stanol rich margarines and salad dressings such as Take Control or Benecol -- up to 2 grams per day.

By James J. Kenney, PhD, RD, FACN

Where Is The Soluble Fiber?

Increase these foods in your diet. They contain 2 or more grams of soluble fiber, which helps lower cholesterol.

Cooked oatmeal	1 cup	breakfast
Oat bran	1 cup	breakfast, muffins
Cooked rye cereal	1 cup	breakfast
Barley, cooked	1 cup	side dish, soups
Avocado	1/2	sandwiches, salads
Broccoli	1 cup	salads, side dish,
Brussels sprouts	1 cup	side dish
Carrots	1 cup	snack, salads
Collard greens	1 cup	stir frys, side dish
Parsnips	1 cup	stir frys, side dish
Sweet potato	1 large	side dish
Beans, cooked	1 cup	salads, pasta, soups
Split peas	1 cup	soups
Lentils	1 cup	salad, pasta, soups
Apricots, figs	1/2 cup	salad, snack, dessert
Prunes	6	snack, dessert
Flax seeds, ground	1/4 cup	cereal, smoothie

Where's The Saturated Fat?

Limit these foods in your diet. They are high in saturated fat, which raises blood levels of cholesterol.

Food	Serving	Sat. fat g	Where
Prime rib	8 oz slice	32	restaurants
Coconut milk	1/2 cup	21	tropical drinks
Dried coconut	1 oz	16	topping, candies
Coconut oil	1 Tbsp	12	processed foods
Palm kernel oil	1 Tbsp	11	popcorn
Cake donut	1 donut	11	bakery
Ricotta cheese	1/2 cup	10	Italian style foods
Ground beef	3 oz	9	burgers, etc...
Butter	1 Tbsp	7.5	spread, etc...
Regular cheese	1 oz	7	pizza, etc...
Cream	2 Tbsp	7	desserts, coffee
Ice cream	1/2 cup	7	dessert
Cream cheese	2 Tbsp	6	bagels, desserts
Croissant/Danish	1 piece	6	bakery
Biscuit	1 each	6	restaurant, home
Cream soup	1 cup	5	restaurant, home
Whole milk	1 cup	5	dairy goods

Sources: Nutr V Database, *Bowes & Churches Food Values of Portions Commonly Used*

Cooking for Your Heart: Substitutions

Instead of:	Portion	Saturated fat (g)	Use:	Saturated fat (g)
Dairy:				
Butter	1 Tbsp	7.5	Vegetable oil* or broth	0
Cream	2 Tbsp	7	Evaporated skim milk	0
Cream cheese	2 Tbsp	6.5	Light cream cheese	3.5
Half and half	2 Tbsp	2	Fat-free half and half	0
Ice cream	1/2 cup	6	Frozen yogurt	1.5
Ricotta cheese	1/2 cup	10	Fat-free ricotta	0
Sour cream	2 Tbsp	3	Fat-free sour cream	0
Whipped cream	2 Tbsp	3	Fat-free whipped cream	0
Whole milk	1 cup	5	Skim milk	0
Whole milk	1 cup	5	1% milk	1.5
Totals		**61**		**7.5**

*Use spray oil or halve total amount.

**Cut amount of cheese in half, or use a small amount of Parmesan cheese

Meat/Poultry				
Bacon	3 slices	3	Turkey bacon	1.5
Beef, ground	3 ounces	7	Ground turkey breast, no skin	0
Beef, ground	3 ounces	7	Vegetarian burger*	0
Beef, prime rib**	3 ounces	12	Beef tenderloin, fat trimmed	3
Beef, T-bone	3 ounces	7	Beef tenderloin, fat trimmed	3
Chicken, dark with skin	3 ounces	3	Chicken breast, no skin, baked	.5
Chicken, fried thigh	1 each	6	Chicken breast, no skin, baked	.5
Lard	1 Tbsp	5	Margarine, trans-fat free	2
Sausage	3 ounces	9	Vegetarian sausage*	0.5
Totals		**54**		**11**

*Read the label, since nutrition facts vary by brand.

**Restaurant portions are often triple this amount, so saturated fat could get to 36 ounces per portion!

Note: For heart-healthier cooking, limit animal protein and emphasize whole grains, beans, soy protein, fish (baked-not fried!), fruits and grains in your meals. Think of meat as a side dish and use less per serving. A 3-ounce serving of meat is about the size of a deck of cards.

Miscellaneous				
Coconut	1 ounce	6.5	Toasted pecans or almonds	1.5
Coconut milk	8 ounces	20	Evaporated skim milk	0
Hydrogenated shortening	1 Tbsp	3+	Vegetable oil or trans-free margarine	0-2
Whole eggs	2	3	Egg white or nonfat egg substitute	0
Gravy with fat	2 Tbsp	5	Defatted gravy	0.5
French fries	4 ounces	4	Baked potato	0

+This product is hydrogenated and contains additional trans-fat that is not listed on the label with saturated fat.

Using Herbs and Spices

Title:
Using Herbs and Spices

Target Audience:
This presentation kit is intended for general audiences.

Lesson Objectives:
• Participants will learn how to use herbs and spices to flavor food.
• Participants will learn that herbs and spices can be excellent and healthy replacements for salt.

Lesson Rationale:
Health authorities have indicated that good nutrition is one of the most important factors in determining long-term health. Poor diet plays a major role in the development of four of the top seven killers in the United States: heart disease, cancer, stroke, and diabetes. Individuals who have the skills to select and prepare nutritious foods can positively impact their present and future health.

Lesson at a Glance:
This lesson introduces participants to new recipes and teaches cooking skills. It also provides nutrition and dietary information that is consistent with the Dietary Guidelines for Americans and MyPlate.

Lesson Materials:
This lesson contains:
• Leader and Activity Guides
• 3 pages of copy-ready recipes and handouts

Preparation:
___ Review leader guide
___ Review handouts
___ Select activities
___ Copy and collect materials for lesson

Activity Ideas:
Activity 1 – Cooking Demo
Use the recipes in this lesson to plan a cooking demonstration. These recipes are for spice mixes, which you can serve in a variety of ways. Some of our favorites are listed below...
Here are serving ideas for the spice mixes:
Stir Fry Mix - Saute a one pound bag of frozen stir fry vegetables and season with light soy sauce and the Stir Fry Seasoning Mix.
Italian Seasoning - Spray whole wheat bread with olive oil spray, top with Italian Seasoning and toast; serve warm.
Salad Shake - Make a simple tossed salad with let-tuce, vegetables, oil and vinegar. Throw in some of the Salad Shake mix.
Sweet Spice - Serve this spice mix over unsweetened apple sauce
Rice Pilaf Seasoning - Use this mix to flavor a quick batch of instant brown rice.
Chili Mix - Use this mix in addtion with nonfat sour cream to top a baked potato.

Activity 2 - Herb and Spice Identification
Use the handout titled, "Do you know how to use herbs and spices" to give participants an overview of how to use herbs and spices. Use the handout "Herb and Spice Buying Guide" to show participants how to buy, store, and use fresh and dried herbs.

Arrange a selection of herbs and spices on a demo table. Allow participants to examine and smell each herb. You might disguise the names and see if they can guess the identity of each one. It would be wise to use salt-free spice blends for sampling. Mix herbs and or herb blends in nonfat sour cream and serve with fresh veggies to allow participants to taste the flavors of various seasonings. For spices, you can sprinkle the spice over unsweetened applesauce and serve in small cups with spoons. Or try some of the options listed in Activity One.

For More Information:
http://foodandhealth.com/blog - Check this site for recipes that use plenty of herbs and spices. Plus, you can find tons of information about the health benefits of a whole bunch of different herbs and spices.

Herb & Spice Blends

Here are some recipes for herb blends that you can make yourself. Herb blends are great because they combine several tasty, versatile ingredients in a single container. The ones we feature here are all made without salt.

Stir Fry Mix

1 Tbsp ground ginger
Generous pinch of ground cloves
2 Tbsp garlic powder
1 tsp red pepper flakes

Stir ingredients together and store in an airtight container at room temperature. Use this seasoning mix (in propotions that work for you) in any and all stir fry dishes.

Italian Seasoning

This seasoning mix is great in pasta dishes, tossed salads, and soups. It is also delicious on garlic toast.

3 Tbsp dried oregano
3 Tbsp dried basil
2 Tbsp dried marjoram
1 tsp dried thyme
1 Tbsp garlic powder

Stir ingredients together and store in an airtight container at room temperature. Season pasta dishes to taste with this mix about 10 minutes before they are done. Usually you use 1 teaspoon of mix for every 4 servings of pasta.

Salad Shake

This spice blend is great on salads - use it with oil and vinegar instead of a salt-laden salad dressing.

2 Tbsp Italian seasoning (use recipe above or buy commercial mix)
2 Tbsp Parmesan cheese
1 tsp dried parsley
1 tsp black pepper
1 tsp garlic powder

Stir ingredients together and store in an airtight container at room temperature. Add this seasoning to salads along with oil and vinegar. Use about 1 tsp per 4 servings.

Sweet Spice

Use this sweet spice blend in fruit salads, cereal, and yogurt.

2 Tbsp ground cinnamon
1 Tbsp ground ginger
1/2 Tbsp ground nutmeg
1 tsp allspice
Pinch ground cloves

Stir ingredients together and store in an airtight container at room temperature. You will find that a shaker container is very convenient to use with this spice mix.

Rice Pilaf Seasoning

This mix is great for rice pilaf, stuffing, and cornbread.

1 Tbsp oregano
1 tsp dried ground sage
1 tsp dried rosemary, crushed
2 tsp onion powder
1 tsp garlic powder

Stir ingredients together and store in an airtight container at room temperature. Use this seasoning mix for rice pilaf, stuffing, and cornbread. You can also add it to bread mixes for loaves of bread, focaccia, bread sticks, etc. Generally, you should use around 1 tsp per 4 servings.

Chili Mix

Great for dips, salads, baked potatoes, chili, and pasta.

3 Tbsp ground pure red chile powder
1 Tbsp garlic powder
1 Tbsp cumin
1 Tbsp dried oregano

Stir ingredients together and store in an airtight container at room temperature. If you toast the chile powder and cumin gently in a warm saute pan, it will enhance their flavor. Use this seasoning mix as you would chile powder, so the amount depends on your preference for spiciness. To start, try 1 tsp per 6 servings.

Herb & Spice Buying Guide

Herb Buying Guide

Use this handy guide to stock your kitchen's herb shelf, determine how to use an herb, or to convert amounts for fresh and dry herbs. Note that some herbs (like tarragon or rosemary) are more potent dry than fresh, while others, like (cilantro or parsley) are less potent when dry. Dried herbs lose their potency after prolonged storage, so buy them in small amounts and replace them at least once a year.

Herb	Forms	Fresh = Dry	Uses
Allspice	dry: whole, ground		baked goods, fruits, poultry or veggies
Anise	dry seeds		pasta sauce, barbecue sauce, soups
Basil	fresh or dry leaves	1 Tbsp = 1.5 tsp	sprinkle over pasta, salads & soups
Bay leaf	dry		soups, chowders, stews, beans
Black pepper	dry: whole, ground		salads, pasta, soups, stews, veggies, beans
Caraway	dry seeds		slaw, cabbage, rye bread, veggies, salads,
Chervil	fresh or dry leaves	1 Tbsp = 1.5 tsp	pasta, salads, soups, veggies
Chives	fresh or dry leaves	1 Tbsp = 1 tsp	baked potatoes, soups, pasta, dips
Cilantro	fresh or dry leaves	1 Tbsp = 2 tsp	salsa, guacamole, pasta, pizza, dips, salad
Cinnamon	dry: sticks or ground		tea, coffee, fruit, cereal, pancakes
Cloves	dry: whole, ground		stew, baked goods, baked or stewed fruit
Coriander	dry: whole, ground		pasta, fish, beans, soups
Dill	fresh or dry leaves	1 Tbsp = 1.5 tsp	potato salad, salads, pasta, soups
Fennel	dry seeds		pasta, barbecue sauce, soups
Garlic	garlic powder	1 tsp = .5 tsp	beans, grains, veggies, fish, poultry
Garlic	fresh		beans, grains, veggies, fish, poultry
Ginger	dry or fresh	1 Tbsp = 1 tsp	stir fry dishes, pasta, salads, baked goods
Marjoram	fresh or dry leaves	1 Tbsp = 2 tsp	pasta dishes, beans, veggies, salads, grains
Nutmeg	dry: whole, ground		beverages, sauces, fruits, baked goods
Oregano	fresh or dry leaves	1 Tbsp = 1.5 tsp	pasta dishes, beans, salsa, veggies, salads
Parsley	fresh or dry leaves	1 Tbsp = 2 tsp	pasta dishes, beans, potatoes, soups, salads
Peppermint	fresh leaves		tea, grain dishes, fruit, yogurt
Rosemary	fresh or dry leaves	1 Tbsp = 1 tsp	beans, poultry, grains, veggies, potatoes
Saffron	dry		rice, seafood
Sage	fresh or dry leaves	1 Tbsp = 1 tsp	stuffing, rice, veggies, grain dishes, beans
Savory	fresh or dry leaves	1 Tbsp = 1.5 tsp	dips, pasta, grains, beans, rice, stuffing
Tarragon	fresh or dry leaves	1 Tbsp = 1 tsp	poultry, rice, veggies, salads, dressings
Thyme	fresh or dry leaves	1 Tbsp = 1.5 tsp	poultry, veggies, beans, soups, potatoes
Vanilla	extract or bean		desserts, fruit, yogurt

How to Use Herbs & Spices

Herbs and spices can really make a difference in your kitchen. They add flavor, heat, and/or zest to many dishes.Here is a guide to help you know which ones to use and ehwn:

Sweet Spices
Try using sweet spices like cinnamon, ginger, nutmeg, allspice, and cloves to add zing to fruit and cooked cereals. Cinnamon is often the most popular and adds a sweet, woody fragrance. It comes from the bark of various laurel trees in Vietnam, China, Indonesia and Central America. Ground nutmeg, allspice, and cloves are all wonderful additions to muffins and breads. Ginger adds a rich, sweet, warm flavor to fruits.

Italian seasonings
Marjoram, basil, oregano, and thyme are all herbs which can be used in Italian-flavored dishes such as pasta, soups, salads, and even garlic toast. Basil is absolutely wonderful when used fresh. Oregano and thyme seem to hold their flavor very well when dried. Marjoram has a mild mint flavor and is similar to oregano - they are best when used together.

Licorice flavors
Fennel seeds, caraway seeds, dill seeds, anise seeds, chervil, and tarragon all taste like licorice. Tarragon is strong and is especially tasty when used to flavor chicken. Chervil is milder and is excellent, along with dill, over seafood. Anise and fennel seeds add a sausage-like flavor to spaghetti sauce. It is best to grind these seeds in a coffee grinder and use a little to enhance soups and sauces.

Fresh flavors
Dill weed, parsley, cilantro, culantro, and savory are all fresh-tasting, light herbs that are much better fresh than dried. Use parsley to flavor soups and potatoes. Use cilantro and culantro to flavor southwestern dishes like salsa, chili, or guacamole. Dill weed is excellent with potatoes and seafood, while savory is a light, peppery herb that goes well in dips and dressings.

All-purpose herbs
Whenever you are making soup and are not quite sure what to use, the answer is usually: parsley, thyme, and a bay leaf. This combination is often used in classic French cooking and is called a bouquet garni. A few whole cloves add a touch of warmth and sweetness; a strip of citrus zest enhances meat-based stews and braises; a sprig of rosemary, sage, or savory sets a Mediterranean tone; and a garlic clove is a welcome addition to almost any selection of herbs. Some cooks tie these together with twine so they can remove all of them easily. Cloves can often be stuck into an orange rind so you can retrieve them at the end.

Fines herbes, a staple in France, traditionally features a blend of chopped herbs including: chervil, chives, parsley and tarragon. Dried fines herbes is widely available in grocery stores, but for a real treat, make your own using fresh herbs. This mixture adds a rich flavor to potatoes, fresh steamed vegetables, fish, poultry, and soups.

Onion family
Garlic, chives, onions, shallots, leeks and scallions all add flavor to any dish. Chives and scallions add a fresh, mild onion flavor to baked potatoes, salads, salsa, and rice. Shallots have a complex, light flavor which resembles a cross between onions and garlic. Leeks and onions are similar - use these for soups, pasta and more. Garlic is a classic herb which goes well with almost anything.

Middle Eastern
Cumin and curry are most often used in Middle Eastern dishes. Curry is strong and adds a sweet, heavy essence to dishes. Use it sparingly to flavor things like curried chicken, curried rice, and curried pumpkin soup. Cumin is one of the most prominent flavors in hummus, which is a dip made from chick peas, tahini paste, and garlic.

Pepper
Cooks have a wide variety of pepper choices. Black pepper, white pepper and green pepper all come from the berry of piper nigrum. The spiciest is black pepper, which comes from berries that are picked unripe. The berries used for white pepper are ripened on the vine and soaked until their outer hulls are easily removed. Green peppercorns are immature berries which are freeze dried or packed in brine for preservation. Out of the three, black pepper has the best flavor and aroma - grind it fresh out of a pepper mill for a real treat.

Paprika, cayenne pepper, chili pepper, red pepper, and bell pepper, are fruits from the capiscum family. Cayenne pepper is the hottest, followed in intensity by red pepper, chili pepper and paprika. Use them sparingly, especially at first.

Latin
Chili, cumin, oregano and coriander are the best herbs for spicing up chili, quesadillas, beans and rice, etc for Latin style dishes.

Leader Guide: Hypertension

Title:
Hypertension

Target Audience:
This presentation kit is intended for general audiences age 13 and up. It covers topics of wellness, aging, diabetes, heart disease, family health, limited resources, cancer prevention, and nutrition.

Lesson Objectives:
• Participants will learn about the DASH diet.
• Participants will learn how to make recipes that are in line with the DASH diet.

Lesson Rationale:
About 1 in every 3 adults in the United States has high blood pressure. High blood pressure increases the risk for heart disease and stroke, which are the first and third leading causes of death in the United States (source: cdc.gov).

Health authorities have indicated that good nutrition is one of the most important factors in determining long-term health. Poor diet plays a major role in the development of four of the top seven killers in the United States: heart disease, cancer, stroke and diabetes. Individuals who have the skills to select and prepare nutritious foods can positively impact their present and future health.

Lesson at a Glance:
This lesson introduces participants to new recipes and teaches cooking skills. It also provides nutrition and dietary information that is consistent with the Dietary Guidelines for Americans and MyPlate.

Lesson Materials:
This lesson contains:
• Leader and Activity Guides; Recipe Leader Guides
• 3 pages of copy-ready handouts and recipes

Preparation:
___ Review leader guide
___ Review handouts
___ Select activities
___ Copy and collect materials for lesson

Activity Ideas:
Introduction
Ask participants if they have ever heard of the DASH diet. Explain that DASH stands for Dietary Approaches to Stop Hypertension.

Activity 1 – Cooking Demo
Use the recipes in this lesson to plan a cooking

demonstration. These recipes are designed to help participants explore healthy and delicious ways to follow the DASH diet. We suggest you make all three recipes Muesli is great for breakfast, corn chowder is great for lunch (pair it with a salad) and the broccoli peanut stir fry is great for dinner. For dessert, you can serve fresh fruit. Check out the recipes in the Fruit and Vegetable lesson for more ways to serve a fruity dessert.

Activity 2 - DASH through the Day
Show participants the handout, "Have you heard of the DASH diet?" As a class activity, plan one day or one week's worth of meals following the DASH plan. This will help participants learn how to structure their meals using the DASH diet. You can also use the handout in the Cooking for One lesson called "Planning Saves You Time and Money."

Activity 3 - Sodium Danger Zones
Bring a variety of high-sodium food packages to class. Include processed cereals, crackers, canned goods, condiments, frozen foods, deli meats, bread and cheese. Outline what to look for when identifying high-sodium foods, and remind particpants that MyPlate also stresses the importance of low-sodium options. At this point, you can compare the high-sodium foods to their low-sodium counterparts.

For More Information:
www.foodandhealth.com - Check out our CPE course on diet, hypertension, and salt toxicity.

http://www.nhlbi.nih.gov/health/dci/Diseases/dash/dash_what.html - Take a look at this link for an in-depth exploration of the DASH diet.

http://www.cdc.gov/bloodpressure/ - Learn about high blood pressure and ways to get it under control at the CDC's website.

Leader Guide: Recipes to Lower Blood Pressure

Muesli
Makes 6 sample servings

Eat this delicious dish for breakfast to increase your calcium intake. It is very convenient to eat on the go.

1/4 cup rolled oats, dry
1/4 cup skim milk
1/2 cup vanilla light nonfat yogurt
1 cup diced fresh fruit
Pinch of cinnamon

Directions:
1. Mix the rolled oats and milk; allow to soak for a few minutes or overnight.
2. Fold in the rest of the ingredients. Eat immediately or refrigerate until ready to serve, up to 1 day. We recommend using a 2 ounce serving for tasting samples.

Equipment:
___ Knife (for cutting fruit)
___ Cutting board
___ Soup spoon
___ Mixing bowl
___ Cup or bowl (for final presentation)
___ Measuring cups and spoons

Shopping list:
___ Rolled oats, dry
___ Skim milk
___ Vanilla nonfat light yogurt
___ Fresh fruit
___ Ground cinnamon
___ Cups, spoons and napkins (for samples)

Cooking skills/nutrition lesson:
This is a perfect DASH breakfast - it uses whole grains, lowfat dairy, and fruit, while steering clear of high-sodium options.

Demo preparation:
1. Wash your hands before you handle food.
2. Cut and measure ingredients.

Garnish/presentation tips:
Place the muesli in a cup or bowl. Top with a few pieces of fresh fruit and a pinch of ground cinnamon.

Number of sample servings: 6

Healthy Pasta Sauce
Makes 32 sample servings

8 oz can no-salt-added tomato sauce
15 oz can no-salt-added stewed tomatoes
6 oz can tomato paste
1/2 cup mixed frozen vegetables
1 tsp dried oregano
1 Tbsp olive oil
1 Tbsp sugar

Directions:
1. Place all ingredients in blender and blend on high speed until smooth.
2. Pour out of blender and into a saucepan. Place pan on the stove, bring to a boil, reduce to a simmer, and cook for 5 minutes. Use on pasta or chill and freeze for later use. Makes one quart.

Note: Commercial varieties of pasta sauce have about 600-800 mg sodium per 1/2 cup!

Equipment:
___ Can opener
___ Blender
___ Measuring cup
___ Stove
___ 2 quart sauce pan
___ Spoon

Shopping list:
___ 8 oz can no-salt-added tomato sauce
___ 15 oz can no-salt-added stewed tomatoes
___ 6 oz can tomato paste
___ Mixed frozen vegetables
___ Dried oregano
___ Olive oil
___ Sugar
___ Cups, spoons, and napkins (for samples)

Cooking skill/nutrition lesson:
This recipe shows participants how to make a pasta sauce that is tasty AND low in sodium.

Demo preparation:
1. Wash hands, measure, and organize ingredients.

Number of tastings: 32 (2 tablespoons each)

Leader Guide: Recipe to Lower Blood Pressure

10 Minute Corn Chowder

Makes 20 sample servings

This tasty corn chowder is easily made in a skillet.

1 tsp oil
1/2 onion, chopped
1 tsp minced garlic
4 tbsp all purpose flour
3 cups skim milk
2 tsp prepared mustard
1/4 tsp dried thyme
Black pepper to taste
2 cups frozen corn kernels
2 Tbsp shredded reduced fat cheddar cheese

Directions:

1. Heat a large, nonstick skillet over medium-high. Add the oil, then onion and garlic and saute until golden, about 2 minutes.
2. Meanwhile, place the milk, flour, mustard, and seasonings in a small bowl and mix well. Add the milk mixture to the skillet, followed by the corn. Mix well until the mixture comes to a boil and thickens, about 3 minutes. Stir frequently to keep the mixture from burning.
3. Divide into four bowls and top each with 1 tablespoon of shredded cheese. We recommend a 2 ounce serving for tasting samples.

Equipment:

___ Knife (for chopping onion)
___ Cutting board
___ 12-inch nonstick skillet
___ Stove
___ Small bowl (to mix flour and milk)
___ Ladle
___ Large soup bowl (for final presentation)
___ Measuring cups and spoons

Shopping list:

___ Oil
___ Onion
___ Jar of minced garlic
___ All purpose flour
___ Skim milk
___ Prepared mustard
___ Dried thyme
___ Black pepper
___ Frozen corn kernels
___ Shredded, reduced fat cheddar cheese
___ Spoons, cups, and napkins (for samples)

Cooking skills/nutrition lesson:

Many of the prepared cream soups on the market are very high in sodium. You may want to bring in a can of cream soup to show that a one cup serving often contains around 800-1200 mg of sodium or a half day's supply. Compare that nutrition information with this homemade version.

Demo Preparation:

1. Wash your hands before you handle food.
2. Cut and measure ingredients. Organize them around the stove and skillet so they are in the order you will add them.

Garnish/presentation tips:

Place a serving of the soup in a large soup bowl and top with cheddar cheese.

Number of sample servings: 20

Leader Guide: Recipe to Lower Blood Pressure

Broccoli Peanut Stir Fry

Makes 12 sample servings

2 tsp oil
1 cup sliced green onion
1 cup sliced carrots
2 cups chopped kale, prewashed
1 cup chopped broccoli
1/2 tsp garlic powder
2 Tbsp light soy sauce
1/4 tsp ground ginger (or 1 Tbsp fresh ground ginger)
1 cup dry roasted peanuts, no salt added
2 cups cooked brown rice
Optional garnish: 4 tsp sesame seeds

Directions:

1. Cook brown rice in microwave according to package directions. (We recommend that you cook it ahead of time or start it before class arrives. It is also handy to have a microwave or rice cooker so you are hands free while it is cooking).
2. Heat a large, nonstick skillet over medium high and add oil. Add the vegetables in the order they appear above. Cover pan and allow to saute for a few minutes before stirring, allowing them to turn golden brown. Saute until vegetables are almost tender then add seasonings and peanuts.
3. Serve over cooked brown rice and garnish with toasted sesame seeds. We recommend 2 ounce portions for tasting samples.

Equipment:

___ Knife (for cutting vegetables)
___ Cutting board
___ Stove
___ 12" nonstick skillet
___ Plastic spoon
___ Kitchen spoon
___ Casserole for cooking rice (we recommend cooking it in the microwave or a rice cooker)
___ Microwave oven (for rice)
___ Measuring cups and spoons
___ Disposable cups (for premeasured ingredients)

Shopping list:

___ Vegetable oil
___ Sesame seeds (optional garnish)
___ Green onion
___ Carrots
___ Fresh kale
___ Broccoli
___ Garlic powder
___ Light soy sauce
___ Ground ginger (or fresh ground ginger)
___ Dry roasted peanuts, no salt added
___ Brown rice
___ Cups, spoons, and napkins (for samples)

Cooking skills/nutrition lesson:

A stir fry dish is an excellent way to increase vegetable consumption. However, some stir fries can be an absolute sodium bomb. This method involves little salt but lots of flavor.

Demo preparation:

1. Wash your hands before you handle food.
2. Cut and measure ingredients. Organize them around the skillet in the order you will be adding them.

Make ahead options:

We recommend that you cook the brown rice before class and demonstrate the rest. Stir fry generally does not reheat well.

Garnish/presentation tips:

Place the brown rice on a large dinner plate and top with the stir fry. You can also sprinkle this dish with sesame seeds. They are delicious, go well with Asian style dishes, and are high in calcium.

Number of sample servings: 12

Recipes to Lower Blood Pressure

Muesli

Eat this delicious dish for breakfast to increase your calcium intake. It is very convenient to eat on the go.

1/4 cup rolled oats, dry
1/4 cup skim milk
1/2 cup vanilla light nonfat yogurt
1 cup diced fresh fruit
Pinch of cinnamon

Directions:

1. Mix the rolled oats and milk; allow to soak for a few minutes or overnight.
2. Fold in the rest of the ingredients. Eat immediately or refrigerate until ready to serve, up to 1 day. Serves 1. Each serving (about 2 cups): 250 calories, 6 g fat, 0.5 g saturated fat, 4 mg cholesterol, 84 mg sodium, 38 g carbohydrate, 6 g fiber, 11 g protein.

Broccoli Peanut Stir Fry

Peanuts add crunch to this delicious stir fry dish.

2 tsp oil
1 cup sliced green onion
1 cup sliced carrots
2 cups chopped kale, prewashed
1 cup chopped broccoli
1/2 tsp garlic powder
2 Tbsp light soy sauce
1/4 tsp ground ginger (or 1 Tbsp fresh ground ginger)
1 cup dry roasted peanuts, no salt added
2 cups cooked brown rice
Optional garnish: 4 tsp sesame seeds

Directions:

1. Cook brown rice in microwave according to package directions. (We recommend that you cook it ahead of time or start it before class arrives. It is also handy to have a microwave or rice cooker so you are hands free while it is cooking).
2. Heat a large, nonstick skillet over medium high and add oil. Add the vegetables in the order they appear above. Cover pan and allow to saute for a few minutes before stirring, allowing them to turn golden brown. Saute until vegetables are almost tender then add seasonings and peanuts.
3. Serve over cooked brown rice and garnish with toasted sesame seeds. (You can toast them in an oven or toaster oven).

Serves 4. Each 1-1/2 cup serving: 280 calories, 12 g fat, 1.5 g saturated fat, 0 mg cholesterol, 290 mg sodium, 35 g carbohydrate, 5.5 g fiber, 9.5 g protein.

10 Minute Corn Chowder

This tasty corn chowder is easily made in a skillet.

1 tsp oil
1/2 onion, chopped
1 tsp minced garlic
4 tbsp all purpose flour
3 cups skim milk
2 tsp prepared mustard
1/4 tsp dried thyme
Black pepper to taste
2 cups frozen corn kernels
2 Tbsp shredded reduced fat cheddar cheese

Directions:

1. Heat a large, nonstick skillet over medium-high. Add the oil, then onion and garlic and saute until golden, about 2 minutes.
2. Meanwhile, place the milk, flour, mustard, and seasonings in a small bowl and mix well. Add the milk mixture to the skillet, followed by the corn. Mix well until the mixture comes to a boil and thickens, about 3 minutes. Stir frequently to keep the mixture from burning.
3. Divide into four bowls and top each with 1 tablespoon of shredded cheese.

Serves 4. Each serving (1-1/4 cups): 232 calories, 5 g fat, 2.5 g saturated fat, 13 mg cholesterol, 191 mg sodium, 35 g carbohydrate, 3 g fiber, 13 g protein.

Healthy Pasta Sauce

8-oz can no-salt-added tomato sauce
15-oz can no-salt-added stewed tomatoes
6-oz can tomato paste
1/2 cup mixed frozen vegetables
1 tsp dried oregano
1 Tbsp olive oil
1 Tbsp sugar

Directions:

1. Place all ingredients in blender and blend on high speed until smooth.
2. Pour out of blender and into a saucepan. Place pan on the stove, bring to a boil, reduce to a simmer, and cook for 5 minutes. Use on pasta or chill and freeze for later use. Makes one quart.

Serves 5. Each serving (2/3 cup): 101 calories, 3 g fat, 0 g saturated fat, 0 mg cholesterol, 53 mg sodium, 16 g carbohydrate, 3.5 g fiber, 3 g protein.

Note: Commercial varieties of pasta sauce have about 600-800 mg sodium per 1/2 cup!

Have You Heard of the DASH Diet?

What is the DASH diet?

DASH stands for Dietary Approaches to Stop Hypertension. In the first DASH study, participants were able to lower their blood pressure by eating more whole grains, fruits, vegetables, beans, and nuts, while consuming less meat than the standard American diet. Low-fat dairy products were also included. The second DASH-Sodium study used the same diets with various amounts of sodium. Lowering sodium intake to 1500 mg per day was the most effective for lowering blood pressure, especially when coupled with the DASH diet itself. This diet lowered blood pressure as much as using blood pressure medication. Here is what participants ate:

Grains and grain products - 7 to 8 servings a day
Serving: 1 slice bread, 1/2 cup dry cereal, 1/2 cup cooked rice, pasta, or cereal

Vegetables - 4 to 5 servings a day
Serving: 1 cup raw leafy vegetable, 1/2 cup cooked vegetable, 6 ounces vegetable juice

Fruits - 4 to 5 servings a day
Serving: 6 ounces fruit juice, 1 medium fruit, 1/4 cup dried fruit, 1/2 cup fresh, frozen, or canned fruit

Lowfat or nonfat dairy food - 2 to 3 servings a day
Serving: 1 cup skim or 1% milk, 1 cup low-fat yogurt, 1-1/2 ounces part-skim or non-fat cheese

Meats, poultry, & fish - 2 or fewer servings a day
Serving: 3 ounces broiled or roasted lean meats, skinless poultry, or fish

Nuts, seeds, & beans - 4 to 5 servings a week
Serving: 1/3 cup nuts, 1/2 cup cooked beans

Added fats and oils - 2 to 3 servings a day
Serving: 1 teaspoon oil or soft margarine, 1 teaspoon regular mayonnaise, 1 tablespoon low-fat mayonnaise, 1 tablespoon regular salad dressing, 2 tablespoons light salad dressing

Snacks & sweets - 5 servings a week
Serving: 1 medium fruit, 1 cup low-fat yogurt, 1/2 cup low-fat frozen yogurt, 3/4 cup pretzels, 1 tablespoon maple syrup, sugar, jelly, or jam, half cup Jell-O, 3 pieces hard candy, 15 jellybeans.

The DASH diet has more servings of whole grains, fruits, vegetables and beans than most people are used to eating. Increase your intake of these slowly and drink plenty of water to avoid gas and bloating.

This diet also helps prevent many diseases, including heart disease, stroke, certain cancers, diabetes, obesity and osteoporosis. For more information, see www.nhlbi.nih.gov/health/public/heart/hbp/dash/.

Blood Pressure Categories for Adults:

	Systolic**		Diastolic**
Optimal	<120 mm Hg	and	<80 mm Hg
Normal	<130 mm Hg	and	<85 mm Hg
High-Normal	130–139 mm Hg	or	85–89 mm Hg
High:			
Stage 1	140–159 mm Hg	or	90–99 mm Hg
Stage 2	160–179 mm Hg	or	100–109 mm Hg
Stage 3	>=180 mm Hg	or	>=110 mm Hg

*Categories apply to people 18 and older and come from the National High Blood Pressure Education Program. The categories are designed for people who are not on high blood pressure medication and who have no short-term serious illness.
** If your systolic and diastolic pressures fall into different categories, the higher category represents your overall status.

Reduce Your Sodium Intake

Where's the Sodium?

DASH Food Groups	Sodium (mg)
Grains	
Cooked cereal, rice, pasta, unsalted, 1 /2 cup	0–5
Ready-to-eat-cereal, 1 cup	100–360
Bread, 1 slice	110–175
Vegetables	
Fresh or frozen, cooked without salt, 1 /2 cup	1–70
Canned or frozen with sauce, 1 /2 cup	140–460
Pasta sauce 1/2 cup	400-800
Prepared salsa 2 ounces	200
Tomato juice, canned 3 /4 cup	820
Fruit	
Fresh, frozen, canned, 1 /2 cup	0–5
Dairy (stick to lowfat or fat free)	
Milk, 1 cup	120
Yogurt, 8 oz	160
Natural cheeses, 1 1 /2 oz	110–450
Processed cheeses, 1 1 /2 oz	600
Nuts, seeds, and beans	
Peanuts, salted, 1 /3 cup	120
Peanuts, unsalted, 1 /3 cup	0–5
Beans, cooked from dried or frozen, without salt, 1 /2 cup	0–5
Beans, canned, 1 /2 cup	400
Meats, seafood, and poultry	
Fresh meat, fish, poultry, 3 oz	30–90
Tuna canned, water pack, no salt added, 3 oz	35–45
Tuna canned, water pack, 3 oz	250–350
Deli turkey meat 2 oz	700
Ham, lean, roasted, 3 oz	1,020
Miscellaneous:	
Frozen and canned prepared meals	
Fettucini Alfredo, 1 serving	700
Chicken Noodle Soup, 1 cup	700
Lasagna, 1 serving	850
Meatloaf dinner, 1 serving	1171
Condiments	
Barbecue sauce, 1/4 cup	1018
Soy sauce, 1 Tbsp	1028

Tips for Eating Less Salt:

- **Choose unsalted grains** such as barley, plain rice, pasta and oats. Look for unsalted versions of cereal such as shredded wheat. Buy bread that is low in sodium. Beware of many packaged mixes that are usually very high in sodium.

- **Buy fresh vegetables or plain frozen vegetables** with no added salt. If you are buying canned vegetables, look for varieties that say no added salt. Many tomato products are now available in no-salt-added versions.

- **Buy fresh poultry, fish and meat** rather than cured, smoked, canned and processed versions which include: deli meat, ham, canned fish and meat, smoked meat, sausage, bacon, etc.

- **Use high-sodium condiments very sparingly**. Examples of these include: ketchup, mustard, mayonnaise, salad dressings, soy sauce, barbecue sauce and other bottled sauces. It helps to use lower-salt versions of these such as light soy sauce, but you should treat these as table salt and use them very sparingly.

- **Limit cheese**, especially hard and processed cheeses which are high in sodium.

- **Instead of buying frozen dinners**, canned soups and other convenience type products, **prepare large batches of your favorite meals and freeze them** in individual portions.

- Use **herbs and spices** instead of salt to flavor your food. Always taste before you shake the salt shaker. Try to gradually wean yourself from using added salt on your food.

- **When eating out try to select foods without added salt** such as salads and baked potatoes. Use oil and vinegar to dress your salad. Ask about preparation methods and specify no added salt where possible.

Leader Guide: Kid's Interactive Snacks & Easy Meals

Title:
Kid's Interactive Snacks and Easy Meals

Target Audience:
This presentation kit is intended for parents, teachers and caretakers of children between the ages of 3 and 10.

Lesson Objectives:
• Participants will learn how to make fun, healthy recipes with (and for) kids.

Lesson Rationale:
Health authorities have indicated that good nutrition is one of the most important factors in determining long-term health. Poor diet plays a major role in the development of four of the top seven killers in the United States: heart disease, cancer, stroke and diabetes. Individuals who have the skills to select and prepare nutritious foods can positively impact their present and future health.

Lesson at a Glance:
This lesson introduces participants to new recipes and teaches cooking skills. It also provides nutrition and dietary information that is consistent with the Dietary Guidelines for Americans and MyPlate.

Lesson Materials:
This lesson contains:
• Leader and Activity Guides; Recipe Leader Guides
• 1 page of copy-ready recipes

Preparation:
___ Review leader guide
___ Review handouts
___ Select activities
___ Copy and collect materials for lesson

Activity Ideas:

Activity 1 – Cooking Demo
Use the recipes in this lesson to plan a cooking demonstration. The recipes in this lesson are designed to making cooking fun for kids. The other goal is to explore ways to make healthy foods that kids will love.

For More Information:
www.foodandhealth.com - Check out our posters and handouts for kids in the Free Resources section.
http://www.recipesource.com/ - Take a look at SOAR's new home for an extensive collection of kids recipes.

Leader Guide: Kids Recipes

Tortilla Pizza

Makes 8 sample servings

2 large tortillas
Pasta sauce
1 cup assorted fresh or frozen veggies
1 cup part skim shredded mozzarella cheese

Directions:

1. Preheat the oven to 350 degrees. Place each tortilla on a large baking pan.
2. Spread a little pasta sauce on each tortilla.
3. Sprinkle 1/2 cup of vegetables on each tortilla. Top each one with 1/2 cup of shredded mozzarella cheese.
4. Bake the pizzas until the vegetables are heated through and the crust is crisp on the bottom, about 15 minutes. Remove from oven, slice each pizza into quarters with the pizza wheel and allow to cool.

Equipment:

____ Oven
____ Baking pans (2)
____ Spoon
____ Measuring cups
____ Oven mitts
____ Pizza wheel
____ Spatula

Shopping list:

____ 2 large tortillas
____ Pasta sauce
____ Assorted fresh or frozen veggies
____ Part skim shredded mozzarella cheese
____ Paper plates and napkins

Demo tips:

1. Have everyone wash their hands.
2. Allow kids to assemble pizzas.
3. The pizzas will be very hot when they are fresh out of the oven. Allow them to cool before cutting and serving.

Number of servings: 8 (1/4 slice each)

Happy Face Sandwiches

Makes 2 sample servings

2 slices of whole wheat bread
Assorted fresh fruit
Peanut butter

Directions:

1. Spread the whole wheat bread with the peanut butter.
2. Arrange the fruit on top in a happy face. For example, you might want to use banana slices and halved grapes for eyes, an orange slice for the nose and a slice of apple for the mouth.

Equipment:

____ Cutting board
____ Sharp knife (to cut fruit)
____ Butter knife (to spread peanut butter)

Shopping list:

____ 2 slices of whole wheat bread
____ Assorted fresh fruit
____ Peanut butter
____ Paper plates and napkins

Demo tips:

1. Have everyone wash their hands.
2. Have an adult cut the fruit and spread the peanut butter. Allow kids to decorate sandwiches.

Number of servings: 2

Leader Guide: Kids Recipes

Magic Spaghetti

Makes 8 sample servings

8 ounces dry spaghetti
26 ounce jar pasta sauce
1 cup fresh or frozen mixed vegetables

Directions:

1. Cook spaghetti according to package directions.
2. Place pasta sauce and vegetables in blender, turn it on and watch the vegetables "disappear."
3. Heat the sauce and serve over spaghetti - it disappears again in a more delicious way as the kids eat their vegetable-rich pasta sauce.

Equipment list:
____ Stove
____ Pot (to cook spaghetti and heat sauce)
____ Colander
____ Blender
____ Measuring cup
____ Spoon

Shopping list:
____ 8 ounces dry spaghetti
____ 26 ounce jar pasta sauce
____ 1 cup fresh or frozen mixed vegetables
____ Paper plates and napkins (for samples)

Demo tips:
1. Have everyone wash their hands. Kids can put the sauce and vegetables in the blender.
2. Make sure an adult stands at the blender. Do not plug it in until the sauce is in and the lid is on. Unplug as soon as you are done.
3. Have an adult handle the cooked spaghetti because it is very hot.

Number of servings: 8

Strawberry Banana Shake

Makes 6 sample servings

2 cups skim milk
1 cup frozen strawberries
1 banana

Directions:

1. Place all items in the blender, put the lid on and puree at full speed until smooth. Pulse if necessary. Pour into glass and serve with a straw.

Equipment list:
____ Blender
____ Measuring cup
____ Spoon

Shopping list:
____ Skim milk
____ Frozen strawberries
____ Bananas
____ Paper cups and straws (for samples)

Demo tips:
1. Have everyone wash their hands. Kids can put the ingredients in the blender.
2. Make sure an adult stands at the blender. Do not plug it in until the ingredients are in and the lid is on. Unplug as soon as you are done.
3. Have an adult help with pouring

Number of servings: 6 (1/2 cup each)

Leader Guide: Kids Recipes

Banana Cereal Split

Makes 4 sample servings

1 ripe banana
1 cup of berries
1 cup of vanilla yogurt
1 cup of whole grain cereal

Directions:

1. Peel banana and slice lengthwise.
2. Spoon 1/2 cup yogurt in center of 2 cereal bowls.
3. Sprinkle cereal over yogurt.
4. Put banana and blueberries in each cereal bowl.

Equipment:

____ Knife
____ Spoon
____ Measuring cup

Shopping list:

____ Banana
____ Berries
____ Vanilla yogurt
____ Whole grain cereal
____ Disposable bowls, spoons, napkins (for samples)

Demo tips:

1. Have everyone wash their hands before handling food.
2. Let kids assemble their splits.
3. Have everyone clean up before they sit down to eat.

Number of servings: 4

Banana Butterfly

Makes 2 sample servings

1 banana
Colored sprinkles
Vanilla yogurt
4 thin pretzel sticks

Directions:

1. Peel the banana and slice it in half widthwise, then again lengthwise.
2. Place the yogurt in the middle of the plate in a shape that suggests the body of a butterfly.
3. Place two quarters of banana next to the yogurt with the inward curve touching the yogurt. Sprinkle the banana quarters with colored sprinkles then add 2 pretzel sticks "antennas."

Equipment:

____ Knife
____ Spoon

Shopping list:

____ Banana
____ Colored sprinkles
____ Vanilla yogurt
____ Thin pretzel sticks
____ Disposable plates, spoons, napkins (for samples)

Demo tips:

1. Have everyone wash their hands before handling food.
2. Let kids assemble their butterflies.
3. Have them clean up before they sit down to eat.

Number of servings: 2

Yogurt Sundae

Makes 4 sample servings

1/2 cup nonfat vanilla yogurt
1/2 cup fresh fruit
Chocolate syrup
Colored sprinkles

Directions:

1. Place nonfat vanilla yogurt in a bowl. Top with fruit, syrup, and sprinkles.

Equipment:

____ Knife
____ Cutting board
____ Spoon
____ Measuring cup

Shopping list:

____ Fruit
____ Vanilla yogurt
____ Chocolate syrup
____ Colored sprinkles
____ Disposable bowls, spoons, napkins (for samples)

Demo tips:

1. Have everyone wash their hands before handling food.
2. Let kids assemble their sundaes, but keep an eye on proportions of fruit, yogurt, sprinkles, and syrup.
3. Have them clean up their work areas before they sit down to eat.

Number of servings: 4

Kids Recipes

Tortilla Pizza

2 large tortillas
Pasta sauce
1 cup assorted fresh or frozen veggies
1 cup part skim shredded mozzarella cheese
Directions:

1. Preheat the oven to 350 degrees. Place each tortilla on a large baking pan.
2. Spread a little pasta sauce on each tortilla.
3. Sprinkle 1/2 cup of vegetables on each tortilla. Top each one with 1/2 cup of shredded mozzarella cheese.
4. Bake the pizzas until the vegetables are heated through and the crust is crisp on the bottom, about 15 minutes. Remove from oven, slice each pizza into quarters with the pizza wheel and allow to cool.

Happy Face Sandwiches

2 slices of whole wheat bread
Assorted fresh fruit
Peanut butter
Directions:

1. Spread the whole wheat bread with the peanut butter.
2. Arrange the fruit on top in a happy face. For example, you might want to use banana slices and halved grapes for eyes, an orange slice for the nose and a slice of apple for the mouth.

Magic Spaghetti

8 ounces dry spaghetti
26 ounce jar pasta sauce
1 cup fresh or frozen mixed vegetables
Directions:

1. Cook spaghetti according to package directions.
2. Place pasta sauce and vegetables in blender, turn it on and watch the vegetables "disappear."
3. Heat the sauce and serve over spaghetti - it disappears again in a more delicious way as the kids eat their vegetable-rich pasta sauce.

Strawberry Banana Shake

2 cups skim milk
1 cup frozen strawberries
1 banana
Directions:

1. Place all items in the blender, put the lid on and puree at full speed until smooth. Pulse if necessary. Pour into glass and serve with a straw.

Banana Cereal Split

1 ripe banana
1 cup of berries
1 cup of vanilla yogurt
1 cup of whole grain cereal
Directions:

1. Peel banana and slice lengthwise.
2. Spoon 1/2 cup yogurt in center of 2 cereal bowls.
3. Sprinkle cereal over yogurt.
4. Put banana and blueberries in each cereal bowl..

Banana Butterfly

1 banana
Colored sprinkles
Vanilla yogurt
4 thin pretzel sticks
Directions:

1. Peel the banana and slice it in half widthwise, then again lengthwise.
2. Place the yogurt in the middle of the plate in a shape that suggests the body of a butterfly.
3. Place two quarters of banana next to the yogurt with the inward curve touching the yogurt. Sprinkle the banana quarters with colored sprinkles then add 2 pretzel sticks "antennas."

Yogurt Sundae

1/2 cup nonfat vanilla yogurt
1/2 cup fresh fruit
Chocolate syrup
Colored sprinkles
Directions:

1. Place nonfat vanilla yogurt in a bowl. Top with fruit, syrup, and sprinkles.

Leader Guide: Meet MyPlate

Title:
Meet MyPlate

Target Audience:
This presentation kit is intended for general audiences age 14 and up. It covers topics of wellness, heart disease, diabetes, weight loss, and nutrition. The recipes and lessons center on ways to create a balanced meal based on MyPlate guidelines.

Lesson Objectives:
• Participants will explore MyPlate's recommendations and rules about healthy eating.
• Participants will learn how to build a balanced plate in the proportions advocated by MyPlate.

Lesson Rationale:
Health authorities have indicated that good nutrition is one of the most important factors in determining long-term health. Poor diet plays a major role in the development of four of the top seven killers in the United States: heart disease, cancer, stroke and diabetes. Students who have the skills to select and prepare nutritious foods can positively impact their present and future health.

Lesson at a Glance:
This lesson introduces participants to new recipes and teaches cooking skills. It explores the rules set forth by MyPlate and examines why following those rules is good for your health.

Lesson Materials:
This lesson contains:
• Leader and activity guide
• Leader guide for recipes
• 3 pages of copy-ready handouts and recipes

Preparation:
____ Review leader guide
____ Review handouts
____ Select activities
____ Copy and collect materials for lesson

Activity Ideas:

Activity 1 - Meet the Plate
Bring samples of a wide variety of foods and arrange them on a table in your classroom. Outline the five basic MyPlate groups, then ask students to organize the samples into MyPlate's categories. While participants are rearranging the foods, review the handouts featured in this lesson and discuss a few of MyPlate's main points. Be sure to include...

• Enjoy your food, but eat less.
• Avoid oversized portions.
• Make half your plate fruits and vegetables.
• Make at least half your grains whole grains.
• Switch to fat-free or low-fat (1%) dairy products.
• Compare sodium in foods like soup, bread, and frozen meals -- and choose the food with lower numbers.
• Drink water instead of sugary drinks

Activity 2 - Make It Over
Place a value meal with a large burger, large fries and large soda on and around a plate. Print out the nutrient analysis from the fast food restaurant. Have participants try to fit the items on the plate and calculate the calories. Then use the same burger and a fast food salad to make my plate. One piece of bun, one piece of burger then half the plate is salad without dressing. What are the results? By our calculations you will go from around 1000 calories to just over 300 calories using the MyPlate method.

Activity 3- MyPlate Trivia
Divide participants into balanced teams and bring on the trivia. The first team to answer each question correctly will earn a point, and the team with the most points at the end of the game wins.
1. How much of your plate should be filled with fruits and vegetables at each meal?
   Answer: Half
2. What should you drink instead of sugary drinks?
   Answer: Water
3. What are the five main MyPlate food groups?
   Answer: Fruits, Vegetables, Grains, Protein, and Dairy
4. Beans and peas are part of two different MyPlate groups. What are those groups?
   Answer: Protein and vegetables
5. Make at least half the grains you eat _____ grains.
   Answer: Whole
6. Name one of the five subgroups of MyPlate's vegetable group. Answer: Varies, but should include either dark green vegetables, red and orange vegetables, beans and peas, starchy vegetables, or other vegetables.
7. How much juice counts as a cup serving of fruit?
   Answer: One cup, but only if the juice is 100% fruit juice. Otherwise, it doesn't fit that category and should actually be avoided.

Leader Guide: Meet MyPlate

(Continued...)

8. How much lowfat dairy should typical adults consume in one day?
   Answer: 3 cup servings
9. What food group do anchovies belong to?
   Answer: Protein
10. How many ounces of seafood should non-vegetarians consume per week?
    Answer: Eight
11. Oils provide essential nutrients. Are they a food group?
    Answer: No
12. True or false: According to MyPlate, no vegetables contain cholesterol.
    Answer: True
13. How many ouces of meat constitute a typical serving of protein?
    Answer: One
14. What food group does cream belong to?
    Answer: None. It is considered a source of empty calories thanks to its low calcium and high saturated fat content per serving.
15. How many cup servings of fruit should women age 31 or older consume each day?
    Answer: One and a half

Activity 4 - Balance that Plate!

Examine a few popular meals. You can bring in restaurant menus, cookbooks, or plastic food to help generate ideas, or you can simply brainstorm a few popular meals. Have participants brainstorm ways to make those meals more balanced in accordance with MyPlate directions. We've listed a few examples below...

• Fish and chips with ice cream for dessert should become a plate that has a smaller serving of grilled fish (3 ounces or so, max) with roasted potatoes instead of fried ones. Then add a side salad dressed with vinegar and a tsp of oil in the remaining space. Finish the meal not with ice cream but with lowfat chocolate pudding. Be sure to top the pudding with 1 cup of fresh, chopped fruit.

• Tuna salad on a bun with a side of chips and a large soda should be deconstructed. Toss a cup of leafy greens with a half cup of fresh, chopped vegetables and dress with balsamic vinegar and a few spritzes of olive oil. Top this salad with a few ounces of drained tuna that had been packed in water and add a small, whole grain roll on the side. Instead of soda, have a glass of nonfat milk and try a piece of fruit for dessert.

• Beef chili on a baked potato can be a great start to a meal, but it isn't quite in step with MyPlate guidelines or proportions. Make that chili vegetarian by swapping in beans and lentils for the beef, or try lowering the fat with a leaner protein source like ground turkey. Keep the baked potato, but add a fruit salad, and top a smaller serving of your chili with a hearty dollop of unsweetened, nonfat Greek yogurt. You can even dip whole grain crackers in the chili if you want to up the grain in this meal.

Activity 5 - Lower the Sodium

MyPlate and the Dietary Guidelines call for most people to keep sodium to 1500 mg or less. Bring in high and low sodium choices from each food group. Have individuals find the lowest sodium choices. Make sure they know to compare the mg of sodium with the calories on the food label to keep the sodium number balanced with the calories. 5% or less is low, too.

Further reading/info/links

www.foodandhealth.com - Check out our blog posts about the latest innovations at MyPlate, or search the site for MyPlate lesson materials. After all, we have everything from posters to powerpoints. You never know what might come in handy!

http://www.choosemyplate.gov/ In addition to reviewing MyPlate's basic guidelines, MyPlate's homepage also provides individualized recommendations based on age, gender, and activity level. You'll also find reasons for their nutrtion advice and lots of benefits of a healthy, balanced diet.

Leader Guide: MyPlate Recipes

Mix and match the following recipes to create balanced MyPlate meals. Remember to keep portions small!

Broccoli Peanut Stir Fry
Makes 12 sample servings

2 tsp oil
1 cup sliced green onion
1 cup sliced carrots
2 cups chopped kale, prewashed
1 cup chopped broccoli
1/2 tsp garlic powder
2 Tbsp light soy sauce
1/4 tsp ground ginger (or 1 Tbsp fresh ground ginger)
1 cup dry roasted peanuts, no salt added
2 cups cooked brown rice
Optional garnish: 4 tsp sesame seeds

Directions:
1. Cook brown rice in microwave according to package directions. (We recommend that you cook it ahead of time or start it before class arrives. It is also handy to have a microwave or rice cooker so you are hands-free while it is cooking).
2. Heat a large, nonstick skillet over medium high and add oil. Add the vegetables in the order they appear above. Cover pan and allow to saute for a few minutes before stirring, allowing them to turn golden brown. Saute until vegetables are almost tender then add seasonings and peanuts.
3. Serve over cooked brown rice and garnish with toasted sesame seeds. We recommend 2 ounce portions for tasting samples.

Equipment:
___ Knife (for cutting vegetables)
___ Cutting board
___ Stove
___ 12" nonstick skillet
___ Plastic spoon
___ Kitchen spoon
___ Casserole for cooking rice (we recommend cooking it in the microwave or a rice cooker)
___ Microwave oven (for rice)
___ Measuring cups and spoons
___ Disposable cups (for premeasured ingredients)

Shopping list:
___ Vegetable oil
___ Sesame seeds (optional garnish)
___ Green onion
___ Carrots
___ Fresh kale
___ Broccoli
___ Garlic powder
___ Light soy sauce
___ Ground ginger (or fresh ground ginger)
___ Dry roasted peanuts, no salt added
___ Brown rice
___ Cups, spoons, and napkins (for samples)

Cooking skills/nutrition lesson:
A stir fry dish is an excellent way to increase vegetable consumption and bring a plate more in line with MyPlate recommendations. Fill out the missing pieces by having fruit and lowfat yogurt for dessert. You can also add firm tofu or chicken breast for a protein boost.

Demo preparation:
1. Wash your hands before you handle food.
2. Cut and measure ingredients. Organize them around the skillet in the order you will be adding them.

Make ahead options:
We recommend that you cook the brown rice before class and demonstrate the rest. Stir fry generally does not reheat well.

Garnish/presentation tips:
Place the brown rice on a large dinner plate and top with the stir fry. You can also sprinkle this dish with sesame seeds. They are delicious, go well with Asian style dishes, and are high in calcium.

Number of sample servings: 12

Leader Guide: MyPlate Recipes

Mix and match the following recipes to create balanced MyPlate meals. Remember to keep portions small!

Lowfat Turkey Burger

1 pound extra lean ground turkey breast
1 tsp garlic powder
1/2 tsp thyme
Black pepper to taste
1 tablespoon no-salt ketchup
Directions:
1. Mix all ingredients together and form four thin burgers. Place the burgers in a glass baking pan with a sprinkle of water.
2. Bake the burgers at 375 for 10 minutes or until firm in the center and no longer pink (about 170F internal temperature).
3. Serve the burgers open-faced on whole grain toast with onion, lettuce and sliced ripe tomatoes. Garnish with apple slices, too, if desired.

Carrot Slaw

1/4 head cabbage, shredded
1 carrot, grated
1 tablespoon mayonnaise
1 tablespoon sugar
1 tablespoon vinegar
sprinkle mustard seeds
sprinkle black sesame seeds
Directions:
1. Mix the mayonnaise with the sugar and vinegar. Add the seeds.
2. Mix the cabbage and carrots with the mayonnaise mixture. Chill until ready to serve.
3. The seeds are optional and add a lot of flavor - find them in the spice section. You can also use poppy seeds or omit them.

Total dinner: 488 calories, 2.5 g fat, 0 g sat fat, 0 g trans fat, 42 mg cholesterol, 489 mg so- dium, 81 g carbohydrate, 11 g fiber, 32 g protein.

Equipment:

____ Oven
____ Knife
____ Cutting board
____ Glass baking pan
____ 2 Mixing bowls, 2 kitchen spoons
____ Hand grater
____ Small peeler
____ Measuring cups and spoons

Shopping list:

____ 1 pound turkey breast
____ Garlic powder
____ Thyme
____ Black pepper
____ No salt ketchup
____ Whole grain bread for toast
____ Assorted veggies for burger: tomato, onion, lettuce
____ Cabbage
____ Carrot
____ Apple
____ Mayonnaise (light)
____ Sugar
____ Vinegar (red wine, cider or regular)
____ Mustards seeds (or powder)
____ Black sesame seeds or poppy seeds
____ Cups, spoons and napkins (for samples)
____ Disposable cups (for premeasured ingredients)

Cooking skill/nutrition lesson:

This easy recipe will show how to make a MyPlate meal out of a popular entree: the hamburger. By making it open faced and adding veggies.

Demo preparation:

1. Wash your hands before you handle food.
2. Measure all ingredients.
3. Organize your work area so everything is easily accessible.

Make ahead options:

You can bake the burgers ahead of time and just assemble. It is fun to ask for help from the audience.

Garnish/presentation tips:

Serve the burger open faced style with veggies on top then add the carrot slaw and the apple slices on the side. You can also show how one burger and one piece of whole grain toast make up 1/2 of the plate and the other half is filled with slaw, veggies for the top of the burger and the sliced apple. Be sure to use skim milk or the dairy dessert on the next page.

Number of sample servings: 8-12

Make mini "MyPlates" with the taste samples for more fun!

Leader Guide: MyPlate Recipes

Mix and match the following recipes to create balanced MyPlate meals. Remember to keep portions small!

Half n Half Meat Loaf

1 pound lean ground turkey
1 pound frozen stew veggies
1 can whole tomatoes, no salt
1/2 tsp onion powder
1/2 tsp garlic powder
1/4 tsp black pepper
1/4 tsp poultry seasoning
1 cup seasoned bread crumbs
Ketchup, about 2 tablespoons
Directions:

1. Cook the veggies in the microwave for 10 minutes or until really tender.
2. Puree the cooked veggies with the tomatoes in a food processor.
3. Stir the turkey, puree, season- ings and bread crumbs together. Place into oiled loaf pan, top with ketchup and bake at 375 for 1 hour or until done.
4. Allow to sit out for 10 minutes; cut and serve from the pan.

Serves 10. Each slice (4 ounces): 100 calories, 1 g fat, 0 g saturated fat, 0 g trans fat, 21 mg cholesterol, 191 mg sodium, 10 g carbohydrate, 1 g fiber, 12 g protein. (Compare to 520 calories and 36 g of fat for regular meatloaf!)

Mashed Cauli Taters

1 pound yukon gold potatoes
1 pound frozen cauliflower florets
1 teaspoon butter
1/4 tsp black pepper
1/2 tsp garlic powder
1/4 cup skim milk Directions:

1. Peel the potatoes and cut them in quarters. Cook them in boiling water with the cauliflower until they are very tender, about 30 minutes.
2. Drain off the water, mash with a potato masher and then whip smooth with electric beaters. Add the but- ter, seasonings and skim milk. Dab with additional butter or margarine. Serve hot.

Serves 8. Each 1/2 cup serving: 66 calo- ries, <1 g fat, 0 g saturated fat, 0 g trans fat, 1 mg cholesterol, 19 mg sodium, 14 g carbohydrate, 2.5 g fiber, 2 g protein. (Compare to 270 calories and 11 g of fat for regular mashed potatoes!)

Equipment:

____ Oven
____ Food processor
____ Rubber scraper
____ Pan to cook veggies
____ Potato masher
____ Colander
____ Kitchen/serving spoon
____ Knife
____ Cutting board
____ Measuring cups and spoons

Shopping list:

____ 1 pound turkey breast
____ 1 pound frozen stew veggies (onions, potatoes, carrots)
____ 1 can whole tomatoes
____ seasonings: onion powder, garlic powder, black pepper, poulty seasoning
____ bread crumbs
____ potatoes
____ cauliflower
____ margarine
____ skim milk
____ Cups, spoons and napkins (for samples)
____ Disposable cups (for premeasured ingredients)

Cooking skill/nutrition lesson:

This easy recipe will show how to make a MyPlate meal and it will show how to sneak in MORE veggies.

Demo preparation:

1. Wash your hands before you handle food.
2. Measure all ingredients.
3. Organize your work area so everything is easily accessible.

Make ahead options:

You can bake the meatloaf ahead of time and just assemble. It is fun to ask for help from the audience.

Garnish/presentation tips:

Add shaved red pepper or sauteed mushrooms.

Number of sample servings: 16

Make mini "MyPlates" with the taste samples for more fun!

MyPlate Recipes

This recipe is a great use of dairy to add to MyPlate meals.

Yogurt Sundae
Makes 8-10 sample servings
1 cup nonfat vanilla yogurt
1 1/2 cups fresh fruit
Garnish: 2 tsp chocolate syrup, cherry
Directions:
1. Layer nonfat vanilla yogurt and fresh fruit in a parfait glass.
2. Top with chocolate syrup and a fresh cherry.

Equipment:
____ Knife
____ Cutting board
____ Spoon
____ Measuring cups and spoons
____ Parfait glass

Shopping list:
____ Fresh fruit (remember the cherry!)
____ Vanilla yogurt
____ Chocolate syrup
____ Disposable bowls, spoons, napkins (for samples)

Cooking skill/nutrition lesson:
This recipe shows participants how to prepare a healthy dessert that includes a balance of lowfat dairy and fruit. It is excellent when served after a meal that features vegetables, protein, and whole grains.

Demo preparation:
1. Wash your hands before you handle food.
2. Chop fruit and measure yogurt.
3. Organize your work area.

Make ahead options:
Chop up fruit before class or buy pre-chopped options. You can also use fruit that doesn't need chopping, like raspberries or blackberries.

Garnish presentation tips:
Layer fruit and yogurt in a parfait glass. Be sure to save some fruit for the top of the glass, then drizzle the chocolate syrup over everything and top with a fresh (not maraschino) cherry.

Number of sample servings: 8-10

Cafe Con Leche
Makes 4 samples (about 3 ounces each)
1/2 cup brewed strong decaffeinated coffee
1 cup non-fat/skim milk
Directions:
1. Heat milk in microwave for 1 to 1 1/2 minutes. Add coffee and mix.

Equipment:
____ Microwave
____ Measuring cup
____ Coffee mug

Shopping list:
____ Instant decaf coffee
____ Skim milk
____ Ground cinnamon for garnish
____ Disposable mini cups (for samples)

Cooking skill/nutrition lesson:
This recipe shows participants how to prepare a healthy coffee drink that includes skim milk.

Demo preparation:
1. Wash your hands.
2. Measure ingredients.
3. Organize your work area.

Make ahead options:
Make instant coffee ahead of time.

Garnish presentation tips:
Garnish with ground cinnamon. For a nice touch you can use a milk frother so you can add a good layer of foam on the milk before adding the coffee.

Number of sample servings: 4

MyPlate Recipes

Mix and match the following recipes to create balanced MyPlate meals.

Lowfat Turkey Burger
1 pound extra lean ground turkey breast
1 tsp garlic powder
1/2 tsp thyme
Black pepper to taste
1 tablespoon no-salt ketchup
Directions:
1. Mix all ingredients together and form four thin burgers. Place the burgers in a glass baking pan with a sprinkle of water.
2. Bake the burgers at 375 for 10 minutes or until firm in the center and no longer pink (about 170F internal temperature).
3. Serve the burgers open-faced on whole grain toast with onion, lettuce and sliced ripe tomatoes. Garnish with apple slices, too, if desired.

Carrot Slaw
1/4 head cabbage, shredded
1 carrot, grated
1 tablespoon mayonnaise
1 tablespoon sugar
1 tablespoon vinegar
sprinkle mustard seeds
sprinkle black sesame seeds
Directions:
1. Mix the mayonnaise with the sugar and vinegar. Add the seeds.
2. Mix the cabbage and carrots with the mayonnaise mixture. Chill until ready to serve.
3. The seeds are optional and add a lot of flavor - find them in the spice section. You can also use poppy seeds or omit them.
Total dinner: 488 calories, 2.5 g fat, 0 g sat fat, 0 g trans fat, 42 mg cholesterol, 489 mg so- dium, 81 g carbohydrate, 11 g fiber, 32 g protein.

Yogurt Sundae
1 cup nonfat vanilla yogurt
1 1/2 cups fresh fruit
Garnish: 2 tsp chocolate syrup, cherry
Directions:
1. Layer nonfat vanilla yogurt and fresh fruit in a parfait glass.
2. Top with chocolate syrup and a fresh cherry.

Half n Half Meat Loaf
1 pound lean ground turkey
1 pound frozen stew veggies
1 can whole tomatoes, no salt
1/2 tsp onion powder
1/2 tsp garlic powder
1/4 tsp black pepper
1/4 tsp poultry seasoning
1 cup seasoned bread crumbs
Ketchup, about 2 tablespoons
Directions:
1. Cook the veggies in the microwave for 10 minutes or until really tender.
2. Puree the cooked veggies with the tomatoes in a food processor.
3. Stir the turkey, puree, season- ings and bread crumbs together. Place into oiled loaf pan, top with ketchup and bake at 375 for 1 hour or until done.
4. Allow to sit out for 10 minutes; cut and serve from the pan.
Serves 10. Each slice (4 ounces): 100 calories, 1 g fat, 0 g saturated fat, 0 g trans fat, 21 mg cholesterol, 191 mg sodium, 10 g carbohydrate, 1 g fiber, 12 g protein. (Compare to 520 calories and 36 g of fat for regular meatloaf!)

Mashed Cauli Taters
1 pound yukon gold potatoes
1 pound frozen cauliflower florets
1 teaspoon butter
1/4 tsp black pepper
1/2 tsp garlic powder
1/4 cup skim milk Directions:
1. Peel the potatoes and cut them in quarters. Cook them in boiling water with the cauliflower until they are very tender, about 30 minutes.
2. Drain off the water, mash with a potato masher and then whip smooth with electric beaters. Add the butter, seasonings and skim milk. Dab with additional butter or margarine. Serve hot.
Serves 8. Each 1/2 cup serving: 66 calo- ries, <1 g fat, 0 g saturated fat, 0 g trans fat, 1 mg cholesterol, 19 mg sodium, 14 g carbohydrate, 2.5 g fiber, 2 g protein.

Cafe Con Leche
1/2 cup brewed strong decaffeinated coffee
1 cup non-fat/skim milk
Heat milk in microwave for 1 to 1 1/2 minutes. Add coffee and mix. Optional: garnish with cinnamon.

Fast and Lean MyPlate Meals

Breakfast

Whole Grains
- Cooked oatmeal
- Cooked whole grain cream of wheat
- Smoothie -- Mix nonfat, light yogurt with 100% fruit juice, fresh or frozen fruit, and uncooked oats.
- Shredded wheat (or another unsweetened wholegrain cereal) with nonfat milk.
- Yogurt parfait -- Layer nonfat, light yogurt with fresh fruit and uncooked oats.
- Two slices of whole grain toast or a whole grain English muffin. Top with light jelly or fresh fruit.

Dairy
- Top cereal with nonfat milk or have a small glass on the side.
- Snack on nonfat, low sugar yogurt.

Fruit
- Banana
- Orange
- Apple
- Pear
- Grapes
- Melon

Beverage
- Coffee
- Tea
- 100% fruit juice
- Nonfat or low-fat milk

Go easy on portions, cream, and sweeteners.

Lunch

Light Entrees
- Pasta with low-fat red sauce
- Fish: poached, baked, grilled
- Stir fry with veggies, brown rice, and lean protein
- Skinless chicken breast: roasted, baked, or grilled
- Tuna salad: Make this with light maynaise and serve on a bed of chopped lettuce
- Chicken breast salad: Make this with light maynaise and serve on a bed of chopped lettuce
- Clear, broth-based soup
- Low-fat chili

Side dishes
- Fresh fruit
- Tossed, low-fat salad (try to include one of these in every meal)
- Steamed or raw vegetables
- Low-fat slaw
- Baked potato with low-fat sour cream

Beverage
- Water
- Skim milk
- Unsweetened iced tea

Dinner

Light Entree
- Pasta with low-fat red sauce
- Fish: poached, baked, grilled
- Stir fry with veggies, brown rice, and lean protein
- Skinless chicken breast: roasted, baked, or grilled
- Low-fat lasagna
- Shrimp cocktail
- Beans and rice
- Low-fat chili

Side dishes
- Fresh fruit
- Tossed, low-fat salad (try to include one of these in every meal)
- Steamed or raw vegetables
- Low-fat slaw
- Baked potato with low-fat sour cream

Beverage
- Water
- Skim milk
- Unsweetened iced tea

Get to Know MyPlate

Key Consumer Messages
- Enjoy your food, but eat less.
- Avoid oversized portions.
- Make half your plate fruits and vegetables.
- Make at least half your grains whole grains.
- Switch to fat-free or low-fat (1%) dairy products.
- Compare sodium in foods like soup, bread, and frozen meals -- choose the food with lower numbers.
- Drink water instead of sugary drinks

Meet the Vegetable Group!
- Vegetables can be raw or cooked, whole, chopped or mashed. They can also be fresh, frozen, canned, or dried/dehydrated. Even 100% vegetable juice is welcome in the vegetable group. Just watch out for high sodium content in frozen and canned varieties.
- One cup serving of veggies is equivalent to...
    - 1 cup of fresh or cooked vegetables
    - 2 cups of leafy greens
    - 1 cup of 100% vegetable juice
- Most people should get between 2.5 and 3 cup servings of vegetables every single day.

Meet the Fruit Group!
- Fruit can be raw or cooked, whole, chopped or pureed. It can also be fresh, frozen, canned, or dried/dehydrated. Even 100% fruit juice is welcome in the fruit group. Remember to steer clear of fruit products with added sugar.
- One cup serving of fruit is equivalent to...
    - 1 cup of chopped fruit
    - 1 medium piece of fruit
    - 1 cup of 100% fruit juice
    - 1/2 cup of dried fruit
- Most people should eat between 1.5 and 2 cup servings of fruit every single day.

Meet the Grain Group!
- The grain group includes food made from wheat, rice, oats, cornmeal, barley, or another cereal grain.
- One ounce serving of grain is equivalent to...
    - 1 piece of bread
    - 1/2 cup cooked rice, cereal, or pasta
    - 1 cup of dry cereal
- Most people should eat between 5 and 6 ounces of grains per day.

Meet the Protein Group!
- Any food made from meat, poultry, seafood, beans and peas, eggs, processed soy products, nuts, and seeds is welcome in the protein group.
- One ounce serving of protein is equivalent to...
    - 1 ounce of chicken, fish, or lean meat
    - 1 egg
    - 1/4 cup of cooked, dried beans
    - 1/2 ounce of nuts
    - 1 tablespoon of nut butter
- Most people should consume 5 to 6 ounces of protein every day.

Meet the Dairy Group!
- All fluid milks, as well as yogurt, milk-based desserts, calcium-fortified soymilk, hard natural cheeses, and soft cheeses are part of this group.
- One cup serving of dairy is equivalent to...
    - 1/3 cup shredded cheese
    - 1 cup skim milk
    - 1.5 ounces of hard, natural cheese
    - 1 cup nonfat yogurt
    - 2 ounces processed cheese
- Most people should consume 3 cup servings of dairy every day.

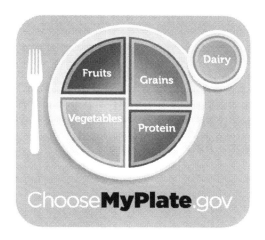

Leader Guide: No Cook Demos

Title:
No Cook Demos for the Classroom

Target Audience:
This presentation kit is intended for general audiences age 14 and up. It covers topics of wellness, heart disease, diabetes, weight loss, and nutrition. These recipes may be used at health fairs, classes, supermarket tours, and any other situation where no-cook food demos would enhance nutrition education.

Lesson Objectives:
• To demonstrate that healthy foods are easy to prepare and taste great.
• To provide food and nutrition specialists with healthy food items that do not require cooking.

Lesson Rationale:
Health authorities have indicated that good nutrition is one of the most important factors in determining long-term health. Poor diet plays a major role in the development of four of the top seven killers in the United States: heart disease, cancer, stroke and diabetes. Students who have the skills to select and prepare nutritious foods can positively impact their present and future health.

Lesson at a Glance:
This lesson introduces participants to new recipes and teaches cooking skills. It also provides nutrition and dietary information that is consistent with the Dietary Guidelines for Americans and MyPlate.

Lesson Materials:
This lesson contains:
• Leader and activity guide
• Leader guide for recipes
• 2 pages of copy-ready handouts and recipes

Preparation:
___ Review leader guide
___ Review handouts
___ Select activities
___ Copy and collect materials for lesson

Activity Ideas:

Activity 1 - Stock it Well
Using MyPlate, show your participants how to stock their kitchens for quick and easy healthy meals.
Here are some ideas:
• Grains: Pasta (preferably whole grain), brown rice, whole grain crackers, whole grain breads, barley, couscous, bulgur wheat, etc.
• Vegetables: Fresh, frozen, canned (stick to low-sodium options in accordance with MyPlate guidelines). Common easy-to-prepare/store items include potatoes, sweet potatoes, lettuce, shredded cabbage, baby carrots, broccoli florets.
• Fruits: Fresh, frozen, dried. Common easy-to-prepare items include: melon, pears, apples, bananas, berries, tree fruits in season, citrus.
• Protein: Beans, tuna, fresh or frozen fish, poultry, lean meat, tofu, nuts, nut butters.
• Dairy: Skim milk, nonfat yogurt, nonfat sour cream, Parmesan, light cheese, fortified soy milk. Remember to keep as many items lowfat or fat free as possible.
• Extras: Salad dressings, light syrup, low sodium condiments.

Activity 2 - Food Demo
Use one or more recipes in this lesson to show how to make easy no-cook meals.

Further reading/info/links
www.foodandhealth.com - Click on the Recipes link in the Free Resources section for additional healthy and delicious options.

Leader Guide: No Cook Demos

Caribbean Bean Salad
Makes 14 sample servings
4 cups ready-to-serve Romaine lettuce or salad mix
1/4 cup red onion
1 cup canned black beans, drained and rinsed
1 orange, peeled and diced
1 tomato, diced
1 Tbsp olive oil
3 Tbsp red wine vinegar
1 tsp dried oregano
Black pepper to taste
Directions:
1. Toss all ingredients together in a large salad bowl.
2. Serve immediately, or refrigerate up to one hour before serving. (We recommend 1/2 cup servings for sample servings).

Equipment needed:
___ Large salad bowl
___ Kitchen spoons (to toss and serve salad)
___ Can opener
___ Knife and cutting board
___ Measuring cups and spoons
___ Large plate (for final presentation)

Shopping list:
___ Ready-to-serve Romaine lettuce or salad mix
___ 1 can black beans
___ 1 orange
___ 1 ripe tomato
___ Olive oil
___ Red wine vinegar
___ Dried oregano
___ Ground black pepper
___ Small plates, forks, and napkins (for samples)

Cooking skill/nutrition lesson:
This recipe shows participants how to make an entree salad and outlines how to dress a salad using a small amount of oil and vinegar. This salad is lower in sodium than one made with commercial salad dressings, and uses foods from three groups of MyPlate: vegetables, fruit, and protein.

Demo preparation:
1. Wash hands before preparing food.
2. Wash produce in cold, running water.
3. Cut and measure produce. Place these ingredients in disposable zip lock bags or plastic containers.
4. Assemble and organize items around the salad bowl.

Make ahead:
You can prepare all produce ahead of time and simply assemble the salad at the demo.

Garnish/presentation tips:
Place the salad on a large plate and top with fresh cracked black pepper.

Number of sample servings: 14

Leader Guide: No Cook Demos

Tuna Salad on Greens
Makes 8 sample servings
Tossed salad:
4 cups ready-to-serve romaine lettuce
1 carrot, peeled and grated
1 tomato
1/4 red onion
1 Tbsp olive oil
3 Tbsp red wine vinegar
1 tsp Italian Seasoning
Fresh cracked black pepper
Tuna Salad:
1 can low-sodium tuna in water, drained
1/3 cup lowfat mayonnaise
1/4 cup celery
1/4 cup green onion
Garnish: 4 whole grain crackers (Try WASA or another brand that is low in fat and sodium)
Directions:
1. Place tossed salad ingredients in a large salad bowl. Toss together.
2. Mix ingredients for tuna salad in another mixing bowl.
3. Assemble tossed salad on a large plate. Top with a scoop of tuna salad, and garnish with the whole grain cracker.

Equipment needed:
___ Cutting board
___ Knife
___ Vegetable peeler
___ Grater
___ Medium mixing bowl
___ Salad bowl
___ 2 kitchen spoons
___ Can opener
___ Large plate (for final presentation)

Shopping list:
___ 1 bag ready-to-serve romaine lettuce
___ 1 carrot
___ 1 tomato
___ Red onion
___ Olive oil
___ Red wine vinegar
___ Italian Seasoning
___ Fresh cracked black pepper
___ 1 can low-sodium tuna
___ Lowfat mayonnaise
___ Celery
___ Green onion
___ WASA crackers
___ Plates, forks, and napkins for tasting

Cooking skill/nutrition lesson:
This recipe shows the audience how to make a delicious, healthy tuna salad that is lower in salt and fat than most commercial preparations. It uses a lot of vegetables and just one cracker, which makes it more filling and lower in calorie density than a tuna sandwich made with 2 slices of bread. These proportions bring the salad into alignmnet with MyPlate guidelines and is excellent for those wanting to eat healthier, trying to lose weight, or following a heart healthy diet. In addition, it outlines tasty ways to dress a salad using less fat and sodium. Finally, gives participants a chance to try lowfat whole grain crackers like WASA. Note: You can vary this recipe by using cooked chicken or canned salmon (with bones!) in place of the tuna.

Demo preparation:
1. Wash your hands before you handle food.
2. Measure all ingredients and place in disposable containers. Organize them around the mixing bowls.

Make ahead:
You can precut all tossed salad ingredients and make the tuna salad ahead of time. Then, when you get to class, simply assemble and serve.

Garnish/presentation tips:
Center a scoop of tuna salad on top of the scattered, tossed salad. Arrange a whole grain cracker to the right of the scoop and sprinnkle the whole thing with fresh cracked black pepper.

Number of sample servings: 8

Leader Guide: No Cook Demos

Barbecue Bean Dip

Makes 12-14 sample servings

1 cup carrot sticks
1 cup celery sticks
1 cup broccoli florets
1 green bell pepper, stemmed, seeded, and cut in rings
2 whole wheat pitas, cut in triangles
Dip:
1 can pinto beans
1 cup no-salt-added tomato sauce
1/2 tsp chili powder
1 Tbsp vinegar
1/2 Tbsp brown sugar
Directions:

1. Arrange vegetables and pita triangles on a large platter. Place a bowl in the center or off to the side for the dip.
2. Place all ingredients for dip in a food processor. Puree on high speed until smooth.
3. Pour the dip into the bowl and serve immediately or cover and refrigerate for later use.

Equipment:
___ Cutting board
___ Knife
___ Vegetable peeler
___ Food processor
___ Spatula
___ Can opener
___ Large platter
___ Bowl for dip

Shopping list:
___ 1 bag carrot sticks, baby carrots, or whole carrots
___ 1 bag celery sticks or stalk of celery
___ 1 stalk fresh broccoli
___ 1 green bell pepper
___ Whole wheat pita bread
___ 1 can pinto beans
___ 1 can (8 ounces) no-salt-added tomato sauce
___ Chili powder
___ Vinegar
___ Brown sugar
___ Plates and napkins (for samples)

Cooking skill/nutrition lesson:
This versatile platter is great to have on hand for everyday snacks, appetizers, and parties. This recipe is an ideal vehicle for increasing the consumption of some of MyPlate's favorite food groups -- protein, whole grains, and vegetables. By using no-salt-added tomato sauce and seasonings, participants will use far less sodium than is found in commercial bean dips and barbecue sauces.

Demo preparation:
1. Wash your hands before you handle food.
2. Wash, peel and cut vegetables. Cut pita triangles. Arrange all on platter and cover with plastic wrap.
3. Measure ingredients for dip and arrange in disposable containers around food processor.

Make ahead options:
You can prepare vegetables, pita triangles, and even the bean dip ahead of time. Then all you have to do, once you get to class, is assemble and serve.

Garnish/presentation tips:
Arrange the vegetables and pita triangles in rows around the bowl for the dip. Top the dip with green bell pepper rings.

Number of sample servings: 12-16

Leader Guide: No Cook Demos

Fruit Kabobs with Yogurt Dip

Makes 8 sample servings

1 cup watermelon chunks
1 cup pineapple chunks
1 cup red seedless grapes
1 cup stemmed strawberries
2 kiwi, peeled and cut in quarters
8 bamboo skewers (6 inches)
1 cup nonfat light strawberry yogurt

Directions:

1. Place fruit chunks on bamboo skewers and arrange skewers on a platter.
2. Place nonfat light strawberry yogurt in bowl. Serve kabobs with yogurt on the side.

Equipment:

___ Knife
___ Cutting board
___ Measuring cups
___ Platter
___ Bowl

Shopping list:

___ Watermelon (buy cubes or a quarter of one melon)
___ 1 package seedless red grapes
___ Pineapple (buy fresh or canned chunks or one whole pineapple)
___ 1 pint fresh strawberries
___ 2 kiwi (look for firm kiwi)
___ 8 ounces nonfat light strawberry yogurt
___ Bamboo skewers
___ Disposable bags or cups (to hold fruit)
___ Plates and napkins (for samples)
___ Optional: fresh mint for garnish - see tips below

Cooking skill/nutrition lesson:

This recipe requires no cooking and very little preparation time. It makes a delicious dessert or snack, which will make it easier for participants get more fruit in their diets. It also highlights light nonfat yogurt's deliciousness as a fruit dip. Be sure to compare the calorie savings for light nonfat yogurt versus yogurt that is sweetened with sugar. Nonfat yogurt options are also recommended by MyPlate, which calls for using low-fat or nonfat dairy in place of full fat dairy foods.

Demo preparation:

1. Wash your hands before you handle food.
2. Cut the fruit and place in disposable bags or cups.
3. Organize your demo table so that the fruit, skewers, platter, and bowl are all within reach. Place the cutting board in the center.

Make ahead options:

You can make the kabobs ahead of time or cut the fruit ahead of time and transport it to the demo.

Garnish presentation tips:

You can arrange the kabobs in an orderly fashion on the platter and garnish with fresh sliced mint. You can also place one kabob on a plate and drizzle with the yogurt.

Number of sample servings: 8

No Cook Recipes

Caribbean Bean Salad

4 cups ready-to-serve Romaine lettuce or salad mix
1/4 cup red onion
1 cup canned black beans, drained and rinsed
1 orange, peeled and diced
1 tomato, diced
1 Tbsp olive oil
3 Tbsp red wine vinegar
1 tsp dried oregano
Black pepper to taste
Directions:
1. Toss all ingredients together in a large salad bowl.
2. Serve immediately, or refrigerate up to one hour before serving.
Serves 4. Each 1 cup serving: 114 calories, 3.5 g fat, 0.5 g saturated fat, 0 mg cholesterol, 207 mg sodium, 17 g carbohydrate, 4.5 g fiber, 4.5 g protein.

Tuna Salad on Greens

4 cups ready-to-serve romaine lettuce
1 carrot, peeled and grated
1 tomato
1/4 red onion
1 Tbsp olive oil
3 Tbsp red wine vinegar
1 tsp Italian Seasoning
Fresh cracked black pepper
1 can low-sodium tuna in water, drained
1/3 cup lowfat mayonnaise
1/4 cup celery
1/4 cup green onion
Garnish: 4 whole grain crackers (Try WASA or another brand that is low in fat and sodium)
Directions:
1. Place tossed salad ingredients in a large salad bowl. Toss together.
2. Mix ingredients for tuna salad in another mixing bowl.
3. Assemble tossed salad on a large plate. Top with a scoop of tuna salad, and garnish with the whole grain cracker.
Serves 4. Each 2 cup serving: 182 calories, 4.5 g fat, 0.5 g saturated fat, 22 mg cholesterol, 250 mg sodium, 23 g carbohydrate, 4.5 g fiber, 14 g protein.

Barbecue Bean Dip

1 cup carrot sticks
1 cup celery sticks
1 cup broccoli florets
1 green bell pepper, stemmed, seeded, and cut in rings
2 whole wheat pitas, cut in triangles
1 can pinto beans
1 cup no-salt-added tomato sauce
1/2 tsp chili powder
1 Tbsp vinegar
1/2 Tbsp brown sugar
Directions:
1. Arrange vegetables and pita triangles on a large platter. Place a bowl in the center or off to the side for the dip.
2. Place all ingredients for dip in a food processor. Puree on high speed until smooth.
3. Pour the dip into the bowl and serve immediately or cover and refrigerate for later use.
Serves 6. Each serving: 122 calories, 1 g fat, 0.5 g saturated fat, 0 mg cholesterol, 299 mg sodium, 25 g carbohydrate, 6 g fiber, 6.5 g protein.

Fruit Kabobs with Yogurt Dip

1 cup watermelon chunks
1 cup pineapple chunks
1 cup red seedless grapes
1 cup stemmed strawberries
2 kiwi, peeled and cut in quarters
8 bamboo skewers (6 inches)
1 cup nonfat light strawberry yogurt
Directions:
1. Place fruit chunks on bamboo skewers and arrange skewers on a platter.
2. Place nonfat light strawberry yogurt in bowl. Serve kabobs with yogurt on the side.
Serves 8. Each kabob: 50 calories, 0 fat, 1 mg cholesterol, 14 mg sodium, 11 g carbohyrdrate, 1 g fiber, 1.5 g protein.

Leader Guide: Recipe Modification

Title:
Recipe Modification

Target Audience:
This presentation kit is intended for general audiences.

Lesson Objectives:
• Participants will learn how to modify recipes to make them lower in fat, sodium, and sugar.
• Participants will taste modified, healthier recipes.

Lesson Rationale:
Health authorities have indicated that good nutrition is one of the most important factors in determining long-term health. Poor diet plays a major role in the development of four of the top seven killers in the United States: heart disease, cancer, stroke and diabetes. Individuals who have the skills to select and prepare nutritious foods can positively impact their present and future health.

Lesson at a Glance:
This lesson introduces participants to new recipes and teaches cooking skills. It also provides nutrition and dietary information that is consistent with the Dietary Guidelines for Americans and MyPlate.

Lesson Materials:
This lesson contains:
• Leader and Activity Guides
• 2 pages of copy-ready recipes and handouts
• PowerPoint show (on CD-ROM)
• Overheads
• Additional handouts (in PDF file on CD-ROM)

Preparation:
___ Review leader guide
___ Review handouts
___ Select activities
___ Copy and collect materials for lesson

Activity Ideas:
Activity 1 – Cooking Demo
Use the recipes in this lesson to plan a cooking demonstration. These recipes are designed to show participants how to modify favorite recipes so they are lower in fat, sodium and sugar. Recipes in this section can also be presented in the overhead and PowerPoint Shows provided in this kit (modify.ppt).

Activity 2 - Change is Good
Use the overheads or PowerPoint show provided in Cooking Demo II to show participants easy ways to modify recipes so that they contain less sodium, fat and sugar. Use the corresponding handout titled, "Recipe Modification," to outline ways to sidestep significant amounts of saturated fat. You can also use the handout in the Hypertension lesson, which reviews how to use reduce sodium.

For More Information:
www.foodandhealth.com - Check out the recipes in the Free Resources section for even more ideas and tips.
http://www.choosemyplate.gov/ - Get personalized dietary recommendations and take a look at MyPlate guidelines to help shape a healthier diet.

Leader Guide: Recipe Modification

Light Lasagna
Makes 20 sample servings

8 ounce box lasagna noodles
2 26-ounce jars pasta sauce
32 ounces fat free ricotta cheese
12 ounce box silken tofu
1 Tbsp Italian seasoning
1 cup shredded mozzarella cheese
Directions:

1. Preheat oven to 350 degrees. Place ricotta, tofu and Italian seasoning in a food processor and blend on high speed.
2. Layer lasagna in a 9 by 12 inch pan. Begin with sauce, then add noodles, then add filling, then repeat in that same order until the pan is full. Finish with extra sauce, then sprinkle with mozzarella cheese. Cover the lasagna with foil and bake for one hour in or until noodles are tender. There is no need to pre-cook the noodles.
3. Allow lasagna to stand for 5 minutes, then cut into 10 cubes and serve hot.

Equipment:
_____ Stove
_____ Oven
_____ Food processor
_____ Spatula
_____ Measuring cups and spoons
_____ 9 by 12 inch pan
_____ Plate (for final presentation)

Shopping list:
_____ 8 ounce box lasagna noodles
_____ 2 26-ounce jars pasta sauce
_____ 32 ounces fat free ricotta cheese
_____ 12-ounce box silken tofu
_____ Italian seasoning
_____ Shredded mozzarella cheese
_____ Fresh basil for garnish
_____ Aluminum foil
_____ Plates, forks, and napkins (for sample servings)

Cooking skill/nutrition lesson:
This recipe shows participants how to lighten a traditional lasagna recipe without sacrificing flavor. The silken tofu mixed with fat-free ricotta cheese makes a great creamy filling.

Traditional lasagna that is made with meat and regular ricotta contains 380 calories, 20 g of fat and 10 g of saturated fat. Our portions (of the same size) contain only 249 calories, 3 g of fat, and 1 g of saturated fat.

Demo preparation:
1. Wash your hands before you handle food.
2. Measure all ingredients.
3. Organize work area.

Make ahead options:
We recommend that you bake one pan of lasagna ahead of time and then demo a second during class time.

Garnish/presentation tips:
Cut the lasagna into 10 squares. Place one square on an attractive dinner plate and garnish with a sprig of fresh basil.

Number of sample servings: 20 (1/2 piece of lasagna per person)

Leader Guide: Recipe Modification

Spaghetti with Lentils

Makes 18 sample servings

1 cup dry lentils

8 oz package dry spaghetti

26 oz jar pasta sauce, preferably low sodium

1 tsp Italian seasoning

4 Tbsp Parmesan cheese

Directions:

1. Fill a large soup pan with water and bring to a boil. Add the lentils and return to a boil. Lower heat to medium and cook for 4 minutes, then add spaghetti.

2. Bring water back to a boil over high heat and cook until spaghetti is al dente and lentils are tender, about 10 minutes. Drain in colander.

3. Place the same pot back on the stove and add pasta sauce and Italian seasoning. Bring to a boil, then add the pasta and lentils.

4. Heat through then serve immediately. Place one portion on a large dinner plate and top with Parmesan cheese. (Use 2 ounce servings topped with a little Parmesan for sample servings).

Equipment:

_____ Large soup pan (3 quart)

_____ Kitchen spoon

_____ Colander

_____ Measuring cups and spoons

_____ Dinner plate to show final presentation

_____ Stove

Shopping list:

_____ 1 package dry lentils

_____ 1 package dry spaghetti

_____ 1 jar pasta sauce

_____ 1 bottle Italian seasoning

_____ 1 bottle grated Parmesan cheese

_____ mini cups, spoons and napkins (for samples)

_____ Disposable cups (for premeasured ingredients)

Cooking skill/nutrition lesson:

This recipe shows participants how to add more fiber and nutrients to spaghetti. It also demonstrates that lentils are easy to cook and taste delicious. Lentils are an excellent source of folate and many other vitamins and minerals.

Traditional spaghetti made with ground beef contains 433 calories and 14 g of fat. This one has only 382 calories and 2.5 g of fat in a serving of the same size.

Demo preparation:

1. Wash your hands before you handle food.

2. Measure all ingredients and arrange them around the stove.

3. Position the colander in a nearby sink (or bucket).

4. Have pot of water covered and simmering on the stove. That way you can add the lentils as soon as class starts.

Make ahead options:

You can make this dish ahead of time and reheat in the microwave for tasting purposes.

Garnish/presentation tips:

Sprinkle the Parmesan cheese over the pasta, letting it fall onto the side and rim of the plate.

Number of sample servings: 18

Leader Guide: Recipe Modification

Oven Fried Potatoes

Makes about 12 sample servings

2 large baking potatoes

1 tsp garlic powder

Black pepper to taste

1/4 cup Parmesan cheese

Garnish: No-salt-added ketchup

Directions:

1. Preheat oven to 400 degrees.
2. Wash potatoes and cut into wedges about 1/4 inch thick. Mix the rest of the ingredients in a small bowl and set aside.
3. Spray a large cookie sheet with vegetable oil spray. Arrange the potato wedges in rows. Spray the top of the potatoes with the vegetable oil spray and place them in the oven.
4. Bake potatoes until golden brown, about 10 minutes. Flip and continue baking until brown on both sides, about 10 more minutes. Place potatoes in serving bowl and toss with seasoning/cheese mixture. Garnish with no-salt-added ketchup.

Equipment:

_____ Oven

_____ Baking pan

_____ Knife

_____ Cutting board

_____ Mixing bowl

_____ Platter (for final presentation)

Shopping list:

_____ 2 large Idaho potatoes

_____ Garlic powder

_____ Black pepper

_____ Grated Parmesan cheese

_____ No-salt-added ketchup (for garnish)

_____ Vegetable oil cooking spray

_____ Plates and napkins (for sample servings)

Cooking skill/nutrition lesson:

This lesson teaches participants how to make french fries in the oven instead of frying them in fat.

The same sized serving of traditional fries contains 350 calories and 16 g of fat. This one contains only 69 calories and 2 g of fat.

Demo preparation:

1. Wash your hands before you handle food.
2. Chop and measure all ingredients.
3. Organize ingredients and work area while preheating the oven.

Garnish presentation tips:

Serve fries on a platter with ketchup on the side.

Number of sample servings: Approximately 12 (2 fries per person).

Leader Guide: Recipe Modification

Chicken Stew

Makes 18 sample servings

2 tsp vegetable oil
1 onion, peeled and cut in chunks
3 carrots, peeled and cut in chunks
1 pound skinless chicken breast cut in chunks
3 potatoes, peeled and cut in chunks
1 can chicken broth
1 cup water
1 bay leaf
1 tsp garlic powder
1/2 tsp dried thyme leaves
1/2 tsp dried ground sage
Fresh ground black pepper to taste

Directions:

1. Place vegetable oil in Dutch Oven pan and place over medium heat. Allow oil to get hot then add the onion and carrots. Saute until lightly browned, about 3 minutes.
2. Add the rest of the ingredients. Cover and bring to a boil. Lower heat to medium-low and cook until the potatoes and carrots are tender, about 30-35 minutes. Serve in soup bowls.

Equipment:

____ Dutch oven pan
____ Stove
____ Spoon
____ Knife
____ Cutting board
____ Vegetable peeler
____ Can opener
____ Measuring cups and spoons
____ Soup bowl (for final presentation)

Shopping list:

____ Vegetable oil
____ 1 onion
____ 3 carrots
____ 1 pound skinless chicken breast
____ 3 potatoes
____ 1 can chicken broth
____ Water
____ Bay leaves
____ Garlic powder
____ Dried thyme leaves
____ Dried ground sage
____ Ground black pepper

____ Disposable cups (for premeasured ingredients)
____ Cups, forks and napkins for sample servings

Cooking skill/nutrition lesson:

This stew uses chicken breast instead of beef and features more vegetables than usual. In fact, this recipe brings stew closer to alignment with MyPlate principles. Plus, the flavor is enhanced with herbs instead of added salt, which makes the stew better for your heart. Traditional beef stew contains 440 calories, 22 g fat and 8 g saturated fat. Our lighter version only contains 254 calories, 4.5 g fat and 0.5 g saturated fat in a serving of the same size.

Demo preparation:

1. Wash your hands before you handle food.
2. Prepare and measure all ingredients.
3. Organize work area and ingredients.
4. If you are using an electric stove, turn the burner to low as participants are entering room.

Garnish/presentation tips:

Place the stew in an attractive soup bowl. Garnish with fresh parsley and a sprig of dried thyme.

Make ahead options:

You can make this stew ahead of time and reheat for sample servings.

Number of servings: 18 (1/2 cup per person)

Recipe Modification

Light Lasagna

8 ounce box lasagna noodles
2 26-ounce jars pasta sauce
32 ounces fat free ricotta cheese
12 ounce box silken tofu
1 Tbsp Italian seasoning
1 cup shredded mozzarella cheese
Directions:
1. Preheat oven to 350 degrees. Place ricotta, tofu and Italian seasoning in a food processor and blend on high speed.
2. Layer lasagna in a 9 by 12 inch pan. Begin with sauce, then add noodles, then add filling, then repeat in that same order until the pan is full. Finish with extra sauce, then sprinkle with mozzarella cheese. Cover the lasagna with foil and bake for one hour in or until noodles are tender. There is no need to pre-cook the noodles.
3. Allow lasagna to stand for 5 minutes, then cut into 10 cubes and serve hot.
Serves 10. Each serving: 249 calories, 3 g fat, 1 g saturated fat, 12 mg cholesterol, 178 mg sodium, 45 g carbohydrate, 7 g fiber, 14 g protein.

Spaghetti with Lentils

1 cup dry lentils
8 oz package dry spaghetti
26 oz jar pasta sauce, preferably low sodium
1 tsp Italian seasoning
4 Tbsp Parmesan cheese
Directions:
1. Fill a large soup pan with water and bring to a boil. Add the lentils and return to a boil. Lower heat to medium and cook for 4 minutes, then add spaghetti.
2. Bring water back to a boil over high heat and cook until spaghetti is al dente and lentils are tender, about 10 minutes. Drain in colander.
3. Place the same pot back on the stove and add pasta sauce and Italian seasoning. Bring to a boil, then add the pasta and lentils.
4. Heat through then serve immediately. Place one portion on a large dinner plate and top with Parmesan cheese.
Serves 4. Each 1-1/4 cup serving: 382 calories, 2.5 g fat, 1 g saturated fat, 4 mg cholesterol, 680 mg sodium, 72 g carbohydrate, 6 g fiber, 17 g protein.

Oven Fried Potatoes

2 large baking potatoes
1 tsp garlic powder
Black pepper to taste
1/4 cup Parmesan cheese
Garnish: No-salt-added ketchup
Directions:
1. Preheat oven to 400 degrees.
2. Wash potatoes and cut into 1/4 inch thick wedges. Mix the rest of the ingredients in a small bowl.
3. Spray a large cookie sheet with vegetable oil spray. Arrange the potato wedges in rows. Spray the top of the potatoes with the vegetable oil spray and place them in the oven.
4. Bake potatoes until golden brown, about 10 minutes. Flip and continue baking until brown on both sides, about 10 more minutes. Place potatoes in serving bowl and toss with seasoning/cheese mixture. Garnish with no-salt-added ketchup.
Serves 4. Each serving: 69 calories, 2 g fat, 1 g saturated fat, 5 mg cholesterol, 118 mg sodium, 9 g carbohydrate, 2 g fiber, 4 g protein.

Chicken Stew

2 tsp vegetable oil
1 onion, peeled and cut in chunks
3 carrots, peeled and cut in chunks
1 pound skinless chicken breast cut in chunks
3 potatoes, peeled and cut in chunks
1 can chicken broth
1 cup water
1 bay leaf
1 tsp garlic powder
1/2 tsp dried thyme leaves
1/2 tsp dried ground sage
Fresh ground black pepper to taste
Directions:
1. Place vegetable oil in Dutch Oven pan and place over medium heat. Allow oil to get hot then add the onion and carrots. Saute until lightly browned, about 3 minutes.
2. Add the rest of the ingredients. Cover and bring to a boil. Lower heat to medium-low and cook until the potatoes and carrots are tender, about 30-35 minutes. Serve in soup bowls.
Serves 4. Each 2 cup serving: 254 calories, 4.5 g fat, 0.5 g saturated fat, 76 mg cholesterol, 200 mg sodium, 19 g carbohydrate, 32 g protein, 3 g fiber.

Recipe Modification

Instead of:	Portion	Saturated fat (g)	Use:	Saturated fat (g)
Dairy:				
Butter	1 Tbsp	7.5	Vegetable oil* or broth	0
Cream	2 Tbsp	7	Evaporated skim milk	0
Cream cheese	2 Tbsp	6.5	Light cream cheese	3.5
Half and half	2 Tbsp	2	Fat-free half and half	0
Ice cream	1/2 cup	6	Frozen yogurt	1.5
Ricotta cheese	1/2 cup	10	Fat-free ricotta	0
Sour cream	2 Tbsp	3	Fat-free sour cream	0
Whipped cream	2 Tbsp	3	Fat-free whipped cream	0
Whole milk	1 cup	5	Skim milk	0
Whole milk	1 cup	5	1% milk	1.5
Totals		**61**		**7.5**

* Use a spray oil or cut amount in half.

** Include only half the cheese or use a small amount of Parmesan cheese

Meat/Poultry				
Bacon	3 slices	3	Turkey bacon	1.5
Beef, ground	3 ounces	7	Ground turkey breast, no skin	0
Beef, ground	3 ounces	7	Vegetarian burger*	0
Beef, prime rib**	3 ounces	12	Beef tenderloin, fat trimmed	3
Beef, T-bone	3 ounces	7	Beef tenderloin, fat trimmed	3
Chicken, dark with skin	3 ounces	3	Chicken breast, no skin, baked	.5
Chicken, fried thigh	1 each	6	Chicken breast, no skin, baked	.5
Lard	1 Tbsp	5	Margarine, trans-fat free	2
Sausage	3 ounces	9	Vegetarian sausage*	0.5
Totals		**54**		**11**

*Read the label, nutrition facts vary by brand

**Restaurant portions are often triple this amount, so you could be getting as much as 36 grams of saturated fat per portion!

Note: For heart-healthier cooking, you should limit animal protein and emphasize whole grains, beans, soy protein, fish (baked-not fried!), fruits ,and grains in your meals. Remember, MyPlate advises people to make their mealtime plates half full of fruits and vegetables, with smaller servings of lean protein and whole grains, and a side of lowfat dairy. A 3-ounce serving of meat is the size of a deck of cards.

Miscellaneous				
Coconut	1 ounce	6.5	Toasted pecans or almonds	1.5
Coconut milk	8 ounces	20	Evaporated skim milk	0
Hydrogenated shortening	1 Tbsp	3+	Vegetable oil or trans-free margarine	0-2
Whole eggs	2	3	Egg white or nonfat egg substitute	0
Gravy with fat	2 Tbsp	5	Defatted gravy	0.5
French fries	4 ounces	4	Baked potato	0

+This product is hydrogenated and contains additional trans-fat that is not listed on the label with saturated fat.

Leader Guide: Soy

Title:
Soy

Target Audience:
This presentation is intended for general audiences.

Lesson Objectives:
• Participants will learn about health benefits of soy.
• Participants will learn how to prepare soy products.

Lesson Rationale:
The Food and Drug Administration (FDA) has authorized the use of health claims about the role of soy protein in reducing the risk of coronary heart disease (CHD). This action was based on the FDA's conclusion that foods containing soy protein, when included in a diet low in saturated fat and cholesterol, may reduce the risk of CHD by lowering blood cholesterol levels.

This health claim is based on evidence that indicates that including soy protein (in a diet low in saturated fat and cholesterol) may help to reduce the risk of CHD. Recent clinical trials have shown that consumption of soy protein (compared to other proteins such as those from milk or meat) can lower total and LDL-cholesterol levels.

Foods that may be eligible for the health claim include soy beverages, tofu, tempeh, soy-based meat alternatives, and possibly even some baked goods. Foods that carry the claim must also be low in fat, saturated fat, and cholesterol.

In order to lower cholesterol, scientific studies show that a person must consume 25 grams of soy protein daily. In order to qualify for this health claim, a food must contain at least 6.25 grams of soy protein per serving. Because soy protein can be added to a variety of things, it is possible for consumers to eat foods that contain soy protein at almost all meals and snacks.

This health claim rule responds to a petition submitted to the FDA by Protein Technologies International. The rule is based on the proposed measure that was published in the Federal Register on November 10, 1998, and comments received by the FDA. Use of the claim in food labeling is authorized immediately.

Health authorities have indicated that good nutrition is one of the most important factors in determining long-term health. Poor diet plays a major role in the development of four of the top seven killers in the United States: heart disease, cancer, stroke and diabetes. Individuals who have the skills to select and prepare nutritious foods can positively impact their present and future health.

Lesson at a Glance:
This lesson introduces participants to new recipes and teaches cooking skills. It also provides nutrition and dietary information that is consistent with the Dietary Guidelines for Americans and MyPlate.

Lesson Materials:
This lesson contains:
• Leader and Activity Guides
• 3 pages of copy-ready recipes and handouts

Preparation:
___ Review leader guide
___ Review handouts
___ Select activities
___ Copy and collect materials for lesson

Activity Ideas:

Activity 1 – Cooking Demo
Use the recipes in this lesson to plan a cooking demonstration. These recipes are designed to show participants how to prepare and serve soy foods.

Activity 2 - Discover the Joy of Soy
Buy several soy foods from your local grocery store. This might include soy milk, cooked tofu, soy energy bars, or veggie burgers. Allow participants to look at, handle, and taste these products.

For More Information:
The web is full of information on soy and soy products these days. Check out the following links and search for the word "soy" to get a plethora of information at your very fingertips.
http://vrg.org
http://eatright.org
http://thesoyfoodscouncil.com

Leader Guide: Soy Recipes

Stir Fry with Tofu

Makes about 20 sample servings

4 cups cooked brown rice
2 cups diced firm tofu (not silken)
4 Tbsp light soy sauce
2 tsp corn starch
1/2 cup orange juice
1 Tbsp sesame oil
1 tsp vegetable oil
2 tsp minced garlic
1 Tbsp grated fresh ginger
1/2 cup sliced carrots
1 cup sliced mushrooms
1 cup broccoli florets
Pinch red pepper flakes

Directions:

1. Marinate the tofu in a small bowl with the soy sauce, cornstarch, orange juice, and sesame oil.
2. Heat a large, nonstick skillet or wok over high heat. Add the oil and then the garlic and ginger. Saute until the garlic is nutty brown, about 1 minute.
3. Add the rest of the veggies and saute until crisp-tender, about 4-5 minutes. Add the tofu along with the marinade and cook briefly. Serve hot over brown rice.

Equipment:

____ Knife
____ Cutting board
____ Vegetable peeler
____ Grater
____ Nonstick skillet or wok
____ Stove
____ Large salad bowl
____ 3 kitchen spoons
____ Plate (for final presentation)
____ Measuring cups and spoons
____ Small bowl

Shopping list:

____ 1 pound package diced firm tofu (not silken)
____ Light soy sauce
____ Corn starch
____ Orange juice
____ Sesame oil
____ Brown rice
____ Vegetable oil
____ Minced garlic*
____ Fresh ginger
____ Carrots*
____ Sliced mushrooms*
____ Broccoli florets*
____ Red pepper flakes

*Tip: Look for precut (and even mixed) versions of these items.

Cooking/nutrition lesson:

This recipe shows participants how to get more soy in their diets. A stir fry packs more vegetables per serving than most other dishes.

Demo preparation:

1. Wash your hands before you handle food.
2. Chop and measure all ingredients.
3. Organize work area.

Garnish/presentation tips:

Place this stir fry dish on a large decorative plate and set chopsticks on the side. You can drizzle the plate with a little additional soy sauce and sesame oil.

Number of sample servings (1/4 cup): about 20

Leader Guide: Soy Recipes

Soyliscious Lasagna
Makes 20 sample servings

8 ounce box lasagna noodles
2 26-ounce jars pasta sauce
16 ounces fat free ricotta cheese
2-12 ounce boxes silken tofu
1/4 cup Parmesan cheese
1 Tbsp Italian seasoning
1 cup shredded part skim mozzarella cheese
Directions:

1. Preheat oven to 350 degrees. Place ricotta, tofu, Parmesan, and Italian seasoning in a food processor and blend on high speed.
2. Layer lasagna in a 9 by 12 inch pan. Begin with sauce, then add noodles, then add filling, then repeat in that same order until the pan is full. Finish with extra sauce, then sprinkle with mozzarella cheese. Cover the lasagna with foil and bake for one hour in the oven or until noodles are tender. (There is no need to precook the noodles).
3. Allow lasagna to stand for 5 minutes, then cut into 10 squares and serve hot.

Equipment:
____ Stove
____ Oven
____ Food processor
____ Spatula
____ Measuring cups and spoons
____ 9 by 12 inch pan
____ Plate (for final presentation)

Shopping list:
____ 8 ounce box lasagna noodles
____ 2 26-ounce jars pasta sauce
____ 16 ounces fat free ricotta cheese
____ Grated Parmesan cheese
____ 2-12 ounce boxes silken tofu
____ Italian seasoning
____ Shredded part skim mozzarella cheese
____ Fresh basil (for garnish)
____ Aluminum foil
____ Plates, forks, and napkins (for samples)

Cooking skill/nutrition lesson:
This recipe shows participants how to lighten a traditional lasagna recipe without sacrificing flavor. The silken tofu mixed with the fat-free ricotta cheese makes a great, creamy filling.

Demo preparation:
1. Wash your hands before you handle food.
2. Measure all ingredients.
3. Organize your work area.

Make ahead options:
We recommend that you make/bake one pan of lasagna ahead of time and then prepare a second one during class.

Garnish/presentation tips:
Cut the lasagna into 10 squares. Place one square on an attractive dinner plate and garnish with a sprig of fresh basil.

Number of sample servings: 20 (1/2 piece of lasagna per person)

Leader Guide: Soy Recipes

Strawberry Smoothie

Makes 4 sample servings

This smoothie contains soymilk and silken tofu.

1 cup soymilk
1/4 cup silken firm tofu
1 cup fresh sliced strawberries or frozen mixed berries
1 tsp vanilla extract

Directions:
1. Place all ingredients in a blender.
2. Blend on high speed until smooth. Pour into a glass and enjoy.

Equipment:
____ Blender
____ Spoon
____ Measuring cups and spoons
____ Glass (for final presentation)

Shopping list:
____ Soymilk
____ Silken firm tofu
____ Fresh strawberries or frozen mixed berries
____ Vanilla extract
____ Disposable cups (for premeasured ingredients)
____ Disposable cups and napkins (for samples)

Cooking skill/nutrition lesson:
This recipe outlines an easy and delicious way to introduce people to soy. It contains soy in a few different forms (soymilk and silken tofu), yet looks approachable and tastes great. You can sweeten further if you'd like, but be sure to keep things balanced and healthy.

Demo preparation:
1. Wash your hands before you handle food.
2. Prepare and measure ingredients.
3. Organize work area and ingredients.

Garnish/presentation tips:
Place this smoothie in a tall glass and garnish with a straw.

Number of sample servings: 4 (1/2 cup each)

Fruit with Peach Dip

Makes 4 sample servings

4 cups assorted, fresh, cubed fruit
12-ounce package silken tofu
1 can peaches in juice, with juice
2 Tbsp sugar
1 tsp cinnamon
1/2 tsp almond extract

Directions:
1. Prepare the fresh fruit and arrange on a platter. Cover and chill until ready to use.
2. Combine the tofu, peaches with juice, sugar, cinnamon, and almond extract in a blender or food processor. Blend until smooth. Pour into a small serving bowl and chill until ready to serve, at least one hour.

Equipment:
____ Food processor and rubber spatula
____ Can opener
____ Knife and cutting board
____ Platter and bowl (for final presentation)
____ Measuring cups and spoons

Shopping list:
____ 4 cups assorted fresh diced fruit
____ Silken firm tofu
____ 1 can peaches in juice
____ Almond extract
____ Sugar
____ Cinnamon
____ Disposable cups (for premeasured ingredients)
____ Plates, forks, and napkins (for samples)

Cooking skill/nutrition lesson:
This recipe outlines an easy and delicious way to introduce people to soy. It contains soy in a few different forms (soymilk and silken tofu), yet looks approachable and tastes great. Plus, it's a fantastic way to balance servings of fruit and protein.

Demo preparation:
1. Wash your hands before you handle food.
2. Prepare and measure ingredients.
3. Organize work area and ingredients.

Garnish/presentation tips:
Place the chilled bowl of dip in the center of the platter and surround with the sliced, fresh fruit.

Number of sample servings: 4 (1/2 cup each)

Soy Recipes

Stir Fry with Tofu

4 cups cooked brown rice
2 cups diced firm tofu (not silken)
4 Tbsp light soy sauce
2 tsp corn starch
1/2 cup orange juice
1 Tbsp sesame oil
1 tsp vegetable oil
2 tsp minced garlic
1 Tbsp grated fresh ginger
1/2 cup sliced carrots
1 cup sliced mushrooms
1 cup broccoli florets
Pinch red pepper flakes
Directions:

1. Marinate the tofu in a small bowl with the soy sauce, cornstarch, orange juice, and sesame oil.
2. Heat a large, nonstick skillet or wok over high heat. Add the oil and then the garlic and ginger. Saute until the garlic is nutty brown, about 1 minute.
3. Add the rest of the veggies and saute until crisp-tender, about 4-5 minutes. Add the tofu along with the marinade and cook briefly. Serve hot over brown rice.

Serves 4. Each 2 cup serving: 399 calories, 11 g fat, 1.5 g saturated fat, 0 mg cholesterol, 536 mg sodium, 59 g carbohydrate, 5.5 g fiber, 17 g protein.

Soyliscious Lasagna

8 ounce box lasagna noodles
2 26-ounce jars pasta sauce
16 ounces fat free ricotta cheese
2-12 ounce boxes silken tofu
1/4 cup Parmesan cheese
1 Tbsp Italian seasoning
1 cup shredded part skim mozzarella cheese
Directions:

1. Preheat oven to 350 degrees. Place ricotta, tofu, Parmesan, and Italian seasoning in a food processor and blend on high speed.
2. Layer lasagna in a 9 by 12 inch pan. Begin with sauce, then add noodles, then add filling, then repeat in that same order until the pan is full. Finish with extra sauce, then sprinkle with mozzarella cheese. Cover the lasagna with foil and bake for one hour in the oven or until noodles are tender. (There is no need to precook the noodles).

3. Allow lasagna to stand for 5 minutes, then cut into 10 squares and serve hot.

Serves 10. Each serving: 235 calories, 3.5 g fat, 1 g saturated fat, 8 mg cholesterol, 629 mg sodium, 31 g carbohydrate, 3 g fiber, 19 g protein.

Strawberry Smoothie

This smoothie contains soymilk and silken tofu.
1 cup soymilk
1/4 cup silken firm tofu
1 cup fresh sliced strawberries or frozen mixed berries
1 tsp vanilla extract
Directions:

1. Place all ingredients in a blender.
2. Blend on high speed until smooth. Pour into a glass and enjoy.

Serves 1. Each 1-1/2 cup serving: 279 calories, 4 g fat, 0 g saturated fat, 0 mg cholesterol, 120 mg sodium, 55 g carbohydrate, 7 g fiber, 30 g sugars, 10 g protein

Fruit with Peach Dip

4 cups assorted, fresh, cubed fruit
12-ounce package silken tofu
1 can peaches in juice, with juice
2 Tbsp sugar
1 tsp cinnamon
1/2 tsp almond extract
Directions:

1. Prepare the fresh fruit and arrange on a platter. Cover and chill until ready to use.
2. Combine the tofu, peaches with juice, sugar, cinnamon, and almond extract in a blender or food processor. Blend until smooth. Pour into a small serving bowl and chill until ready to serve, at least one hour.

Serves 4. Each serving: 153 calories, 2.5 g fat, 0.5 g saturated fat, 0 mg cholesterol, 35 mg sodium, 28 g carbohydrate, 7 g protein, 4.5 g fiber.

Soy Facts

❖What is Soy?

Soy is a loose term that is used to describe foods made with soybeans. Tofu, soymilk, soynuts, tempe, textured vegetable protein, and veggie burgers are just a few examples. According to MyPlate, soybeans are part of the vegetable AND protein food groups.

❖What are its benefits?

Soy protein improves blood lipid status by lowering LDL or "bad cholesterol" levels. A meta-analysis of 38 controlled studies, published in the New England Journal of Medicine (1995), indicated that replacing animal protein with soy protein achieved an average:

- 9.3% decrease in total cholesterol
- 12.9% decrease in LDL-cholesterol
- 10.5% decrease in triglyceride

The FDA later authorized the use of health claims in food labeling when it came to the association between soy protein and reduced risk of coronary heart disease. Consuming 25 grams of soy protein a day, as part of a diet low in saturated fat and cholesterol, may reduce the risk of coronary heart disease. In order for a food to bear this claim, one serving must provide at least one-fourth of this minimum daily amount.

❖Does soy have other possible benefits?

Most soyfoods are rich in isoflavones, a class of phytoestrogens that are weak but highly beneficial plant versions of human estrogens. Menopausal women in Asian countries with high soy intakes have a much lower incidence of symptoms of menopause. Three of the four studies published to date have shown that soy even has a modest effect on hot flashes, though studies are needed.

Isoflavones are one of soy's several anti-cancer compounds and appear to reduce the risk of certain cancers by binding to body cell estrogen receptors to prevent full access by stronger human estrogen (which can be tumor promoting).

For men, phytoestrogens may reduce testosterone's promotion of prostate cancer, with no adverse effects on virility. For premenopausal women, phytoestrogens may inhibit the initial growth of endometrial and breast cancers. But, for breast cancer survivors and older women, there is controversy. Mark Messina, PhD, former head of soy research for the National Cancer Institute, says that it is important to proceed carefully with this issue because we can't rule out the fact that the data suggests that soy has both an estrogenic and anti-estrogenic effect on breast tissue.

Where's the protein?

Soyfood	Isoflavones (mg)	Calories	Protein (g)
Soy nuts, 1/4 cup (1.5 ounces)	60	193	17
Tempeh, 1/2 cup	40	165	16
Soybeans, cooked, 1/2 cup	38	150	14
Textured soy protein, dry, 1/4 cup	35	80	12
Soy flour, 1/3 cup	38	130	11
Tofu, raw, firm, 3 ounce serving	32	90	10
Green Soybeans, 2/3 cup	30	73	7
Soy milk, full fat, 1 cup	33-40	80-130	6-7
Mori-Nu Silken Tofu, firm, 3 oz serving	26	50	6
Roasted Soy Butter, 2 Tbsp	38	170	6
Mori-Nu Silken Tofu, Lite, firm, 3 oz serving	18	31	5

Sources: USDA Nutrient Data Lab, Manufacturers' Data, The Simple Soybean & Your Health, and Indiana Soybean Board.

How to Put More Soy in Your Diet

❖Smoothies
Make a smoothie using silken tofu, soy milk, and fruit. You can usually find tofu in the produce section of most grocery stores. Soymilk usually hides out in both the refrigerator and dry good shelves.

❖Stir Fry dishes
Cube firm tofu and add it to stir fry dishes. Tofu takes on the seasonings and flavors you are using and adds a delicate custard-like texture that compliments the crisp vegetables in your stir fry.

❖Sandwiches and salads
Try baked tofu in sandwiches and salads. It comes in many flavors and tastes similar to turkey or ham, especially when you slice it thinly. Use it in a sandwich with lettuce and tomato.

❖Soymilk
Replace milk with soymilk in some of your favorite recipes. If you choose to replace milk entirely, make sure you buy a soymilk that is fortified with calcium and vitamin D. For regular cooking and baking, use plain soymilk. Keep in mind that each brand of soymilk tastes different.

❖Nuts
Soynuts taste a lot like peanuts. Try them in stir fry dishes, as a snack, or sprinkled over yogurt. Soy nuts are usually found with other nuts in the grocery store.

❖In place of ground beef
Tempeh is a pressed cake that is made from cooked soybeans. It is delicious when crumbled and used in place of ground beef in most skillet dishes. You can find tempeh in the refrigerator section of food stores.

Textured vegetable protein (TVP) can also be used in place of ground beef. It is a dry product that needs to be reconstituted and you can find it in dry goods sections of food stores.

Veggie burgers are in the freezer section of most grocery stores. They just need to be heated a minute or two in the microwave.

❖Vegetables and medleys
Edamame are immature, green soybeans that are still in their pods. You can find them freezer section. They're super easy to prepare: just steam and serve.

Actual soybeans come dried and in canned form. The dried form needs to be soaked and cooked, just like any other bean, while the canned versions are ready to use. Add them to soups, chilis, and salads.

❖Dessert
Silken tofu is excellent in desserts, especially pudding and cream pie. Look for recipes and more information regarding soy and soy products at www.foodandhealth.com.

Tofu Success Tips:
- Use the right tofu for the job:
  - Silken tofu comes in an asceptic package. It is smooth and custard-like, and can be best used in recipes that need a blender, like desserts, smoothies, lasagna filling, salad dressings, etc.

  - Regular tofu is more firm and looks like a sponge. It often comes in a large plastic package with water. This tofu is excellent in stir fry dishes or on kabobs because it holds its shape easily and has a more meaty texture than silken tofu.
- Think of tofu as an ingredient, rather than a stand-alone food. For example, you would not eat plain flour, yet you could easily enjoy cakes and bread.
- Refrigerate regular tofu. Once opened, it should be stored in a covered container. Under proper temperatures, regular tofu should keep refrigerated for about a week.
- Silken tofu in asceptic packaging can be stored at room temperature until opened. Once opened, it should be stored in a covered container in the refrigerator.

Leader Guide: Vegetarian Cooking

Title:
Vegetarian Cooking

Target Audience:
This presentation is intended for general audiences.

Lesson Objectives:
• Participants will explore the health benefits of a vegetarian diet.
• Participants will learn how to prepare vegetarian recipes.

Lesson Rationale:
Health authorities have indicated that good nutrition is one of the most important factors in determining long-term health. Poor diet plays a major role in the development of four of the top seven killers in the United States: heart disease, cancer, stroke and diabetes. Individuals who have the skills to select and prepare nutritious foods can positively impact their present and future health.

Lesson at a Glance:
This lesson introduces participants to new recipes and teaches cooking skills. It also provides nutrition and dietary information that is consistent with the Dietary Guidelines for Americans and MyPlate.

Lesson Materials:
This lesson contains:
• Leader and Activity Guides
• 2 pages of copy-ready recipes and handouts

Preparation:
___ Review leader guide
___ Review handouts
___ Select activities
___ Copy and collect materials for lesson

Activity Ideas:

Activity 1 – Cooking Demo
Use the recipes in this lesson to plan a cooking demonstration. These recipes are designed to show participants how to prepare and serve vegetarian foods. Sample servings of each recipe will also provide participants with ways to try new and delicious vegetarian meals.

Activity 2 - Why Vegetarian?
Use the handout "Vegetarian Diet Facts" to explain the health benefits of a vegetarian diet and to answer questions regarding this topic.

Activity 3 - Where's the Beef?

Purchase a variety of soy meat alternatives - examples include veggie burgers and soy breakfast sausage. There are also frozen sandwich pockets made with soy ham and soy cheese. Prepare items according to package directions and allow participants to sample each one. As they are trying these foods, explain that people still need to read the labels of these types of foods because some are very high in sodium.

Activity 4 - A Vegetarian Day
Using a blackboard, flip chart, or dry erase board, show participants what a day of vegetarian meals could be like. Here is one example (ovo-lacto):

Breakfast:
Shredded wheat or cooked oatmeal - 1 cup
Skim milk - 1 cup
Banana - 1

Morning Snack:
Apple - 1
Celery sticks - 1 cup
Nonfat light yogurt - 6 ounces

Lunch:
Baked Potato Salad - 2 cups
Diced melon - 1 cup

Afternoon Snack:
2 slices 100% whole wheat bread
2 Tbsp unsalted old-fashioned peanut butter
1 sliced kiwi or 1/2 cup berries

Dinner:
Cooked penne pasta - 1 cup
Black Bean Marinara Sauce - 1 cup
Steamed spinach - 1/2 cup
Raw carrots - 1 cup
Orange - 1

Evening Snack:
Nonfat light yogurt - 6 ounces
Berries - 1/2 cup
Nutritional analysis: 2050 calories, 35 g fat, 7 g saturated fat, 5 mg cholesterol, 1344 mg sodium, 385 g carbohydrate, 58 g fiber, 135 g sugars, 72 g protein.

For More Information:
www.vrg.org - This site is the home of the Vegetarian Resource Group, which provides a bounty of information. Check it out to learn about everything from nutrition to health statistics to food's impact on the environment.

Leader Guide: Vegetarian Recipes

Easy Stir Fry With Tofu
Makes 16 sample servings

4 cups cooked brown rice
Juice of 1 orange
1/4 cup chicken broth
1 Tbsp corn starch
4 Tbsp light soy sauce
1 Tbsp sesame oil
1 cup diced firm tofu (not silken)
1 Tbsp oil
1 Tbsp minced garlic
1 Tbsp grated fresh ginger
1 pound package frozen stir-fry vegetables

Directions:
1. Cook the rice according to package directions.
2. Mix the orange juice, chicken broth, corn starch, soy sauce, sesame oil, and tofu in a small mixing bowl. Stir well and set aside.
3. Meanwhile, heat the oil in a large nonstick skillet or wok over high heat. Saute the garlic and ginger until golden, about 3 minutes. Add the frozen veggies and cook until tender, about 6 minutes. Add sauce and cook until the mixture is heated through. Serve the veggies and tofu over the cooked brown rice.

Equipment:
____ Stove
____ Wok or large nonstick skillet
____ Spoon
____ Knife and cutting board
____ Can opener
____ Measuring cups and spoons
____ Grater
____ Mixing bowls
____ Pot
____ Plate (for final presentation)

Shopping list:
____ Brown rice
____ 1 orange
____ Chicken broth
____ Corn starch
____ Light soy sauce
____ Sesame oil
____ Firm tofu (not silken)
____ Oil
____ Minced garlic
____ Fresh ginger
____ 1 pound package frozen stir-fry vegetables
____ Disposable cups (for premeasured ingredients)
____ Plates, forks, and napkins (for sample servings)

Cooking skill/nutrition lesson:
This recipe teaches participants how to make a basic stir fry. It uses frozen vegetables to cut preparation time, but you can also use fresh assorted vegetables. This stir fry brings the dish closer to alignment with proper MyPlate proportions and is an easy way to increase vegetable consumption.

Demo preparation:
1. Wash your hands before you handle food.
2. Prepare and measure all ingredients.
3. Organize your work area. If you are using an electric stove turn it on low as participants arrive.

Make ahead options:
Make the brown rice ahead of time and have it ready before class starts. For 4 cups of cooked brown rice, you need 1-1/3 cups of rice and 2-2/3 cups of water.

Garnish/presentation tips:
Place the rice in the center of the plate, making a well for the stir fry. Place the stir fry in the well and serve hot.

Number of sample servings: 16 (1/2 cup each)

Leader Guide: Vegetarian Recipes

Red Beans and Rice

Makes 18 sample servings

This dish is very filling, yet the cost per serving is only .26!

2 cups brown rice

5 cups water

6 tsp low sodium beef bouillon granules

2 cups cooked or canned kidney beans

1/4 cup dried onion

1 tsp oregano

1 tsp paprika

1 tsp garlic powder

Pinch cayenne pepper

Black pepper to taste

Directions:

1. Place all ingredients in large soup pot and bring to a boil. Lower heat to simmer, cover pot, and cook on low until rice is done, about 30 minutes.
2. Serve hot or refrigerate/freeze for later use.

Equipment:

___ Large soup pan

___ Stove

___ Knife

___ Cutting board

___ Kitchen spoon and ladle

___ Can opener

___ Measuring cups and spoons

___ Soup bowl (for final presentation)

Shopping list*:

___ 2 cups brown rice

___ Water

___ Low sodium beef granules

___ 2 cups cooked kidney beans

___ 1/4 cup dried onion

___ 1 tsp oregano

___ 1 tsp paprika

___ 1 tsp garlic powder

___ Pinch cayenne pepper

___ Black pepper to taste

___ Disposable cups (for premeasured ingredients)

___ Cups, spoons, and napkins (for samples)

Cooking skill/nutrition lesson

This lesson shows how to make a healthy, economical dish using beans and rice. Beans are one of MyPlate's featured foods because they can count as either a protein source or a vegetable, depending on what else a person is eating. Check out http://www.choosemyplate.gov/ for details.

Demo preparation:

1. Wash your hands before handling food.
2. Cut and measure all ingredients.
3. Arrange pan and all ingredients around the stove.
4. Preheat stove as participants are coming into the room.

Make ahead options:

You can make the soup ahead of time and reheat and serve for class.

Garnish/presentation tips:

Serve the red beans and rice on a pretty plate with a sprinkle of paprika on top.

Number of sample servings: approximately 18.

Leader Guide: Vegetarian Recipes

Skillet Chili

Makes 10 sample servings

1 tsp oil
1 cup zucchini, chopped
1 cup mild chili peppers, chopped
1 cup chopped veggie burger
2 cups canned kidney beans, drained and rinsed
1 15-ounce can no-salt-added diced tomatoes
1/2 cup no-salt-added ketchup
1 cup water
1 tsp chili powder
1 tsp garlic powder

Directions:

1. Heat a 12" nonstick skillet over high heat. Add the oil and saute the zucchini and peppers until golden brown, about 3 minutes.
2. Add the rest of the ingredients, bring to a boil and reduce to a simmer. Cook until sauce is thick.
3. Serve over cooked brown rice, a baked potato, or 100% whole wheat toast.

Equipment:

_____ Stove
_____ Skillet
_____ Colander (to drain beans)
_____ Can opener
_____ Kitchen spoon
_____ Knife and cutting board
_____ Measuring cups and spoons
_____ Plate or bowl (for final presentation)

Shopping list:

_____ 1 tsp oil
_____ 1 zucchini
_____ 1 mild green chili pepper
_____ 1 box frozen veggie burgers
_____ 2 cans (15 oz each) kidney beans
_____ 1 can (15 oz) no-salt-added tomatoes
_____ No-salt-added ketchup
_____ Water
_____ Chili powder
_____ Garlic powder
_____ Plates, forks, napkins (for samples)
_____ Plastic cups (for premeasured ingredients)

Cooking skill/nutrition lesson:

This recipe shows everyone how to make a vegetarian version of a well-loved food. By using veggie burgers instead of meat and adding beans you will increase the fiber and lower the saturated fat, both of which is very good for your health.

Demo preparation:

1. Wash your hands before you handle food.
2. Measure all ingredients.
3. Organize your work area.

Garnish presentation tips:

Top the chili with fresh cracked black pepper.

Number of sample servings: Approximately 10 (Use a 1/2 cup portion for tastings.)

Leader Guide: Vegetarian Recipes

Chocolate Mousse with Berries

Makes 8-12 sample servings

1 box (12 ounces) silken tofu
1/3 cup sugar
1/4 cup cocoa powder
2 cups assorted berries: sliced strawberries, raspberries, blueberries, etc.
Nonfat whipped cream
Directions:

1. Puree tofu, sugar, and cocoa powder in a food processor. Divide between four tall stemmed glasses. Refrigerate until ready to serve or immediately proceed to step two.
2. Mash berries in a bowl and divide among four glasses, placing them on top of the chocolate mousse.
3. Top each glass with about 2 tablespoons of nonfat whipped cream.
4. Optional garnish: Dust the top of the whipped cream with cocoa powder.

Equipment:

____ Food processor
____ Knife
____ Cutting board
____ Sieve (for cocoa powder)
____ Four tall stemmed glasses
____ Measuring cups and spoons

Shopping list:

____ 12 ounce box silken tofu (we recommend Mori-Nu Firm)
____ Sugar
____ Cocoa powder
____ Fresh berries
____ Fat free whipped cream - 1 can
____ Cups, spoons and napkins (for samples)
____ Disposable cups (for premeasured ingredients)

Cooking skill/nutrition lesson:

This creative recipe is a great way to introduce participants to soy, a healthy protein source. They will be surprised at how good a mousse/pudding can taste when it's made from tofu and includes fresh fruit and nonfat whipped cream.

Demo preparation:

1. Wash your hands before you handle food.
2. Measure all ingredients (except for whipped cream - that should come out of the can at the last minute).
3. Organize your work are so everything is easily accessible.

Make ahead options:

You can make the mousse ahead of time and just bring it to class and serve. We recommend you ask for volunteers to help you assemble the final desserts.

Garnish/presentation tips:

Put this mousse in a tall, elegant glass. Layer berries and whipped cream on top, then dust the whipped cream with cocoa powder. It is best if you place the cocoa powder in a sieve, then lightly tap said sieve with a spoon or knife so that just a little falls down on the whipped cream.

Number of sample servings: 8-12

We recommend that you split one dessert between 2 or 3 people.

Vegetarian Recipes

Easy Stir Fry With Tofu
4 cups cooked brown rice
Juice of 1 orange
1/4 cup chicken broth
1 Tbsp corn starch
4 Tbsp light soy sauce
1 Tbsp sesame oil
1 cup diced firm tofu (not silken)
1 Tbsp oil
1 Tbsp minced garlic
1 Tbsp grated fresh ginger
1 pound package frozen stir-fry vegetables
Directions:
1. Cook the rice according to package directions.
2. Mix the orange juice, chicken broth, corn starch, soy sauce, sesame oil, and tofu in a small mixing bowl. Stir well and set aside.
3. Meanwhile, heat the oil in a large nonstick skillet or wok over high heat. Saute the garlic and ginger until golden, about 3 minutes. Add the frozen veggies and cook until tender, about 6 minutes. Add sauce and cook until the mixture is heated through. Serve the veggies and tofu over the cooked brown rice.

Serves 4. Each 2 cup serving: 398 calories, 11 g fat, 1.5 g saturated fat, 1 mg cholesterol, 538 mg sodium, 59 g carbohydrate, 5 g fiber, 16 g protein.

Red Beans and Rice
2 cups brown rice
5 cups water
6 tsp low sodium beef bouillon granules
2 cups cooked or canned kidney beans
1/4 cup dried onion
1 tsp oregano
1 tsp paprika
1 tsp garlic powder
Pinch cayenne pepper
Black pepper to taste
Directions:
1. Place all ingredients in large soup pot and bring to a boil. Lower heat to simmer, cover pot, and cook on low until rice is done, about 30 minutes.
2. Serve hot or refrigerate/freeze for later use.

Serves 4. Each 1-1/2 cup serving: 323 calories, 2 g fat, 0.5 g saturated fat, 0 mg cholesterol, 12 mg sodium, 65 g carbohydrate, 6 g fiber, 10 g protein.

Skillet Chili
1 tsp oil
1 cup zucchini, chopped
1 cup mild chili peppers, chopped
1 cup chopped veggie burger
2 cups canned kidney beans, drained and rinsed
1 15-ounce can no-salt-added diced tomatoes
1/2 cup no-salt-added ketchup
1 cup water
1 tsp chili powder
1 tsp garlic powder
Directions:
1. Heat a 12" nonstick skillet over high heat. Add the oil and saute the zucchini and peppers until golden brown, about 3 minutes.
2. Add the rest of the ingredients, bring to a boil and reduce to a simmer. Cook until sauce is thick.
3. Serve over cooked brown rice, a baked potato, or 100% whole wheat toast.

Serves 4. Each serving: 259 calories, 2.5 g fat, 0.5 g saturated fat, 40 mg cholesterol, 408 mg sodium, 32 g carbohydrate, 10.5 g fiber, 26 g protein.

Chocolate Mousse with Berries
1 box (12 ounces) silken tofu
1/3 cup sugar
1/4 cup cocoa powder
2 cups assorted berries: sliced strawberries, raspberries, blueberries, etc.
Nonfat whipped cream
Directions:
1. Puree tofu, sugar, and cocoa powder in a food processor. Divide between four tall stemmed glasses. Refrigerate until ready to serve or immediately proceed to step two.
2. Mash berries in a bowl and divide among four glasses, placing them on top of the chocolate mousse.
3. Top each glass with about 2 tablespoons of nonfat whipped cream.
4. Optional garnish: Dust the top of the whipped cream with cocoa powder.

Serves 4. Each 3/4 cup serving: 159 calories, 3.5 g fat, 0.5 g saturated fat, 1 mg cholesterol, 35 mg sodium, 25 g carbohydrate, 3 g fiber, 7.5 g protein.

Vegetarian Diet Facts

❖What is a vegetarian?
Vegetarians are people who eat vegetables, fruits, grains, and beans, but do not eat animal flesh. Lacto-ovo vegetarians include milk and eggs in their diet, while Vegans avoid any foods that come from animals.

❖Why are some people vegetarians?
People become vegetarians for different reasons. Common examples include spiritual beliefs, the desire to protect the environment, and concerns about the treatment of animals. Many people also choose a vegetarian diet for their health.

❖What are the health benefits of a vegetarian diet?
Vegetarians are at decreased risk for heart disease, certain types of cancer, hypertension, diabetes and obesity. They also have lower rates of gallstones, kidney stones and diverticular disease. Vegetarian diets may even be beneficial in treating some diseases.

❖What makes a well-balanced vegetarian diet?
Omitting meat from your diet is not the only step you need to take in order to become a healthy vegetarian. Vegetarians need to make good food choices, just like everyone else. This means skipping high fat foods, decreasing consumption of highly processed items, and constructing healthy meals in decent proportions. MyPlate provides a fantastic guide to crafting healthy, delcious meals. Check it out at http://www.choosemy-plate.gov/ and remember that half your plate should be fruits and veggies at each meal, at least half of all the grains you consume should be whole grains, most (if not all) of the dairy products you consume should be lowfat or fat-free, and that portions should reasonably sized.

❖Can people get all the nutrients they need from a vegetarian diet?
As long as the vegetarian is consuming dairy or eggs, the answer is yes. Vegans must eat foods that are fortified with vitamin B12 or take a B12 supplement.

Vegetarian diets are high in plant foods, which means that they offer many nutritional advantages over diets that rely on meat. Vegetarian diets tend to be higher in fiber, antioxidants, and other health-promoting substances found in plants. At the same time, vegetarian diets tend to be lower in fat and cholesterol.

❖What about omega-3 fatty acids?
Vegetarians should include foods rich in linolenic acid (such as ground flax seed, canola oil, and full-fat soy products) in their daily diet. They should also minimize their intake of trans fatty acids. This will help their body produce DHA, a long-chain omega-3 fatty acid that may reduce the risk for heart disease and provide other health benefits.

❖What about protein, iron, zinc and calcium?
Protein - Vegetarian diets provide enough protein, as long as the vegetarian is conscious of the need for balance. Vegetables, beans, peas, and grains all contain protein. It is not necessary to eat these foods in special combinations, as long as people choose a variety of these foods over the course of a day. Lacto-ovo vegetarians also get protein from milk and eggs.

Most Americans get more protein than they need. The RDA for adult protein consumption is 0.8 g/kg (children, the elderly, and elite athletes need more). This means that a 138 lb person would need to consume about 50 grams of protein per day, which can be pretty easy. In fact, when you eat lean protein, a proper daily dose comes to 200 calories worth of protein. That's 10% of the calories in a 2000 calorie diet! Vegans tend to get that amount or a little more, and lacto-ovo vegetarians get even more than vegans. Omnivorous diets in this country provide about one and a half times the RDA for protein, if not more.

Iron - It is true that the iron in meat is more readily absorbed than the iron in plants, but vegetarian diets tend to be higher in iron, which compensates for decreased absorption.

Zinc - Most people don't consume enough zinc. However, outright zinc deficiency is rare in the U.S. Fortified breakfast cereals are excellent sources of zinc, but this mineral is also in legumes, nuts, grains, and dairy products.

Calcium - Vegans can meet their calcium needs by choosing plant foods that are rich in calcium, such as tofu made with calcium sulfate, collard greens, kale, figs, navy beans, sesame seeds and almonds, as well as soymilk and orange juice that have been fortified with calcium.

By Cheryl Sullivan, MA, RD.

❖For more information:
Check out he Vegetarian Resource Group at
www.vrg.org

Leader Guide: Weight Loss Cooking

Title:

Weight Loss Cooking

Target Audience:

This presentation is intended for general audiences who are are looking for healthy ways to lose weight.

Lesson Objectives:

• Participants will learn to prepare recipes that are high in fiber and low in calorie density, both of which promote weight loss.

• Participants will explore the benefits of maintaining a healthy weight.

Lesson Rationale:

Health authorities have indicated that good nutrition is one of the most important factors in determining long-term health. Poor diet plays a major role in the development of four of the top seven killers in the United States: heart disease, cancer, stroke and diabetes. Individuals who have the skills to select and prepare nutritious foods can positively impact their present and future health.

Lesson at a Glance:

This lesson introduces participants to new recipes and teaches cooking skills. It also provides nutrition and dietary information that is consistent with the Dietary Guidelines for Americans and MyPlate.

Lesson Materials:

This lesson contains:

• Leader and Activity Guides

• 4 pages of copy-ready recipes and handouts

Preparation:

___ Review leader guide

___ Review handouts

___ Select activities

___ Copy and collect materials for lesson

Activity Ideas:

Activity 1 – Cooking Demo

Use the recipes in this lesson to plan a cooking demonstration. These recipes are designed to show participants how to prepare and serve foods that are high in fiber and low in calorie density. Participants will get a chance to sample these items and taste the ways that healthy cooking aids weight loss without sacrificing flavor.

Activity 2 - Compare the Calories

Use the handout, "Lowfat Saves Calories" to show your audience how lowfat meat, dairy, salad dressings, band other ingredients can reduce fat and calories. Use the handout, "Whole Usually Means Less" to show them that whole, unprocessed, fruits, vegetables, and grains are usually lower in fat and calories. Bring along cereal bars, processed cereal, and packages of muffins to show the number of calories per ounce (or 28 gram serving). These foods are all much higher in calories than fruits, vegetables, salads, beans and potatoes.

For More Information:

http://www.foodandhealth.com/continuinged.php - Follow this link for excellent articles on diet and weight loss. Explore foodandhealth.com for more recipe options and diet advice.

Other lessons in this ki are valuable for weight loss classes. Take a look at...

- High Fiber Cooking

- Recipe Modification

- Cooking for One

- Heart Healthy

- Beans

- Fruits & Vegetables

- Cooking on a Budget

- Cooking and Eating on the Run

- Healthy & Ethnic: Italian, African American, Hispanic and Asian

- Desserts

Leader Guide: Recipes for Weight Control

Tuna Salad Redux

Makes about 4 sample servings

1/2 can tuna in water, drained
1 lowfat whole grain cracker

Salad:
2 cups ready-to-serve romaine lettuce
1 sliced tomato
1/2 cup sliced cucumber
1 Tbsp chopped red onion
1 tsp olive oil
2 Tbsp flavored vinegar
Black pepper (to taste)
1/2 tsp dried oregano

Directions:
1. Toss salad ingredients in a large bowl. Place the salad on a dinner plate.
2. Top the salad with tuna and the cracker.

Equipment:
____ Mixing bowl
____ Knife
____ Cutting board
____ Can opener
____ Spoons (to toss and serve salad)
____ Measuring cups and spoons
____ Dinner plate (for final presentation)

Shopping list:
____ 1 can tuna
____ Lowfat whole grain crackers (like WASA)
____ Ready-to-serve romaine lettuce
____ 1 tomato
____ Cucumber
____ Red onion
____ Olive oil
____ Flavored vinegar
____ Black pepper
____ Dried oregano
____ Plates, napkins, and forks (for samples)

Cooking skill/nutrition lesson:
This recipe shows participants how to make a large salad that is filling, yet low in calories - great for a weight control program. It balances proper proportions of three MyPlate food groups -- grains, vegetables, and protein. Add a bit of fruit and lowfat dairy for a full, healthy meal.

Demo preparation:
1. Wash your hands before you handle food.
2. Measure all ingredients.
3. Organize your work area.

Garnish/presentation tips:
Place the salad on a large dinner plate. Top with tuna and a cracker, then garnish with fresh cracked black pepper.

Number of sample servings: Approximately 4

Super Soup

Makes about 4 sample servings

1 cup frozen mixed vegetables
1 cup canned healthy (low fat, low sodium) soup

Directions:
1. Combine vegetables & soup in a microwave-safe container.
2. Microwave on high until soup comes to a full boil.
3. Pour into soup bowl. We suggest you accompany this meal with a large tossed salad.

Equipment:
____ Microwave
____ Microwave container
____ Spoon
____ Can opener
____ Insulated thermos
____ Measuring cup

Shopping list:
____ Frozen mixed vegetables
____ 1 can healthy soup
____ Lowfat whole grain crackers (like WASA)
____ Plates, napkins, and spoons (for samples)

Cooking skill/nutrition lesson:
This recipe shows how to modify canned soup, making it both healthier and heartier. You can also discuss strategies for picking healthy soups (look at the label, compare brands, etc).

Demo preparation:
1. Wash your hands before you handle food.
2. Measure all ingredients and organize work area.

Garnish/presentation tips:
Pour the soup into the thermos. Place next to a spoon and napkin.

Number of sample servings: Approximately 4.

Leader Guide: Recipes for Weight Control

Chili Rice Pot
Makes 10 sample servings

1 cup instant brown rice
15 oz can diced Mexican tomatoes
15 oz can pinto beans, drained and rinsed
1/2 cup water
1 tsp garlic powder
Optional garnish: Fat free sour cream
Directions:
1. Place all ingredients into a 2 quart microwave-safe container. Cover and microwave on high until rice is done, about 8-10 minutes.
2. Stir well and serve hot. Garnish with a dollop of fat free sour cream.

Equipment:
____ Microwave
____ 2 quart microwave container
____ Kitchen spoon
____ Can opener
____ Measuring cups and spoons
____ Plate (for final presentation)

Shopping list:
____ 1 box instant brown rice
____ 1 can (15 oz) diced Mexican-flavored tomatoes
____ 1 can (15 oz) pinto beans
____ Water
____ Fat free sour cream (optional, for garnish)
____ Garlic powder
____ Plates, forks, napkins (for samples)
____ Plastic cups (for premeasured ingredients)

Cooking skill/nutrition lesson:
This recipe only contains 5 ingredients, but manages to feature foods from three different MyPlate groups: grains, protein, and veggies. It features instant brown rice and can be made in one pot in the microwave. This recipe demonstrates that healthy cooking doesn't have to be fussy and time-consuming.

Demo preparation:
1. Wash your hands before you handle food.
2. Measure all ingredients, open cans.
3. Organize your work area.

Garnish/presentation tips:
Top this dish with nonfat sour cream.

Number of sample servings: Approximately 10

(use a 1/2 cup portion for tastings).

Beanut Butter
Makes 30 sample servings

3/4 cup cooked white beans, drained and rinsed
1/2 cup peanut butter, no added salt
1/2 cup water
Directions:
1. Add beans and peanut butter to food processor. Blend on high speed, adding water slowly until smooth.
2. Use immediately or refrigerate until ready to use.

Equipment:
____ Food processor
____ Spatula
____ Can opener
____ Measuring cup
____ Knife (to spread peanut butter)

Shopping list:
____ Canned white beans
____ Peanut butter, natural - no added salt
____ Water
____ Crackers
____ Napkins (for samples)

Cooking skill/nutrition lesson:
This recipe outlines how to make peanut butter lower in fat and calories. Without modifications like this, people who are trying to lose weight often have to give up favorite foods that are too high in fat and calories.

Demo preparation:
1. Wash your hands before you handle food.
2. Measure ingredients.
3. Organize work area and ingredients.

Garnish/presentation tips:
Serve "beanut butter" on small, lowfat crackers. We recommend using pieces of a WASA whole grain cracker.

Number of sample servings: 30 (1 Tbsp each)

Leader Guide: Recipes for Weight Control

Golden Split Pea Soup
Makes 20 sample servings

This savory soup is made with yellow split peas. It is high in fiber, but low in fat, which will fill you up, not out.

2 tsp vegetable oil
2 cups chopped onion
2 cups diced baking potatoes, skin on
12 ounces yellow split peas (1-1/2 cups)
5-6 cups low-sodium chicken broth
1 cup water
1/2 tsp onion powder
1 tsp poultry seasoning
Optional garnish: diced tomato

Directions:

1. Place the vegetable oil in a large soup pot or Dutch-oven style pan. Heat over medium-high. Add the onion and saute until golden, about 2-3 minutes.
2. Add the rest of the ingredients and mix well. Bring to a boil, then lower to simmer. Cook uncovered until the split peas are tender, about 45 minutes. Serve hot.

Cooking skill/nutrition lesson:

This recipe teaches participants how to make split pea soup. This soup is high in fiber and must be eaten slowly since it is hot and holds heat well. It is perfect for those trying to lose weight.

Equipment list:
____ Stove
____ Soup pot or Dutch-oven style pan
____ Spoon
____ Ladle
____ Measuring cups and spoons
____ Can opener
____ Cutting board
____ Knife
____ Bowl (for final presentation)

Shopping list:
____ Vegetable oil
____ Onion
____ 1 tomato (for garnish, optional)
____ Baking potatoes
____ 12 ounces yellow split peas (1-1/2 cups)
____ 5-6 cups low-sodium chicken broth
____ Water
____ Onion powder
____ Poultry seasoning
____ Disposable cups (for premeasured ingredients)
____ Cups, spoons, and napkins (for samples)

Demo preparation:
1. Wash your hands before handling food.
2. Measure and prepare all ingredients.
3. Organize work area and ingredients.

Make ahead options:
We recommend that you make this recipe ahead of time and reheat for class. Alternatively, you could get it started and discuss other topics while it is cooking.

Garnish/presentation tips:
Ladle this soup into an attractive soup bowl and top with a little chopped tomato.

Number of sample servings: 20 (1/2 cup each)

Recipes for Weight Control

Tuna Salad Redux

1/2 can tuna in water, drained
1 lowfat whole grain cracker
Salad:
2 cups ready-to-serve romaine lettuce
1 sliced tomato
1/2 cup sliced cucumber
1 Tbsp chopped red onion
1 tsp olive oil
2 Tbsp flavored vinegar
Black pepper (to taste)
1/2 tsp dried oregano
Directions:
1. Toss salad ingredients in a large bowl. Place the salad on a dinner plate.
2. Top the salad with tuna and the cracker.

Serves 1. Each serving: 193 calories, 2 g fat, 0 g saturated fat, 45 mg cholesterol, 422 mg sodium, 22 g carbohydrate, 4 g fiber, 25 g protein.

Golden Split Pea Soup

2 tsp vegetable oil
2 cups chopped onion
2 cups diced baking potatoes, skin on
12 ounces yellow split peas (1-1/2 cups)
5-6 cups low-sodium chicken broth
1 cup water
1/2 tsp onion powder
1 tsp poultry seasoning
Optional garnish: Diced tomato
Directions:
1. Place the vegetable oil in a large soup pot or Dutch-oven style pan. Heat over medium-high. Add the onion and saute until golden, about 2-3 minutes.
2. Add the rest of the ingredients and mix well. Bring to a boil, then lower to simmer. Cook uncovered until the split peas are tender, about 45 minutes. Serve hot and garnish with diced tomato.

Serves 4. Each 1-1/2 cup serving: 224 calories, 3 g fat, 0 g saturated fat, 18 mg cholesterol, 196 mg sodium, 33 g carbohydrate, 12 g fiber, 17 g protein.

Chili Rice Pot

1 cup instant brown rice
15 oz can diced Mexican tomatoes
15 oz can pinto beans, drained and rinsed
1/2 cup water
1 tsp garlic powder
Optional garnish: Fat free sour cream
Directions:
1. Place all ingredients into a 2 quart microwave-safe container. Cover and microwave on high until rice is done, about 8-10 minutes.
2. Stir well and serve hot. Garnish with a dollop of fat free sour cream.

Serves 4. Each serving: 181 calories, 1.5 g fat, 0 g saturated fat, 0 mg cholesterol, 274 mg sodium, 33 g carbohydrate, 6 g fiber, 6.5 g protein.

Super Soup

1 cup frozen mixed vegetables
1 cup canned healthy (low fat, low sodium) soup
Directions:
1. Combine vegetables & soup in a microwave-safe container.
2. Microwave on high until soup comes to a full boil.
3. Pour into soup bowl. We suggest you accompany this meal with a large tossed salad.

Serves 1. Each serving: 145 calories, 0.5 g fat, 0 g saturated fat, 0 mg cholesterol, 475 mg sodium, 29 g carbohydrate, 8 g fiber, 6.5 g protein.

Beanut Butter

3/4 cup cooked white beans, drained and rinsed
1/2 cup peanut butter, no added salt
1/2 cup water
Directions:
1. Add beans and peanut butter to food processor. Blend on high speed, adding water slowly until smooth.
2. Use immediately or refrigerate until ready to use.

Serves 14. Each 2 Tbsp serving: 70 calories, 4.5 g fat, 0.5 g fat, 0 g saturated fat, 0 mg cholesterol, 54 mg sodium, 4.5 g carbohydrate, 1 g fiber, 3 g protein.

3 Magical Steps to Weight Management

1. Think Positive!
• Know that weight loss "magic" is within you. There is no magic fad diety or pill.
• Talk about your goals in a positive way. Say things like "I am ready to change my life. Today is the best day to start."

2. Control Your Environment
• Find a buddy or group of friends who will join you in your weight management journey.
• Keep the right foods on hand. Be sure to include plenty of fruits and vegetables, whole grains, canned or dried beans, nonfat dairy and fish or lean poultry. Advanced meal planning makes it easier to eat healthy meals at home.
• Choose restaurants that offer a variety of menu items that are good for you and your goals.

3. Choose the Right Strategies
• Avoid fad diets and follow a healthy, balanced lifestyle. Remember, MyPlate advises people to enjoy food, but eat less of it and avoid oversized portions.
• Eat only when you're actually hungry. Smaller, frequent meals are better than one or two large ones, especially if you are trying to lose weight.
• Use MyPlate's guidelines and make half your plate fruits and veggies, and at least half of the grains you eat whole grains.
• Stay hydrated.
• Eat a healthy breakfast every day.
• Exercise for at least 30 minutes on most days of the week.

Golden Split Pea Soup
This savory soup is high in fiber and will fill you up, not out.

2 tsp	vegetable oil
2 cups	chopped onion
2 cups	diced baking potatoes, skin on
12 ounces	yellow split peas (1-1/2 cups)
5-6 cups	low-sodium chicken broth
1 cup	water
1/2 tsp	onion powder
1 tsp	poultry seasoning

Place the vegetable oil in a large soup pot or Dutch-oven style pan. Heat over medium-high heat. Add the onion and saute until golden, about 2-3 minutes. Add the rest of the ingredients and mix well. Bring to a boil then lower to simmer. Cook uncovered until the peas are tender, about 45 minutes. Serve hot. **Serves 8.** Each 1 cup serving: 181 calories, 1.5 g fat, 0 g saturated fat, 0 mg cholesterol, 135 mg sodium, 28 g carbohydrate, 10 g fiber, 4 g sugars, 14 g protein.

10 Steps I will do right now to perform my own "magic:"

1. _____
2. _____
3. _____
4. _____
5. _____
6. _____
7. _____
8. _____
9. _____
10. _____

Stumped? Try any of the following suggestions...

Eat more fruits and vegetables, find an exercise partner or class to help you increase your amount of exercise, develop more healthy dishes to prepare at home, take a walk after dinner instead of watching TV, bring a healthy lunch and snacks to work, or eat a healthy breakfast every day.

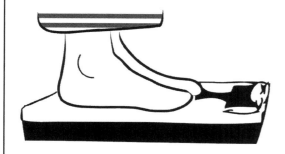

Whole Usually Means Less

Compare the foods at the top with the foods at the bottom. The ones at the top are high in sugar, white flour, and calories per ounce. Whole foods in their natural form are usually higher in fiber and lower in calories than processed foods.

Processed Food:	Calories Per Ounce
Brownies	80-120
Cake (without frosting)	90-120
Cereal (dry)	120-150
Cereal bars/granola bars	110-130
Cookies	100-140
Crackers	101-113
Danish, donuts, pastries	120-140
Muffins	70-80
Potato chips, tortilla chips	110-130
Pretzels	90-111
Rice cakes	101-124
Toaster pastries	110-130

Whole food:	Calories Per Ounce
Apple	16
Baked potato	20
Banana	26
Bean chili	18
Cooked oatmeal or cream of wheat	12
Carrot sticks	12
Celery sticks	4
Cooked pasta	39
Cooked rice	31
Lowfat soup with pasta, rice or beans	9
Orange	13
Sweet potato	30

Reduce Fat to Lower Calorie Intake

Choose fat-free dairy products:

Try using:	Instead of:	Save Fat(g)	Save Calories:
Salsa for Baked Potato (2 Tbsp)	Sour Cream & Butter (1 Tbsp each)	15	122
Evaporated Skim Milk (2 Tbsp)	Heavy Cream (2 Tbsp)	11	79
Nonfat Cream Cheese (2 Tbsp)	Cream Cheese (2 Tbsp)	10	77
Skim Milk (1 cup)	Whole Milk (1 cup)	8	65
Nonfat Ricotta (1/4 cup)	Whole Milk Ricotta (1/4 cup)	8	60
Low-fat Cheddar (1 ounce)	Cheddar Cheese (1 ounce)	7	56
Fat-Free Frozen Yogurt (1/2 cup)	Ice Cream (1/2 cup)	9	50
1% Milk (1 cup)	Whole Milk (1 cup)	5.5	48
Fat-Free Cottage Cheese (1/2 cup)	4% Cottage Cheese (1/2 cup)	7	38
Reduced-Fat Cheddar (1 ounce)	Cheddar Cheese (1 ounce)	4	30
Roasted Garlic for bread (1 clove)	Butter/Margarine (1 tsp)	3.7	28
Nonfat Sour Cream (2 Tbsp)	Sour Cream (2 Tbsp)	5	15

Choose lean or lowfat protein products:

Try using:	Instead of:	Save Fat(g)	Save Calories:
Lowfat Veggie Burger (3 ounces)	Hamburger (3 ounces)	19	170
Lowfat Ground Turkey (3 ounces)	Ground Beef (3 ounces)	18	165
Chili Made With Beans (1 cup)	Chili Made With Ground Beef (1 cup)	14	160
Lean Pork (3 ounces)	Pork (roast, ribs, 3 ounces)	4-9	76-139
Lean Beef, (3 ounces)	Beef (rib, brisket, chuck, 3 ounces)	5-17	49-129
Skinless Chicken Breast (3 ounces)	Dark Chicken with Skin (3 ounces)	8	59

Miscellaneous substitutions:

Try using:	Instead of:	Save Fat(g)	Save Calories:
Broth (1/4 cup)	Margarine/Butter/Oil (1/4 cup)	54	472
Flavored vinegar or lemon (1 Tbsp)	Salad Dressing (2 Tbsp)	12	134
Spray oil (2 second spray)	Free Pouring Oil (1 Tbsp)	13	120
Mustard (1/2 tsp)	Mayonnaise (1 Tbsp)	11	95
Fat-Free Mayonnaise (1 Tbsp)	Regular Mayonnaise (1 Tbsp)	11	90
Fat-Free Salad Dressing (2 Tbsp)	Salad Dressing (2 Tbsp)	12	84
Egg Whites (2)	Whole Eggs (1)	5	49

BONUS: Our Favorite Recipes and Fun Lessons

This section includes a bonus leader guide, a selection of more of our favorite recipes and a recipe index.

Bonus Leader Guide

This leader guide will help you incorporate the recipes and handouts from other lessons in a wider range of circumstances and classes.

Diabetes:
Most of the recipes in this kit are excellent for people with type 2 diabetes.
- Use the recipes and handouts in the Heart Healthy lesson to help them lower their risk of heart disease.
- Use the recipes and handouts in the Fiber and Beans and Grains lessons to explore how to increase fiber intake for better blood sugar control.
- The Dessert lesson emphasizes the use of healthy, fruit-based desserts, and will make a charming addition to any healthy eating discussion. The chocolate mousse recipe can be made with Splenda instead of sugar to further lower calories and carbohydrates.
- Discuss recipe modification for people with diabetes. You can use the PowerPoint show (modify.ppt) or overhead show to explore how to make healthier versions of favorite foods. There is also an excellent recipe modification handout in the Heart Lesson. That handout highlights ways to lower saturated fat.

Cancer Prevention/Treatment Classes:
There are several lessons in this kit that work well when addressing cancer.
- Use the Antioxidant lesson to demonstrate how to eat a healthier, anti-cancer diet. This lesson stresses the importance of fruits and vegetables.
- The Bean, Grain, Soy and Fruits & Vegetables lessons emphasize the importance of a plant-based diet and give tips and recipes for making these foods healthy and easy to prepare.

Cooking/Wellness:
The ethnic food classes are fun in cooking and wellness classes. Our goal for the healthy ethnic classes was to take healthy ethnic ingredients, that can be found in most any grocery store, and use them in recipes that can be made quickly in an American kitchen.

You can also use the Herb and Recipe Modification lessons for cooking/wellness. See the leader guide for activity ideas. We have provided an extra PowerPoint show to accompany the recipe modification exploration.

Summer

The no-cook demos are a great way to prepare healthy and attractive dishes without turning on the stove or oven. This keeps things nice and cool in the kitchen.

Heart Healthy:
There are many lesson plans that can be used for this topic. The most obvious is the Heart Healthy Cooking lesson, but others include:

Beans - Beans are an excellent source of folate and soluble fiber. This lesson reviews a variety of ways to prepare healthy and delicious bean recipes.

Fiber - This lesson helps people include more of the right ingredients in meals and recipes.

Fish Twice Per Week - This section is based on the American Heart Association recommendation to eat omega-3 rich fish twice per week. Plus, it aligns nicely with MyPlate's call to eat 8 ounces of seafood every week.

Flax - This seed is rich in omega-3 fatty acids and fiber. It makes a great substitute for eggs, fat and flour in most recipes.

Folate - This lesson features another important nutrient. Folate can help lower homocysteine levels

Fruits and Vegetables - People should increase their consumption of these in order to increase fiber and lower calorie density.

Herbs and Spices - This lesson will help participants use less sodium. We have designed spice mixes that can take the place of boxed mixes and prepared sauces

Hypertension - This class uses the DASH diet to help lower blood pressure. Up-to-date materials reflect the findings of the DASH-Sodium trials. We recommend that you feature the low-sodium recipe for pasta sauce, especially after an exploration of how much sodium can be found in most commercial blends of pasta sauce.

Recipe Modification - This lesson shows how to modify recipes and almost always includes specific moves to increase heart health.

Soy - This lesson includes excellent ways to use less meat and include more plants in everyone's diet.

Vegetarian Cooking - This class is great for introducing participants to the idea of meatless meals

Weight Loss - This lesson is short and sweet. It outlines ways to prepare recipes that are lower in calories. We recommend highlighting "Beanut Butter," a neat way to lowers the fat and calories in a serving of

Quick & Heart Healthy

Pasta Primavera

Fresh veggies, basil and a tasty broth go well with penne pasta.

3 cups dry penne pasta[1]
1/2 tsp minced garlic
1 cup nonfat chicken broth[2]
3 cups assorted fresh or frozen vegetables
1 15-ounce can of Italian stewed tomatoes, diced
1 Tbsp chopped fresh basil[3]
4 Tbsp Parmesan cheese

Directions:

1. Cook pasta according to package directions. Drain in colander and set aside.
2. Spray a large, nonstick skillet with vegetable oil cooking spray and heat over medium high heat. Add garlic and saute until nutty brown. Add broth, vegetables and tomatoes and bring to a boil. Reduce heat to a simmer and cook until vegetables are tender - about 5 minutes.
3. Toss sauce with cooked pasta and fresh basil. Serve each portion with 1 tablespoon of Parmesan cheese.

Serves 4. Each 1-1/2 cup serving: 330 calories, 2.5 g fat, 1 g saturated fat, 5 mg cholesterol, 380 mg sodium, 61 g carbohydrate, 6 g fiber, 16 g protein. Diabetic exchange: 3 bread, 1/2 meat, 2 veg.

Italian Chopped Salad

This easy salad goes well with any pasta dish, especially the Pasta Primavera.

4 cups Romaine lettuce, washed, dried, and chopped
1 Tbsp dried Italian Seasoning Herb Mix[4]
2 cups chopped salad vegetables
3 Tbsp balsamic vinegar[5]
Fresh cracked black pepper

Directions:

1. Toss all ingredients together. Spray lettuce leaves with a little olive oil for added flavor.
2. Salad tips: Always dry your lettuce after washing. Keep it stored in a bag or covered container until ready to use. Experiment with different colors and varieties of lettuce leaves, this presents an interesting salad with a more diverse flavor profil. To add even more of a kick, include fresh, chopped herbs like parsley and basil.

Serves 4. Each 1-1/2 cup serving: 80 calories, 1 g fat, 0 g saturated fat, 0 mg cholesterol, 35 mg sodium, 14 g carbohydrate, 3 g fiber, 4 g protein. Diabetic exchange: 3 veg.

Cook's Notes:

1. Pasta used for this recipe can be any small-shaped pasta. Try whole wheat options whenever possible.
2. Look for chicken broth with less than 500 mg sodium per serving.
3. If you don't have access to fresh basil, you can use a half tablespoon of dried basil instead.
4. Italian herbs can be substituted with a half tablespoon each of dried oregano and basil.
5. Red wine or cider vinegar may be substituted for balsamic vinegar.

Recipe brought to you by:

Quick & Healthy Pasta Dishes

Spaghetti Bolognese

This zesty meat sauce has lots of fresh veggies.

8 oz. dry spaghetti

1 onion, diced

1 tsp minced garlic

12 oz. extra-lean ground turkey breast (skinless)

1 fresh tomato, cored and chopped

1 zucchini, sliced

1 cup sliced fresh mushrooms

2 tsp Italian seasoning herb mix[1]

Pinch cayenne pepper

1 28 ounce jar pasta sauce[2]

Directions:

1. Cook spaghetti according to package directions, drain in colander, and reserve until ready to serve.
2. Lightly spray large, nonstick skillet with vegetable oil cooking spray and heat over medium-high heat. Add garlic and onions and cook until lightly brown. Add the turkey in small chunks and cook until no longer pink. Add the rest of the ingredients and bring to a boil. Cook until vegetables are tender, about 3 minutes.

Serves 4. Each 2 cup serving: 440 calories, 3 g fat, 0 g saturated fat, 55 mg cholesterol, 740 mg sodium, 69 g carbohydrate, 7 g fiber, 34 g protein. Diabetic exchange: 3 bread, 2 meat, 5 veg.

Angel Hair Pasta with Marinara

Roasted vegetables make a thick, flavorful marinara sauce.

8 ounces dry angel hair pasta[3]

2 large, ripe tomatoes, cored, halved and seeded

1/2 onion, peeled and quartered

1 clove garlic, cut in half

1/2 green bell pepper, cored

1/4 cup fresh basil[4]

4 Tbsp grated Parmesan cheese

Fresh cracked black pepper

Directions:

1. Cook pasta according to package directions. Drain and set aside in colander until ready to serve.
2. Meanwhile, preheat your oven broiler. Place tomatoes, onion, garlic and bell pepper skin side up on a flat cookie tray. Roast under the broiler until skins turn very brown and blister- about 10 minutes. Place all vegetables into your food processor or blender. Add fresh basil and puree until smooth. Reheat sauce and serve over cooked angel hair pasta. Sprinkle 1 Tbsp grated Parmesan and fresh cracked black pepper over the top of each portion.

Serves 4. Each 1 cup serving: 270 calories, 3 g fat, 1.5 g saturated fat, 5 mg cholesterol, 125 mg sodium, 50 g carbohydrate, 3 g fiber, 11 g protein. Diabetic exchange: 3 bread, 1 veg, 1/2 meat.

Cook's Notes:

1. Italian herbs can be substituted with a teaspoon each of dried oregano and basil.
2. Pasta sauce should be low in fat and sodium. Check the label to be sure fat does not exceed 1 gram and sodium does not exceed 500 mg per ½ cup serving.
3. You can also use regular spaghetti.
4. You can also use one tablespoon of dried basil.

Bone Up With More Calcium

Lasagna Roll Ups

This easy recipe makes delicious lasagna for two. It also has over 750 mg of calcium per serving.

4 cooked lasagna noodles[1]
1 14 ounce can stewed diced tomatoes- no-added-salt
1 cup nonfat ricotta cheese
1/2 tsp each: garlic powder, oregano, dried basil
2 Tbsp Parmesan cheese
2 Tbsp nonfat grated mozzarella

Directions:

1. Combine seasonings with ricotta cheese and Parmesan in a small mixing bowl.
2. Spread the cheese mixture by the spoonful onto each cooked lasagna noodle.
3. Roll up the lasagna noodles and place seam side down in a casserole dish.
4. Pour tomatoes on top of the noodles, cover the dish with a glass lid or plastic wrap and microwave for 10 minutes.
5. Sprinkle cheese on top of the tomatoes and return the dish to the microwave for 30 more seconds or until cheese melts. (You can also bake lasagna for 20 minutes at 375° - add cheese at the end and cover with tinfoil instead of glass or plastic).

Serves 2. Each 2 roll serving: 400 calories, 3.5 g fat, 1.5 g saturated fat, 15 mg cholesterol, 440 mg sodium, 60 g carbohydrate, 5 g fiber, 31 g protein. Diabetic exchange: 3 bread, 2 veg, 2-1/2 meat.

Cook's Notes

1. You can cook and freeze a batch of lasagna noodles to have on hand for things like these roll-ups. You can also freeze the prepared rollups so that all you will have to do later is heat and serve.
2. You can also use other fruits and berries.
3. You can also use fat free cookies or fat free blondies in this smoothie.

Angel-Devil Smoothie

This smoothie is pureed with strawberries and nonfat chocolate brownies. Each delicious serving has 250 mg of calcium.

2 cups nonfat plain yogurt
2 cups frozen sliced strawberries[2]
2 chocolate nonfat brownies[3] (broken in small pieces)
1/4 cup skim milk

Directions:

1. Combine all items in blender or food processor.
2. Pulse until mixture becomes a fine puree and serve immediately.

**Our test kitchen has also found a hand-held vertical chopper/blender to be well-suited to this recipe.

Serves 4. Each 1 cup serving: 0 g fat, 0 g saturated fat, 5 mg cholesterol, 135 mg sodium, 26 g carbohydrate, 2 g fiber, 8 g protein.

Quick, Inexpensive, & Healthy

Chili Macaroni

Make macaroni fun and nutritious with beans and a zesty tomato sauce. This easy dish can made in a single skillet.

2 cups dry elbow macaroni
2 and 1/2 cups water
1/2 cup prepared salsa
3 Tbsp tomato paste
1 15 ounce can kidney beans, rinsed & drained
1/2-1 tsp chili powder[1]

Directions:

1. Place all ingredients in a nonstick skillet. Bring to a boil, then reduce to a simmer.
2. Cook uncovered, stirring frequently, for 8-10 minutes or until macaroni is tender and excess liquid is evaporated.
3. Serve with your favorite steamed vegetables.

Serves 4. Each 1-1/2 cup serving: 290 calories, 1.5 g fat, 0 g saturated fat, 0 mg cholesterol, 35 mg sodium, 57 g carbohydrate, 5 g fiber, 13 g protein. Diabetic exchange: 3 bread, 1 veg.

Chunky Spaghetti

Beans make this spaghetti sauce rich and hearty.

12 ounces spaghetti, cooked
1/2 medium onion, diced
1 28 ounce can crushed tomatoes[4] with juice
1 Tbsp sugar
1 Tbsp Italian Herb Mix[2]
1 15 ounce can kidney beans[3], rinsed & drained
4 Tbsp Parmesan cheese

Directions:

1. Heat a 3 quart sauce pan and spray with oil. Add onion and cook 3-5 minutes until tender.
2. Add crushed tomatoes, sugar and herbs. Simmer 5 minutes. Stir in drained beans and reheat.
3. Serve sauce over cooked spaghetti with 1 tablespoon Parmesan on top of each serving.

Serves 6. Each 1-1/2 cup serving: 370 calories, 1.5 g fat, 0 g saturated fat, 0 mg cholesterol, 360 mg sodium, 74 g carbohydrate, 8 g fiber, 15 g protein. Diabetic exchange: 3-1/2 bread, 1 veg.

Cook's Notes:

1. Chili powder should be added according to your personal heat preferences.
2. You can switch in a teaspoon of oregano and a teaspoon of basil for the Italian Herb Mix.
3. You can also use 1¾ cups of any cooked bean.
4. Stewed, diced tomatoes can be substituted for crushed tomatoes.

Quick, Inexpensive, & Healthy

Chicken Noodles

This simple pasta dish uses fresh chicken.
3 cups dry whole wheat rotini noodles[1]
1 cup diced celery
1 cup diced onion
1 cup diced carrot
1 cup frozen peas
Pinch each: dried thyme, garlic powder, black pepper
8 ounces chicken breast, cut in bite-size pieces
2 cups lowfat, low-sodium chicken broth[2]
1/2 cup water
Directions:
1. Spray a 12-inch nonstick skillet with cooking spray and heat over medium-high heat.
2. Add celery, onion, carrots and chicken and saute until golden.
2. Add noodles, soup and water and bring to a boil. Reduce heat to a simmer and cook until noodles are tender. Add more water if needed. Serve hot.

Serves 4. Each 1-1/4 cup serving: 370 calories, 3 g fat, 0.5 g saturated fat, 40 mg cholesterol, 320 mg sodium, 60 g carbohydrate, 5 g fiber, 27 g protein. Diabetic exchange: 3 bread, 1-1/2 meat, 2 veg.

Macaroni with Tomatoes & Broccoli

Here's a hearty pasta dish that's easy to make and fun to eat.
2 cups dry macaroni[1]
1 14 oz. can diced stewed tomatoes with Italian herbs[3]
1 15 oz. can kidney beans, drained and rinsed
1 cup nonfat, low sodium chicken broth
2 cups broccoli florets[4]
Directions:
1. Place noodles, tomatoes, beans and broth in skillet; bring to a boil, reduce heat to medium high, cover and cook 10 minutes or until noodles are tender.
2. Add broccoli florets during the last 3 minutes of cooking. This dish is done when the noodles and broccoli are tender. We recommend serving with a little Parmesan on top.

Serves 4. Each 1-1/2 cup serving: 340 calories, 1.5 g fat, 0 g saturated fat, 0 mg cholesterol, 220 mg sodium, 65 g carbohydrate, 9 g fiber, 18 g protein. Diabetic exchange: 4 bread, 1 veg.

Cook's Notes:

1. You can also use any small-shaped pasta such as macaroni, penne, rotini or shells.
2. You can find chicken broth with no add sodium in most grocery stores or dilute half and half with water.
3. Tomatoes with Italian herbs and garlic are usually called Italian Style. You can also used diced stewed tomatoes and add ½ tsp each: garlic powder, oregano and basil.
4. Florets of broccoli are the flowery heads. Cut them close off the stems of broccoli for best results.

High-Fiber, Low-Fat

Tomato Barley Risotto

Barley isn't just for soups and pilafs anymore. In fact, today we're going to use it to make a risotto-style one-pot meal.

1/2 cup chopped onion
1 cup pearl barley, dry
1 15 ounce can diced stewed tomatoes, no added salt
1 6 ounce can tomato paste, no added salt
2 cups water
1 15 ounce can chicken broth[1]
1/2 Tbsp each: garlic powder, dried oregano, dried basil
Black pepper to taste
4 Tbsp Parmesan cheese

Directions:

1. Combine all ingredients (except for the Parmesan cheese) in a large microwave container.
2. Microwave on full power for 30-40 minutes or until barley is tender. You can also cook on top of the stove.
3. Stir occasionally during cooking. The barley risotto is done when the barley is tender and most of the liquid is evaporated. Sprinkle the top of each portion with 1 tablespoon of Parmesan cheese.

Serves 6. Each 1-1/2 cup serving: 200 calories, 2 g fat, 1 g saturated fat, 5 mg cholesterol, 160 mg sodium, 37 g carbohydrate, 8 g fiber, 9 g protein. Diabetic exchange: 2 bread, 1 veg.

Shells with Black Bean Sauce

This lively, Latin-style dish is super simple.

3 cups dry small shell pasta[2]
2 cups water
1 15 ounce can black beans, rinsed and drained
2 14 ounce cans peeled, diced tomatoes with Italian herbs and garlic[3], with juice
1/2 tsp chile powder
1 tsp cumin
4 Tbsp Parmesan cheese

Directions:

1. Combine all ingredients into a shallow microwaveable container. Cover and microwave on high for 15-18 minutes or until shell pasta is tender.
2. Stir well and serve each portion with 1 tablespoon of grated Parmesan cheese sprinkled over the top. Accompany with a green tossed salad with oranges, tomatoes, and balsamic vinegar.

Serves 4. Each serving: 460 calories, 3.5 g fat, 1.5 g saturated fat, 5 mg cholesterol, 160 mg sodium, 87 g carbohydrate, 8 g fiber, 20 g protein. Diabetic exchange: 5 bread, 1/2 meat.

Cook's Notes:

1. Chicken broth should be low in fat and relatively low in sodium. Look for one with less than one gram of fat and 400 mg of sodium per half cup serving.
2. Shell pasta may be substituted with any small shaped pasta such as macaroni, rotini, penne, etc...
3. Tomatoes with Italian herbs and garlic are usually called Italian Style. You can also used diced stewed tomatoes and add ½ tsp each: garlic powder, oregano, and basil.

High-Fiber, Low Fat

Pasta Cannellini

This hearty pasta with a tomato and white bean sauce is especially excellent when served alongside fresh steamed vegetables or a tossed salad.

2 cups dry penne pasta[1]
1/2 tsp. garlic, minced
1/2 onion, sliced
1/2 red bell pepper, sliced
2 cups pasta sauce[2]
1/2 cup water
1 15 oz. can white cannellini beans[3], rinsed and drained
1/2 tsp dried oregano

Directions:

1. Cook the pasta according to package directions. Drain in colander.
2. Spray a large, nonstick skillet with vegetable oil cooking spray and heat over medium-high heat.
3. Add garlic and saute until lightly golden. Add the rest of the ingredients and bring to a boil.
4. Cook until the onions are tender, then toss the pasta with the sauce.

Serves 4. Each 1-1/2 cup serving: 270 calories, 1.5 g fat, 0 g saturated fat, 0 mg cholesterol, 400 mg sodium, 53 g carbohydrate, 6 g fiber, 12 g protein. Diabetic exchange: 2-1/2 bread, 2- 1/2 veg.

Pasta Fagioli

This hearty and delicious pasta dish can made in a single pot.

1 cup chicken broth[4]
3 cups frozen Italian style mixed vegetables
1 tsp each: thyme, garlic powder, oregano
1 bay leaf
1 15 oz. can stewed, diced tomato with onions and green peppers
2 Tbsp tomato paste
1 10 oz. can kidney beans, drained and rinsed
1 cup dry macaroni[1]

Directions:

1. Add all ingredients to a large, covered microwave-able container.
2. Microwave on full power for 12-15 minutes or until pasta is tender. Stir every 4 minutes. Serve in pasta or soup bowl.

Serves 4. Each 2 cup serving: 310 calories, 2.5 g fat, 0 g saturated fat, 0 mg cholesterol, 110 mg sodium, 58 g carbohydrate, 9 g fiber, 15 g protein. Diabetic exchange: 2 bread, 4 veg.

Cook's Notes:

1. You can also use any small shaped pasta such as macaroni, penne, bowtie, rotini, or shell.
2. Use a pasta sauce that is low in fat and relatively low in sodium. Try to find one with less than one gram of fat and 400 mg of sodium per half cup serving.
3. You can use any variety of white bean.
4. Chicken broth should be low in fat and relatively low in sodium. Look for one that has less than one gram of fat and 400 mg of sodium per one half cup serving.

Marvelous One-Dish Meals

Broccoli Sesame Stir fry

This delicious stir fry if full of good sources of non-dairy calcium. There is 244 mg of calcium per serving.

8 ounces dry spaghetti noodles
1 mild green chile pepper, seeded and diced
2 cups sliced mushrooms
1/2 cup green onion, sliced
3 Tbsp sesame seeds
2 Tbsp red wine vinegar
1/4 cup light soy sauce
2 cups calcium-fortified orange juice
1-1/2 Tbsp cornstarch
3 cups broccoli florets[2], cooked

Directions:

1. Break spaghetti noodles in half and cook according to package directions. Strain in colander and hold to side.
2. Lightly spray a 12-inch nonstick skillet with vegetable oil cooking spray and heat over medium high. Saute chile pepper, mushrooms, onion and sesame seeds until lightly brown.
3. Combine vinegar, soy sauce, orange juice and cornstarch. Add to pan and stir rapidly to make smooth sauce.
4. Toss with spaghetti noodles and cooked broccoli and serve with a crisp vegetable garnish.

Serves 4. Each 1-1/2 cup serving: 370 calories, 5 g fat, 0 g saturated fat, 0 mg cholesterol, 550 mg sodium, 68 g carbohydrate, 5 g fiber, 14 g protein. Diabetic exchange: 3 bread, 1 veg, 1 fruit. Diabetic exchange: 3 bread, 1 veg, 1 fruit.

Cook's Notes:

1. You can use regular orange juice if you don't have any calcium-fortified orange juice, but you will have less calcium per serving.
2. Florets of broccoli are the flowery tips. Cut them off close to the stem for best results.
3. Pasta sauce should be low in fat and relatively low in sodium. Try to find one with less than one gram of fat and 400 mg of sodium per one half cup serving.

Macaroni Spinach Bake

A great pasta casserole, this recipe features a heavenly layering of ricotta, Parmesan, spinach and beans.

1-1/2 cups dry macaroni
1 28 ounce jar pasta sauce, heated[3]
1 pound package frozen cut leaf spinach, thawed and drained, with excess water pressed out
1 15-ounce can kidney beans, rinsed and drained
1/2 cup nonfat ricotta cheese
1/4 cup Parmesan cheese
1 Tbsp garlic powder
1/4 cup nonfat grated mozzarella

Directions:

1. Cook macaroni according to package directions. Drain in colander and place in medium mixing bowl.
2. Toss with spinach, beans, ricotta, Parmesan and garlic powder.
3. Spray an 8 inch by 8 inch glass casserole dish with vegetable oil cooking spray.
4. Place one third of spaghetti sauce in bottom of casserole dish. Layer half of pasta mixture on top, follow with another third of sauce then the rest of the pasta mixture and last third of sauce.
5. Cover and bake in microwave oven until heated through, about 15-20 minutes. Top with cheese and bake until the cheese melts, about 3 minutes.

Serves 6. Each 1-1/2 cup serving: 270 calories, 2.5 g fat, 1 g saturated fat, 5 mg cholesterol, 590 mg sodium, 45 g carbohydrate, 7 g fiber, 17 g protein. Diabetic exchange: 2 bread, 1/2 meat, 3 veg.

Summary Picnic Baskets

Tuna Macaroni Salad

This simple salad is delicious for a quick, light dinner or lunch. The tuna is tossed with chopped fresh vegetables, macaroni, and dressing, then served over fresh greens.

1 cup dry elbow macaroni[1]
1/2 cup chopped green onion
1 cup cucumber, peeled, diced
2 ripe tomatoes, diced
6 mushrooms, sliced
2 6.5 oz. cans of tuna[2], drained
1/2 Tbsp red wine vinegar
1/2 cup nonfat Italian Salad Dressing
4 cups ready-to-serve romaine lettuce[3]

Directions:
1. Cook macaroni according to package directions. Drain and rinse with cold water in a colander.
2. Place the vegetables in a medium-sized mixing bowl. Add the tuna, using a fork to break up the chunks. Toss with the vinegar, dressing and macaroni.
3. To serve: Place the tuna salad mixture over the top of the greens.

Serves 4. Each serving: 190 calories, 1 g fat, 0 g saturated fat, 15 mg cholesterol, 580 mg sodium, 28 g carbohydrate, 3 g fiber, 16 g protein. Diabetic exchange: 1 bread, 1-1/2 meat, 1/2 veg.

Turkey Waldorf Salad

This recipe is a perfect entree salad for nights when you just don't feel like cooking. You can also use leftover cooked chicken in place of the turkey.

1/4 cup each: light mayonnaise, nonfat plain yogurt
3 Tbsp cider vinegar[4]
1/2 tsp curry powder
1 pound cold, roasted, skinless turkey breast, cubed
2 large apples, peeled, cored, diced
1/2 cup diced celery
1/4 cup raisins
3 Tbsp walnuts, chopped
4 cups dark green lettuce leaves

Directions:
1. Whisk mayonnaise with yogurt, vinegar and curry powder.
2. Add turkey, celery and raisins and mix well.
3. Serve over lettuce with walnuts sprinkled on top. This salad also goes well in a pita.

Serves 4. Each 1-1/2 cup serving: 310 calories, 4.5 g fat, 0.5 g saturated fat, 95 mg cholesterol, 290 mg sodium, 29 g carbohydrate, 38 g protein. Diabetic exchange: 1 fat, 1 fruit, 5 meat.

Cook's Notes:
1. You may also use any small-shaped pasta such as rotini, bowtie, or shells.
2. Buy tuna that is packed in water.
3. Ready-to-serve Romaine lettuce has been washed, dried and chopped. You can also prepare it yourself.
4. You can use any mild flavored vinegar such as rice, red wine or balsamic.

Heart Healthy Entertaining

Sicilian Pasta Primavera

This dish is so spicy and flavorful, your guests will think that you spent all day in the kitchen.

2 cups dry rotini pasta[1]
1 16 oz. bag Italian style frozen vegetables
1/2 cup white wine[2]
2 cups pasta sauce[3]
Pinch cayenne pepper
2 Tbsp grated Parmesan cheese

Directions:

1. Cook the pasta according to package directions. Drain in colander.
2. Place the vegetables and wine in a medium-sized sauce pan. Cook over medium high heat until wine evaporates. Add pasta sauce, cayenne pepper, and bring to a boil. Simmer until vegetables are tender.
3. Toss the pasta with the sauce and the vegetables. Sprinkle ½ tablespoon of ground Parmesan cheese on each serving.

Serves 4. Each 1-1/2 cup serving: 300 calories, 3.5 g fat, 0.5 g saturated fat, 0 mg cholesterol, 490 mg sodium, 55 g carbohydrate, 4 g fiber, 12 g protein. Diabetic exchange: 2 bread, 5 veg.

Raspberry Chicken

A creative, festive chicken dish that always satisfies meat lovers. We recommend serving with roasted potatoes and your favorite vegetables.

1/2 onion, sliced thin
1/2 cup frozen or fresh raspberries
2 Tbsp tomato paste
1 Tbsp raspberry marmalade
4 4-ounce boneless, skinless chicken breast halves

Directions:

1. Preheat oven to 350°. Place sliced onion in 8 inch by 8 inch glass casserole dish and spray lightly with vegetable oil cooking spray.
2. Saute in microwave until onion is tender. Add raspberries, tomato paste and marmalade. Microwave until mixture comes to a boil.
1. Stir well and add chicken breasts. Spoon sauce over chicken, cover and bake until chicken is done- about 15 minutes.

Serves 4. Each 6 ounce serving: 160 calories, 1.5 g fat, 0 g saturated fat, 70 mg cholesterol, 80 mg sodium, 8 g carbohydrate, 1 g fiber, 28 g protein. Diabetic exchange: 2-1/2 meat.

Cook's Notes:

1. You may also use any small-shaped pasta such as macaroni, shell, or rotelle.
2. You can substitute vegetable or chicken broth for the white wine.
3. Pasta sauce should be low in fat and sodium. Check the label to be sure fat does not exceed 1 gram and sodium does not exceed 400 mg per ½ cup serving.

Breakfast With a Smile

Whole Wheat Pancakes

These pancakes are delicious with cherry syrup, and both are easy to make. This recipe yields 12 small pancakes.

Dry Ingredients:
1 cup whole wheat flour
1/3 cup rolled oats
1/3 cup all-purpose flour
2 tsp baking powder
1/2 tsp ground cinnamon
Liquid Ingredients:
1/2 cup nonfat buttermilk
3/4-1 cup skim milk
Directions:

1. Mix the dry ingredients together in a large bowl. Add the liquid ingredients and mix until incorporated. Vary the amount of milk according to how thick you like your pancakes.
2. Lightly spray a 12 inch nonstick skillet with cooking spray and heat over medium heat. Spoon the pancake batter into the skillet to form 4-inch pancakes.
3. Flip the pancakes over after they brown on the bottom and the tops start bubbling. Brown well on the other side and remove from the skillet. Repeat until all of the batter is gone.
4. Serve with your favorite fruit and syrup.

Serves 4. Each serving (3 pancakes): 210 calories, 1.5 g fat, 0 g saturated fat, 0 mg cholesterol, 270 mg sodium, 39 g carbohydrate, 5 g fiber, 9 g protein. Diabetic exchange: 2 bread, 1/2 milk.

Muesli

Muesli means mix. This wonderful mixture of oats, yogurt, fruits, and almonds is great any time of day.
2 cups rolled oats
2 cups skim milk
2 Tbsp dark seedless raisins
1 apple- cored and chopped
1 banana- sliced
1 orange peeled and cubed
1 Tbsp sliced almonds[1]
1 cup plain nonfat yogurt
Directions:

1. Mix the rolled oats and skim milk before you prepare the other ingredients. Add the rest of the ingredients and mix well. Eat right away or refrigerate for later.
2. If you want to make Muesli ahead of time, leave the banana out until you're ready to serve. The rest of the ingredients will keep for 2 days.

Serves 8. Each 1 cup serving: 160 calories, 2 g fat, 0 g saturated fat, 0 mg cholesterol, 55 mg sodium, 28 g carbohydrate, 3 g fiber, 8 g protein. Diabetic exchange: 1 bread, 1/2 milk, 1/2 fruit.

Cook's Notes:
1. Almonds are optional. You can also use any other type of nut such as pecans or walnuts.

Easy Bean Cuisine

White Chili

This variation of chili is made with white beans.

2 cups cooked brown rice[1]
1 can white Northern beans[2], rinsed and drained
1 cup shredded cabbage
3/4 cup prepared salsa[3]
1/2 tsp each: oregano, garlic powder
Garnish: 4 Tbsp nonfat sour cream and 1/2 cup nonfat grated mozzarella

Directions:

1. Combine beans, cabbage, prepared salsa and seasonings together in medium-sized sauce pan. Bring to a boil, reduce to a simmer, and cook for 2-3 minutes or until cabbage is tender.
2. Lightly mash beans to help thicken chile. Serve chile over brown rice and top each serving with 2 tbsp grated mozzarella and 1 tablespoon sour cream.
2. This recipe is delicious served over a baked potato or sweet potato. You can also serve it with a salad and whole grain bread.

Serves 4. Each 1 cup serving: 250 calories, 1 g fat, 0 g saturated fat, 0 mg cholesterol, 480 mg sodium, 42 g carbohydrate, 7 g fiber, 17 g protein. Diabetic exchange: 2-1/2 bread, 1/2 meat.

BLT

The BLT stands for beans, lettuce, and tomato!

4 large, lowfat flour tortillas
1 cup canned kidney beans, drained, rinsed, and lightly mashed
4 Tbsp nonfat ranch salad dressing
1 cup shredded Romaine lettuce
1/2 cup diced fresh tomato

Directions:

1. Lightly warm the tortillas to make them pliable.
2. Divide all ingredients between the tortillas, placing everything in a line down the center of each tortilla.
3. Roll up the tortillas and serve seam side down. These BLTs go well with slaw and fresh carrot sticks. You can also use salsa in place of the nonfat Ranch salad dressing.

Serves 4. Each 6 ounce serving: 240 calories, 3 g fat, 0.5 g saturated fat, 0 mg cholesterol, 330 mg sodium, 44 g carbohydrate, 6 g fiber, 8 g protein. Diabetic exchange: 3 bread.

Cook's Notes:

1. To make 2 cups of cooked brown rice, use 1 cup of instant brown rice and 1 cup of water and cook until tender, about 5-10 minutes. Or you can cook 2/3 cup brown rice with 1 1/3 cups water until tender, about 30 minutes.
2. You can use any type of white bean.
3. Prepared salsa adds many ingredients with the convenience of one. Try to find one that has less than 200 mg. of sodium per 2 tablespoon serving. You can also use pureed Mexican Recipe tomatoes for lower sodium content.

Popular Makeovers

Oven-Fried Parmesan Chicken

Bread crumbs and Parmesan cheese give chicken a crispy, savory coating. Serve with corn pudding and your choice of either a fresh vegetable or salad.

4 boneless, skinless chicken breast halves
1 cup nonfat plain yogurt
3/4 cup plain bread crumbs
4 Tbsp Parmesan cheese
2 Tbsp all-purpose flour
1 Tsp paprika
Pinch cayenne pepper

Directions:

1. Place chicken breast halves in yogurt and refrigerate while you get the rest of the items ready.
2. Mix the rest of the ingredients together in a medium-sized mixing bowl. Preheat oven to 425° and lightly spray a cookie tray with vegetable cooking oil.
3. Coat each piece of chicken with yogurt and dredge it in the crumb mixture, pressing down on both sides and turning several times to create a thick coat of crumbs. Place chicken on a tray and spray the top with vegetable cooking oil. Bake for 15-20 minutes or until chicken is fork tender and juices run clear.

Serves 4. Each serving (1 breast): 280 calories, 6 g fat, 2 g saturated fat, 75 mg cholesterol, 420 mg sodium, 22 g carbohydrate, 1 g fiber, 34 g protein. Diabetic exchange: 1-1/2 bread, 3 meat.

Corn Pudding

This recipe is total comfort food, and we find it to be a nice change from mashed potatoes or pasta.

2 cups skim milk
1 Tbsp butter granules[1]
4 Tbsp honey[2]
1/2 cup corn meal
2 cups frozen corn kernels
1 cup diced green and red bell pepper

Directions:

1. Place all ingredients in a medium-sized sauce pan. Bring to a boil, stirring frequently.
2. Cook briefly, stirring constantly, until vegetables are tender and pudding is thick, about 3-5 minutes. Scoop onto a plate and serve.

Serves 4. Each 1 cup serving: 270 calories, 1 g fat, 0 g saturated fat, 0 mg cholesterol, 120 mg sodium, 58 g carbohydrate, 4 g fiber, 8 g protein. Diabetic exchange: 2 bread, 1/2 milk, 1 veg.

Cook's Notes:

1. Butter flavored granules can be found in the spice section of your grocery store. Popular brands are Butter Buds and Molly McButter.
2. You can substitute two tablespoons of sugar for the honey in this recipe.

Popular Makeovers

Turkey Loaf & Mushroom Sauce

This meatloaf is moist and tasty.

1/2 cup plain bread crumbs
1/4 cup skim milk
1/4 cup fat free egg substitute
1-1/2 pounds ground turkey breast[1]
3/4 cup prepared mild salsa[2]
1/2 tsp each: oregano, sage, garlic powder, black pepper

Mushroom Sauce:
1 cup lowfat ready-to-serve cream of mushroom soup
1 cup sliced mushrooms

Directions:

1. In a large bowl, combine the bread crumbs, skim milk, and egg substitute. Add the turkey, salsa and seasonings. Mix well and transfer mixture to a loaf pan. Smooth the top, then cover and refrigerate until ready to bake.
2. Preheat oven to 350°. Bake loaf until it is firm in the center, about 45-50 minutes. Allow to sit for 5 or 10 minutes before cutting and serving.
3. To make the mushroom sauce, combine the soup with the mushrooms and microwave on high for 6-8 minutes or until the mushrooms are tender.

Serves 8. Each serving (1/8th loaf): 160 calories, 1.5 g fat, 0 g saturated fat, 60 mg cholesterol, 480 mg sodium, 9 g carbohydrate, 1 g fiber, 28 g protein. Diabetic exchanges: 1 bread, 2 meat.

Cook's Notes:

1. Make sure the ground turkey that you buy is skinless. You can always get the butcher to grind it fresh for you if you are not sure about the skin or if ground turkey is not available in your store.
2. Salsa adds the flavor of many ingredients in one nifty jar. Look for a salsa that is not too high in sodium - less than 200 mg. per 2 tablespoon serving.
3. Buy a chicken broth that is lowfat and not too high in sodium. Look for one with less than one gram of fat and 400 mg of sodium per half cup serving.
4. You can also use ½ tablespoon of dried basil in this recipe.

Recipe brought to you by:
Florentine Mashed Potatoes

Chicken broth, spinach, and Parmesan cheese add great flavor to these fluffy mashed potatoes.

2 pounds baking potatoes
3/4-1 cup lowfat chicken broth[3]
1 cup frozen chopped spinach, thawed
1/2 tsp garlic powder
1/4 cup grated Parmesan cheese
1 Tbsp fresh chopped basil[4]
Pinch of black pepper

Directions:

1. Peel and cube potatoes; place in large sauce pan, cover with water and bring to a boil. Simmer until tender, about 20 minutes.
2. Drain the water and place the potatoes on a stove over medium heat. Mash potatoes using hand mixer or potato masher. Add broth slowly until desired consistency is reached.
3. Add the rest of the ingredients, stir well and reheat. Serve hot.

Serves 6. Each 1 cup serving: 170 calories, 1 g fat, 0.5 g saturated fat, 5 mg cholesterol, 125 mg sodium, 32 g carbohydrate, 4 g fiber, 6 g protein. Diabetic exchange: 2 bread.

Lip Smacking Soup Meals

Tortilla Soup with Baked Chips

This delicious, hearty soup that comes together very quickly.

1 15-ounce can kidney beans, drained and rinsed
1 cup prepared salsa[1]
1 cup frozen corn kernels
1/2 cup white rice
3 cups water
1 tsp each: oregano, garlic powder, cumin
2 cups baked tortilla chips[2]

Directions:

1. Add all ingredients except tortilla chips to a large dutch oven (4-6 quart) and bring to a boil.
2. Cover, reduce heat to a simmer and allow to cook for 12-15 minutes or until rice is done.
3. Serve in bowls with ½ cup of tortilla chips floating on top of each one. A teaspoon of nonfat plain yogurt make an additional tasty garnish.

Serves 4. Each 1 cup serving: 260 calories, 1 g fat, 0 g saturated fat, 0 mg cholesterol, 540 mg sodium, 50 g carbohydrate, 7 g fiber, 13 g protein. Diabetic exchange: 3 bread.

Chicken Corn Chowder

This hearty chowder is delicious for lunch or dinner and is a snap to make. In addtion to a tasty treat, you'll also get 216 mg of calcium per serving.

1 4-ounce boneless, skinless chicken breast, diced
1 can lowfat, condensed cream of broccoli and potato soup[3]
1-1/2 cups skim milk
2 cups frozen corn kernels
1 14-ounce can stewed diced tomatoes with no added salt

Directions:

1. Toast corn kernels under broiler for 3-5 minutes or until golden brown.
2. Place all items in medium-sized sauce pan and bring to a boil over medium-high heat. Stir well and reduce to a simmer, stirring occasionally.
3. Cook for 5-7 minutes or until chicken is done and corn is tender. Serve in a soup bowl and garnish with dots of Tabasco.

Serves 4. Each 1 cup serving: 210 calories, 2 g fat, 1 g saturated fat, 20 mg cholesterol, 380 mg sodium, 34 g carbohydrate, 3 g fiber, 15 g protein. Diabetic exchange: 2 bread, 1 meat, 1 milk.

Cook's Notes:

1. Salsa adds the flavor of many ingredients in a single nifty jar. Look for a salsa that is not too high in sodium - less than 200 mg. per 2 tablespoon serving.
2. This is a good way to get rid of the small pieces of baked tortilla chips that are often left in the bottom of the bag.
3. You can use any lowfat cream soup. Try to find one that is not too high in sodium - less than 400 mg. per one half cup serving.

Quick & Healthy

The Fastest Stir Fry on the Planet

We are always striving to create a faster, tastier stir fry. We think you will agree that this is it!

8 ounces dry linguine noodles, cooked
1 cup presliced fresh mushrooms
2 cups preshredded cabbage
1 pound frozen festive stirfry vegetable medley
1 can lowfat, ready-to-serve chicken noodle soup[1]
1 Tbsp light soy sauce
1 tsp ground ginger[2]

Directions:

1. Spray a large nonstick skillet with nonstick cooking spray and place over medium-high heat.
2. Saute mushrooms until golden brown and add the rest of the ingredients, except the linguine noodles.
3. Turn heat to high and cook for 3 minutes or until vegetables are heated through.
4. Add cooked linguine noodles and stir everything together. Serve hot with fresh steamed broccoli florets on top (broccoli is optional, of course).

Serves 4. Each 1 cup serving: 320 calories, 2.5 g fat, 0.5 g saturated fat, 10 mg cholesterol, 500 mg sodium, 60 g carbohydrate, 4 g fiber, 15 g protein. Diabetic exchange: 3 bread, 2 veg.

Macaroni with Tomatoes & Broccoli

A hearty pasta dish that's easy to make and fun to eat.

2 cups dry macaroni noodles
1 14½ oz. can diced stewed tomatoes with Italian herbs
1 15½ oz. can kidney beans, drained and rinsed
1 cup nonfat, low sodium chicken broth[3]
1½ cups broccoli florets[4]

Directions:

1. Place noodles, tomatoes, beans and broth in skillet; bring to a boil, reduce heat to medium high, cover and cook for 7 minutes.
2. Add broccoli florets and cook 3 minutes more (or until noodles are tender).

Serves 4. Each 1-1/2 cup serving: 340 calories, 1.5 g fat, 0 g saturated fat, 0 mg cholesterol, 220 mg sodium, 65 g carbohydrate, 9 g fiber, 18 g protein. Diabetic exchange: 4 bread, 1 veg.

Cook's Notes:

1. Try to find a chicken noodle soup that is low in fat and relatively low in sodium. Look for one with less than one gram of fat and 400 mg of sodium per one half cup serving.
2. You can also use a pinch of ground ginger.
3. Try to find a chicken broth that has less than one gram of fat and 400 mg of sodium per one half cup serving.
4. The florets of the broccoli are the flowery tops.

Speed Scratch Cooking

Skillet Lasagna

This lasagna has all the flavor and none of the fussiness of traditional lasagna.

6 ounces dry mini lasagna[1]
1 medium zucchini, thinly sliced
1 cup presliced mushrooms
1 cup cooked ground turkey breast (or lean beef or chicken)
3 cups no-salt-added tomato sauce
1 Tbsp Italian seasoning mix[3]
1 cup fat-free cottage cheese
4 Tbsp grated Parmesan cheese
Directions:

1. Cook pasta according to package directions and drain in a colander.
2. Meanwhile, coat a large pot or skillet with nonstick cooking spray and place over medium-high heat. Saute zucchini and mushrooms until tender.
3. Add cooked ground turkey and pasta sauce and bring to a boil. Stir in cheeses and mix well.

Serves 4. Each 2 cup serving: 350 calories, 6 g fat, 1.5 g saturated fat, 5 mg cholesterol, 500 mg sodium, 47 g carbohydrate, 6 g fiber, 26 g protein. Diabetic exchange: 2 bread, 2 meat, 2 veg.

Popeye's Spaghetti

Add chopped, frozen spinach leaves to your pasta sauce and you'll have a colorful creation that is high in nutrients.

8 ounces dry spaghetti noodles[4], cooked
2 cups lowfat pasta sauce[5]
2 cups frozen chopped spinach
1 cup presliced mushrooms
Directions:

1. Cook spaghetti noodles according to package directions, drain in colander and set aside.
2. Meanwhile, prepare sauce by adding the rest of the ingredients to a medium-sized sauce pan. Bring to a boil over medium-high heat.
3. Allow to simmer until mushrooms and spinach are tender, about 2-3 minutes. Serve over cooked, hot spaghetti.

Serves 4. Each 1-1/2 cup serving: 290 calories, 1 g fat, 0 g saturated fat, 0 mg cholesterol, 380 mg sodium, 57 g carbohydrate, 6 g fiber, 13 g protein. Diabetic exchange: 3 bread, 2 veg.

Cook's Notes:

1. Mini lasagna noodles may be substituted with any small-shaped pasta such as penne, macaroni, rotini or bowtie.
2. Veggie burger crumbles are in the freezer section of your grocery store. You can also use ground, skinless turkey breast. If you add sub in turkey, cook it in the skillet first and then proceed with the rest of the recipe.
3. Italian seasoning mix may be substituted with a half tablespoon each of oregano and basil.
4. You can also use any long, thin pasta for this recipe. Try linguine, angel hair or fettucine.
5. Try to find a pasta sauce that has less than one gram of fat and 400 mg of sodium per one half cup serving.

Speed Scratch Cooking

7 Minute Vegetable Soup

This delicious, homemade soup takes advantage of ingredients that are already prepared so that you won't have to chop anything! It is a favorite of Carol Coughlin, RD and her family.

1 cup frozen diced onion[1]
2 tsp minced garlic[2]
2 8-ounce cans no-salt-added tomato sauce
1 15-ounce can Italian recipe stewed tomatoes
2 cups frozen mixed vegetables[3]
1 tsp dried basil

Directions:
1. Spray a medium sized soup pan or large nonstick skillet with cooking spray and place over medium-high heat.
2. Add onion and saute briefly. Add garlic and saute until both are golden brown.
3. Add tomato sauce and tomatoes and chop tomatoes coarsely with a spatula. Add vegetables. Season with basil.
4. Heat soup until vegetables are cooked. This can also be made in the microwave. Serve hot with whole grain bread.

Serves 4. Each 1-1/2 cup serving: 150 calories, 0 g fat, 0 g saturated fat, 0 mg cholesterol, 300 mg sodium, 30 g carbohydrate, 9 g fiber, 6 g protein. Diabetic exchange: 4 veg, 1/2 bread.

Cook's Notes:
1. Diced onion is found in the freezer section of your grocery store. You can also dice fresh onions on your own.
2. Minced garlic can be bought packed in water or oil. You can also mince your own or use a half teaspoon of garlic powder.
3. You can substitute any 2 cups of fresh vegetables for frozen, though cooking time may need to be reduced.

More Speed Scratch Ideas:

Speed scratch cooking is a way of assembling home-made meals by using a combination of prepared ingredients. Here are more ideas to help you save time and serve a good meal.

- **Buy a rotisserie chicken** from your grocery store. Serve it with reheated frozen veggies and cooked instant brown rice for a fancy dinner that takes only a little time.

- **Chili** - Make a quick chili by mixing stewed tomatoes (with no added salt), canned beans, frozen corn and mixed frozen veggies. Season it with a little garlic powder, chili powder, and cumin. Bring to a boil and cook until the veggies are tender, around 8 minutes. Serve with a little salad.

- **Chicken Caesar Salad** - Here is a way to use up leftover cooked chicken. Toss ready-to-serve romaine lettuce with cooked chicken, various garden veggies (buy them from the salad bar in the grocery store), fat-free Caesar dressing, and a little Parmesan Cheese. This salad is even heartier if you add cooked instant brown rice.

Healthy Inexpensive Meals for 2

Broccoli Cheese Potato

Potatoes contain complex carbohydrates and supply protein and ample vitamins. They are also delicious when dressed up with broccoli and cheese.

2 hot, baked potatoes[1]
1 cup nonfat cottage cheese
1 cups cooked broccoli florets[2]
1/4 cup sliced green onion
2 Tbsp nonfat grated mozzarella

Directions:

1. Cut baked potatoes in half lengthwise and dig out the insides. Mix potato innards with cottage cheese, broccoli, and green onion.
2. Place filling back into potato skins and top with mozzarella. Microwave for 2 minutes per potato or until filling is hot and cheese is melted.

Serves 2. Each serving (1 5-ounce potato): 350 calories, 0 g fat, 0 g saturated fat, 0 mg cholesterol, 460 mg sodium, 61 g carbohydrate, 8 g fiber, 25 g protein. Diabetic exchange: 4 bread, 2 meat, 1 veg.

Lime Rice, Chili

Ingredients:
1 cup brown rice
2 cups water
dash coriander, garlic, pepper
2 limes, cut in wedges
1 can no-salt kidney beans, und- rained
1 can no-salt diced tomatoes with basil and oregano, undrained
1 tablespoon minced onion
1/2 can tomato paste (1/4 cup)
1/4 cup water
1 tsp chili powder
1 tsp cumin
1/2 tsp garlic powder Directions:

1. Cook rice, water and coriander/garlic/pepper in pan or rice cooker until done, about 30 minutes. Add the juice of one lime, fluff with a fork and allow to stand.
2. Meanwhile, cook chili by add- ing kidney beans, diced tomatoes, minced onion, tomato paste, water and the rest of the seasonings to a medium skillet; bring to a boil then lower to a simmer.
3. To serve the chili, mold the rice in a small cup and place in the center of a bowl. Surround with chili.
4. Garnish with lime wedges.

Optional: you can also add cooked turkey or chicken to this chili. We also like the addition of corn for a variation.

Servings: Serves 4. Each serving: 2 cups.

Per Serving: Calories: 233, Total Fat: 2g, Saturated Fat: 0g, Trans Fat: 0g, Cholesterol: 0mg, Sodium: 55mg, Carbohydrates: 25g, Dietary Fiber: 8.5g, Protein: 15g

Cook's Notes:

1. Bake potatoes in your oven (1 hour) or microwave (10 minutes per potato) until tender.
2. Florets are the flowery tops of the broccoli.
3. You can also use any small-shaped pasta such as macaroni, shell, or penne.
4. Try to find a chicken noodle soup that has less than one gram of fat and 400 mg. of sodium per one half cup serving.

Great Easy Weekday Meals

Oven-Fried Fish Dinner

Ingredients:

2 tablespoons bread crumbs

1 pound fillet white fish olive oil

1 pound yukon gold potatoes[1]

2 tablespoons fresh basil

2 cloves garlic, minced

Skim milk

1 pound asparagus

Directions:

1. Heat oil in a nonstick skillet over medium-high heat. Preheat oven to 375F.
2. Press bread crumbs on one side of the fish then saute crumb side down in 2 tea- spoons of olive oil until golden, about 2 minutes.
3. Turn the fish over and place in the oven until done, about 15 minutes.
4. Boil the potatoes then strain in colander.
5. Saute the garlic with a tiny drizzle of olive oil and add the basil; saute briefly then add the potatoes.
6. Mash them with a little bit of skim milk then season with garlic powder and black pep- per.
7. Roast the asparagus in a toaster oven.

Servings: Serves 4. Each serving: 3 cups.

Per Serving: Calories: 276, Total Fat: 7g, Saturated Fat: .5g, Trans Fat: 0g, Cholesterol: 0mg, Sodium: 108mg, Carbohydrates: 31g, Dietary Fiber: 6g, Protein: 25g

See this meal with picture directions at foodandhealth.com/blog

Cook's Notes:

1. Yukon gold potatoes have a fine, light brown skin and yellow, buttery flesh. You can also use regular baking potatoes.
2. The florets are the flowery tops to the broccoli.

Gold Broccoli Potato

Yukon gold potatoes have the look and texture of a buttered potato, without the fat.

4 medium sized yukon gold potatoes, baked[1]

3 cups hot steamed broccoli florets[2]

1 cup nonfat sour cream

1/2 cup nonfat grated cheese

Directions:

1. Split baked potatoes lengthwise down the center. Mash lightly with a fork.
2. Mash ¼ cup nonfat sour cream into each potato; add ¾ cup steamed broccoli florets to each potato and top with nonfat grated cheese.
3. Arrange potatoes on a platter. Make sure they are evenly spaced and not touching each other. Microwave on high for one minute per potato or until cheese melts over broccoli.

Serves 4. Each 1-1/2 cup serving: 350 calories, 0.5 g fat, 0 g saturated fat, 0 mg cholesterol, 200 mg sodium, 70 g carbohydrate, 8 g fiber, 17 g protein. Diabetic exchange: 4 bread, 1/2 meat, 2 veg.

Meatless Meals for Better Health

Skillet Chili

1 medium onion, chopped[1]
2 garlic cloves, minced[2]
1 small bell pepper, diced
1/2 cup crushed tomatoes
2 15-ounce cans pinto beans, including liquid
1 diced mild green chile peppers
1 tsp cumin
Pinch oregano
Directions:

1. Heat ½ cup water in a large skillet or pot. Add the onion, garlic, and bell pepper and cook over high heat, stirring often, until the onion is translucent, about 5 minutes.
2. Stir in the remaining ingredients and simmer, stirring occasionally, for 15 minutes.

Serves 6. Each 1 cup serving: 160 calories, 1 g fat, 0 g saturated fat, 0 mg cholesterol, 450 mg sodium, 30 g carbohydrate, 9 g fiber, 8 g protein. Diabetic exchange: 1-1/2 bread, 1 veg.

Vegetarian Sloppy Joes

This fun dish makes a spicy, easy meal. It's a healthy twist on an old classic.
4 whole wheat rolls, halved and toasted
1/2 cup each, sliced: zucchini, green onion, mushrooms
1/2 cup kidney beans, drained and rinsed
1 15-oz. can stewed diced tomatoes, drained
1/2 cup barbecue sauce
1/4-1/2 tsp chili powder
Directions:

1. Heat a large, nonstick skill over medium-high heat. Add vegetables, beans, tomatoes, barbecue sauce and chili powder and bring mixture to a boil, stirring well.
2. Reduce heat to a simmer and cook until vegetables are tender, about 4-5 minutes.
3. Serve mixture over toasted bun halves, open face style. This dish goes well with a tossed salad or lowfat slaw. You can also cook everything together in the microwave.

Serves 4. Each serving: 180 calories, 1.5 g fat, 0 g saturated fat, 0 mg cholesterol, 580 mg sodium, 33 g carbohydrate, 5 g fiber, 7 g protein. Diabetic exchange: 2 bread, 1 veg.

Cook's Notes:
1. You can find chopped onion in the freezer section of your grocery store.
2. You can also use 2 tsp of minced garlic. Find this in the produce or spice section of your grocery store.

Healthy Desserts

Chocolate-Banana Pudding Pie

This chocolate pie is rich and smooth. For a real treat, serve with fresh sliced bananas on top.

Filling:

1 12-ounce package of light, silken tofu[1]

1/2 cup cocoa powder[2]

1/3 cup sugar

1 Tbsp vanilla extract

3 ripe bananas

Crust: 1-1/2 cups fat free chocolate cookies

Directions:

1. Preheat the oven to 350 degrees. Lightly spray a 9" glass pie pan with cooking spray.
2. Grind the cookies in a blender or food processor. Press them into the bottom and sides of the pie pan, staying below the rim.
3. For the filling, place all of the ingredients into a food processor and blend until smooth.
4. Pour filling into the pie pan until it comes slightly above the top edge of the crust (this prevents burning). Bake for 30 minutes, or until firm in the center. Chill before serving and serve with fresh sliced bananas on top.

Serves 8. Each serving (1/8th pie): 200 calories, 1.5 g fat, 0 g saturated fat, 0 mg cholesterol, 65 mg sodium, 38 g carbohydrate, 5 g fiber, 8 g protein. Diabetic exchange: 1-1/2 bread, 1 fruit, 1/2 meat.

Raisin Streudal Oatmeal

This cereal makes a great standby for any cookie urge. It's delicious for breakfast, an afternoon pick-me-up or bedtime snack. Better still, it can be made in 4 minutes.

1 packet instant oatmeal[3] (¼ cup)

1 Tbsp dark seedless raisins

1 tsp brown sugar

1/4 tsp cinnamon

1/2 cup boiling water

2 Tbsp skim milk

1 Tbsp lowfat granola[4]

Directions:

1. Place first four ingredients in a coffee mug or cereal bowl.
2. Pour boiling water into the mug/bowl, stir and steep for 2 minutes. Top with skim milk and lowfat granola.

Serves 1. Each 1 cup serving: 190 calories, 2.5 g fat, 0 g saturated fat, 0 mg cholesterol, 115 mg sodium, 36 g carbohydrate, 4 g fiber, 6 g protein. Diabetic exchange; 2 bread, 1/2 fruit.

Cook's Notes:

1. Silken tofu comes in an asceptic package. Mori-Nu is a popular brand.
2. Cocoa powder should be Dutch Process for maximum flavor and color.
3. Instant oatmeal comes in premeasured packets. If you use quick cooking oatmeal, you must cook the oatmeal for one minute longer on low power in your microwave.
4. Lowfat granola without nuts or raisins is best for this recipe.

Healthy Desserts

Caramel Peach Crunch

This fast, microwaved dessert takes advantage of fresh, seasonal peaches.

4 ripe peaches[1], pitted and cut in wedges (3 cups)
1/4 cup brown sugar
1/2 cup lowfat granola[2]
Directions:

1. Toss peaches with brown sugar and place in a glass baking pan. Cover with plastic and microwave for 6-8 minutes on high or until peaches are tender.
2. Serve in individual bowls with lowfat granola sprinkled over the top. This goes well with a scoop of nonfat vanilla frozen yogurt. You can also use a one pound bag of frozen peach wedges. If you do this, increase cooking time to 12-15 minutes or until fruit is tender and mixture is bubbly.

Serves 4. Each 1/2 cup serving: 140 calories, 0.5 g fat, 0 g saturated fat, 0 mg cholesterol, 30 mg sodium, 31 g carbohydrate, 2 g fiber, 2 g protein. Diabetic exchange: 1 bread, 1 fruit.

Raspberry Chocolate Crunch

This chocolate raspberry pie is very simple, yet tastes very sinful.

1 cup fat free chocolate cookies, ground[3]
1 pint chocolate sorbet[4]
1 pint raspberry sorbet[4]
1/4 cup semisweet chocolate chips
Garnish: chocolate sauce, cocoa powder
Directions:

1. Lightly spray a glass pie pan with cooking oil spray. Press ground chocolate cookies on the bottom and up the sides.
2. Alternately scoop chocolate sorbet and raspberry sorbet into the pie pan and press flat.
3. Top with chocolate chips and refreeze for at least 2 hours. Sprinkle with cocoa powder and serve with chocolate sauce.

Serves 8. Each serving (1/8th slice): 240 calories, 2 g fat, 1.5 g saturated fat, 0 mg cholesterol, 35 mg sodium, 53 g carbohydrate, 2 g fiber, 2 g protein. Diabetic exchange: 3-1/2 bread, 1/2 fat.

Cook's Notes:

1. You can use any type of firm fruit, like blueberries, cherries, apples, pears, or apricots. Avoid melon or strawberries - they are too soft.
2. Lowfat granola without raisins or nuts works best in this recipe.
3. Grind cookies in a plastic bag using a glass. You can also grind them in a food processor or blender.
4. Sorbet is similar to sherbet but does not contain dairy products. It's also generally firmer and less sweet. Our favorite brand to use in this recipe is Haagen Dazs.

Light Beverages

White Sangria

This light sangria-esque spritzer features luscious, colorful fruits and will please your family and guests.

1 orange, seeded and sliced
1 lime, seeded and sliced
1/2 cup frozen cherries[1], thawed, rinsed, and drained
2 cinnamon sticks
2 cups white grape juice
2 cups sparkling mineral water or club soda, chilled

Directions:
1. Place fruit and cinnamon sticks in a large glass pitcher.
2. Pour white grape juice over the fruit and refrigerate until ready to use, preferably overnight.
3. At serving time, pour chilled sparking mineral water into the pitcher, mix, and pour into glasses with ice. Garnish each glass with fruit and serve.

Serves 4, 130 calories per serving. Each 1 cup serving: 90 calories, 0 g fat, 0 g saturated fat, 0 mg cholesterol, 10 mg sodium, 22 g carbohydrate, 0 g fiber, 1 g protein. Diabetic exchange: 1-1/2 fruit.

Mocha Latte

A chocolate coffee drink made with milk is a fancy alternative to hot chocolate. You also get 309 mg of calcium per serving.

2-1/2 tablespoons instant coffee powder (decaf)
1-1/4 tablespoon cocoa powder
1-1/4 tablespoon sugar
4 cups skim milk

Directions:
1. Place 1 tablespoon instant coffee, ½ tablespoon cocoa powder and ½ tablespoon sugar into each large glass mug.
2. Add some of the milk and mix until you have a stiff paste.
3. Gradually add the rest of the milk until you have 1½ cups of milk per mug. Stir well.
4. Microwave 2 minutes per mug or until very hot. Do not boil. Stir well and serve. Optional garnish: fat free whipped cream and a dash of cocoa powder.

Serves 4. Each 1 cup serving: 110 calories, 0.5 g fat, 0 g saturated fat, 5 mg cholesterol, 130 mg sodium, 18 g carbohydrate, 0 g fiber, 9 g protein. Diabetic exchange: 1 milk.

Cook's Notes:
1. Dark, pitted, sweet cherries work best for this recipe

Great Easy Fruit Desserts

Cherry-Apple Skillet Pie

Sweet and sour cherries are a natural partner to apples in this easy dessert.

1 cup frozen, pitted cherries[1]
3 baking apples[2], peeled, cored and sliced
2 Tbsp sugar
1/2 tsp cinnamon
2 cups fat-free pancake batter[3]

Directions:

1. Preheat oven to 350°. Lightly spray a large, nonstick skillet with vegetable oil cooking spray and heat over medium high heat.
2. Place cherries, apples, sugar, and cinnamon in pan and saute until apples are tender - about 4-6 minutes.
3. Shake fruit so that it's level in the pan. Pour pancake batter over the top of the fruit and place the pan in the oven. Bake until top is golden brown, about 12 minutes.

Serves 4. Each serving (1/4th pie): 200 calories, 1 g fat, 0 g saturated fat, 0 mg cholesterol, 370 mg sodium, 45 g carbohydrate, 4 g fiber, 3 g protein. Diabetic exchange: 2 bread, 1 fruit.

Citrus Cup

Grapefruit and orange sections are enhanced with a warm lemon-lime glaze.

3 oranges, peeled, seeded and diced
1 ruby grapefruit, peeled, seeded and diced
Zest of 1 lemon[4]
Zest of 1 lime[4]
1/3 cup pineapple juice concentrate

Directions:

1. Add zest to pineapple juice concentrate. Bring to a boil in a sturdy pot and pour over the orange and grapefruit pieces. Toss together and place into a serving bowl or individual dishes.

Serves 4. Each serving (3/4 cup): 120 calories, 0 g fat, 0 g saturated fat, 0 mg cholesterol, 0 mg sodium, 28 g carbohydrate, 3 g fiber, 2 g protein. Diabetic exchange: 2 fruit.

Cook's Notes:

1. Dark, sweet, pitted cherries work best in this recipe.
2. Baking apples such as Rome or Pippin work best for this recipe.
3. Look for fat free pancake mix in your grocery store or make some from a mix or recipe.
4. The zest is the fine outer skin of the citrus fruit. Grate it off gently so you don't get the white, bitter pith underneath.

Great Easy Fruit Desserts

Blueberry Pandowdy

Warm, plump blueberries are baked with bits of cereal bars to create a neat new dessert.

3 cups frozen blueberries
1/4 cup grape juice concentrate
1/4 cup water
1/2 Tbsp corn starch
3 Lowfat apple cereal bars[1], chopped into 1-inch pieces

Directions:

1. Preheat oven to 350°. Combine all ingredients in a mixing bowl. Mix well and pour into a ceramic bakeproof bowl.
2. Cover bowl with foil or glass lid and bake for 35-40 minutes or until bubbly. Stir and serve warm. Optional garnish: Top with 2 Tbsp frozen, nonfat, vanilla yogurt.

Serves 4. Each 3/4 cup serving: 180 calories, 1 g fat, 0 g saturated fat, 0 mg cholesterol, 50 mg sodium, 41 g carbohydrate, 6 g fiber, 2 g protein. Diabetic exchange: 2 bread, 1 fruit.

Berry Tostada

Crispy cinnamon sugar corn tortillas are topped with sorbet and fresh fruit.

4 corn tortillas
3 Tbsp sugar
1/2 tsp ground cinnamon
Vegetable oil cooking spray
1 cup fresh sliced strawberries
1 cup frozen mango sorbet[2]
2 lowfat cereal bars[1], chop into fine pieces

Directions:

1. Preheat oven to 375°. Combine cinnamon and sugar in medium-sized mixing bowl.
2. Spray corn tortillas on both sides with canola oil spray. Dredge in cinnamon sugar on both sides and place flat on cookie sheet without overlapping.
3. Bake for 5 minutes and turn over; bake an additional 5 or 10 minutes until golden and crispy.
4. While tortillas are still warm, top with fruit, then sorbet, then sprinkle crumbled, nonfat cereal bars over the top.

Serves 4. Each serving (1 tostada): 170 calories, 1 g fat, 0 g saturated fat, 0 mg cholesterol, 40 mg sodium, 40 g carbohydrate, 2 g fiber, 2 g protein. Diabetic exchange: 1-1/2 bread, 1 fruit.

Cook's Notes:

1. Lowfat cereal bars may be any flavor that you like.
2. You can use any flavor of fruit sorbet. A sorbet is similar to sherbet, except that it is not as sweet and does not contain dairy products.

Easy Way To 4.5 Cups Per Day

Tomato Bean Potpourri
Kidney beans, green beans, and tomatoes are delicious, especially when served with raspberry dressing.
1 cup canned kidney beans, drained and rinsed
1 cup cooked green beans
1 cup shredded kale[1]
1 cup diced ripe tomatoes
2 Tbsp nonfat raspberry salad dressing[2]
1 Tbsp balsamic vinegar[3]
Directions:
1. Toss all ingredients together. Serve on a bed of dark green lettuce.

Serves 4. Each 3/4 cup serving: 100 calories, 0.5 g fat, 0 g saturated fat, 0 mg cholesterol, 125 mg sodium, 18 g carbohydrate, 5 g fiber, 5 g protein. Diabetic exchange: 1 bread, 1 veg.

Peach Slaw
Ripe peaches tossed with cabbage and tangy dressing make a great summer slaw!
3 Tbsp nonfat plain yogurt
3 Tbsp nonfat mayonnaise
1 ripe peach, grated
1 Tbsp sugar
1/2 Tbsp vinegar
2 cups shredded savoy cabbage[4]
Directions:
1. Make the dressing by combining all ingredients except cabbage in medium-sized mixing bowl.
2. At serving time add shredded cabbage and toss well.

Serves 4. Each 1/2 cup serving: 70 calories, 0 g fat, 0 g saturated fat, 0 mg cholesterol, 170 mg sodium, 14 g carbohydrate, 2 g fiber, 2 g protein. Diabetic exchange: 1/2 bread, 1 veg.

Cook's Notes:
1. Kale can be substituted with any green. Try spinach, chard, or beet greens.
2. Raspberry salad dressing is best for this recipe, but you can also use fat-free Italian salad dressing.
3. Balsamic vinegar can be substituted with red wine vinegar or cider vinegar.
4. Savoy is a fancy curly cabbage. You can also use regular cabbage.

Easy Way To 5 A Day

Red Slaw

It's fun to enjoy a salad that's bright red and vitamin-rich too.

Dressing:

2 Tbsp balsamic vinegar[1]

2 tsp sugar

1 tsp Italian herb seasoning mix[2]

Salad:

2 cups red cabbage, finely shredded

2 cups regular cabbage, finely shredded

1 bunch fresh red beets and greens

1/4 cup red onion, diced

Directions:

1. Whisk dressing ingredients together in medium bowl and set aside.
2. Cut tops and stem off the beets. Blanch in boiling water for two minutes and let cool. Peel off skins and discard.
3. Finely shred skinned beets with a hand shredder or in a food processor.
4. Finely chop beet greens, discarding stems.
5. Toss cabbage, shredded beets, beet greens, diced pepper and onion with dressing. Chill for one hour before serving.

Serves 4. Each 1-1/2 cup serving: 210 calories, 0 g fat, 0 g saturated fat, 0 mg cholesterol, 140 mg sodium, 48 g carbohydrate, 5 g fiber, 3 g protein. Diabetic exchange: 1 bread, 2 veg.

Oriental Broccoli Salad

Sweet and sour dressing goes well with crisp fresh vegetables.

2 carrots, peeled and sliced thin

2 cups broccoli florets[3]

2 cups shredded cabbage

1 Tbsp light soy sauce

2 Tbsp balsamic vinegar[1]

1 tsp sugar

2 Tbsp nonfat plain yogurt

Directions:

1. Steam broccoli florets until just crisp-tender.
2. Toss broccoli with the rest of the ingredients.
3. Chill for 2-3 hours and mix again. Serving suggestion: Top with toasted sesame seeds.

Serves 4. Each 1-1/2 cup serving: 200 calories, 0 g fat, 0 g saturated fat, 0 mg cholesterol, 190 mg sodium, 43 g carbohydrate, 4 g fiber, 5 g protein. Diabetic exchange: 1 bread, 2 veg.

Cook's Notes:

1. Balsamic vinegar may be substituted with cider vinegar or red wine vinegar.
2. You can also use a half teaspoon each of oregano and basil.
3. Broccoli florets are the flowery tops of the broccoli.

Easy Snacks For All Ages

Fruit and Nut Sandwiches

4 slices whole wheat bread
1/3 cup chopped dried fruit[1]
1/4 cup chopped nuts[2]
1/2 cup lowfat ricotta cheese
1/4 tsp lemon juice

Directions:

1. Combine all ingredients in a small bowl, then spread onto 2 slices of the whole wheat bread. Top with remaining 2 slices of bread.
2. Cut each sandwich in half diagonally. These sandwiches go well on a snack platter with veggie sticks, baked chips, and fresh fruit.

Serves 4. Each serving (1/2 sandwich): 170 calories, 6 g fat, 0.5 g saturated fat, 5 mg cholesterol, 190 mg sodium, 23 g carbohydrate, 3 g fiber, 7 g protein. Diabetic exchange: 1 fat, 1 fruit, 1/2 meat.

Spinach Dip

Serve this dip with fresh vegetables, or as a spread for sandwiches or lowfat crackers.

1 cup lowfat ricotta cheese
1 cup nonfat plain yogurt
2 cups chopped, washed and dried fresh spinach[3]
2 garlic cloves, chopped
1/8 tsp fresh ground black pepper
Pinch of nutmeg

Directions:

1. Combine all ingredients in a blender or food processor. Puree until almost smooth.
2. Serve with an assortment of raw or lightly cooked vegetables, such as carrot sticks, broccoli florets, jicama sticks, radishes, celery sticks, and bell pepper wedges.

Serves 8. Each 1/4 cup serving: 40 calories, 0 g fat, 0 g saturated fat, 0 mg cholesterol, 150 mg sodium, 4 g carbohydrate, 0 g fiber, 6 g protein. Diabetic exchange: 1/2 meat, 1/2 veg.

Cook's Notes:

1. We like dried apricots and cranberries.
2. Toasted pecans and almonds are delicious.
3. You can also use one cup of frozen spinach.

Recipe Index

For more recipes and ideas visit:
http://foodandhealth.com
Click on "*What's Cooking*" for up to the minute ideas from our kitchen, complete with photos. Or click on "*Recipes*" to search our extensive database.
Email us from our home site, too!

Made in United States
Orlando, FL
25 April 2024